Suddenly, nearly a half-dozen NVA soldiers broke through the dense brush twenty meters from the team. Macias and Barr were the first Rangers to initiate contact, dropping two or three of the enemy soldiers with their opening bursts. Screaming *"Dinks...dinks... dinks!"* the two Rangers dropped their empty magazines at their feet and jammed home new ones as a number of ChiCom grenades sailed out of the brush and landed among the patrol. One of the grenades exploded under Wells, flipping him on his back. . . .

As the Rangers fought back desperately, word came over the radio that the weather back at Camp Eagle was beginning to break and the helicopters were cranking up. Now they only had to manage to stay alive for another twenty minutes until the cavalry arrived. . . .

Also by Gary A. Linderer
Published by Ivy Books:

THE EYES OF THE EAGLE: F Company LRPs in Vietnam,
1968
EYES BEHIND THE LINES: L Company Rangers in
Vietnam, 1969

Also in this series:

SIX SILENT MEN: Book One
by Reynel Martinez

SIX SILENT MEN: Book Two
by Kenn Miller

SIX SILENT MEN

101st LRP/Rangers: Book Three

Gary A. Linderer

IVY BOOKS • NEW YORK

Ivy Books
Published by Ballantine Books
Copyright © 1997 by Gary A. Linderer

http://www.randomhouse.com

Library of Congress Catalog Card Number: 97-93362

ISBN 0-8041-1567-2

Printed in Canada

First Edition: November 1997

10 9 8 7 6

This book is dedicated to my son, Bryan, whose untimely death in 1995 left his brothers, his mother, and me heartbroken. Bryan was a special child who accomplished much more in his sixteen short years than many of us do in a lifetime. He was my inspiration.

To Command Sergeant Major Neal Gentry, L Company, 75th Infantry (Ranger), First Sergeant from August 14, 1970, to December 15, 1971. He was the backbone of the company during its final years in Vietnam. His death in 1990 deprived us of one of our finest leaders.

To Terry Clifton, my good friend and comrade. When he died in battle at my side on November 20, 1968, my life changed forever. He is still in my prayers.

To all my Lurp and Ranger brothers—those we followed and those who followed us. Sharing in your glory and your camaraderie has made all the trauma and the sacrifice worthwhile.

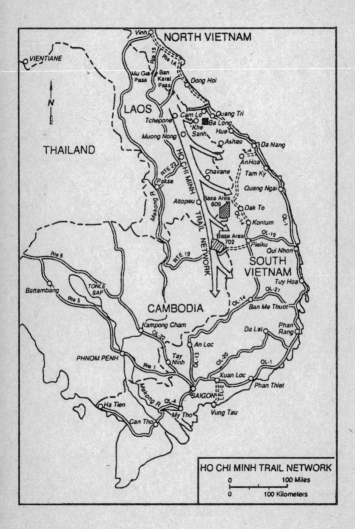

HO CHI MINH TRAIL NETWORK

0   100 Miles

0   100 Kilometers

PROLOGUE

When Rey Martinez, Kenn Miller, and I decided to take on the task of recording the history of the Long Range Patrol companies that served under the command of the 101st Airborne Division during the Vietnam War, little did we realize that we were beginning an almost four-year project that would reach herculean proportions. The original manuscript was intended to be a shared work by the three of us, incorporating complete histories of the 1st Brigade LRRP Detachment (Provisional), F Company, 58th Infantry (LRP); and L Company, 75th Infantry (Ranger). Three years later, and over fourteen hundred pages of recorded history, we realized that we'd only scratched the surface. To make matters worse, we had exceeded the six to eight hundred pages that our contract called for. That's when we began to realize we were in big trouble.

Owen Lock, our editor at Ivy Books, took compassion on us, agreeing to extend our deadline and rewrite our contract to allow us to publish three separate works. Now, after almost forty-six months of personal and telephone interviews, transcribed notes, and follow-up reviews, *Six Silent Men*—Books I, II, and III are complete. We have kept faith with our teammates. Their history is now a matter of public record, and their story will never die.

We have purposely omitted stories of our brother Lurps and

Rangers when printing them would surely have caused pain and anguish to loved ones, friends, and relatives. We have also avoided airing our dirty laundry for all to see. We took care of our own problems when they came to light—we still do. We ask forgiveness in advance from anyone we may have offended. It was not always possible to interview each man involved in a particular story. Some are dead, some do not wish to resurrect old memories, and some we have not yet located. Accepting the fact that each participant in any action will have a totally different perspective of the events that occurred, please forgive us if we did not quite address your perspective. Our intent was honorable and the effort sincere.

You must read each installment of the *Six Silent Men* series in order to understand the true history of this outstanding military unit. I say "unit," even though our predecessors in the 1st Brigade LRRPs were a distinct and separate organization. But they must know that the groundwork they established became the "lessons learned" that kept us alive. We kept the faith and carried on the torch they had ignited. Those who followed us fanned the flames even higher.

Today, our brothers in the Long Range Surveillance Detachment (LRSD) of the 101st Airborne Division carry the fire. They are us. We were them. It was a privilege to serve in this legendary unit. And the legend lives on.

1

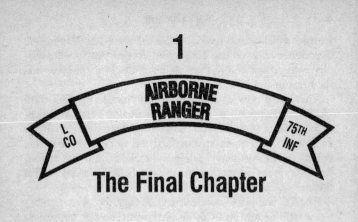

AIRBORNE RANGER

L CO

75TH INF

The Final Chapter

On February 1, 1969, thirteen Long Range Patrol (LRP) and Long Range Reconnaissance Patrol (LRRP) companies and detachments serving throughout the Republic of South Vietnam were summarily deactivated by the Department of the Army. Simultaneously, the Department of the Army activated the first thirteen letter companies of the 75th Infantry Regiment (Ranger). There was no fanfare, no parades, no physical transfer of unit personnel, no change of command, no relocation, no turn-in or reissuance of weapons, gear, and equipment, and no additional training. It was little more than a paper transaction conducted under the auspices of military protocol that affected only unit designation, unit heritage, and the exchange of one unauthorized shoulder scroll for another.

The units affected were small groups of volunteers, most between the ages of eighteen and twenty-one. But they were warriors who prosecuted their war deep behind enemy lines. They fought the NVA and VC on his own turf, bringing the war to the enemy. In their limited numbers they searched out and hunted the enemy in his sanctuaries. And when they found him, they brought the wrath of God and the U.S. military down on his head.

They had little formal training for what they did, most of them learning their stock-in-trade as they went. Those who

3

learned quickly survived and passed their knowledge and experience on to others. Those who learned slowly were usually weeded out before they managed to get themselves and their teammates killed.

The Lurps saw this organizational metamorphosis from "LRP" to "Rangers" as just another confusing example of Pentagon politics at its finest. It didn't affect them individually or as a unit. Their mission remained the same—to locate the enemy on his own playing field and make certain that he paid the full price of admission into the war he had created. And at this they excelled.

The VC and NVA soon learned that they, too, were fighting a war with no rear areas, no secure havens, no safe houses, no place where death and destruction could not seek them out and destroy them. They were being given a taste of their own brand of warfare by these small teams of Americans they soon came to call "the men with painted faces." It was a name that struck fear into the hearts and souls of the best troops the enemy sent to the field.

Up and down the length of South Vietnam, four- to six-man American Long Range Patrols prowled the vast expanses of enemy-controlled territory, exposing troop concentrations, base camps, hospitals, and weapons and supply caches. And when the enemy forces went on the offensive or infiltrated new units into South Vietnam, it was the U.S. Long Range Reconnaissance Patrols that waited to welcome them with deadly ambushes, devastating air strikes, and thundering artillery barrages.

F Company, 58th Infantry (LRP), 101st Airborne Division was one of the Long Range Patrol companies forced to undergo this strange mutation. The company had arrived in South Vietnam in November 1967. Activated at Fort Campbell, Kentucky, just prior to the division's deployment to Southeast Asia, the Long Range Reconnaissance company as a unit was inexperienced and untested in combat. But the swamps, jungles, mountains, and valleys of South Vietnam would soon become its proving ground.

In the fifteen months of its brief existence, the Long Range Patrol company would go through an extended metamorphosis of its own—sometimes satisfying, sometimes painful. Arriving in Vietnam without an organic unit history with the division, the Long Range Patrollers soon found themselves the "butt boys" of Division Headquarters. They were frequently utilized as a special assignment element and given every odd job in the division that other units could not or would not perform. They pulled perimeter security at the division rear. They rode shotgun for a Screaming Eagle general during his post-Tet '68 quest through I Corps in search of a choice piece of real estate on which to construct a new home for the division. They conducted numerous short-notice infantry sweeps in search of enemy raiders, sappers, and saboteurs.

Sandwiched between those too frequent attempts by higher command to keep the "troublesome malcontents" busy, the Lurp company begged, borrowed, and stole whatever Long Range Patrol missions it could get its hands on. And by trick or treat, trial and error, F Company, 58th Infantry (LRP) managed to add to the legacy established by its predecessor, the legendary LRRP detachment of the 1st Brigade, 101st Airborne Division.

Then, on February 1, 1969, the story of the Long Range Patrollers of F Company, 58th Infantry (LRP) came to an ignoble end. With the sudden deactivation of all Long Range Patrol companies in Vietnam, and the simultaneous activation of "lettered" Ranger companies, F Company, 58th Infantry (LRP) ceased to exist. However, its members soon rose Phoenixlike from the ashes to man the rolls of L Company, 75th Infantry (Ranger), and so began the final chapter of their long and glorious odyssey in the Vietnam War. During seven bloody years of loyal and unselfish service as the "Eyes and Ears of the Screaming Eagles," the Long Range Patrollers built a legacy that glorifies the division to this day.

This is the final chapter—this is their story.

2

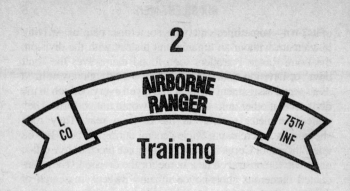

AIRBORNE RANGER

L CO

75TH INF

Training

The transition of the 101st Airborne Division from "airborne" to "air mobile" resulted in a new approach to combat mobility. This change didn't occur overnight, but developed slowly over a period of three years of intense counterguerrilla and conventional warfare. It was the product of a new type of combat mandated by the conditions and circumstances that evolved during the Vietnam conflict. Except in the coastal lowlands and in a few large, fertile valleys, airborne—parachute—operations were difficult if not impossible among the mountainous, jungle-covered terrain of Indochina.

The French had enjoyed somewhat limited success with airborne operations during their war in Vietnam, more often than not using this capability to reinforce or resupply beleaguered combat bases surrounded by enemy forces. But as an offensive combat arm of its own military forces, the French believed that airborne operations had a limited use in dealing with the mobile and highly elusive Viet Minh. A dozen years later, U.S. forces would discover that they suffered the same handicap in conducting combat operations against the Viet Cong.

Beginning in 1965, the 1st Air Cavalry pioneered helicopter warfare in combat operations against main force VC and NVA units. Their initial success promised a slow but steady transition from airborne tactical combat entry to the more flexible, quick response, heliborne operations that came to characterize the Vietnam War. As the air-mobile concept was quickly perfected, the enemy began ambushing and booby-trapping all large open areas in the immediate vicinity of their base camps that could be used by the Americans and their allies as multiple-ship landing zones for heliborne combat assaults. This created the need for a more subtle means of entry into small, single-ship landing zones, and—especially in the case of small Long Range Reconnaissance Patrols—into virtually nonexistent openings in dense jungle terrain. Insertion by rope ladder or free rappel became the two methods of choice, and by 1969 they were utilized by nearly all U.S. Long Range Patrol, Ranger, SEAL, Force Recon, and Special Forces recon teams operating in Vietnam.

With new refinements in technique, and with the 101st Airborne Division's own operational requirement for putting infantry and combat engineers onto remote, heavily vegetated mountain peaks to carve out temporary fire support bases, someone had to provide rappelling training on a mass scale. This became the job of L Company, 75th Infantry (Ranger).

Blessed with a small number of former Special Forces NCOs and young team leaders experienced in free-rappelling techniques, the Rangers began to conduct rappelling classes on their company helicopter pad. Initially, elements of the division's 326th Engineer Battalion arrived to learn how to rappel onto a virgin mountaintop with their chain saws and explosive charges to quickly carve out a single-ship chopper pad from the surrounding jungle. This gave the division the capability of relocating artillery positions almost at will to support combat operations that were designed to plunge unannounced into the vast reaches of the enemy's sanctuaries in the Chaîne Annamatique.

Moving quickly to avoid attracting attention, an air strike or artillery prep on a selected mountaintop knocked down enough of the overhead cover to enable a small group of combat engineers and their Ranger or infantry security force to rappel into the site and clear away the underbrush. Within hours Chinook helicopters were sling-loading small caterpillars, backhoes, rolls of concertina wire, pallets of sandbags, bridge timbers, perforated steel planking (PSP), and all the other items necessary to construct and man a fully operational fire support base. This technique gave the division the capability of effectively taking the war to the enemy anywhere at any time within its area of operations, and to do so before NVA forces could mount an effective response or withdraw from the area.

Later, 101st Airborne Rangers provided the same training for the 2/17th Cav's aero-rifle troopers and the division's regular infantry, along with their South Vietnamese counterparts. The ability to rope into restricted areas gave Allied forces access to the enemy that had previously been denied by the rugged terrain and dense vegetation of South Vietnam.

"Slack-jumping" was an experimental method of rappelling from a helicopter which incorporated the principles of free-falling and the art of free-rappel. It allowed the participant to achieve unimpeded maximum velocity during the descent, yet enabled him to control his landing upon reaching the ground. In practice it was not nearly as confusing as it sounds. The originators of slack-jumping were supposedly looking for a means to enable rappelling soldiers to reach the ground faster than they did using conventional rappelling techniques. In theory, the shorter the time on the rope, the shorter opportunity the enemy had to make a target of you, and the shorter the time the helicopter had to remain in a vulnerable hover over the landing site.

Slack jumping involved snapping onto the 100- to 120-foot rappelling rope at a point seventy to eighty feet below where it was secured to the rigging in the helicopter, then stepping off the skid into a vertical free fall, which ended when the participant reached the end of his "slack line." At that point he would gently but firmly apply pressure with his "brake" arm, resulting in a rapid deceleration, culminating in a standard free rappel the remaining distance to the ground.

There were some inherent dangers involved with this technique that prevented its practice on combat operations, but it was still used on occasion by rappelling instructors to impress and terrify their new students.

Such an occasion occurred on March 1, 1969, when Ranger

Platoon Sergeant Richard "Bernie" Burnell decided to put on a slack-jumping demonstration to introduce rappelling to a new group of combat engineer trainees from the division's 326th Engineer Battalion.

Burnell, a Ranger school instructor back in the States, had already earned a reputation as "one tough son of a bitch." Besides being fearless in combat and hard-driving in the field, Burnell's legendary barroom feats of derring-do were the talk of the division. He would sit at a table chugging a glass of beer, and then when he had finished drinking, proceed to eat the glass. His taste for the inedible included lightbulbs and double-edged razor blades, which he would snap in half before swallowing. No one could understand how he survived these frontal assaults to his gastrointestinal tract, but Burnell seemed to thrive on it, which only elevated his stature in a company of warriors to almost mythical proportions.

Burnell was also famous for his "tough-man" tests, which fortunately produced few challengers. When Bernie ran into some blowhard who he considered a possible challenger to his undisputed claim as the "toughest son of a bitch in the Rangers," he would invite him to sit down with him at a table in the Ranger lounge or one of the Division NCO clubs. After an appropriate audience had formed, Sergeant Burnell would place his bare arm alongside the bare arm of his unsuspecting antagonist, then calmly drop a freshly lit cigarette in the seam formed by their two forearms. He would quickly admonish the startled individual that the first one who flinched or moved his arm was a "pussy." Soon, the smell of burning hair and charred flesh had the weaker observers running for the door with their hands over their mouths. No one recalls Burnell ever being a pussy, nor does anyone remember a challenger lasting the full length of a cigarette. Platoon Sergeant Richard Burnell, forearms cratered like the surface of the moon, was indeed the toughest son of a bitch in the Rangers.

As he stood balanced on the skid of the Huey hovering over the penta-prime chopper pad at the Ranger compound, Burnell looked over his shoulder at the ground and then at the hundred or so Rangers and engineers surrounding the helipad, and he smiled. His audience was in place and the show about to begin. The Rangers knew what was coming, but the engineers thought they were about to witness a standard rappelling demonstration. The only thing standard about "Bernie" Burnell was his height—everything else was bigger than life.

Bernie looked back inside the helicopter and watched for his bellyman, who was wired into the aircraft's intercom, to give him a signal. Suddenly, the pilot nodded and gave the bellyman the word that they had reached an altitude of 110 feet and it was okay to go. The bellyman turned to the waiting Ranger platoon sergeant and screamed, *"Do it!"* Burnell stepped back off the skid in a perfect upright, tight body position and dropped like a rock toward the all-weather chopper pad. A collective gasp went up from the engineers. The Rangers only smiled. Bernie had done this act before. They knew he would hit the end of his slack twenty or thirty feet above the ground, and top it off with a perfect rappel. But it wouldn't happen that way this time.

No one knows for certain exactly when Bernie realized that he had more slack rope between himself and the helicopter rigging than he had altitude, but something told him that his "shit was weak," which compelled him to execute a perfect airborne PLF (parachute landing fall) a split second before he slammed into the chopper pad. The instinctive parachute landing fall probably saved his life. The helicopter pilot had misread his altimeter and had given the "go" when the chopper was only seventy-five feet above the ground. With eighty feet of slack between Bernie's D-ring and the helicopter rigging, the Ranger NCO had in essence "jumped" seventy-five feet from a hovering helicopter onto a rock-hard surface.

This would have killed a normal man, probably even a normal Ranger, but Sergeant Richard Burnell was not a normal man, nor was he a normal Ranger. Miraculously, he survived the impact. Suffering a shattered pelvis and two broken legs—some estimate it could have been as many as three—Burnell was rushed to the surgical hospital at Phu Bai. Every medical specialist at the 85th Evac believed that if he survived his injuries, he would never walk again. But they were wrong. They didn't know Platoon Sergeant Bernie Burnell. He would go on to retire years later as a brigade command sergeant major in the 82nd Airborne Division, still a Ranger, still a legend, and still one tough son of a bitch.

Another incident occurred in April 1969, when Staff Sergeant Julian Dedman, an L Company team leader, was flying bellyman on a 101st Aviation Battalion lift ship. The mission was a midday insertion designed to get an engineer team and an infantry squad into a jungle-choked ridgeline just east of the Ashau Valley. Their task was to open up a high spot on the crest of the ridge to accommodate a 105mm artillery battery scheduled to be flown in and set up later that evening.

Dedman, one of the Ranger NCOs who had served as a rappelling instructor to the engineers, had been ordered to rig three helicopters with rappelling harnesses to insert the engineer team and the grunts. When he finished rigging the aircraft, Dedman volunteered to fly bellyman on the lead ship going into the ridgeline. In addition to the Ranger NCO and the four-man air crew, six combat engineers from the 326th Engineer Battalion were also on board.

Just before noon on April 23, 1969, the heavily loaded helicopter was approaching the high point on the ridgeline where the firebase was to be constructed. Dedman was standing up in the center of the cabin snapping a pair of combat engineers onto the two rappelling ropes secured to the rigging on the floor of the helicopter. The two men were holding the weighted sandbags containing the coiled rappelling ropes and were waiting to toss them out of the cabin on Dedman's command. The aircraft was just slowing to a hover when the B-40 rocket flashed out of the jungle and turned the Huey into a giant fireball. There were no survivors.

In early February 1970, a lot of new 11 Bravo infantrymen (i.e., riflemen) were coming into the 101st Airborne Division as replacements. Since the division had in effect ceased to be an "airborne" division in 1968, and was operating as an airmobile or air-assault division, it became imperative that these new replacements be taught the air-assault method of inserting into a tight LZ. And in the "new" 101st Airborne Division this method of insertion meant rappelling.

Since no one in the division had mastered the fine art of mountaineering better than the division's Rangers, it became their task to train these new recruits. The 326th Engineer Battalion had constructed an outstanding rappelling tower in their battalion area. As nearly all of them had been trained to rappel during the previous months by Ranger instructors, they generously permitted the Rangers to use their tower to conduct their rappelling course. Depending on the size of the class, it seldom took more than a day or two to put the entire group through a tower phase of training and an aircraft phase. At the end of the course, the students were familiar, if not proficient, with the technique of rappelling from a helicopter.

The 326th Engineer's training tower consisted of two distinct faces—one, a solid, walled face, made up of vertical sheets of PSP grating, was used to simulate rappelling down the face of a cliff or the side of a building; the other, a "free" or open face, simulated rappelling from a suspended platform or a helicopter. The two methods of vertical rope descent provided new skills to the combat proficiency of the Screaming Eagle soldiers who were already building a reputation as the finest U.S. infantrymen in South Vietnam.

The Rangers' job was to take each replacement off the walled side of the tower until he felt comfortable with the procedure, then move around to the opposite side of the tower to take him off the free side. This was more than just a familiarization, since most of them would soon be using the technique in the field. After the Ranger instructors completed the tower segment of the training, they moved the recruits to the final phase—rappelling from a helicopter.

One morning a number of Ranger instructors had just taken a batch of newbies through the tower segment of training and had stopped for their usual midday lunch break. During the meal, instructor Sergeants Riley Cox, Joe Bielesch, and Dave Bennett decided to have a little fun with the recruits during the afternoon helicopter phase of training.

When chow was over, a demonstration team of L Company Rangers went up in the helicopter to show the trainees exactly what was expected of them. While the six Rangers went through their paces on board the aircraft, Ranger NCO Dave

Bennett stood before the class and went over the importance of rigging a "Swiss seat" properly, clipping onto the D-ring, exiting from the aircraft, applying the "brake" and completing the rappel. He stressed again and again how critical it was to feed the rappelling rope through the D-ring twice.

When the instructors felt that their pupils had a good grasp of what was expected of them, they excused the demonstration team and loaded the first batch of neophytes into the waiting aircraft. Before the Huey left the ground, Bennett, Cox, and Bielesch once more rechecked each man's Swiss rappelling harness to make sure it was properly tied. When everything was ready, Bielesch signaled for the pilot to lift off while Cox and Bennett remained on the ground to handle the belay rope.

In each training cycle there were always a couple of loud-mouths who had a smart comment or a wise answer for everything the instructors had to say. This batch of trainees was no different; three or four of them were taking frequent liberties with the Ranger instructors, liberties that didn't go unnoticed.

At lunch the three Ranger NCOs concocted a scheme to deal with the know-it-alls. During the helicopter phase, they would make sure that at least one of the loudmouthed troublemakers was part of each group of trainees that was taken up. The instructor aboard the aircraft would make certain that the first trainee rigged on the line was one of the perpetrators. Each trainee had been taught that prior to making his rappel, he was to first step out on the skid, then turn and face the cabin, making sure the "brake" hand with the leading end of the rappel line was firmly positioned in the small of his back. Then, gripping the secure end of the line in his "control" hand, he was to lean back away from the skid until he was nearly horizontal to the ground, thereby reaching a "point of no return." On command from the instructor, the trainee was to step off the skid and slide under the helicopter to rappel the remainder of the way to the ground.

Sergeant Bielesch went up with the first group. He designated one of the troublemakers to go first and told him to hook up to the rope. He watched silently as the trooper stepped out on the skid and turned to face the cabin. As instructed, the soldier began playing out line until he was nearly horizontal to the skid.

Just as the man reached the critical point of no return, Sergeant Bielesch stepped forward to the edge of the cabin, looked down at the nearly horizontal soldier, and screamed, *"Hey, that's not right!"*

Immediately, the shocked trainee panicked and let go of the rope just as he stepped off the skid and dropped beneath the aircraft. Sergeant Cox, on the other end of the line, jerked the belay rope tight to prevent the wildly thrashing trainee from completing an out-of-control slide into the ground. When the stunned soldier finally collected himself enough to reach up and recover the rope, Cox gave him a little slack and let him finish his rappel. Upon reaching the ground, the trainee fed the remainder of the rope through his D-ring, then moved quietly to the rear, embarrassed over his performance and panic. Fortunately, the noise of the helicopter had drowned out the words of the instructor that had caused the soldier's panic, thus preventing anyone on the ground from realizing what had happened.

Bennett went up with the second group, and when the next troublemaker leaned back away from the skid, Bennett dropped down on his hands and knees and moved to the edge of the cabin floor. When the man leaned back and reached the point of no return, Sergeant Bennett leaned out over the edge, pointed toward the snap link and yelled, *"That's not right!"* As before, the new replacement immediately panicked and released his rope. As he began to fall, he reached up and grabbed Bennett's nearest hand and pulled him out of the aircraft. Unfortunately, Bennett was not hooked up to the rappelling rope, nor was he connected to the helicopter by means of a lifeline. Both soldiers began to fall.

Bennett, motivated by sheer survival instinct, reached out and snagged the rope in his right hand. This enabled him to slow his free fall from a hundred plus miles per hour to about sixty. And as he continued his uncontrolled slide down the rope, he slammed head first into the trainee who was also desperately attempting to retard his descent. Stunned by the force of the collision, Bennett once more released the rope and resumed his uncontrolled fall toward the ground.

Cox, on the ground manning the belay rope, saw Bennett

jerked from the helicopter and reacted instantly, pulling the rope tight and backing away from the projected point of impact. But when he saw Bennett collide with the trainee and begin to fall toward the ground again, he swung the rope he was holding wide to one side, and somehow managed to snag Bennett's right leg, tangling him in the line. Bennett responded immediately by doing the only thing he could do. In total desperation, he latched onto two large handfuls of nylon rappelling rope and squeezed it for all it was worth—all the way to the ground. There he suffered his second collision in as many seconds, driving head first into Ranger Sergeant Riley "Dozer" Cox. And Cox hadn't been given the nickname "Dozer" because he liked to sleep a lot.

When the gravitational pull of the Earth finally gave up on Sergeant Bennett, he lay in a heap on the ground, a spent projectile still tangled in the rappelling lines. But he was still not out of danger. He now faced the very real prospect of the pilot's climbing up and away from the chopper pad. If he did, the hapless Ranger NCO would be dragged back into the air. And somewhere above him, still attached to the rope, was a suitably humbled ex-loudmouth trainee who was still trying to understand what had happened.

Cox and Bielesch stepped back from under the aircraft and signaled wildly for the pilot to slide the helicopter to one side or the other while they attempted to get Bennett and the now thoroughly confused and frightened trainee off the rope without another collision.

The pilot finally recognized the problem and slowly lowered the helicopter in stages until the two men were removed from the ropes. When they were free and had been carried away from the chopper pad, the pilot landed the aircraft amid a choking cloud of dust and debris. Bielesch and Cox immediately rushed to get the injured Ranger back on board the helicopter, and shouted instructions to the pilot to get him down to the surgical hospital at Phu Bai.

Bennett showed up back at the company later that afternoon none the worse for wear. But he had so many bandages on both hands that everyone started calling him Mickey Mouse after the white-gloved Disney rodent on TV back in the World. In addition, the Ranger also suffered nasty rope burns on both legs, both arms, and across his chest, and he was still somewhat shaken from his head-first dive toward the asphalt chopper pad. Otherwise, the veteran Ranger would live to train again.

His only comment to his grinning comrades: "Dozer, if you'd have gotten the hell out of my way, I probably would have been able to see my life pass before my eyes."

Rappelling was just one of a Ranger's many methods of inserting into his area of operations. There were many more skills he would have to master.

Upon a volunteer's arrival in the company, he was immediately assigned to a team, specifically for training purposes. This not only served to keep the teams fully manned, but also allowed the new man to feel he'd become part of something special, something he could bond to—a team. Of course, a newly assigned but untrained Ranger was a long way from being a valuable component of a team, but his assignment to one gave him an immediate sense of belonging, and a strong desire to do well and contribute his part to the team effort. And if he did not quickly demonstrate that sense of loyalty, his days as a Lurp/Ranger would swiftly come to an end.

Once this sense of belonging was fully instilled and the new Ranger's loyalty established, the team began the process of breaking in the FNG ("fucking new guy"), educating him in the finer arts of long range patrolling. Several weeks of rugged physical training, immediate action drills,* weapons' zeroing, map and compass reading, radio communication, first aid, and insertion/extraction techniques—all performed alongside his teammates—provided the neophyte with most of the basic techniques of long range patrolling. Then, after individual sessions with his team leader and assistant team leader and other patrol members demonstrating the proven methods of setting up one's LBE (load bearing equipment), packing rucksacks,

---

*Immediate action drills were frequently rehearsed, team-size maneuvers to be used automatically under specific situations, usually enemy contact to the patrol's front, rear, or flanks.

setting out claymore mines, loading magazines, weapons care, prepacking Lurp rations, understanding the CAR-codes, field first aid and medications, patrol technique, silent movement, hand signals, break-in patrols, booby-trapping, escape and evasion, rendezvous points, directing artillery fire and air strikes, and the myriad other skills designed to successfully survive on a Long Range Patrol, the new man was finally ready to go out on his first mission.

But a Lurp/Ranger never stopped learning. When he did, or when he thought that he knew enough—well, that's when he would make a mistake, and mistakes were what got him "fatally" killed. "Fatally" killed was the worst way to die.

There was no diploma, no graduation ceremony for the new Lurp/Ranger, because the training never ended. When a new man's teammates thought he was ready to be a part of the team, they let him know that they would now permit him to accompany them on a mission. It didn't mean he was accepted on the team, and it didn't mean that he was a Ranger. It only meant that he'd earned the right to be on probation, and that if he didn't fuck up and get himself or a teammate killed, they just might continue to let him fill a spot on a team. At some point down the line he would know when the probation period was over and he was finally accepted as a full-fledged member of the team and a "real" Ranger.

Those who paid their dues and excelled at the art were usually recognized as potential team leaders and assistant team leaders. These Rangers were normally assigned one of the limited slots at MACV Recondo School at Nha Trang. Run by the 5th Special Forces Group, this was the "finishing school," the Juilliard of long range patrolling. Its successful graduates returned to their units with the self-confidence and polish necessary to lead other Rangers on the lonely long range patrols behind enemy lines. Probably the finest school of its kind anywhere in the world, even those who failed to complete the course and earn the school certificate and the right to wear the MACV Recondo patch were still a notch above those who failed to attend the school at all.

It was the tradition that the honor graduate of each class at MACV Recondo School be awarded a Gerber commando dagger by the school's staff. During the school's illustrious history, a large number of 101st Airborne Division Lurp/Rangers won that coveted award, a testament to the quality of men who served in the division's Long Range Patrol units.

3

AIRBORNE RANGER

L CO   75TH INF

The Perfume River

On February 27, 1969, I was the newly appointed team leader of Team 2-2. I was surprised at the appointment. Having been wounded three days prior to my class date for MACV Recondo School in Nha Trang, I sat out my schooling at the 6th Convalescent Center in Cam Ranh Bay. It was a policy in our company that to obtain one of the scarce slots for Recondo School, you not only had to be team leader/assistant team leader material, but you had to have six months left in-country when you started class. When I was released from the hospital just before Christmas 1968, and from my physical profile a month later, I was down to just over four months left in-country. There was no point wasting a slot on someone who would be into double numbers when he graduated. So I missed my opportunity to wear the coveted MACV Recondo "arrowhead" patch, and I missed my opportunity to attend the finest long range patrolling course in the world. So it's probably understandable that I was flabbergasted when told that I would be taking out my own team.

I was assigned a two-day reconnaissance mission into an area along the Perfume River southwest of Camp Eagle and just north of Leech Island. The recon zone sat along the east side of the river in the evening shadows of the Annamatique mountain range that rose quickly from its foothills just across the blue line, which was the river, designated by a blue line on the map. It was typical river bottom with a narrow band of single canopy trees and spotty to heavy vegetation running along the shoreline.

A hundred meters east of the river there were sparsely covered, rolling hills common to the coastal piedmont. The west side of the river provided much better cover and concealment for a six-man long range patrol, but for reasons unknown to me or anyone in the company, Division Intelligence (G-2) had selected the east side of the river as our recon zone. Our mission was to set up an observation post and remain there in hiding for two nights to monitor enemy boat traffic. We were supposed to count boats—not fire them up, just count them. Some guys get no respect!

Intelligence had been receiving numerous reports of light-to-moderate sampan traffic on a portion of the Perfume River that shouldn't have been getting any at all. I remember wondering who in the hell was making the reports. But I guess Division still needed someone to confirm them. That part of the river was in a free-fire zone, all the villages in the area having long ago been relocated closer to the coast. If the NVA units in the mountains were using the Perfume River at night to move supplies from Hue back into their sanctuaries, Division wanted to know about it.

My patrol was also ordered to look for signs of river crossings within the boundaries of our recon zone. Enemy troop concentrations moving from the mountains out into the piedmont and coastal areas had to be crossing in a number of places. Division wanted to know at what points they were fording.

Besides myself, Team 2-2 consisted of two other veteran Rangers—Sergeant Jim Schwartz, my assistant team leader and point man, and Sergeant Ken Munoz, Senior RTO; and three newbies—Privates First Class Marvin Hillman, Dean Groff, and Charles Kilburn. We weren't the most experienced team in the company, but then we weren't going into an area that was known for heavy enemy activity.

Our patrol inserted at dusk on February 27. Because of the open terrain and the high ground across the river, the insertion slick and the chase ship engaged in a series of false insertions and leapfrog tactics designed to confuse the enemy. Suddenly, our insertion aircraft flared over a stretch of open ground fifty feet from the tree line that bordered the river. I hollered *"Go"* and Schwartz and I were off the skids and running for cover while the chopper was still six feet above the ground. I looked over my shoulder. The rest of the team was right behind us.

Our helicopter dropped its nose to pick up forward momentum, and was already racing down the shoreline and out of sight even before we reached the safety of the trees along the river.

We lay panting in a tight circle facing out, fighting to get our breathing under control. It's difficult to listen for sounds of the enemy when the sound of your own heartbeat is pounding in your ears, but sprinting twenty yards with a hundred pounds of gear on your back will drain the wind from anyone's lungs.

While Munoz established radio contact with the TOC (tactical operations center) at Camp Eagle, I quickly double-checked my map to make sure that our position was correct. My calculation showed that we were a hundred meters too far north. It was only a slight pilot error on the insertion, but it was a mistake that would be difficult if not impossible to correct in the thirty minutes of daylight that was left; my patrol was to cover three hundred meters of single canopy cover choked with thick clusters of bamboo to reach a little knob of high ground overlooking the river. Three hundred meters in thirty minutes doesn't sound like a difficult task, but if you're trying to accomplish it without walking into an ambush or making unnecessary noise that might alert the enemy to your presence, it's next to impossible.

Thirty minutes later Schwartz stopped the team among the trees twenty feet back from where we could hear the river. It was now pitch-black along the water. To move forward another foot while "night blind" was too risky to chance. I decided to hold the team in place until the moon rose. According to our premission briefing, it was supposed to appear in the eastern sky in about thirty minutes.

We waited in standard patrol formation, stretched out over twenty meters. Schwartz faced upstream, Hillman downstream, with the rest of us alternating from east to west between them.

Nearly half an hour passed before the moon slowly began to appear above the eastern horizon. When Schwartz felt that he could once again advance without breaking brush and ricocheting off trees, he turned and signaled me. I nodded and turned to pass the word back to the rest of the patrol to get ready to move out. Soon my point man was easing through the heavy cover again, working his way slowly around the thicker clusters of mature bamboo. Only the sound of the river flowing past us ten meters to our right disturbed the silence of the night.

It took almost another thirty minutes to cover the final hundred meters to our OP (observation post) site, but we made it without incident. Schwartz knew he'd reached it when he stepped out of the brush and found himself looking down at the dark slash of a fresh trail running up from the edge of the river. The trail had been so heavily used that a shallow trench was worn into the sandy soil of the riverbank. Glancing to his right, Schwartz saw where the trail disappeared into a thicket overlooking the Perfume River.

I was ten meters back from the point when Schwartz stopped the patrol. Not knowing what was going on, I moved up slowly to see what had caused the halt. When I reached Schwartz, he nodded toward the river, and I spotted the trail. I whispered to Schwartz to remain there with the rest of the team while I followed the trail down to where it cut through the riverbank and entered the water. He nodded.

There were a number of muddy footprints on the trail just up the bank from the edge of the river, and they were fresh. This was the northern crossing Schwartz and I had spotted from the air during the overflight late that morning.

I returned quickly to the team and pulled them back into some heavy bamboo. The spot offered good cover and overlooked the river to the west. It was less than fifteen meters back from the edge of the footpath and was an excellent spot from which to monitor both the river and the trail.

Without waiting for my instructions, Schwartz took two of the new men and began to set out five claymores to cover the land approaches to our position. They left uncovered only the high riverbank on our right. When they were finished we settled back into the undergrowth to watch and listen.

At 0230 in the morning the silence was interrupted by the dull throb of a motor out on the river, perhaps a hundred meters upstream. The sound was moving in our direction. When approximately thirty to forty meters away, the engine suddenly changed pitch and slowed down to an easy idle. We listened anxiously as the sampan swung in toward the shoreline on our side of the river, then suddenly killed its engine. We waited breathlessly for at least thirty minutes, expecting the worst at any moment, but it was the last we heard of the sampan. It was almost as if the night had swallowed it completely.

I whispered for Munoz to call the 105 battery on Fire Support Base Brick and request that it stand by to fire a single "willie pete" (white phosphorous) round in the river fifty meters upstream from our position. There would be little time to adjust a fire mission if the enemy suddenly turned up in our faces. Munoz also took the initiative to alert the TOC of our situation. Not knowing what to expect, we remained at one hundred percent alert for the remainder of the night.

By dawn it had become obvious that the enemy had somehow moved out. I instructed my teammates to sanitize the NDP (night defensive perimeter/position) and pull in their claymores. I then put them on line with Schwartz on the left and myself on the edge of the river. When they were ready, we moved cautiously up to the edge of the trail. We had heard nothing more from the sampan or its occupants after the engine had shut down during the night, nor had we seen the enemy boat moving past us out on the river. The only other possibility was that it lay somewhere ahead of us, pulled up on the shoreline. I wondered if the enemy was up ahead waiting for us.

We hesitated for several minutes at the edge of the trail, listening and scanning the brush to our immediate front. Finally, I signaled for Schwartz to stay back with the new men while Munoz and I scouted ahead. Ten meters beyond the trail, we walked up on what appeared to be an old roadbed cut deep into the ground, running parallel to the river. It looked like one hell of a good place for an ambush. I radioed Schwartz and whispered for him to bring the rest of the team up on the left flank of the roadbed while Munoz and I scouted out the right flank.

Ten minutes later Schwartz was back on the air reporting that they had found a large bunker and a newly constructed, open-sided lean-to. I told him to sit tight while Munoz and I checked out the rest of the roadbed. When we were finished, we would swing around, cross over to his side and link back up with him.

A few feet ahead I looked down over the edge of the river-bank and saw that someone had pulled a boat ashore in the mud and then taken a few steps up the bank. Whoever it was had returned to the boat without coming all the way up to the roadbed. There was no explanation for the enemy's actions, but, for whatever reason, the occupant of the boat had decided not to land on shore nor continue downstream. It was spooky!

Thirty meters ahead the sunken roadbed played out. Munoz and I swung around 180 degrees and returned down the opposite side of the cut to where Schwartz sat waiting in the cover with the rest of the team.

The six-by-ten-foot bunker that Schwartz had found appeared to be only a couple of weeks old, constructed not as a fighting position, but as a hiding place secure from aerial reconnaissance. The lean-to was larger than the bunker and poorly constructed. Both structures showed recent use.

I set up security then took several quick photos of the two structures and the roadbed with a small Penn double-E 35mm camera that G-2 had furnished. When I was finished, I motioned for the team to get back into patrol formation and move out toward a second river crossing twelve hundred meters to the south. Schwartz and I had spotted it during the overflight, and I wanted to inspect it up close before dark.

It took six hours to cover the distance through the vine-choked brush and heavy bamboo along the river. When we finally reached the crossing, I was disappointed to discover that it was thickly overgrown and apparently hadn't been used in several years.

By then it was past 1600 hours (four P.M., in civilian) and less than two hours of daylight remained. I debated moving back to the first crossing for the final night of the mission or staying where we were. We'd covered a lot of ground during the day as we moved through the narrow stretch of trees that flanked the river, and were often in full view of anyone who might be posted up in the mountains on the west side of the Perfume. Because of the poor cover along the river, that couldn't be helped. There was a good possibility that we'd been observed by enemy scouts on the high ground.

It would be growing dark soon and I was beginning to have some major misgivings about spending another night along the river. We had already accomplished our mission, and I guess I was looking for a good excuse to get out of there. The hair on the back of my neck was beginning to stand at attention, and my sphincter was starting to draw shut—warning signs that should never be ignored. We had already ascertained that the enemy was using the river. One of the two crossings in the AO (area of operations) was definitely being used, while the other was not. And we had located a squad-size overnight rest area on the east side of the river that was less than two weeks old. It was all the intelligence we were going to gather without a very personal contact with an enemy unit.

It was enough for me! I had succeeded in convincing myself that to stay was to die. I got on the radio and called Captain Cardona back at Camp Eagle to request an extraction at last light. The captain wanted to know why I was requesting an early extraction. I knew he wouldn't buy the standing hair and the tight asshole, so I gave him all those "other" reasons I had managed to rationalize.

He denied the request. I could tell by the tone in his voice that he was also questioning his judgment in giving me a team. He stated that unless we made contact, the patrol would be extracted at 0900 the next day—as planned. Well thank you, sir!

In the past it had always been the team leader's call on the ground to decide when and where his patrol would come out, but this new commanding officer had different ideas. He had determined that the final decision to end a mission prior to the scheduled extraction would fall under his domain as the officer in charge. That was a bad decision and it would result in future casualties and shatter the confidence the Long Range Patrols had in their own ability to survive deep behind enemy lines.

I led the patrol back away from the river and into the thickest cover we could find. But in the narrow band of trees between the river and the open piedmont to the east, no cover was thick enough to prevent a determined and resourceful enemy from locating us. It would likely be a long night.

We set out three claymores and sat back to await the arrival of darkness. The consensus among us was that we were very vulnerable if we remained where we were. Schwartz, Munoz, and I were trying real hard not to alarm the new men, but we could tell from the looks on their faces that they sensed our anxiety.

As darkness began to settle in, our sense of despair and foreboding increased. Finally, I whispered to my teammates to pull in their claymores and prepare to move out. I wasn't sure where we were going, but I knew we weren't going to stay in the trees along the river that night. My teammates seemed relieved at my decision and told me that I was doing the right thing. Great for the libido, bad for the *cojones*!

With a sense of urgency born of desperation, we moved quickly from the thicket and out into the open piedmont. The grass-covered, gently rolling terrain east of the river had all the cover and concealment of a newly constructed golf course, but to my now fully spooked team the open country would buy us time—time to spot an enemy patrol looking for us, and for us to deal with it.

A hundred meters from the trees we came upon a low hill rising perhaps ten to fifteen feet above the surrounding terrain. There was no cover or concealment near the hill, but in the total darkness that preceded the rising moon, the hill itself offered a barrier between us and whatever danger, real or perceived, existed back in the trees along the river.

I posted two men on the crest, one facing the river, the other facing east, and took the rest of the team with me to string out six claymores around the knoll. From our new vantage point on top of the hill the two observers would be able to spot enemy activity in time to alert the rest of the team. I cautioned the two guards to remain prone, to minimize their movement, and in particular to avoid standing out against the skyline. If the enemy came at us from across the open ground, the clay-mores would give us the time we needed to E&E or to get a reaction force out from Camp Eagle.

It was almost 0230 when Kilburn slid down off the back side of the knoll and gently shook me awake. He whispered in my ear that he had just seen a light in the tree line close to where we had set up in the brush just before dark. He said that it had looked like a match or a cigarette lighter, but he couldn't be sure. It had only lasted a few seconds, but it was long enough to assure him that it hadn't been a firefly or a figment of his imagination. I asked him if Schwartz had also seen it, only to be told that the ATL had been looking in the opposite direction and had seen nothing.

Shaking the sleep out of my eyes, I told Kilburn to take a break, that I would relieve him a little early. With the nervous newbie safely ensconced behind the limited protection of the hill, I crawled up next to Schwartz, who was now looking intensely at the spot where Kilburn had seen the light.

"Did you see anything, Schwartzy?" I asked in a hushed whisper, my voice betraying my nervousness.

"Not really, but I was looking the other way when he saw it. I've been watching the spot ever since and I haven't seen a thing."

The two of us remained in that position for the rest of the night. If there had been some kind of a light in the trees along the river, it never revealed itself again.

At 0900 that morning, a single Huey slick landed in a low open spot thirty meters from the knoll. Six Rangers sprinted the final distance to the helicopter and scrambled quickly aboard. The Huey rose slowly and turned to the east before dipping its nose to gain forward momentum.

When the mission was over, the patrol back in the relatively safe confines of Camp Eagle, I questioned Kilburn before the debriefing, and believed the kid when he told me he'd definitely seen a light in the trees. There had been no reason for him to make up such a story.

When everything was said and done, each of the Rangers on Team 2-2 was satisfied that the enemy had indeed been in the tree line along the river that night. Had we remained where we

were instead of moving away from the river, we might not have
survived until daylight.

Sometimes it's skill that saves a recon team deep in enemy
territory, and sometimes it's luck. But on the night of February
28–29, it was something else entirely that caused us to move
out of the trees and take up a position in the open. It's a difficult thing to explain, and maybe I'm not altogether convinced
myself. But then maybe you just had to be there to understand!

4

Find Our Pilots!

Vietnam-era Lurp/Rangers possess an almost unnatural respect and appreciation for the courageous helicopter pilots and crewmen who supported their operations. Well, maybe it's not so unnatural. Without the sacrifices and risks taken by those pilots and crewmen, most of those Lurp/Rangers wouldn't be around at all.

A Ranger's lifeline for survival was the control stick in the hands of the slick (transport) and gunship pilots who routinely flew through massed enemy small-arms and antiaircraft fire to support six-man recon teams trapped deep in enemy territory.

A Ranger's lifeline for survival was the butterfly trigger grips on the M-60s in the able hands of the door gunners who, often hanging in space secured only by a nylon lifeline, fought tenaciously from the open hellholes of hovering Hueys to drive back charging VC/NVA soldiers trying to prevent the escape of a trapped recon team.

A Ranger's lifeline for survival was the thin steel cable supporting the torpedo shape of the jungle penetrator that lifted him, wounded and bleeding, from the double and triple canopy jungles of South Vietnam.

A Ranger's lifeline for survival was the thin red hose of minigun tracers and the deadly 2.75 rockets of Huey and Cobra gunships that kept him alive when all else failed.

Ask any Lurp/Ranger why he'll never let a helicopter pilot or crewman pay for a drink when he's around, and maybe then you'll begin to understand that the respect, and the appreciation, and the "love," is something that doesn't need to be explained.

Now that you know how Rangers feel about the helicopter jocks and their shotguns, you'll be more inclined to understand what singular thought goes through a Ranger's mind when the call *"Chopper down!"* goes out.

On March 7, 1969, L Company Rangers were called upon to perform an unusual mission. The rescue of two downed helicopter crews was originally intended to involve only two Ranger teams and last no more than three hours. Before it was over, two additional Ranger teams would be inserted, an infantry company would join the operation, and the mission would take seven full days to complete.

The warning order reached the company area just after lunch. Earlier that morning a Cobra gunship from the 77th ARA (Aerial Rocket Artillery) flying a combat strike in low cloud cover had gone down in the mountains south of Camp Eagle. A short time later an LOH (pronounced "Loach") scout helicopter was dispatched to locate the downed Cobra. It, too, disappeared into a cloud bank over the same area. The brigade commander realized that because of the poor weather conditions an aerial search would likely produce nothing but more aircraft losses. He contacted Division headquarters and asked for a rescue team that could rappel into the crash sites. Rappelling meant a Ranger team.

Staff Sergeant Ron Bowman, recently transferred into L Company from the 3/506th LRP detachment at Phan Thiet, was the new platoon sergeant of Lima Company's second platoon. When he got the warning order, he scoured the company for a Ranger team to volunteer for the mission. But there wasn't a single operational recon team in the rear at that time. With six teams out on patrol, and a large number of Rangers on R&R, extension leave, or away at MACV Recondo School in Nha Trang, there were fewer than twenty Rangers available in the entire compound.

Sergeant Richard Fadeley and I were enjoying a few days'

stand-down when we got the word that the TOC was looking for a couple of teams to rescue two downed air crews. Recalling all the times that our bacon had been pulled from the fire by helicopter crews, we immediately volunteered to lead the two rescue teams.

However, neither of us had a full team on hand in the company area. We quickly realized that we would have to go through the platoon barracks to locate enough fill-ins to put together two complete teams. After our alert, Division made the decision to put a single twelve-man ("heavy") team into the area around the crash site because it was suspected that the Cobra might have been brought down by enemy fire.

This changed our plans. Fadeley, as the senior man, would take charge of the combined teams once we were on the ground. I would serve as his ATL (assistant team leader) and would take my six-man team in on the first lift ship. Fadeley's team would follow right behind us in the second lift ship and insert into the same LZ.

We were told to go in light with weapons and load-bearing equipment (suspenderlike harnesses on which small pieces of equipment, ammunition, etc., are hung)—no rucks, no food, no extra water. They told us we wouldn't be in that long. Staging out of Fire Support Base Tomahawk, we were to carry in nothing that would interfere with a quick insertion right on top of the downed aircraft. It would take no more than thirty minutes to an hour to locate and extract the air crews or their bodies, and another thirty minutes to strip the aircraft of weapons and radios. Then a short "string" ride back to Firebase Tomahawk and it would be over. It all sounded so simple!

Fadeley and I took a quick swing through the barracks asking for volunteers to accompany us on the rescue mission. It didn't take us very long to throw together a couple of teams. Sergeants Larry Saenz, Dave Biedron, and Ken Munoz, and Spec 4s Mike Kilburn and Dean Groff, made up my team. Fadeley wasn't as lucky, rounding up Sergeant Phil Myers and four new E-4s. Fadeley and I each designated an RTO and ordered the two men to tie their PRC-25 radios to pack frames rather than carry them in an empty ruck.

Some of the more experienced Rangers grabbed bags of

claymores and some extra grenades from the ammo bunker, and threw together strobe lights, a few pen-gun flares, and a compass or two. There was no time to run an equipment check or to test-fire our weapons. We knew that was a bad way to start a mission, but those pilots had to be rescued before "oh-dark-thirty," while we could still see to support them.

We grabbed our weapons, web gear, an extra bandoleer or two of ammunition, and headed for the company chopper pad. There had been no time to change into cammies or to apply camouflage face paint, or even to double-check weapons and gear. In the excitement of the moment even the older veterans among us had failed to notice that few of the SOP safeguards and premission rituals had been followed. None of us had even had enough time to get nervous. Well, what the hell! They told us we would be back at Camp Eagle by dark!

We scrambled into our Swiss seat rappelling harnesses while waiting on the chopper pad for the arrival of the two slicks that would ferry us out to the crash sites. The wait ran to thirty minutes while two of the company's senior NCOs, Staff Sergeants Johnson and Bowman, went over to the Cav compound to rig the aircraft for rappelling. Johnson and Bowman would also act as bellymen during the insertions.

When the Cav slicks finally set down on our chopper pad, we boarded immediately, anxious to get under way. We wanted to make certain we got in and out before dark, before the NVA got to the pilots and the enemy located the downed aircraft and set up a special welcome for the rescue party.

As we flew south across the open, rolling hills between Camp Eagle and Firebase Tomahawk, Staff Sergeant Bowman shouted that he had just gotten word that we'd been ordered to land at the firebase to receive a final briefing from a division staff officer, and to await the arrival of a pair of Cobra gunships to escort us into the area where the two aircraft had gone down.

Both were good news, but we knew that any delay meant less time on the ground to complete our mission. With the day already wearing late, time was becoming a critical factor to the success of the operation.

The two helicopters landed on the small, two-ship, perforated-steel-planking chopper pad just outside the firebase perimeter wire. To avoid wasting any more time than necessary, Fadeley and I instructed our teammates to wait with the aircraft while we attended the briefing. As we walked across the firebase toward a tight cluster of officers standing near the command bunker, a tall, thin lieutenant ran up and ordered us to form up our teams along the outer edge of the chopper pad. Perturbed by such an unwarranted and useless delay, we turned and beckoned our teammates to join us.

When we had formed up, an LOH scout helicopter popped up over the edge of the already crowded helipad, then sidled over to the center of the firebase, settling down in an open area next to a large command bunker. Seconds later two officers stepped down and walked toward us. One was a tough-looking, full-bird colonel (that is, not merely a lieutenant colonel), the other was Major General Melvin Zais, commander of the 101st Airborne Division.

Zais, dressed in starched ODs (olive-drab fatigues) and looking every bit the commanding general, walked smartly over to where we stood waiting. We started to snap to attention but he waved us "at ease." Then he smiled warmly and thanked us for volunteering to go out on a dangerous rescue mission. He explained that in the 101st every effort was made to recover missing soldiers. Of course, it was unnecessary to explain this to us; our dedication to the aviation crews who supported us was already well-established, and we had a rich—and valuable—tradition in the Rangers of never leaving our own behind.

The general went on to say that there were five good men out there in the jungle, either alive or dead—it didn't make any difference. If they were still alive and not in the hands of the enemy, they would be anxiously waiting for rescue; if dead, their bodies had to be recovered and returned to their families and loved ones. One way or the other, it was our mission to go in and get them out.

All of the missing soldiers were division officers—three warrants, a captain, and a lieutenant colonel. With a gesture and a final expression of his personal gratitude, General Zais turned the briefing over to the staff officer standing beside him.

The colonel said that the two helicopters had gone down no

more than a couple of hundred meters apart. The Cobra had most likely been shot down by a .51-caliber machine gun while attacking a bunker complex. It had broken in two on impact in double canopy jungle about halfway up a steep mountainside. Thirty minutes later the LOH had flown into a low cloud bank looking for the gunship and had failed to come out. Another LOH inched its way into the clouds and located the Cobra, and after a brief search reported that it had also found the wreckage of the scout helicopter. It appeared to have gone down two hundred meters west of the Cobra on the same mountainside. The pilot also reported that the scout aircraft had apparently burned on impact.

Intelligence had also reported a couple of NVA battalions were working in the area and had been active over the past few days. There were no maps of the crash site available on short notice, so artillery fire support would be out of the question. However, the colonel did promise that four Cobra gunships would be placed on standby alert, ready to come to our aid if needed.

One of the Rangers behind me whispered, "That's all we need to hear! Four more gunships down in the middle of those mountains! It'll take us a month to get everybody out." The mission was beginning to assume the customary trappings of a well-organized gang fight.

After the briefing, Fadeley and I decided to go in simultaneously, as close to each other as the pilots of the two ships could get us. Our two teams would rappel into the jungle then link up and move to the site of the downed Cobra first. From the description of the two crash sites, the Cobra crew seemed much more likely to be found alive. It would also be a lot easier to get two live men out than three dead ones. In addition, there was the factor of the cloud cover settling in over the higher crash site first. Fadeley and I estimated our time on the ground at ninety minutes to two hours. If the mission ran any longer, darkness and the weather would likely prevent the recovery, a possibility no one wanted to consider.

We quickly boarded the two slicks and flew off toward the mountains. We picked up a pair of Cobras a couple of klicks west of Tomahawk. We could no longer see the mountains ahead, only the fluffy cottonlike blanket of a thick fog bank.

The four helicopters began to lose airspeed as they approached the dense fog bank. The Cobras went into a wide orbit a mile or two behind us. The pilots of the two slicks put fifty meters between the two aircraft, then slowly began to inch their ships into the fog. A hundred meters inside, the aircraft suddenly broke out into a gauzy pocket of dim, gray clouds. It was like being in the eye of a hurricane, except there was no sky overhead. It was a new and alien experience for both the air crews and the Rangers, sitting quietly aboard the helicopters. Only the tops of tall trees jutting up through a thick blanket of ground fog enabled the pilots to tell up from down without relying entirely on their instruments. Somewhere ahead of them in the clouds, they knew, was a pretty high mountaintop.

Somehow, some way, the pilot of the lead aircraft determined that he was directly over the downed Cobra, and he gave the "green light" to begin the insertion. Staff Sergeant Bowman kicked a weighted sandbag out each side of the Huey. The bags held coiled nylon ropes that fed out as the bags fell toward the ground. Biedron and I were hooking ourselves onto the ropes even before the bags had fully deployed.

Stepping out onto the left skid of the lead helicopter, I took one look down at the vegetation being whipped into a froth by the chopper's downdraft and stepped off into space. It took only seconds to reach the ground. As I braked to a stop I found myself standing in the middle of a six-foot-wide, high-speed trail. My skin began to crawl as I fed the excess rope through my D-ring and stepped back to belay for the next man on the rope. But something was wrong, I could feel it! Dropping the belay rope, I pulled my weapon over my head and whirled around. A newly constructed *concrete* bunker, not yet camouflaged, sat facing me less than three meters back from the trail. It was empty. I would never have spotted it if the rotor wash from the hovering aircraft above me had not beaten down the surrounding vegetation.

I turned back to my teammates rappelling to the ground around me. Munoz, Biedron, and Groff were all on the ground already moving to set up security. But five feet up the rope Kilburn was having trouble. Somehow during his descent, the stocky Ranger had gotten the coiled radio handset cord entangled in the rappelling rope and was now stuck fast just out of my reach. Saenz, the last man to rappel, was already out on the skid ready to rope down as soon as Kilburn reached the ground.

Bowman peered down from the edge of the cabin floor unable to do anything to free the young Ranger from his end. Finally, he signaled for me to get Kilburn off the rope one way or another.

I pulled my K-Bar and tried to cut the rope above the trapped Ranger, but it was just out of my reach. I motioned for Bowman to get the pilot to lower the aircraft. As it dropped two feet closer to the ground, I leaped up and sliced through the rope just a foot above the tangled radio cord.

Finally free of the rope, Kilburn dropped to the ground in a heap. Seconds later Saenz was on his way down the rope, free-falling the last six feet as he ran out of line. Freed of its burden, the Huey drifted off into the clouds and we were alone in the muffled stillness of the jungle.

Something was wrong! Where was the other aircraft? It should have been within sight, with six more Rangers coming down ropes. I told Munoz to try and raise Fadeley's team on the radio, but only loud static answered his call. Munoz contacted the C&C ship circling just out beyond the fog and asked what had happened to the second Huey. The reply was quick and disturbing. The other team was on the ground already— but no one knew where.

When Munoz tried to reach Fadeley's team on the radio, all he got was the aircraft out beyond the fog. C&C ordered us to stay alert and pay attention, Fadeley was preparing to fire a pen-gun flare. Minutes passed but we never spotted the flare.

At that point I made a critical decision. I asked the C&C aircraft to relay the message to Fadeley that I was going to fire a single rifle shot in an attempt to mark my location. Fadeley was to shoot an azimuth to the sound of the shot and then move toward my position. It was a calculated risk, but I knew that the enemy would have little chance of pinpointing the location of a single shot if they weren't expecting it.

Seconds after I fired my weapon, the C&C ship called to report that Fadeley had a sound fix on the shot and was moving toward us. When I asked from what azimuth, he reported that Fadeley didn't really know. No one on his team had a compass.

Fifteen minutes passed. While we waited for Fadeley's team to show up, I moved my own team into thick cover away from the trail and the nearby bunker. I was beginning to realize that the mission would not be over in two or three hours. The weather had already changed the rules, and it would likely get worse before it got better. No maps, no food, no poncho liners, no bug juice, no SOI (signal operating instructions) code book, no artillery, no air support. The original orchestration was out the door. Now it was "play by ear."

"Yo, Rangers!" It was Fadeley, shouting at the top of his lungs somewhere out in the middle of the jungle. It sounded like he was a half klick away, but the heavy fog and the damp jungle muffled the sound; Fadeley's team, we'd discover, was only fifty meters away.

"Rangers! Over here!" I shouted back, cringing as the sound of my voice rang out in the jungle. I hoped my response was clear enough to guide Fadeley's team in because I didn't want to have to yell again. But with the diffusion of sound in the fog and jungle, we were each forced to shout two more times to effect the link-up. By then every NVA soldier in the valley had to have a pretty good idea where we were.

Fadeley's point man, Sergeant Phil Myers, cut the high-speed trail just above the concrete bunker. They turned and followed the trail down to where my team lay hidden in the jungle. We were relieved to be together again. After a brief discussion on what to do next, we decided to get our people on line four or five meters apart and sweep up the ridge to try to locate the downed Cobra. If we didn't find the wreckage by the time we reached the crest, we would move fifty meters along the ridge and then sweep back down again. If the pilot of the lead Huey had been anywhere close to the right spot during the insertion, we would eventually find the wreckage.

A hundred meters up the slope Fadeley walked right into the fuselage and cockpit of the Cobra gunship. He passed the word up and down the line that he'd found the wreckage, and soon we were all setting up security at the crash site. There was no sign of the pilot or the copilot, but the gunship's canopy was standing open and there was no blood or body tissue in the cockpit.

Fadeley left three members of his team with the wreckage while the remainder of us got back on line and continued our sweep uphill. Twenty minutes later we found a flight helmet and a single jungle boot, but there was no sign of the two airmen. There was no indication that there had been a struggle, nor any clue to suggest that the NVA had gotten to the crew ahead of us. The only conclusion we could draw was that the two airmen had survived the crash and, assuming that there would be no rescue attempt until the weather broke, had gone on an E&E (escape and evasion) route of their own choosing.

We called in a sit rep (situation report) but could only reach the artillery battery on Firebase Tomahawk. The fire control officer relayed our current intel to the Ranger TOC back at Camp Eagle and then passed the word back to us that we were to remain in the field until morning. That was no surprise to us, yet it was still somewhat unnerving to hear it over the radio. Hopefully, the weather would break in the morning, enabling us to locate the other chopper and complete our mission.

Fadeley and I discussed splitting up the teams during the night, moving them apart a hundred meters from each other; it was difficult to hide a twelve-man group in the jungle. The proximity of the high-speed trail and the concrete bunker were cause for major concern. Finally, we decided that it would be better for us to remain together in case we got hit in the middle of the night. But Fadeley decided that we still needed to get away from the wreckage. If the NVA knew they had the wrecks of two U.S. helicopters somewhere on the ridge, they would be out in force looking for them.

We moved up the slope a hundred meters away from the crash site and soon located a poorly concealed but level spot about six meters in diameter nestled back among a group of large mahogany trees. It provided an adequate place for us to lay up for the night and afforded enough protection to shield us from direct fire should the enemy hit us before daylight.

There wasn't a lot of concealment, but the dense, swirling

ground fog made it almost impossible to see more than five or six feet anyway. We settled in for the night hoping just to be left alone until morning.

My team had brought three claymores, so I had three of my teammates put them out, one on each flank and the third one facing directly up the ridge, covering what would become our E&E route should we have to run during the night. Our rendezvous point, should we get split up, was an imaginary spot on the crest of the ridge directly above our present position.

When we had first gotten the word on the mission, a few of us had grabbed some "lifer bars" and a handful or two of stateside snacks and stuffed them in our pockets. These "rations" were now the only food we had, and were divided equally among us. It would not satisfy the hunger already gnawing at our stomachs, but it would sustain us through the night. We had all been hungry before for a day or two, and a little more discomfort would not affect our performance. Not yet, anyway.

Fortunately, we each had two quarts of water on our LBE, the standard ration we carried on our web gear when we were in the field. And with the heavy humidity, water would not be a problem for two or three days. Our biggest concern was the lack of poncho liners to protect us from the elements. With the amount of moisture in the air, and the dense cloud cover, the temperatures in the jungle at night could plummet all the way into the fifties, posing a very real threat of hypothermia.

I recommended that we post two-hour guard shifts with three men on duty at a time, but Fadeley nixed the idea, opting for twelve one-man shifts of forty-five minutes each, beginning at 2100 hours.

As the jungle turned dark gray, then black around us, we settled in for the night. Each of us knew that the helicopters, the shouting, and the rifle fire had been heard by the NVA. Would they come in the middle of the night looking for us? Or would they leave us alone as long as we didn't get too close to whatever they were hiding out there. Only time would tell!

A little after 0200, I woke with a start. I looked at the luminescent hands of my Army-issue watch. Something had awakened me, but I didn't know what it was. As I tried to focus my eyes in the eerie illumination of the cloaking ground fog, something moved just outside my line of vision. I turned my head but only managed to catch a fleeting glimpse of something dark and sinister disappearing into the mist. I couldn't even be certain I had seen something. Was it an apparition, or a trick of imagination, or had something really been there? I looked down at the Ranger lying beside me. It was Kilburn. He was on his back with his weapon across his chest. At first I thought he was asleep, and I grew angry. It was his turn to be on guard. I reached over to waken him, and when I felt the young soldier's arm shaking, I realized that he was trembling uncontrollably. He was not only awake, he was terrified.

I moved closer to ask him what was wrong. With a sudden gasp Kilburn whispered that three enemy soldiers had just walked into our perimeter. Kilburn had not even noticed them until they were standing among the sleeping Rangers. He whispered that he had tried to swing his weapon around, but a sapling on his right side was in the way. He was forced to watch in horror as one of the NVA soldiers bent down to get a closer look at one of the sleeping Americans. Just as Kilburn was ready to scream out a warning, he'd felt me tense next to him as I awakened. The NVA must have also sensed it, for they immediately stepped over the sleeping bodies of the Rangers and disappeared back into the mist.

I listened in shocked disbelief. There *had* been something there after all! I told Kilburn to start waking everyone, then turned to my left and woke Biedron and Munoz. When everyone was up and alert, I moved over to Fadeley and reported to him and his ATL what had happened. There were still another four hours until daylight, and some precautions had to be taken at once.

There was no longer any doubt that the enemy knew where we were. I wanted to E&E immediately to the crest of the ridge. But Fadeley felt that it would be best to remain where we were. Yes, the enemy had scouted us and now knew our strength, but there had to be a reason they hadn't already attacked. Maybe they didn't yet have the edge they needed, or maybe they were waiting out there somewhere for us to move into a well-prepared ambush. Fadeley's advice made sense. At least where we were, we had a few claymores out and would have some protection should the enemy attack.

We remained on a hundred percent alert for the remainder of the night. When we tried to call in a sitrep at 0400, we discovered that we no longer had commo with the fire control center on Firebase Tomahawk, or anyone else for that matter. The final two hours of darkness before the dull, misty gray half-light of dawn arrived were terrifying for the entire patrol.

At 0600 Munoz was able to radio the fire control officer on Tomahawk. Munoz requested that he relay a message to the Ranger TOC. The message read that the patrol had been compromised during the night, and requested an immediate extraction or a reaction force.

Ten minutes later a message came back from Captain Cardona, L Company's commanding officer, ordering the team to stay put until he reached the area in his command and control aircraft. The artillery officer on Tomahawk broke in to report that the entire area was now socked in and it didn't appear that the fog was going to burn off anytime in the immediate future.

We knew now that we were in a precarious situation, and we began to realize that the NVA had not returned because they, too, were having a difficult time moving around or finding anything in the heavy fog. For the present, at least, we were probably out of immediate danger if we remained where we were. But time was working against us.

At 1000 hours we received a radio message from Captain Cardona informing us that C Company, 2nd Battalion, 327th Infantry, was moving into the area to link up with us and to assist us in our search for the missing pilots. Their call sign was Alpha Tango. At that time they were only a klick away from us, and were on a line of march that would bring them along the crest of the ridge directly above us.

Two hours later the line company contacted us by radio. Its commanding officer told Fadeley he thought that his unit was somewhere just above our position. He announced he would have his point element shout to mark its location.

We soon heard the shouting, but according to the apparent direction of the infantry company's point element, they were still 150 meters east of where they thought they were.

When Fadeley reported the discrepancy, the infantry commander told him to fire a couple of shots to mark his position. Fadeley answered that he didn't think that was advisable. A short time later the infantry captain radioed back to tell us to move straight up the ridge to meet up with his point element. He reported that they were above us on a ridgetop trail and making good time.

Again Fadeley rejected the advice, telling the officer that after he had established a patrol base up on the crest of the ridge, we would prefer having a squad or two come down to help us in our search for the missing pilots. The officer didn't seem to like that idea, but Fadeley finally convinced him that he wasn't bringing his patrol up the ridge without making one more effort to find the two missing aviators. At last the infantry commander agreed to send his recon element down to link up with us.

We could now hear American voices less than sixty meters away directly above our position. Suddenly, a long burst from an automatic weapon sounded from the vicinity of the line company. The infantry commander was on the radio immediately reporting that his point element had just been ambushed. He had four men down. He shouted a warning over the radio that there were NVA between his position and ours.

Seconds later we heard the distinct sound of brush breaking above us. Someone was coming directly at us and coming hard. From the amount of noise, we knew that it was no more than one or two men. But whoever it was, they were making no effort to be quiet.

The *snap-click-snap* of selector switches being thumbed from "safe" to "fire" were the only sounds coming from our perimeter. Fadeley knelt at the edge of the shallow berm on the uphill side of our position trying to get a look at who was coming our way. I rose slowly to a squat on the downhill side of the perimeter and readied my weapon. That's when a single NVA soldier suddenly broke through the brush twenty-five feet away.

He was bearing down on us, running at full sprint. Dressed in olive-drab shorts and a short-sleeve shirt, and wearing a red bandanna around his neck, the NVA soldier was holding a pair of Ho Chi Minh sandals and an AK-47 over his head in his left hand. He was using his right hand to push through the brush as he ran.

He spotted us sprawled in his path at nearly the same instant we saw him. To his credit, he responded immediately, dropping his weapon and squeezing off a long, one-handed burst from shoulder level. The rounds missed Fadeley and me by inches. Fadeley turned and dove for cover as he screamed, *"Blow the claymore . . . Blow it, blow it!"* I, too, dove for cover. I couldn't believe that the NVA had missed us.

Munoz grabbed the claymore firing device and squeezed the handle. The instantaneous explosion was devastating at that range, but it missed the NVA soldier completely. He had cleared the claymore mine and was already on the back side of the seven hundred steel ball bearings when it detonated. Fortunately for us, the claymore's back blast took out the NVA's legs at a distance of three feet.

When the smoke and debris finally settled, we could hear the NVA moaning in pain less than five feet away on the back side of the berm. Myers responded immediately by leaping to his feet and firing a short burst from his M-16 directly into the wounded man's body. When the NVA only moaned louder, I jumped up and put another quick burst into the enemy soldier at point-blank range. When the moaning still continued, Biedron pulled the pin on a fragmentation grenade and dropped it over the top of the berm, directly on the wounded NVA. The resulting explosion ended the moaning for good.

No one moved or breathed for several long, very pregnant moments as we waited to see what would come next. It had all happened so fast that no one had had time to think, only to react. Realizing that the grunts on the ridge above us needed to know what had just gone down at our position, Fadeley picked up the handset and radioed Alpha Tango Six to tell him that the NVA trail watcher that had shot up his point element was now a KIA. The line commander acknowledged the transmission and responded that he had four WIA on top of the ridge, and still didn't know for certain how many "November Victor Alphas" we had between them and us.

Biedron and Myers stepped over the berm to check on the

enemy soldier. There was little doubt that he was now dead. The claymore's back blast had shattered both of the man's legs. There were numerous bullet wounds and fragmentation injuries caused by Biedron's grenade. The NVA soldier had been a very difficult man to kill.

They returned seconds later with a damaged AK-47, a plastic billfold that contained a photo of a pretty Vietnamese girl and a letter written in Vietnamese. The only ammo the enemy soldier had was the single magazine in his weapon, which was now empty.

Alpha Tango Six called back to tell us that combat patrols had been sent out to sweep the flanks of the ridge. The NVA trail watcher had been alone. The officer no longer wanted to divide his command, and requested that Fadeley bring his team up to the line company's location. Fairly certain that there were no more enemy soldiers between us and the top of the ridge, Fadeley agreed. He ordered Myers to take the point then told everyone else on the team to laugh, talk, and make all the noise we could, so the trigger-happy grunts wouldn't mistake us for the enemy.

We moved out a few minutes later. It was around 1230 hours. Thirty meters away Myers broke through some heavy vegetation and walked headlong into two paratroopers squatting behind an M-60 machine gun. The two grunts stared at each of us as we filed past. One of them muttered his thanks to us for killing the enemy soldier who had shot his buddies. We nodded in silent reply.

When we reached the crest of the ridge, we found the infantry company strung out on both sides of a saddle. Most of them were busy eating C-rats or boiling canteen cups of water for coffee or cocoa. They had posted security out over the edge of the ridge at a number of places, but for the most part they had already put the recent shooting behind them.

Fadeley dropped off his patrol in the middle of the perimeter while he and I walked down to the saddle to report to Charlie Company's commander. Captain Ross was a young, baby-faced infantry officer who would have looked more at home in a Brigham Young basketball uniform than a set of jungle ODs, but his men appeared to have a lot of respect for him, and he seemed comfortable in his role as a field commander. Fadeley and I found him talking to a couple of his lieutenants as we walked up.

When the officer saw us standing off to one side, he stopped his conversation, introduced himself, and shook our hands. He told us that his company had been running search and destroy operations in this area off and on for nearly four months. They had lost a number of people trying to dislodge a couple of NVA battalions. They had been standing down until the weather broke when they got the word to move back into the mountains to link up with our Ranger patrol. Ross was now trying to get a medevac in for his wounded, and the prospects were looking rather dismal. The weather report from Division promised three more days of heavy fog. The high humidity, cool weather, and the total absence of surface winds were responsible for the thick overcast.

Captain Ross asked Fadeley and me if we wanted to be extracted if Division could manage to get a couple of birds in to pick us up. Fadeley told the officer that he would prefer to complete his mission first, but his people had not come in in prepared to stay. He reported that we had no food, water, or poncho liners.

Captain Ross immediately called one of his platoon sergeants and ordered him to scare up some extra C-rations and water for us. He told us he would attempt to get a couple of slicks in once he got his wounded medevacked. Then the busy company commander excused himself and turned to rejoin his lieutenants.

A short time later Ross sent a runner for us and told us that an Eagle dustoff (medevac) aircraft had just made two unsuccessful attempts to reach the company's location; the fog was still too thick. This forced Ross to make the decision to walk his company out, carrying his wounded. There was just no other choice. The two downed helicopters and their missing crews would have to wait until the weather broke.

As the paratroopers and Rangers were preparing to move out down the ridgeline, a Cobra pilot radioed that he and his wingman were going to try to bring their aircraft in through the fog. They had some C-rations and fresh radio batteries on board. The two gunships were from the same aviation unit as the downed helicopters and they wanted to do their part to make sure the rescue effort succeeded. They were not aware that the line company was coming out without even conducting a search.

Captain Ross instructed the Cobra pilots to come in high, then he would attempt to talk them down through the fog by listening to the sounds of their engines. Soon the first Cobra broke through the fog and landed in a clearing on the opposite side of the saddle. Five minutes later the second Cobra was also on the ground, coming to rest on a large, nearly flat limestone shelf thirty meters up the west side of the saddle.

After distributing a small amount of food, some extra radio batteries, and a couple of jerry cans of water, the pilots suggested that they could try to take out the four wounded paratroopers on the armament bay doors on either side of the Cobras' fuselages. The doors had been pressed into extraction situations in the past and served rather well as a narrow jump seat in an emergency such as this.

Soon the four wounded troopers were secured against the outer fuselages of the two gunships. All of them had received painful leg wounds, but injections of morphine had made their unorthodox medical extraction as comfortable as possible. Each pilot flashed a "good luck" wave, then slowly lifted his aircraft straight up into the overhanging clouds and disappeared.

After the successful medevac, Captain Ross came over and told us that he was now going to keep his company in the field to look for the missing air crews. That was the promise he'd given to the Cobra pilots in appreciation for taking out his wounded. Ross had decided to send one of his platoons down to the Cobra wreckage we'd discovered to search the area once more. He told us he'd also radioed his headquarters to obtain the exact coordinates of the LOH crash site. When he got a definite fix, he would send his recon element along with us to locate it.

An hour later Ross came back and reported that the LOH crash site was not anywhere near where it was first thought to be, but well over a thousand meters to the west. Someone had really screwed up, and now a simple rescue mission was being turned into a major search operation.

Fadeley commented that because of the distance we had to cover, there was not enough time to reach the wreckage of the scout helicopter before dark. But Captain Ross had already been in touch with our commanding officer, who'd informed him that, weather permitting, he intended on rappelling an additional "heavy" Ranger team into the second crash site early the next morning.

The infantry platoon returned from the downed Cobra just before dark. They reported that the NVA had been all over the wreckage since we'd been there. The radios were taken from the cockpit, but the rockets and miniguns were still in place. The platoon had swept the area but found no sign of the pilot or his gunner. Before the grunts left the scene, they set explosive charges on the aircraft set to go off in thirty minutes. The grunts had also located our NDP from the previous night. The body of the dead NVA soldier we'd killed had already been removed.

From the enemy activity in the area, there had to be a base camp somewhere below the ridgeline. The trail watcher we'd taken out had not just been trying to escape from the American line company; he had been heading "toward" something. The concrete bunkers along the trail were fighting positions, and the NVA always built fighting positions around areas they wanted to protect. The base camp had to be somewhere near the bunkers, and the NVA would likely be waiting for us there.

The demolition of the Cobra 150 meters away rocked the jungle all the way to the crest of the ridge. It signified the completion of half the mission. But there was still another aircraft out there in the jungle somewhere to our west, and the fate of its crew was yet to be determined.

That night, the twelve of us divided up into groups of three, trying to stay warm with a single poncho liner shared by each group. The grunts had established a long oval perimeter along the crest of the ridge and stretching away from the saddle on both sides. They set out a few claymores and trip flares, then curled up and went to sleep without visibly posting any guards. None of us could believe what we were seeing. That night, twelve wide-eyed Rangers pulled guard duty for an entire infantry company.

The next day proved uneventful. The weather was so bad that the infantry company and our Ranger patrol remained in the perimeter and cleaned weapons, ate, and tried to make ourselves as comfortable as possible. But everything was damp from the terrible humidity, and attempts to get comfortable were futile. Because of the thick fog, no patrols were sent out in search of the scout aircraft.

Around 0830 hours on March tenth, Captain Ross's runner approached us with the word that the other heavy Ranger team was inserting into the crash site of the scout helicopter at that very moment. The cloud cover had finally opened up enough to allow another LOH to locate the wreckage, and, as soon as the pilot had confirmed the coordinates, the Rangers rappelled in to secure the site, almost three klicks away from Charlie Company's perimeter. Someone up at Division had flunked Map Reading 101!

At the crash site, the Rangers reported that the scout chopper had apparently flown into a treetop and exploded, killing all three of the men on board. Body bags were being dropped to the two teams, and they began the unpleasant task of removing the charred remains of the three airmen. The twelve Rangers set up security around the crash site then placed the body bags individually in a wire basket lowered from a medevac aircraft. They watched in silence as the remains were winched up through the trees.

Just as the Rangers completed the recovery operation, the thick fog closed back in over them and forced their extraction aircraft to abandon any attempt to lift them out of the jungle. It was to have been a string extraction, tricky enough in good weather. But now there were twelve more Rangers stranded deep in the mountains south of Camp Eagle. Like us, they had also come into the crash site "light," believing it was an "in and out" operation. All the ingredients were now in place for a potential major catastrophe. The Rangers, ably led by Sergeants Joe Bielesch and John Sours, would have to spend the night in the jungle and hope for a break in the weather the next day.

On the morning of the eleventh, Fadeley told Captain Ross that he wanted to take his Rangers down to sweep the hillside one last time for any sign of the missing Cobra pilots, then patrol west to link up with the other Ranger team. With two battalions of NVA running around out there, the other Rangers, without air and artillery support, were in constant danger of being discovered and destroyed. Twenty-four Rangers would have better than twice the odds of surviving than twelve. Ross said that he understood and generously offered to send his thirteen-man recon element along with us. Fadeley thanked him profusely and accepted his offer—as far as we were concerned, the more the merrier. Ross also promised to keep the remainder of Charlie Company on top of the ridge as a ready reaction force until our two Ranger elements linked up then moved back up to rejoin them.

At 1100 hours our combined Ranger/recon force slipped over the side of the ridge and worked its way down to the site of the destroyed Cobra. Charlie Company had done a good job of leaving nothing of value for the enemy. After a prolonged search of the area, we still had found no sign of the missing pilots, so Fadeley decided to take the twenty-five man patrol and move down into the valley below. The Charlie Company recon element put out flankers and set out on point with the Rangers bringing up the rear. They cautiously zigzagged back and forth to confuse the enemy and to decrease chances of walking into an ambush.

Maps borrowed from Charlie Company indicated that there was a wet-weather stream down in the valley. Since everyone was just about out of water, Fadeley and the staff sergeant in charge of the recon element decided to go to the stream to fill our canteens. Once this was accomplished, we would then turn west and follow the blue line until we linked up with the other Ranger element.

Our patrol reached the stream at 1530 hours and quickly set up security on both sides. While five men filled their canteens at a time, the remainder faced outward toward the jungle, nervously watching the thick vegetation surrounding us. While this was going on Fadeley tried to raise the other Ranger patrol on the radio, but he could not yet get through to them. The weather and the terrain were making radio communication all but impossible. Even commo with Charlie Company, five hundred meters up the ridge from us on high ground, was very, very faint.

With only a couple of hours of daylight left, Fadeley decided to attempt to link up with the other team before dark. In single file, with our Rangers now at point, the column snaked its way slowly up the heavily forested valley. We attempted to stay away from the stream as much as possible, but continued to cross from one side to the other every hundred meters or so, just to keep the enemy off balance.

Just before dark, Fadeley realized that we weren't going to make it to the other team's location by nightfall, but we finally did establish radio contact with Sergeant Joe Bielesch's patrol, only to discover that they were still at the crash site a full klick and a half away. Fadeley advised him to find a good, defendable spot nearby and stay put for the night, then move his team down into the valley in the morning. Eventually, our two elements would effect a link-up somewhere along the stream. We would maintain continuous radio contact to prevent the two patrols from firing each other up when we met.

Our patrol moved a little farther up the valley and located a high earthen mound in the upper loop of an S-shaped curve in the stream bed. It possessed good natural cover and concealment, and would be easy to defend against anything but a determined ground attack.

Our combined elements set up security, then put out eight claymore mines covering all the approaches to the mound. Fadeley established four-man guard shifts to get us through the hours of darkness, then everyone sat back to wait out the night. A lot of nocturnal animals were moving around near the water, and their sounds kept us awake and alert most of the night. Despite several false alerts during the early hours of the morning, we made it through the night uneventfully.

The next morning brought only more of the same weather. The constant moisture and lack of food was beginning to take its toll on all of us, and immersion foot was beginning to develop, especially among some of the Rangers. As it got worse, cracking, bleeding, and then the peeling of skin would make it difficult for anyone with this condition to walk.

We moved out in single file, continuing in a westerly direction up the long valley. Within three hundred meters of our overnight halt the valley began to narrow. Around noon we reached a point where a secondary ridge branched off the main ridge above us and hooked downslope to parallel the stream. This unusual terrain feature forced us to recross the stream to go around it, but it did enable us to get a fix on our position. According to the map, we were less than three hundred meters from Bielesch's last NDP.

Fadeley reached Bielesch on the radio. The two leaders agreed to move their teams toward each other, maintaining constant communication to keep track of each other. An hour later Myers, moving at point, stopped the patrol with a hand signal. He'd just spotted Sergeant John Sours's blond-red hair up ahead, sticking out from behind an old dead tree on the opposite side of the stream.

When the link-up was complete, Bielesch reported to us that his team had just crossed a fresh trail a hundred meters back upstream. This confirmed that NVA patrols were still active in the area and were likely monitoring our progress.

Anxious to put the valley behind us and link back up with Charlie Company, our combined patrols quickly turned around and headed back downstream. Now thirty-seven strong, we were feeling a lot better about our chances of making it. Rucker and Sours took over at point.

When we reached the secondary ridge, to avoid retracing our previous route, we moved away from the stream and climbed fifty meters into the heavy vegetation on the north slope. It was one fine place to walk into an ambush, and with the enemy active in the area, none of us wanted to take any more chances than was necessary.

Fadeley stopped the patrol again an hour later to reestablish radio contact with Captain Ross. When we finally picked up his weak signal, Ross reported that one of his platoons had stumbled across the Cobra aircraft commander during a routine security patrol below the crest of the ridge. The warrant officer reported that he and his gunner had initially tried to

remain close to the wreckage of their aircraft, but when no
rescue force showed up, they moved uphill toward the crest of
the ridge. The gunner had been wounded in the foot and was
having a difficult time keeping up. The two aviators had been
forced to hide from an enemy patrol that first night in the
jungle, and somehow had gotten separated in the dark. The
pilot stated that he never saw his gunner again.

Ross advised us to return to his location as soon as possible.
The pilot was in bad shape from exposure and hunger, and his
own soldiers were getting critically low on food and water.
Captain Ross wanted to make a forced march out of the mountains to reach Highway One to their east.

Back down in the valley, we were having our own problems.
Biedron, Kilburn, and two of the recon squad were suffering
from advanced cases of immersion foot. The four men were
in no condition to climb back up the ridge and then force-
march overland six klicks back to civilization. When Fadeley
apprised Captain Ross of our situation, Ross radioed back that
he understood and recommended that we spend one more night
near the stream, then patrol down into the valley the next day
to where an ARVN armored platoon was laagered up outside
an occupied village. Fadeley readily agreed; under the circumstances, it was the only thing we could do.

Captain Ross also informed us that he'd just received word
from Division that the weather might break the following day,
allowing extraction by helicopter if we could locate a suitable
LZ. Fadeley told him we would not get our hopes up.

Our patrol reached the mound where we'd spent the first
night away from the ridge at 1600 hours. Fadeley decided that
this was as good a position to defend as anyplace else we'd
found, although it would now be somewhat overcrowded, with
thirty-seven bodies instead of twenty-five.

The night once again proved uneventful, even though at
0130 hours in the morning everything suddenly grew quiet. It
was as if the frogs and crickets had just gotten the word to stop
chirping on cue. The sentries noticed it immediately and began
to quietly awaken those sleeping nearby. Then two or three
minutes later, as mysteriously as it had stopped, the sounds of
nature once again.

At dawn on the seventh day of the mission, the Rangers and recon troopers rose to a chilly wet mist. It had rained lightly a couple of hours before daylight, soaking everyone and chilling us to the bone. Fadeley sent out a patrol to sweep around the perimeter to make certain that we weren't walking out into an ambush when we moved on. The patrol found nothing out of the ordinary.

We now had five cases of severe-to-advanced immersion foot. The staff sergeant in charge of the infantry recon element reported to Fadeley that he didn't believe his men could make it three meters, let alone three klicks. Fadeley didn't want to tell him that our Rangers were in no better shape.

Fadeley and I and the recon NCO put our heads together and finally agreed to continue moving down the valley until we could find an area open enough to bring in a medevac. If we could accomplish that, we would at least be able to extract the five worst cases of immersion foot. The rest of us would then attempt to walk out down the floor of the valley. There was no other solution to the problem.

We moved out at 1100 hours, crossing to the south side of the stream. The going soon got easier, as our patrol reached an area where the recent monsoon runoff had washed away much of the surrounding undergrowth. The valley also appeared to be widening out, making it somewhat easier for a helicopter to reach us without running the risk of flying into the side of a mountain.

Two hundred meters downstream from our NDP our point element discovered an old, overgrown field where much of the jungle had once been cleared away. With a little work it could be turned into a single-ship landing zone. In any case, the five cases of immersion foot were unable to go on.

Fadeley and the recon leader put half our force in a security screen around the LZ, while the remainder of the patrol cleared away the brush and small trees. When we had finished an hour later, fewer than a half-dozen trees twenty to thirty feet high still stood in the clearing. It would take hours to chop them down with the four dull machetes that the recon squad had with them, so Fadeley decided to save time by using our claymores to blow the trees down just above ground level.

We strapped a claymore mine to each of the five trees, taking care to aim each of them to the south and away from the patrol. The back blast alone would provide enough explosive force to remove the trees. We fed the claymore wires back toward the stream before connecting them to our firing devices. We planned to blow them ten minutes before the first of the helicopters arrived.

Waiting for the medevac to show, we set up in a horseshoe-shape defense perimeter around the clearing. Twenty minutes later we noticed that the fog was beginning to burn off. When Fadeley contacted Charlie Company, which was still up on the ridge above them, Captain Ross told him that his battalion command post had reported that a breeze had come in from offshore and was quickly pushing the fog to the west and out of the area. Ross had been ordered to remain on the ridge and wait for extraction by helicopter.

Fadeley radioed Captain Cardona, who was orbiting in his C&C ship out near Firebase Tomahawk. The CO reported that the fog was indeed burning off, and that he had six lift ships and a pair of Cobras on the way out to Tomahawk for the specific purpose of extracting the patrol. He'd already canceled the two medevacs that had been laid on.

At 1300 hours Fadeley once again contacted the CO in the C&C aircraft and reported some open sky over the patrol's location. He requested an immediate extraction. At 1315 the lift aircraft radioed that they were three klicks out and closing fast; we blew the claymores.

When the smoke and falling debris had settled back down on the LZ, the clearing was open except for a single twelve-inch-thick hardwood that had somehow resisted the explosive charge strapped to its base. Two of our Rangers ran out into the LZ and began rocking the damaged tree back and forth until it fell over with a loud crash.

The C&C confirmed that the slicks were coming up the valley and would set down in the LZ, one ship at a time. Because of the heavy fog farther up the valley, each Huey would have to turn around and go back out the same way it had come in. This would take time, but it was less risky than trying to climb out through the fog. There were still a lot of high mountains in the immediate area of our patrol.

Fadeley tossed a purple smoke grenade out into the center of the LZ. Soon the first slick thundered up the valley three hundred feet above the ground. It banked hard to the right and came around toward the LZ facing back down the valley. I ran out into the clearing and directed the aircraft into the LZ.

As soon as it touched down, seven troopers from the recon element were up and running for the open cabin. The fully loaded aircraft had some difficulty achieving transitional lift, but the pilot finally managed to manhandle it into the air.

The second chopper came in just as the first ship was clearing the LZ, setting down hard enough to damage a skid support. The pilot held the ship just off the ground while the remainder of the recon element scrambled aboard.

As the third Huey flared out over the LZ, I yelled for Fadeley to take Biedron and Kilburn and get out on that lift. Fadeley wanted to stay, but with me already out in the LZ directing the lift ships, he had no choice in the matter.

Eighteen Rangers were left on the ground when the fourth aircraft approached the LZ. Bielesch quickly designated six Rangers from his patrol to go out on that lift ship. Down to a dozen people on the ground, Bielesch yelled for me and the remainder of my team to go out on the next aircraft. I sprinted around to the opposite side of the Huey, and my five teammates ran across the clearing to pile in from the other side. As the slick lifted away from the LZ, I thought I heard someone shout, "Gooks . . . they got gooks on the perimeter!"

The pilot of Chalk Five was already taking evasive action. He had spotted enemy soldiers closing in on the clearing as he was coming out. He immediately radioed Chalk Six and warned them that there were NVA on the LZ. Much to his credit, the aircraft commander of Chalk Six tried to come in anyway.

Back on the ground, the remaining six Rangers knew nothing of the threat until an NVA soldier stood up in the brush on the far edge of the LZ as Chalk Five was lifting off. Rucker and Sours killed the enemy soldier before he could lift his weapon. As Bielesch's team quickly set up in a loose wagon-wheel defense perimeter, the team leader grabbed the radio and screamed for Chalk Six to abort the extraction. The NVA were already on top of them.

As the Huey flared off, Bielesch tossed a red smoke grenade out into the LZ and instructed the gunships to shoot up everything east, west, and south of the red smoke. The two Cobras responded by rolling in with 40mm cannons firing. They chewed up everything around the clearing but the tiny piece of real estate occupied by the six Rangers.

The Cobras made another pass as the Rangers hugged the ground. Then Bielesch asked them to make a third and final run with miniguns as the extraction aircraft attempted to sneak in while the NVA had their heads down.

As the Huey approached low and fast, Rucker killed a second NVA soldier squatting behind a bush on the opposite side of the LZ. Sours, Bielesch, Rucker, Anderson, Peterson, and Glasser were up and running for the aircraft as it flared over the clearing. Just as they reached the slick, Rucker turned and fired a final burst at a third enemy soldier who had risen up in the brush directly in front of the helicopter. Then Rucker turned and scrambled aboard as the Huey pulled away from the clearing. During the entire extraction, not a single round was fired by the NVA.

The slicks made a final stop at Firebase Tomahawk to drop off the recon squad and let us accept the thanks of a grateful General Melvin Zais, who had flown back out to Tomahawk just to greet his Rangers. He promised us there would be a special meal waiting for us when we got back to Camp Eagle, and he didn't let us down. The Cav mess hall was waiting with a wonderful feast of grilled steaks, baked potatoes, and fresh salad for us—all we could eat.

5

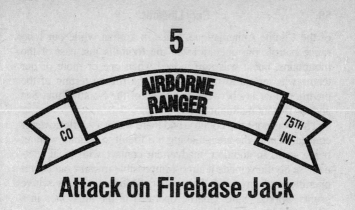

Attack on Firebase Jack

The primary mission of L Company, 75th Infantry (Ranger), in early 1969 was still long range reconnaissance. Walk-off patrols from U.S. fire support bases was the job of line companies and battalion recon units. But occasionally Rangers were tasked with the job. It wasn't their SOP and it was never their choice. Such patrols had certain inherent dangers that were compounded by the fact that on most Lurp missions, less is best. But if one assumes that most U.S. base camps, especially those in the middle of "Indian country," were under constant observation by the enemy, then running small reconnaissance teams through the wire and out into the surrounding bush made it difficult to do so clandestinely. And operational security was necessary for successful long range reconnaissance patrols.

On March 27, 1969, L Company found itself tasked with a walk-off mission. Before it ended it would become one of the legendary patrols of the unit.

Late in the afternoon on the twenty-seventh, four Huey slicks from the 2/17th Cav were inbound to Firebase Jack carrying three six-man Ranger recon teams, and a radio relay element, from L Company, 75th Infantry (Ranger). This was to be an unusual mission for us. Most of our patrols were conducted deep in the mountainous jungles and the dense, verdant valleys of the Chaîne Annamatique. Once in a great while our long range patrols ran operations in the foothills just east of the mountains, but it was rare indeed when one or more of our teams was tasked to run patrols in the rolling terrain of the piedmont that lay between the coast of the South China Sea and the distant mountains.

This was not Lurp country, and there was very little cover or concealment in the area, making it difficult to operate without being seen. In addition, inadvertent contact with local Vietnamese civilians made it almost impossible to carry out covert operations of any kind. This was the kind of country where grunts worked. Sure, Charlie operated in the area once in a while, but it was usually just a brief interlude coinciding with the rice harvest or some type of resupply. But in spite of all the hazards incidental to this type of terrain, this was to be our AO for the next three days.

Unlike most 101st Airborne Division fire support bases located on dominant terrain features in and along the Chaîne Annamatique, Firebase Jack lay sprawled across a low, circular mound rising above a vast sea of five- to eight-foot-high elephant grass, broken only by an occasional raggedy tree line, a cluster of bamboo thickets, or a dense stand of scrubby underbrush. The site sat in the transition zone between the low, level coastal plains to the east and the open, rolling piedmont that extended for three to four thousand meters to the west before ascending steeply into the thickly jungled mountain range beyond. It was in those distant mountains that we Rangers usually plied our trade.

None of us could understand why we had been selected to check out recent signs of increased enemy activity in the vicinity of Firebase Jack. It was a job for the grunts guarding the firebase, not for specially trained six-man long range reconnaissance patrols. How much trouble would it have been to send out a few daylight patrols, followed by a night ambush or two? That was the normal way to determine if Charlie was in the neighborhood. But for some reason unknown to us Rangers, we had been called in to do the job.

Among the Rangers assigned to the mission were veteran NCO team leaders, Sergeants Ray Zoschak, Bill Marcy, Rich

Fadeley, Larry Closson, Phil Myers, Kenn Miller, Joe Bielesch, and myself. Sergeants Ron Rucker, Bill Garrison, Jim Schwartz, Ken Munoz, and Spec 4 Marvel McCann provided an added pool of experienced and talented Lurps who had spent their share of dark nights in the bush. Spec 4s Rick "New Guy" Lawhorn and Robert "Doc" Glasser, along with PFCs Marvin Hillman, Charles Kilburn, Dan Croker, George Thomas, Greg Krahl, and Dean Groff were some of the newer Rangers who, even though they'd only been in-country four months, had already earned their positions on teams. I was going along as Closson's ATL, with Rucker, Hillman, Lawhorn, and Krahl filling out the rest of the team.

When the four Hueys settled onto the dirt road just outside the back gate of Firebase Jack, two dozen Rangers hopped down onto the dusty surface and moved in team file up to the rear entrance. None of us were overly impressed by the security that existed on the compound's perimeter. The back gate was little more than a few strands of barbed wire stretched crisscross over a reinforced rectangular metal frame. Guarded only by a single four-man sandbagged bunker, the gate would not present a serious challenge to an NVA sapper team bent on penetrating the outer perimeter. And as far as we could see in two directions, the firebase was surrounded by a vast sea of eight-foot-high elephant grass, the perfect concealment for a large NVA force moving up to attack.

But in spite of Jack's obvious weaknesses, there were also some strong points. A full infantry company provided perimeter security for the towed 155mm battery set up on the south side of the compound. In addition, the firebase was strategically situated between LZ Sally, a battalion-size permanent base camp to the south, and Camp Evans, a brigade-size forward operating base to the north. There were multiple artillery batteries at each location and a full aviation battalion with a company of Cobra helicopter gunships stationed at Evans. In case of an attack, fire support and reinforcements would not be long in coming.

And finally, it was a foregone conclusion that if Charlie assaulted a major U.S. fire support base this far from the security of his beloved mountains, he would do so knowing he'd get chopped to pieces trying to withdraw. No, Firebase Jack might have tempted the enemy, but it could bite back with a vengeance.

As we entered the compound through the open rear gate, a large number of paratroopers and artillerymen came out of their bunkers to watch. Obviously, they had already heard all the stories about the insane people who volunteered to go out on terrifying long range patrols deep into the mountains with only five or six men, but few of them had actually seen one before. Yet here was an entire platoon of these crazy idiots. We looked different, all right. We were heavily armed and camouflaged and were humping one hell of a lot of gear. But there was something else about us, too, something in our demeanor, that set us apart.

While we were dumping our rucks in a tight circle along the edge of the dirt road crossing the firebase, a middle-aged sergeant first class approached us and introduced himself as the operations NCO for the infantry company providing security at Jack. After our three team leaders introduced themselves and the rest of the formalities were taken care of, the senior NCO briefed us on the enemy situation outside the firebase.

Motioning for everyone to huddle around him, he quickly filled us in on the reasons why we had been requested to run reconnaissance patrols outside the firebase. Every day during the past two weeks the infantry company's external security patrols had been running across newly made trails out in the elephant grass surrounding the perimeter. All of them seemed to head directly toward the firebase. Overnight ambushes set up about a thousand meters outside the wire had netted kills from small parties of NVA, but yielded little good intelligence on what the enemy was up to. However, during the previous night, one of the infantry company's ambush teams had killed a single NVA soldier and recovered a map, drawn to scale, showing all the bunkers, gun emplacements, and claymores along Jack's outer perimeter. The guy was no interior decorator. He was an armed NVA scout, and he had gone to a lot of trouble to recon the firebase. It was not a good sign.

Firebase Jack's commander was beginning to get a little concerned over the increased enemy activity outside his wire, especially since, during the past three nights, listening posts set up in the grass a couple of hundred meters out had reported movement all around them. It was becoming pretty obvious even to a lay person that Firebase Jack was about to get its clock cleaned.

After the briefing ended, the three team leaders decided to wait until after dark to move their patrols out. We would slip through the wire on the east side of the firebase, away from the direction where most of the enemy activity had been occurring. Then moving together, the three teams would circle around the south side of Jack before breaking apart and deploying west toward separate recon zones (RZs). During our infiltration, the three patrols would remain in an echelon formation— Marcy's team on the right, Zoschak's team in the center, and Closson's team on the left. When we reached a point roughly a mile from the firebase, we would split apart and move to our designated recon zones, arriving no later than 2100 hours. Once inside our RZs, we would set up OPs to monitor enemy troop movement heading in the direction of Firebase Jack. We hoped to be in place long before the enemy's scouts left their hiding places and moved back into the grass around Jack to continue with their observations. This time we would be waiting for them when they showed up. It was our turn to observe the observers, and if the opportunity presented itself, maybe even put an ignoble end to a good number of them.

Marcy's team was scheduled to move to the northwest, setting up an OP in an abandoned French fortress overlooking a newly discovered high-speed trail running directly toward the firebase. Zoschak's team was scheduled to patrol straight ahead for another klick after the three teams broke apart, then set up over the junction of three well-established trails that meandered down into the elephant grass from somewhere back in the mountains. Closson's team was to swing to the southwest and establish a third OP at a point where a heavily used high-speed trail ran parallel to a shallow stream that eventually ran past Firebase Jack to the south.

It was a good plan, and it probably would have worked if a certain single event hadn't occurred that changed everything. But I'm getting ahead of myself. . . .

The senior RTOs of each team had previously established a "break squelch" code between them to enable the teams to remain in direct radio contact as they infiltrated through the dense elephant grass to their OPs. The three teams were to each move on the same 270-degree azimuth but maintain an interval of twenty to thirty meters between them. Effective communication during this phase of the operation would be crucial.

Our teams had to avoid each other yet be ready to move to each other's assistance in case one of them ran headlong into the enemy. No one among us had to remind himself that elephant grass would not stop errant bullets; once they left the end of your barrel, they weren't "friendly fire" any longer.

Just after dark, as instructed, the infantry commander pulled in his ambush teams and his LPs. When the last man had moved back into the perimeter through the back gate, our three Ranger teams slipped quietly out the front of the compound through a hole in the wire and moved in single file around to the south side of the firebase. At the jump-off point, the three teams split into a three-pronged echelon formation and moved out slowly westward through the high grass. Against the dark night sky the deeper shadows of the distant mountains stood out against the horizon.

We moved slowly, stopping every few meters to listen. Surprisingly, we made very little noise as we patrolled cautiously through the thick, razor-edged grass. Leather rappelling gloves protected our hands, but the sharp grass still took its toll on the exposed flesh of our faces and necks. We were good at this type of work, and with luck we would reach our recon zones without alerting the enemy.

Zoschak's team, in the center, broke squelch three times to signal pauses, then twice to alert the teams that it was time to move out again. The silence was deafening during those long halts when we stopped to listen. There were no crickets, no night birds, no frogs—nothing. Back in the jungle, where we normally patrolled, that type of cold, stony silence usually meant there were strangers about.

I was proud of my teammates and their professionalism in the field. I was fortunate just to be one of them. How a group of eighteen- to twenty-one-year-old boys can be turned into a well-oiled team of warriors in such a short time is a tribute to America's youth and its veteran military cadre. We were good at what we did, and our leadership was outstanding. Few career soldiers had survived the early teams of long range patrolling, back when the patrols were made up almost entirely of NCOs and were lead by E-7s. Things were different now, but the quality of soldiering and the camaraderie were still there. We lacked nothing but the old-timer's experience and temperament. We were still a bad bunch when cornered.

During our infiltration, each team's rear security man continually attempted to sterilize its backtrail, but in the grass, it was futile. The narrow, broken trail left by our passage was a shining beacon of our presence to any NVA scout who happened upon it. Fortunately for us, there seemed to be a multitude of other trails crisscrossing the savanna where others had passed earlier—grunts out of Firebase Jack or NVA scouts from far back in the mountains.

About eight hundred meters out from the firebase, our team abruptly stopped its forward movement. Squelch breaks went out immediately to halt the other two teams. The word was passed back down the line in a whisper to where I was waiting in the drag position that Closson wanted me up front. Our point man, Sergeant Ron "Mother" Rucker, had just discovered a strand of light-colored commo wire running east to west through the elephant grass. Someone had made a halfhearted attempt to conceal the wire, but it still stood out in the faint illumination cast by the quarter moon overhead—an unnatural horizontal line amid the natural vertical lines of standing elephant grass. Rucker's trained eye had seen it immediately.

When I reached the front of the patrol, Closson whispered in my ear that he'd already halted the other two teams, which at the time must have figured that it was just another pause in the patrol movement to wait and listen. Closson was understandably concerned about the commo wire. Rucker's discovery had changed everything in our game plan. If our three Ranger patrols continued moving in the same direction we were going, we would run the risk of stumbling into whomever or whatever was at the other end of this line of commo wire. And the odds of our not being detected as we approached the terminus of the wire were odds that none of us wanted to bet on. Because of our training and the precautions we always took, few Rangers had ever been in the "kill zone" of a well-prepared ambush, and none of us wanted to experience one firsthand in the middle of the elephant grass.

Closson signaled the other two teams to stand by for a message, then keyed the handset slowly three times, paused, then keyed it again, this time rapidly four times—the signal to assemble on the transmitting team.

The other teams responded by breaking squelch once, then twice, to acknowledge the transmission and to signal their compliance. Closson then turned and passed the word down through our team that Marcy's and Zoschak's teams would be coming into our positions from the right. He cautioned us to be alert and not to fire up the "friendlies."

Ten minutes later, after the link-up had been successfully completed, the three teams formed up in a tight circular defensive perimeter facing outward while the three team leaders huddled in muted conference in the center. The enemy commo wire was an unknown variable; it was time to alter the original plan.

Zoschak immediately wanted to put one team on the wire, with the other two teams on each flank, and follow it right to its source outside the concertina wire in front of Firebase Jack. He opined that we could catch the NVA observation team with its pants down, trapping them between us and the perimeter guards.

Marcy favored the same kind of tactic, but was worried about the grunts and redlegs on the firebase opening up on us. So he suggested that we attempt to patrol in the opposite direction, to capture the enemy's receiver. He figured that the enemy commo section had to be set up somewhere to the west and would probably not be as alert as the team of scout/observers hidden in the grass outside the firebase.

Closson listened to each of his counterparts, then wisely counseled caution. Going after either NVA commo section in the dark could turn out to be a disaster, since they were likely to hear us moving into position. If the NVA detected us before we discovered them, they would either set up a hasty ambush in the grass or escape before we could close with them. Besides, Closson offered, a running gun battle in the elephant grass, regardless of who had the most firepower, was likely to result in casualties on both sides.

After a brief discussion, the three NCOs decided the best course of action was to move their teams to the north, harboring up for the night in the old French fortress assigned as an OP to Marcy's team. At first light we would move in silently behind the enemy to cut off his escape route, then radio the infantry commander on Firebase Jack to send out a platoon of his grunts to sweep the grass between the firebase and our positions. With proper execution and a little luck the grunts would flush the NVA right into the waiting arms of eighteen heavily armed Rangers. All agreed that this was the best of the three plans, and would successfully eliminate most of the risks inherent in the first two.

More cautiously than before, we moved out in single file on an azimuth of 310 degrees. We left one hell of a trail through the grass, but there was nothing we could do to prevent it or cover it. Hopefully, if the enemy stumbled across it in the dark they would think it was just another one of the old line-doggie (infantry) paths that crisscrossed the savanna from every direction. After another hundred meters the height of the grass began to run a little shorter, until it was little more than five feet high.

Sergeant Bill Marcy's team was at point, with our team bringing up the rear. We knew the old French compound couldn't be too far away, but no one wanted to miss it in the dark. After another fifty meters Marcy's point man suddenly threw up his right hand to halt the column. Just ahead a dark shadow rose above the elephant grass. The point man took a few more steps and was able to identify the solid shape of an eight-foot-high earthen berm. We'd found the old French fortress.

Closson and Zoschak pulled their teams into a tight oval perimeter out in the grass, while Marcy took his people inside to recon the fortress. Twenty years of abandonment and neglect had taken their toll, leaving the structure little more than a grass-choked enclosure with scattered clusters of bamboo, brush, and small trees fighting to maintain a toehold among crumbling mounds of laterite. Nearly fifty meters in diameter, the compound was much larger than we'd expected and much too large an area for eighteen men to defend.

When Marcy had assured himself that no one was waiting for us inside, he radioed for the rest of the Rangers to move up. In single file we entered the enclosure and set up a defensive perimeter across the structure's southwest corner. The berm would offer some protection on two sides if the enemy happened to stumble across us in the darkness.

By 2230 hours we'd set out our claymores and settled in for the night. One Ranger from each team was assigned to pull security, while the remainder of his teammates tried to catch a little sleep.

Sitting up under some overhanging shrubs, Zoschak pulled a poncho liner over his head and shined his penlight on the acetate-covered map stretched across his lap. As soon as he determined our exact coordinates, he snatched the handset from his RTO and called in a sitrep to the relay team at Firebase Jack. He asked the radio man to relay the message to the Ranger TOC informing the CO of our discovery and of our plans for dealing with it. A half hour later the relay team radioed back and ordered us to stay put until our CO, Captain Lannie Cardona, could get out over the firebase in the morning in his C&C helicopter. The Old Man wanted to attempt an aerial recon of the commo wire before we moved in.

Zoschak was visibly upset. Our recon teams had gone to a lot of trouble setting up an early morning surprise party for the NVA, and now some showboat officer was attempting to step in and undo all our work.

During the night, frequent aerial flares from the firebase illuminated the surrounding countryside. Flitting shadows cast by the descending flares oscillated back and forth, playing tricks with our night vision and keeping us on edge. The only consolation was that it had to be doing the same to the enemy.

The soldiers and artillery on Firebase Jack were also nervous because word about the wire had gotten back to them, confirming their own fears that they were being scouted for a possible attack. They now knew for certain that something big was coming and they felt that it was only a matter of time before something bad happened.

Out in the grass, the Rangers tucked away in the corner of the old French compound also sensed that something was about to happen. We could smell it in the warm, humid air that hung over the abandoned fortress.

At first light three of the Rangers crawled carefully up to the top of the brush-covered berm to scope out the surrounding countryside. On the horizon well over a thousand meters to the east, they could just make out the skyline of Firebase Jack. As they watched, the morning sun—bright orange and pulsating—seemed to rise from within the confines of the firebase, almost like a nuclear explosion. It was a prophetic sight that none of them would ever forget.

By 1000 hours the "red line" had reached a hundred degrees inside the fortress. Not a hint of a breeze rippled the sea of elephant grass. We tried to make use of what little shade was available as we waited for our commander's C&C ship to arrive.

At the noon sit rep the relay team radioed Zoschak to tell him to keep us where we were until "higher-higher" decided what it wanted us to do. Captain Cardona was no longer calling the shots. He'd gotten Division involved, and now it was out of his hands. Someone at Division HQ had crashed our party.

Suddenly, Rucker, who had been scoping out the territory around our location, observed something fishy in the tree line two hundred meters south of our position. He called me over, handed the binoculars to me and indicated an area in the tree line. Not knowing exactly what I was looking for, I took a full two minutes to scan it. Then I saw what had caught Rucker's attention. It seemed to be something man-made; something rigidly vertical that was totally out of place among the forked diagonal branches of the scrubby trees bordering the elephant grass. After staring at it a little longer, I realized that it couldn't be anything but a radio antenna, and the ones used in the bush by U.S. and ARVN forces weren't nearly that tall.

I handed the binoculars back to Rucker, patted him on the back and told him to keep his eye on the tree line while I went to report his discovery to the team leaders. When I returned a short while later with Closson, Marcy, and Zoschak in tow, Rucker was still up on the berm scanning the distant tree line. The three team leaders each took a turn with the binoculars and soon confirmed Rucker's sighting. The antenna was likely sitting atop the western terminus for the enemy commo wire we'd found in the grass the night before. If it was, we now had the enemy's position pinpointed.

Zoschak had his senior RTO bring his radio up to the berm, where he called in an unscheduled sit rep to report this new bit of intelligence. Where there was a radio antenna, there had to be a transmitter/receiver nearby!

Knowledge of the exact location of the enemy commo team now opened up several new options for us. We could proceed with our original plan to catch the enemy in a classic hammer and anvil operation. We could sit safely back where we were and call in artillery or even an air strike on the enemy position. Or we could wait where we were until late that night, then maneuver silently into position around the antenna site and take them by surprise at first light the next morning. A live prisoner or two could provide a lot more intelligence about the enemy's surveillance operation than a couple of bullet-riddled bodies.

It didn't take Division long to confirm its choice. The final plan would center around an attempt to capture one or more of the NVA at the receiver location. We were ordered to move out shortly after dark, set up by midnight, and then take the enemy position at first light. It all sounded so damned simple, but it was an undisputed fact that Murphy's Laws of Combat always managed to come into play on fourth down and short yardage.

All eighteen of us moved out of the fortress at 2315 hours on a compass heading of 190 degrees. We knew we were taking a sizable risk, sneaking blindly through the elephant grass in the middle of the night, but there was no other way to get into position to hit the NVA commo site at dawn. We advanced slowly and cautiously, maintaining two yard intervals, each man careful to keep track of the man to his front. There were no flankers and no point element out ahead of the patrol. There was no reason to suspect that the enemy knew of our presence, and the likelihood of running into an ambush in such a wide expanse of high elephant grass was virtually nonexistent. The only real danger would come when we began to infiltrate the final twenty or thirty meters to the tree line. If the enemy detected us then, they would either be half way to Hanoi . . . or waiting for us.

We had nearly five hours to cover two hundred meters and get into position, and we planned on using every minute of it. Zoschak's team was in the lead with Schwartz walking point. His slack man made sure that he stayed on the proper heading, and Zoschak's junior RTO counted the paces so we'd have an estimate of the distance traveled. The plan involved moving to within twenty meters of the enemy position in the tree line then pivoting and swinging on line, using the tall tree that held the antenna as a reference point. It was a good plan, but it had some inherent risks that made all of us more uncomfortable than we would have liked.

Forty-five minutes after pulling out of the fortress, we'd covered nearly half the distance to the tree line. Our team was still situated in the center, and Marcy's team was bringing up the rear. Suddenly, both Closson's and Marcy's RTOs stopped dead in their tracks. Zoschak's senior radio operator was rapidly breaking squelch, signaling that there was danger at the head of the column.

Everyone immediately froze in place, not sure of what was happening but fully aware that something was wrong somewhere in the column. Closson and Marcy moved up to take the handsets from their RTOs in an attempt to determine what exactly was coming down. After a few seconds both team leaders turned and held their trigger fingers up to their lips, the sign for absolute silence. They followed this with the hand signals that indicated there was "enemy" to our front.

We waited several minutes in motionless silence before the word was finally passed down from the head of the column that Zoschak's point man had just reported that a large enemy force had crossed in front of him, heading from west to east toward Firebase Jack. Zoschak's team was already falling back on our team, and Marcy's team was moving up to join us. We were going to set up a defensive perimeter right where we were and stay put until we found out what was happening.

As this was transpiring, Sergeant Phil Myers, Marcy's point man, moved up and whispered to Closson and Zoschak that he, too, had movement, but this time it was behind them.

It didn't take a mental genius or a Pentagon general to figure out what was going on. We were caught between a couple of sizable enemy elements moving up through the grass to hit Firebase Jack. The bad news was that this second NVA unit must have crossed the back trail we'd left the night before. If the enemy recognized it for what it was, they could easily turn around and roll us up before we had a chance to set up a defensive perimeter.

Without a moment to spare, Zoschak's and Marcy's point and drag teams tied in with our patrol, forming a rough oval-shaped perimeter facing outward in the high grass. There was plenty of concealment, but absolutely no cover. Elephant grass would not stop AK-47 rounds or even hand grenades. The only thing around us that would accomplish that was the body of a fellow Ranger.

For the next ten minutes our heavy breathing was met by total silence out in the grass around us. Then Zoschak began moving cautiously through our tiny perimeter, positioning men here and there to make sure all the approaches were covered. Because of the density of the grass no one could see anyone else, other than the man kneeling on either side of him. Zoschak whispered to each of us to use grenades if the enemy closed in on us. Rifle fire would only give away our positions.

Finally, when some semblance of a defensive perimeter had been established, the three team leaders gathered in the middle to establish a command center. Few of the Rangers failed to notice that each of the NCOs had already pulled fragmentation grenades from their gear and placed them on the ground around them. There wouldn't be much time to dig through one's LBE and rucksacks if an enemy attack came.

Several minutes elapsed before word was passed around the perimeter that every other man on the line was to crawl about five meters out into the grass and set up a claymore, making certain it was pointed obliquely away from the perimeter. With only the elephant grass to act as a backstop, the back blast from an exploding claymore would be just as deadly as the frontal discharge. Afterward each of us felt a little more secure knowing there were now eight deadly antipersonnel mines between us and the enemy. It would be enough to stop the NVA's initial assault dead in its tracks, and give us the time to break contact and scatter on our E&E routes.

Zoschak had already radioed the relay team, giving them our coordinates and warning them that at least two large enemy units were heading in their general direction. He knew that this was not a scouting party, there were simply too many of them for that. He also gave them four artillery preplots, one on each side of our perimeter. If the enemy suddenly hit us, there would be no time to figure locations and call in artillery coordinates. The artillery fire control officer radioed back that he was going to transfer our fire mission to Fire Support Base Rakkassan, twelve klicks away. He told us that our current position was too close to Firebase Jack for it to provide effective fire support.

Beads of perspiration were running down our backs, sending cold shivers coursing through our bodies. Most of us blamed it on the moisture, the humidity—not the waiting. Nervously, we glanced at the luminous faces on our watches. It was a little after midnight. It would be another six full hours before first light arrived, and a lot could happen in six hours.

At 0100 hours Zoschak radioed in a negative sit rep. The relay team reported everything quiet on their end. No one was breathing any easier. Tension was still running high.

At 0200 hours Sergeant James Van Leuven, commanding the relay team on Firebase Jack, reported that the crickets in the grass outside Jack's perimeter had just stopped chirping. The base had already been put on full alert. The battery of 155s had been lowered to fire point-blank at the likely approaches to the firebase, and were loaded with flechette rounds to accommodate massed infantry.

At exactly 0220 the NVA launched their attack on Firebase Jack. It began with the sharp "crump" of a claymore going off. Then the staccato sounds of M-16s and -60s joining in, quickly rising to a feverish pitch.

We cringed and waited for the deeper sounds of the AKs and RPDs to begin, but after a few minutes of hearing nothing but

U.S. weapons, we began to wonder if the enemy was going to respond.

The heavy mortars began firing, *toop . . . toop . . . toop*. We couldn't tell for sure whose they were, but someone was working out with them. Then there were more claymores . . . or were they satchel charges? Could the enemy have breached the perimeter so soon—or was it the weakly defended rear gate that had gotten them in? God, we hoped not, since our relay team had set up in a bunker near that gate!

Fifteen minutes into the firefight, a pair of Cobra gunships from nearby Camp Evans suddenly appeared over the firebase and began to wreak their own deadly havoc in the grass outside Jack's perimeter. Tracers from the Cobras and the 60s and 50s on Jack began ricocheting out across the savanna and over our heads as we lay hidden in the grass, driving us even closer to the ground.

Suddenly, there seemed to be a new sound coming from the grass surrounding our perimeter. It was only faint at first, like the sound of water rushing in from a very great distance, but as it got closer it grew louder and louder until it seemed it would sweep away everything in its path. It was at that very moment that each of us squatting or kneeling in the grass realized exactly what it was. Enemy soldiers—dozens of them—were moving through the field double-time, heading in the direction of the firebase!

This was the main enemy attack, the first one had only been a diversion. The NVA commander had held back the main body of his troops far outside the danger zone until the American forces on Jack had committed themselves. Now that the claymores and the phou gas barrels were gone, the Cobras had expended their ammo, and the base camp perimeter wire had been breached by sappers, the main attack moved in to hit Jack hard—and eighteen Rangers were lying right in its path.

We crouched in panic as the noise from the onrushing NVA swept over us. Each Ranger's eyes darted back and forth, desperately searching for the first enemy soldier to break through the elephant grass and into our tiny perimeter. There had to be hundreds of them out there in the thick cover, advancing on Firebase Jack.

Abruptly, as if on cue, the rushing noise stopped. But seconds later it began once again as if nothing had happened. This madness lasted for nearly thirty minutes before it finally ended. Miraculously, the enemy battalions moving up on Jack failed to stumble over the eighteen Rangers waiting in their path. And fortunately for the enemy—and for us Rangers—no one panicked and blew a claymore or tossed a frag as the NVA swirled past us less than ten meters away.

Hopeful that the last of the enemy soldiers had finally moved on, Zoschak broke radio silence to call in a desperate warning to the relay team on Firebase Jack. In a muffled whisper he told them that the initial enemy assault had only been a diversion, that the real one was still coming.

The news left the radio relay team audibly shaken. They'd just finished personally dealing with the sappers who had broken through the defenses at the back gate, and were not ready to handle the knowledge that their most recent battle had only been a warm-up for what was yet to come. This new threat was the other side of the hurricane after the eye had passed overhead.

From our location out in the grass we heard the main attack begin. It was initiated by a deep crackling sound that started slowly and built quickly into a crescendo of deafening explosions. At first we couldn't understand what it was, until it dawned on us that what we were hearing were scores of exploding RPG rounds. None of us had ever heard anything like it before. The devastation and destruction of multiple volleys of rocket-propelled grenades had to be catastrophic for the defenders of Firebase Jack. To us Rangers it sounded like heavy automatic weapons fire at first, except that each of those "bullets" exploded on contact with enough force to knock out a heavy tank.

More enemy reinforcements began moving up through the grass, pushing past our tiny perimeter, this time even closer than before. We knew that the defenders on Firebase Jack would be hard pressed to survive this onslaught without help. Why was the enemy expending this much manpower on a second-rate U.S. firebase sitting harmlessly down in the lowlands? None of us had a clue, but we knew that the redlegs and grunts on Jack were going to be lucky to survive the night.

Suddenly, a deafening explosion erupted just outside our perimeter. Someone on Marcy's team had blown his claymore. In the ringing silence immediately following the blast, the sounds of multiple selector switches snapping from "safe" to "full-auto" were the only noises that could be heard.

Zoschak whispered loudly, "No weapons . . . no weapons! Only grenades and claymores. Make sure you know where they are before you blast 'em."

Several minutes passed but nothing else of any importance occurred. The sounds of the enemy soldiers rushing past out in the grass trailed off dramatically after the claymore discharged. They must have been focusing on the firebase, and decided to deal with this new threat later.

Just as we began to breathe a little easier, we heard them coming again. The enemy knew our general location but still didn't know exactly what they were facing. This group hesitated, unsure exactly what to do. We could hear them chattering in low, muffled tones. Myers and Garrison from Marcy's team tossed a couple of frags that exploded among the voices twenty meters outside the perimeter, then the rest of us followed up with an overdose of more of the same.

Shrapnel was flying everywhere. We knew we had to keep the enemy off balance and away from our position. If we were to survive until dawn, the enemy would have to be kept at bay.

The ground attack on Firebase Jack had been going on full-tilt while we fought our own battle for survival. Over the racket of exploding grenades we could hear the main battle for the firebase build to a massive crescendo, peter out, then rise again to a deafening roar. The NVA attackers were still firing massive barrages of RPG and B-40 rounds at the base.

The Cobras supporting Jack had departed to rearm and refuel. In their absence the NVA soldiers moved out of the grass to launch heavy ground assaults on the north and west sides of the firebase. We could hear the tremendous booming sounds of the 155s firing beehive canisters into the massed enemy formations, breaking up their assault waves before they could reach the perimeter wire.

A C-47 "Spooky" gunship arrived on station and went into a tight orbit a couple thousand feet above the besieged firebase. In seconds it threw a wall of 7.62 caliber tracers in a crimson curtain around Firebase Jack. Nothing could stand in the open against such tremendous and overwhelming firepower.

Van Leuven radioed the news to us out in the grass that the ground attack had been broken. The paratroopers manning the perimeter defenses were just mopping up a few stragglers inside the wire, but for all practical purposes the enemy's main ground assault was over. Then, almost as an afterthought, he warned us to be careful—the surviving NVA were withdrawing in our direction.

In less than ten minutes we heard them coming. They were still forty to fifty meters out, and the NVA were making no effort to keep down the noise of their withdrawal. They were scattered out over a wide area and coming fast.

Zoschak got on the horn and requested "Spooky" over our position. The danger had now shifted from Firebase Jack to the eighteen Rangers caught out in the open. If the enemy managed to discover our positions before we could get Spooky over us, the NVA would streamroller us in a matter of seconds.

Spooky came up on the Ranger push and requested a bearing and range to our location from the firebase. Zoschak gave the pilot a heading of 265 degrees then turned and shouted over his shoulder, "Who's got a strobe?" Rucker and I both answered in the affirmative. The team leader told Rucker to take up a position in the center of the perimeter and switch on his strobe as soon as he gave him the word.

In seconds the blacked-out C-47 was over the Rangers. Zoschak pulled the handset away from his face and shouted, "Okay, Mother, hit the strobe—now." The pulsating, blinding light began blinking crazily, marking our position for the gunship—and for every NVA soldier within a thousand meters with an urge to become a hero.

Suddenly, above us, a noise that sounded a lot like someone unzipping a jacket over an intercom tore through the night. But no one made zippers that long. A thousand feet overhead a bright red hose began snaking its way down toward our perimeter. Eighteen young Americans saw their lives flash before them as they realized they were about to die. But at the last minute the deadly red undulating hose found its own sense of direction and began to harvest the grass just outside our perimeter. Everything thirty meters beyond us died . . . just like that. No muss, no fuss, no fur, no feathers! For the next sixty minutes Spooky did its thing, keeping the enemy away from us.

Just when we started to make some serious plans beyond this night, a grenade exploded on the south side of our perimeter. And it wasn't American made. McCann shouted that he'd been hit. Marcy moved over to check him and discovered he had been hit in the neck by shrapnel from a ChiCom fragmentation grenade. It wasn't too serious, and McCann said he could carry on. Enemy soldiers were still in our immediate area.

At 0345 Spooky radioed that he was returning to Da Nang to rearm and refuel. He gave Zoschak's senior RTO the call sign for another Spooky gunship that was en route to the area, but he cautioned that the other aircraft was still ten minutes out. Ten minutes was more than enough time to die.

At that moment, a Cobra pilot came up on the Ranger push and requested that we mark our location with the strobe light again, saying he would see what he could do about "keeping Mr. Charles occupied." Within seconds, 2.75 in. rockets were impacting uncomfortably close to our perimeter. But it worked. Mr. Charles kept his distance!

Then Marcy screamed that Fadeley, his ATL, had been hit by shrapnel from one of the rockets. Zoschak shouted into the handset, *"Break off, break off! You're hitting us."* The Cobra broke off immediately. The pilot, sounding unnerved and broken, apologized and said he wouldn't make another pass.

With all of the supporting aircraft off station, Rucker let out his breath, groaned aloud, then sagged back into the matted grass. The Ranger point man was totally exhausted from kneeling in the center of the perimeter holding the strobe light high above his head for the better part of an hour and a half. He'd earned the rest.

But a few minutes later the second Spooky arrived on station and took up an orbit over our position. Seeing that Mother had had it, I grabbed my own strobe and moved to the center of the perimeter to spell him at marking our location as the second gunship picked up where his partner had left off. It would be daylight in ninety minutes, and for the first time during the night we felt that we might survive until morning. We knew that the enemy would be gone with the coming dawn.

When the sky finally began to lighten, we breathed a collective sigh of relief. The NVA were indeed gone, the battle was over, and we had survived. The U.S. paratroopers on Firebase Jack had taken casualties but had beaten back a determined NVA massed ground assault. It could have been worse, much, much worse.

The presence of eighteen Rangers in the right place at the right time had prevented a committed and determined effort by the NVA to overrun and destroy a U.S. fire support base sitting out in the open terrain between two major 101st Airborne Division base camps. The total destruction of Firebase Jack would have been much more than just another military victory. It would have shown the American soldiers that there was nowhere in I Corps they could be safe. The enemy's gambit backfired.

6

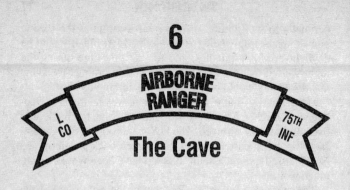

AIRBORNE RANGER

L CO

75TH INF

The Cave

Rangers are widely known to be resourceful, not afraid to tackle anything, but it always helped to have a basic grounding in some of the technical skills necessary to complete a wide range of missions, especially those being assigned to the newly activated L Company, 75th Infantry (Ranger). Medical training, communications, engineering, and demolitions were specialty skills that didn't often surface on the DD-214 of a newly arrived volunteer. Sometimes, having a man on patrol with one or more of those skills would have made the difference in the success or failure of the mission.

On April 5, 1969, Team 2-2 received a warning order for its third reconnaissance mission in the past three months along a stretch of the Song (river) Bo. Ironically, this third mission was slated to go into the same RZ as the previous two. In the business of intelligence-gathering behind enemy lines, it is never good policy to establish patterns. But Sergeant Larry Closson, Team 2-2's leader, had to admit that the OP site at the southern edge of the RZ was an ideal location from which to monitor the river. It was an excellent position twenty feet above the water, offering the optimum in cover and concealment. The only problem was that the previous two missions had both culminated after run-ins with the enemy. If the local NVA commander had his act together, he'd have had his miniature bully boys pulling punishment tours staked out on every clearing in the area large enough to handle a helicopter. Fortunately for us, this had not occurred to the NVA.

Closson would be going out with basically the same team he'd taken in on the first two missions—I would serve as ATL and point man; Senior RTO was Sergeant Ron "Mother" Rucker; Spec 4s Rick Lawhorn, William Gillette, and Dean Groff made up the remainder of the team. Rucker and I were experienced Rangers with over fifty missions between us. The other three members of the team had only been out on patrols for two or three months. They weren't cherries anymore, not by a long shot, but they were still unknown factors in a combat equation.

The patrol went in at last light on the crest of a secondary ridgeline just four hundred meters north of the Song Bo. The ridge sloped gently to the south, ending abruptly twenty feet above the river. The OP site was situated in a small, bowl-shaped depression just back from the end of the ridge. It was surrounded by thick stands of bamboo that offered concealment from the river and from the brush-covered ridgeline that ran out to it. Just big enough to hold a six-man Lurp team, the depression offered adequate cover from grazing fire directed at the team from anywhere behind them or from the other side of the river. Only hand grenades or indirect fire from enemy mortars were an immediate threat. It was an ideal fighting position, with the river providing 180 degrees security. Yet that same river also cut down on the team's available escape routes if it was forced to E&E.

Once on the ground, I took point and immediately led the patrol north, away from the river, in an effort to fool the enemy into believing our real interests lay elsewhere. Two hundred meters from the LZ we circled back to the south and set up a night defense position on the western slope of the same ridge, right in the middle of a thick stand of single canopy vegetation. We were only twenty meters below our own back trail and would be able to hear anyone who was attempting to follow us in the dark. Quietly, we put out three claymore antipersonnel mines, then lay back in silence to listen and to wait. No one ate, no one talked, no one moved, no one broke wind. Each of us knew that the first night on the ground was always the critical period of any patrol, and on our third trip into that AO, we were beginning to feel that we were pushing our luck.

At sunrise the next morning we were up and moving. The night had been quiet—almost too quiet. There had been twenty or thirty seconds of intense small-arms fire less than five or six klicks to the south. Judging from the area, the time of night, and the intensity of the gunfire, some U.S. infantry unit had blown an ambush. It was too far away to determine if any of the firing came from enemy weapons.

Our patrol had to cover six hundred meters before we reached the OP site along the river. There was little but single-canopy vegetation and waist-high underbrush all the way to the water, which made it very difficult for us to stay concealed from the opposite ridgeline. Before I moved out on point, Closson cautioned me to take my time covering the distance to the river. He didn't mind if it took the entire day to reach our destination. He pointed out that it would actually be better if we moved into the OP site at last light. I nodded in agreement and smiled, telling him I'd already come to that conclusion. I had decided that when I reached the OP site, I would move across it and on down along the river, just to make certain that no one had been there since the last mission a month earlier. I would keep the team hidden in the thick cover along the river until shortly after dark, then lead it back into the site under cover of darkness.

Zigzagging, we moved slowly toward the river, even crossing and recrossing our own tracks upon occasion to confuse anyone who might be following us. Rucker, at rear security, took extra precautions to sterilize our back trail, even dropping off to the side of the trail for ten to fifteen minutes every two hundred meters or so just to see if we were being followed. We weren't.

In the middle of the afternoon we intersected a fresh trail running down from the opposite ridgeline and up across the same ridge our patrol had gone in on. This was bad! Had someone come to check on the helicopter activity the day before? Maybe they were tracking us even then. I fought back an uncontrollable urge to move out for the tactical safety of the

OP site immediately. After all, it was our ultimate destination, and the site offered protection that the sparsely covered hillside did not afford. But panicking was no way to handle the situation, so I swallowed hard to overcome my apprehension, then stepped over the trail and continued moving toward the river.

Three hours later I dropped to one knee, raised my hand and stopped the team. We were still in the waist-high brush, but less than fifty feet from the bamboo thicket out on the tip of the ridge. We listened intently for any sound that might give away an enemy force waiting in ambush. There was none, nor were there any obvious signs that anyone had been in the area.

Thirty minutes later it was beginning to grow dark. To play it safe, we waited until the nocturnal birds and insects began their normal evening chatter, a good indication that no alien creatures were moving in the vicinity of the point. Then it was time for us to move. Cautiously, we crossed over the end of the ridge, skirting the shallow depression just inside the bamboo. The OP site was already in heavy shadow and we could see very little within the thick cover.

We moved slowly until we dropped over the end of the ridge and down into the thick grass along the riverbank, where we waited for perhaps ten minutes before moving out again, this time going around the end of the point and back up into the bamboo from the opposite side. When we reached the OP site and moved quickly inside, we could tell that no one had been there since we'd left it a month before. There were still signs of the terrible damage inflicted by the crashing rounds of the sixteen-inch naval guns of the USS *New Jersey*, which had fired in our support when an enemy patrol tried to cut us off on the point. Severed branches, splintered bamboo, and dry, yellow leaves littered the depression. Carefully, three of my teammates cleared away the rubbish while the remainder pulled security.

When Closson was satisfied that the depression was clear of brush and dried leaves, he pulled everyone inside, then sent Rucker on a one-man scout down off the end of the ridge to check out the riverbank below the OP site. At the same time, he sent me out in the brush behind us to circle north to determine if we'd been followed. Both of us returned in less than fifteen minutes to report that our areas were clear. As the full moon began to rise in the eastern sky, half the team slipped outside the perimeter to set out eight claymores in an overlapping circle around our OP. When we finished, we crawled silently back into the depression, hooked up the firing devices, and settled in for the night.

Much to the surprise of the patrol, the night of April eighth was uneventful, as was the following day. But during the night of the ninth, there was a sudden noise in the valley a hundred meters west of the OP. It sounded like someone attempting to catch himself as he fell over a log or slipped off a rock. Then came the unmistakable sound of a body thumping as it hit the ground. Animals weren't that clumsy. It had to have been human.

We went on a hundred percent alert for the next half hour, but nothing happened during the remainder of the night. Closson called in a sit rep to report the noise, and he doubled the security, from one man on watch at a time to two, then told everyone else to go back to sleep.

On the morning of April tenth Captain Cardona radioed the patrol to report that the 2/17th Cav was sending a scout helicopter to check out the valley west of the patrol. Closson didn't like the idea, since it would only confirm to the enemy that someone was nearby monitoring their activities. When he protested to Cardona, the Ranger commander told him that it was too late, the chopper was already on its way.

A little before mid-morning the LOH buzzed up the river fifty feet above the surface of the water. It shot past Team 2-2's OP on the point of the ridge and hooked hard to the right as it flew north of the valley where the noise had occurred the night before. Suddenly, the Ranger radio relay element on Firebase Rakkassan radioed the patrol and reported that the Cav chopper had just spotted fresh sandal tracks in the wet sand along a secondary stream in the next valley west of our OP. The scout aircraft followed the tracks upstream until they disappeared into the narrow opening of a cave just above the stream bed. The pilot got a fix and reported the location of the cave at five hundred meters north of the stream's confluence with the Song Bo.

Captain Cardona radioed our team that he was going to rein-force us with two more Ranger teams. They would be bringing in enough C-4 explosives to destroy the cave. But before then, he wanted his Rangers to move in to check it out. He ordered Closson to move his team two hundred meters west to a gravel bar at the confluence of the Song Bo and the secondary stream.

We pulled in all our claymores, policed up our perimeter, and moved west toward the gravel bar. We reached it at 1000 hours, pulled back into the brush surrounding the gravel bar and set up a security perimeter. The high ground across the river offered the enemy a shooting gallery on the gravel bar. We were extremely nervous to be sitting so close to ground zero.

Thirty minutes later the relay team radioed that the two addi-tional Ranger teams were airborne and en route to our location. They were still twenty minutes out. It was ample time for enemy forces to prepare a welcoming party.

Our radio crackled to life. It was the pilot of the LOH reporting that he would remain in the vicinity of the cave as long as he could but was running low on fuel. He encouraged us to get there quickly.

Captain Cardona broke in and reported that the slicks were now five minutes out. Suddenly, a second scout helicopter shot overhead past our position and flew up the valley toward the cave. It was Captain Cardona in the C&C ship. Seconds later Cardona was on the radio ordering Closson to pop a smoke grenade out on the LZ.

Rucker pitched a yellow smoke grenade out in the center of the gravel bar just as the first Huey came in low from down-stream. The slick flared over the LZ, disgorging Zoschak's team. The six Rangers were off and running for the cover of the brush before the ship could even touch down. Two minutes later Gregory's team was on the ground and linking up with Zoschak and Closson.

As the sound of the choppers faded in the distance, the three Ranger team leaders quickly decided on a plan of action and prepared to move out along the stream bed. Zoschak's team, carrying forty pounds of C-4, plus det cord, blasting caps, and a crimping tool, took the west side of the stream, while Closson and Gregory moved their patrols up the east side.

Heavy vegetation along the east bank immediately forced the two teams on that side of the stream to move inland ten to fifteen meters to maneuver around it. A hundred meters ahead Zoschak radioed that his team had run up against a sheer bluff that extended all the way to the water's edge. They were forced to either move out into the stream or climb the ridge to get around the obstruction. Both options were dangerous and exposed them to enemy ambush, but all things being equal, wading the shallow stream would at least keep Zoschak's team in close proximity to support from our two teams on the opposite side of the water.

Sergeant Zoschak radioed to the scout helicopter circling the cave and requested the pilot to fly to his location and make a low-level aerial reconnaissance of the shoreline between the cave and his patrol.

The LOH was over them in less than two minutes. It had already scouted the eastern bank on its way down to Zoschak's location. Finding nothing unusual ahead of Closson's and Gregory's teams, the scout aircraft circled over Zoschak's team then turned and raced up the west bank. When the pilot was safely back hovering over the cave again, he radioed Zoschak that everything looked clear from above. He also reported that the location of the cave was only two hundred meters ahead of the patrol.

Zoschak's team moved out into the shallow stream in staggered patrol file and reached the cave twenty minutes later. Zoschak was busy setting out security on the ridge above the target when we finally broke through the dense vegetation along the eastern edge of the stream. We immediately spread out along the opposite shoreline and set up security.

The "cave" turned out to be little more than a narrow crevasse in the face of the limestone bluff bordering the stream. Four Rangers from Zoschak's Team 2-3 had already fanned out as a security screen in the thin cover above the cave, while Zoschak and his ATL, Sergeant Jim Schwartz, moved up to the mouth of the cave with a rucksack full of C-4 explosives. While Schwartz covered him with his CAR-15, Zoschak slipped up to the narrow opening and tossed a CS canister back into the recesses. If anyone was still hiding inside, the CS gas would soon drive him out.

We waited in silence as a cloud of noxious white smoke billowed out of the cave and drifted up the face of the cliff, but after several minutes no one emerged from the entrance. Zoschak, unwilling to accept the fact that no one was home, moved back up to pitch a concussion grenade into the mouth of the cave. A muffled explosion blew out a spray of fine debris and gravel, but still there was no indication the cave was occupied.

Zoschak waited nearly ten minutes before dropping his rucksack and moving back up onto the limestone shelf in front of the opening in the bluff. Boldly, he peered inside. Seeing nothing, he stepped back and began to remove one-pound sticks of C-4 plastique from his rucksack. Sergeant Joe Gregory, who had some experience with explosives, waded across the stream to help Zoschak set the charges. Schwartz moved up to cover the entrance of the cave with his weapon as the two team leaders silently worked to prepare the explosives.

Soon the two Ranger NCOs had attached four one-pound sticks of C-4 along the roof of the cave approximately five feet in from the entrance. Gregory ran a ten-foot section of det cord to a blasting cap, crimped it, then pushed it deep into the explosive charge. The two men backed slowly out of the cave, feeding the det cord behind them as they went. When they had joined up with Schwartz out on the ledge, Zoschak turned and looked across the river with a big grin on his face. In his crowning moment of glory, he shouted, "FIRE IN THE HOLE!" then turned and ignited the det cord with a fuse lighter. As the fuse burned toward the explosives, Zoschak stepped off the ledge and calmly waded out into midstream while Gregory and Schwartz ran back along the shoreline to a place of safety.

When it came, the resulting explosion was loud but unimpressive. After the smoke cleared and the dust settled, it was relatively easy to see that the blast had accomplished little more than chip away a few pieces of limestone from the area around the entrance of the cave. The explosive charge had been too

light to cave in the roof of the grotto. A second, more powerful effort would be necessary.

Zoschak, wet to the crotch, waded ashore and dropped to a
squatting position on the ledge to study the problem. Gregory
walked up behind him, surveyed the minuscule damage, and
said, "Well, what do you think, Zo?"

Zoschak pondered the situation silently for another full
minute, then answered, "Ten pounds, ten pounds will do it!"
With that he pulled out ten one-pound sticks of C-4 and placed
the charges. Finished in twenty minutes, he backed out of the
cave with Gregory beside him, lit the det cord, then calmly
turned and waded back out to midstream, where he climbed
up on a large boulder to watch the fireworks. Gregory and
Schwartz, withdrawing much quicker than Zoschak, moved
thirty meters downstream and tucked themselves into a niche
in the cliff face. On the opposite side of the stream eleven
Rangers watched in silence as the det cord burned slowly
toward the charges.

The second blast was much more powerful than the first.
This time it succeeded in dislodging several large boulders
from the roof of the cave and blowing a large fan of jagged
gravel and fist-size rocks out into the stream. But after the
smoke and dust had cleared, the cave was still intact. Except
for a hairline crack in the ceiling, it had suffered no apparent
structural damage. If anything, the charge had only widened
the passage to make it easier to access the innermost reaches
of the cave. This was beginning to get embarrassing for the
mighty "Zo"—and for all of us who were witnessing his
failure.

Outside the cave, most of the Rangers were now openly
smiling. Zoschak, a legendary Ranger team leader, a man who
everyone in the company looked up to, was failing miserably
at destroying a tiny cave.

Zoschak didn't find the situation even remotely comical. For
the third time he stepped up on the rock ledge. Going into his
"full concentration" pose, and ignoring snickers from across
the stream, he studied the most recent damage to the target with
the deliberate eye of a trained demolition expert—which he

wasn't. When he had finished, he turned to Gregory and announced, "It's gonna take the rest of the explosives."

Gregory picked up the rucksack containing the remaining twenty-six pounds of C-4 and moved back into the cave with Zoschak. They shoved the charges inside a narrow fissure in the roof of the cave that had been opened up by the last blast. When they finished packing the charges, they ran another ten-foot length of det cord out to the entrance of the cave. Once again, Zoschak knelt to ignite the cord, yelling *"Fire in the hole!"* this time with a little more conviction than before. Satisfied that everything was going according to plan, he calmly turned and waded back out to his perch on the boulder rising in midstream. Behind him and across the stream, above the cave, the remaining fifteen Rangers were still grinning openly.

This time Gregory and Schwartz ran down the shoreline nearly fifty meters through the shallow water and sought shelter behind a large limestone outcropping.

The third explosion was devastating, much greater than the previous two. Those of us who witnessed it felt it bordered somewhere between a volcanic eruption and a tactical nuke. The four Rangers on the bluff above the cave were knocked completely off their feet by the force of the blast, as were most of us strung out across the stream. Dirt, debris, bits of vegetation, and rocks of all sizes suddenly began raining down from above, subjecting the Rangers to a meteor shower of cataclysmic proportions.

When the smoke cleared and the dust finally settled, someone yelled that Zoschak was gone. He had disappeared from his perch in the middle of the stream, causing most of his fellow Rangers to believe that he'd been vaporized in the blast. This was a tragic mishap and an extremely sad day for L Company. The legendary Zo had done to himself what the NVA had never been able to do.

But as we were struggling to recover from the effects of the mighty explosion, Zoschak, spitting muddy water, rose from where he'd been submerged in the stream thirty feet behind his perch on the boulder. The force of the blast had apparently tossed him like a rag doll, but the water had saved him from serious injury.

As for the cave in the limestone bluff, there was nothing left but a deep, open crevasse running all the way up to the top of the bluff. The humor of the situation was lost on no one, even Sergeant Zoschak. Smiling proudly at his success, the dripping team leader looked around at the other Rangers, who were still picking themselves up, and said, "I think that last one did it!" In spite of the fact that we were deep in Indian country, everyone broke out laughing.

Security and discipline had gone to hell as most of us moved across the stream to admire Zoschak's recent handiwork. But we soon got back in line when Closson announced, "That explosion will bring every damned gook in I Corps down on our heads. Party's over, let's get the fuck out of here."

All three teams quickly formed up in single-patrol formation, with each Ranger spacing out ten meters apart, and began moving quickly downstream toward the gravel bar on the north shore of the Song Bo. It was the closest LZ available, unless we wanted to go out by ladder from midstream, and no one seemed to like that idea. Even though we were dangerously exposed out in the open stream bed, speed was now more important than caution.

Gregory got on his radio and called for an extraction at the gravel bar in ten minutes. He was told that the extraction ships were ready to crank up and would reach us in approximately thirty minutes. This caused much consternation among the eighteen Rangers who knew that any enemy units in the vicinity of the blast would already be reacting to the explosions. Time was now at a premium.

Rucker and Schwartz took point and were moving fifteen meters out in front of the patrol. Knowing what to expect on the return trip, we covered the distance downstream to the river much faster than the trip upstream. Suddenly, Rucker threw up his right hand, pointed to the ridgeline to our west, and held up two fingers. The point man had just spotted two NVA soldiers back in the trees on the crest of the ridge. They were moving parallel to our route of march.

Realizing that there was no point in trying to be silent any longer, Zoschak shouted for everyone to keep moving and pick up the pace. If we had to make a stand until the slicks arrived on station, he wanted it to be as close to the Song Bo as possible. At our present location, we were literally up the creek without a paddle. He got on the horn and requested immediate gunship cover, but was informed that the gunships were escorting the slicks which were still over twenty minutes away.

Our point element could see the river through the trees up ahead. Realizing that we were getting close to our LZ, Zoschak held up the column in the heavy cover along the western shoreline of the stream while Schwartz and Rucker crossed over to the other side and performed a quick cloverleaf reconnaissance of the riverbank bordering the gravel bar. When they were certain it was clear, they moved back to signal Zoschak to bring up the rest of the patrol. The remaining Rangers quickly crossed over through the waist-deep water just above the mouth of the stream and scattered out in the brush along the riverbank.

Zoschak was already on the radio reporting the NVA when the first shot rang out from the ridgeline west of the patrol. *"Bam . . . zinggggg!"* A second shot ricocheted off the gravel bar, then a third round passed overhead. NVA were firing on the LZ from somewhere back on the ridge between the river and the cave. The shots were coming from a very long distance and were not accurate, but all of us hiding in the brush were well aware that even wild, random shots could kill you just as dead as well-aimed ones.

Several of us stood up in the waist-high cover and returned fire. We were not certain of our targets but we instinctively felt the need to shoot back at something. Gregory screamed for Mike Penchansky, his M-79 grenadier, to lob a few high-explosive rounds up on the ridge.

Penchansky quickly put out a half-dozen rounds spaced erratically along the military crest of the ridge. When he'd finished his fire mission, he broke open the weapon to reload the canister round that he usually carried in the chamber. As he slammed it closed, a loud bang sounded. The weapon had accidentally discharged.

At that second, sergeant John Renear, another veteran Ranger from Gregory's team, screamed in pain and shouted that he'd been hit. Closer scrutiny revealed that he had been struck in the right thigh by a few of the pellets from the accidental discharge of Penchansky's 40mm shotgun round. Though very painful, the wound looked much worse than it actually was. It would not cause him permanent damage, but Renear would still need to be medevacked to a surgical facility as quick as possible.

Zoschak grabbed one of the radios and requested an immediate dustoff, while one of the team medics dropped to his knees next to Renear and began treating the wound. Surprisingly, there was not a great deal of blood loss, but it was apparent there was some serious tissue damage to the NCO's leg.

Zoschak returned the handset to the RTO and turned to announce that a medevac was on the way from Camp Evans. Then two more shots rang out from the ridgeline, prompting more sporadic return fire from the scattered Rangers. Zoschak got back on the horn and reestablished contact with Dustoff Control. He requested that the medevac pilot approach the gravel bar from downstream and warned him that the LZ was "hot."

A single Huey helicopter soon raced up the river from the east, a bright red cross on a white border painted on its nose. The Huey slowed as it flared over the gravel bar, but its forward momentum forced the pilot to slam it down on the back of its skids into the LZ. One of the skid supports snapped on impact, causing the aircraft to list as it settled in. The pilot immediately brought it back light on the skids and held it there while two Rangers picked up Renear in a fireman's carry and brought him over to the open cabin. The dustoff medic and crew chief quickly pulled the wounded Ranger into the aircraft, and the pilot nosed the ship forward and away from the gravel bar. Banking hard to the left as it gained forward airspeed, the medevac turned out over the river and headed back downstream toward the field hospital at Camp Evans.

The lift aircraft were late, and all of us who were exposed out on the gravel bar were growing a bit nervous. Another shot whistled overhead from an NVA position high on the ridge on the far side of the stream. This prompted Zoschak to move over to where Gregory and Closson were squatting, discussing the possibility of escape and evading east along the Song Bo to get away from the sniper.

At that moment we heard the loud *whop . . . whop . . . whop* of approaching Hueys. What a beautiful sound! Once you hear it in that type of situation, you never forget it. The slicks had finally arrived.

I popped a purple smoke grenade and tossed it along the edge of the gravel bar to mark the LZ, then I scrambled out into the open to guide the aircraft in. Seconds later the first slick was flaring over the gravel bar.

As the lead Huey touched down, Gregory's team sprinted out of the brush and leaped aboard. Closson's team went out on the second ship, Zoschak's on the third. Within minutes all seventeen of the remaining Rangers had been plucked from the exposed gravel bar.

Renear was the only Ranger casualty of the mission, but would return to the company three weeks later. The enemy had missed its chance to trap us on the open gravel bar. But then maybe they knew what they were doing.

The Song Bo had always been a hot spot for L Company reconnaissance patrols, especially for Team 2-2. Three missions, three months, three contacts. It wasn't enough to write home about, but it was enough to last us for a while. The Rangers of L Company would not soon forget this mission nor the area we pulled it in, but we would be back. We always came back.

7

The Premonition

The standing joke around L Company in March and April 1969 was the premonition of one of its team leaders—yours truly. Early in the morning of March 23, I awoke in a cold sweat from a particularly vivid dream, gripping the sides of my cot. Bad dreams are not a rarity among young soldiers in a combat zone, but this one had been a real ass-kicking doozy. Most nightmares leave the recipient somewhat shaken, but they are normally forgotten soon afterward. Some are pure fantasy, others contorted reality, but few actually foretell some future event, especially with the clarity and realism of the one that I had just experienced that fateful day in March.

My nightmare bore all the trappings of a normal bad dream, but it prophesied an ominous event that very nearly became reality one month later. In the dream I saw myself on a patrol deep in the Ashau Valley with fellow Ranger sergeants Larry Closson, John Sours, Ron Rucker, and Larry Chambers. My comrades were high on a hill overlooking an intricate maze of enemy high-speed trails that completely circled our position. Large numbers of NVA soldiers were coming and going through the network of trails as if it were downtown Hanoi on May Day, yet for some reason they seemed totally oblivious to the Ranger long range recon patrol directly above them.

We radioed a sit rep to our tactical operations center,

reporting thousands of enemy soldiers moving around us in the open. We begged for air support or an emergency extraction, but no one back at the rear would believe us. Finally, someone came up on our push and said, "If you've got that many NVA around you, then go out and capture a few of them and I'll send a helicopter to pull you out."

Sours, Rucker, and I were far too "short" to take those kinds of chances, so we decided to lay dog until the mission ended and we could be extracted. Suddenly, everything began to go to shit. We were spotted, and soon enemy soldiers were coming up the hill at us from all directions. We began firing our weapons, slaying NVA by the dozens. But for every one that fell, another came out of the jungle to take his place.

Finally, we ran out of ammunition and were forced to throw grenades to stop the enemy assault, but to no avail. In my dream, so many enemy soldiers died that those behind them had to climb over the bodies of the dead to get at us. But they were doing just that, and when we blew our claymores in their faces, it seemed to make no difference.

In the beginning of the nightmare everything happened in slow motion, but as the dream progressed it picked up speed until, at the very end, it became a maddening blur.

Suddenly, a tremendous explosion ripped through our tiny defensive position, and when the smoke cleared, everybody was fucked up big-time. From an out-of-body perspective I saw myself lying dead alongside the mangled bodies of Larry Closson and John Sours. Nearby, Larry Chambers was writhing in agony with both legs blown off above the knees. A short distance away Rucker was sitting propped against a tree, screaming and waving the jagged, bloody stumps that used to be his arms. The scene was one of utter devastation and was vivid enough that it jarred me awake. The realism of what I had just "experienced" convinced me that somebody had laced my Tabasco sauce with opium.

Shaking, and in a cold sweat, I lay in bed trying to rationalize what had just happened. At first I attempted to blow it off as just a common, ordinary nightmare, the result of stress and an overactive imagination. But the experience had left me emotionally drained and physically unnerved. It had been too damned real. Still perspiring heavily, I pulled my poncho liner over my head and tried to go back to sleep, but sleep wouldn't come. Somewhere in the recesses of my mind was the thought that maybe, just maybe, the damned dream might come true.

After mulling over the consequences of believing in premonitions, I further rationalized that the entire idea was totally ridiculous. Division hadn't sent a long range patrol into the Ashau in months, and even if it did, the company surely wouldn't send out an understrength five-man Ranger team. Besides, I had never before gone out on a team with Chambers, and even if I did, Sours and Closson were both team leaders who had their own teams to lead.

Thankfully, the dream didn't stand the test of reality, at least not enough to categorize it as a full-blown premonition. Too much of it was impractical and violated basic Ranger SOP. Three team leaders on one team! No way, José! It just wouldn't wash.

But I still couldn't go back to sleep. In spite of myself, I became apprehensive and restless. So I got up, got dressed and went over to the Cav mess hall to grab some breakfast. There, the nightmare still fresh in my mind, I jokingly related the story to my good friend and new ATL, Sergeant Jim Schwartz. This proved to be a major mistake.

Soon, the story of Sergeant Linderer's "bad dream" had evolved into the story of Sergeant Linderer's "premonition," and it quickly spread throughout the Ranger compound. Naturally, this served to mark me for a serious round of lighthearted but merciless ribbing by every Ranger in the company who fancied himself an undiscovered comedian—and in the Rangers a sense of humor was a requirement for anyone who could still fog a mirror.

"Hey, Linderer, can I have your K-Bar when you buy the farm?" "Oh Sarge, you'd better stay away from the valley." "Hey, is it true that you and Closson wasted five thousand dinks all by yourselves . . . just before they waxed you?" "I want to bring my whole platoon out as your reaction force . . . none of us have ever seen that many dead gooks before."

I tried to ignore the ribbing and at the same time clear the image of my death from my mind, but the more I was teased, the more real the idea of my own death became. I suddenly realized just how fragile my own mortality was. With that realization came the acceptance of my fate—not a death wish, but an awareness and a resignation that my future was no longer in my hands.

I probably should have stood my ground and defended myself against my tormentors, but I had previously done my own share of ribbing. In the Rangers, if you gave out medicine when someone was "sick," you took someone else's when you were the one with an ailment.

Nearly a month later, on the morning of April 20, 1969, I was sitting on my cot writing a letter to my fiancée. I was telling her how happy I was about going under forty-five days left in-country, and letting her know that after my upcoming R&R on April 28, I probably would only have one, or at most, two missions left. Suddenly, the screen door at the far end of the hooch opened. Sergeant Larry Closson entered and walked slowly but deliberately down to where I was sitting. Pretending to notice the big shake 'n' bake NCO for the first time, I put down my pen and paper and nodded for Closson to take a seat on the cot facing mine. After a few minutes of general small talk, Closson blurted, "Look, I don't know how to tell you this but I just got a warning order for a mission to go in at last light today. Rucker, Sours, Hillman, Chambers, you, and I are on the team. . . . "

It took a few minutes for Closson's statement to fully register. I hadn't really been paying much attention to the details and had to force myself to refocus on his words. Then it finally began to sink in.

"Hey, would you repeat that one more time?" I asked, squinting at him through half-closed eyes.

He repeated his statement, only much faster than the first time.

"Chambers! Chambers! No way, man! There has to be some mistake here. Not Chambers! Chambers and I never went out on the same team before. And you, Sours, and Rucker, too? No, man, not me. I'm not going out on this mission. Find somebody else. My God, Closson, don't you know about my dream? Jesus Christ, Larry—*the* dream. Tell me you're only joking! Yeah, that's it, isn't it? It's a goddamn joke! Chambers . . . Chambers put you up to it. He's always fuckin' around like this. That son of a bitch! I'll kill him when I get my hands on him. I should have known he'd pull something like this."

But the look of despair on Closson's face remained un-changed. The mission was genuine and I was fucked.

"You aren't kidding, are you?" I finally asked, my voice trailing off as he avoided answering my question.

Closson dropped his head and stared at the floor. I could tell that the big NCO hadn't told me everything. There was more, and it wasn't good.

"Closson, where are we going?"

Nothing!

"Dammit, Closson, *where are we going?*" I demanded, my voice beginning to rise in anger.

Closson looked up, shrugged his shoulders, then shook his head slowly from side to side. "The Ashau . . . yeah, we're going to the Ashau."

I got to my feet, my mouth moving, but unable to utter a word for the moment. As the nightmare played itself back through my mind, the words I wanted to say simply would not come. Closson, too, wanted to say more, but realizing the futility of further discussion, he gave up. Rising slowly to his feet, he turned on his heels and walked quickly from the hooch.

Momentarily lost in thought, I sat back on my bunk. It was all over for me. I wasn't going to make it home after all. I crumpled the letter to my fiancée and threw it angrily across the dirt-stained floor. I would write her another letter, but in that one I could promise her nothing.

Later that day, returning from the ammo bunker where I'd drawn extra bandoleers of ammo, grenades, and claymores for the mission, I ran into First Sergeant Clarence Cardin. The former Special Forces NCO stretched out his hand to stop me as I walked past him.

"Sergeant Linderer, I know all about your dream, and I want you to know that I didn't do this to you on purpose. If there was another way, I would have done it. Every other team is out in the field or understrength. I also realize that you, Sours, and

Rucker are all real short, but I can't send Closson out into the Ashau with a team full of cherries."

There it was! I knew there was no way out of it now. Closson and the others who had played starring roles in my premonition were doomed. Nothing could change the inevitable. It was going to happen no matter what I said or did. It was out of my hands now . . . out of anyone's hands.

I nodded stupidly when he'd finished and muttered something even dumber about understanding, but it didn't really matter . . . nothing really mattered anymore. My teammates and I would accept our fate with the somber fatalism that was characteristic of Rangers about to go out on a long range patrol. We were accustomed to accepting our lot. It was no different this time, except for the fact that we were no longer in control of our own destinies. This time we were nothing more than bit players in someone else's movie.

The mission was a "go." Closson got the nod to lead the team with Sours as his ATL. Rucker was assigned the primary radio, while Chambers was tabbed to walk point on this one. Hillman, the only inexperienced Ranger on the team, was given the unpopular job of humping the artillery radio. I would cover the patrol's back trail.

There was a lot of experience on this team, so its selection had likely taken some forethought on the part of the first sergeant, Lieutenant Jackson (the operations officer), and the two platoon sergeants. However, all the experience in the world couldn't remove the shadow of death that hung over the team like an evil shroud. My "premonition" was playing out its course, and that was all that really mattered to any of us.

The patrol went in late in the afternoon near the foot of a dominant peak that rose from a series of lesser peaks marking the beginning of the western edge of the valley. Within seconds of hitting the ground we discovered that we were in the middle of an old U.S. Army minefield. Some of the antipersonnel mines had been exposed by the torrential rains that frequently hit the Ashau, especially during the monsoon season. If not for the rains, we would have likely found the mines through a much different method.

We froze in place while Rucker established radio contact

with the C&C helicopter standing off out over the valley. He quickly reported our predicament and waited for an answer. It was not long in coming, nor was it the answer we wanted to hear. Captain Cardona came up on the net and informed us that there were indeed old 1st Cavalry Division minefields scattered throughout the area, but that wasn't the least of our problems. After checking his map, Captain Cardona discovered that our patrol had been inserted into the wrong LZ. The pilot flying the insertion aircraft had mistakenly set us down in a clearing three hundred meters west of our primary LZ.

Rather than risk a dangerous extraction from a minefield, the CO ordered us to attempt to extricate ourselves. If we were successful, we were to move toward our planned recon zone and continue our mission. If we weren't successful . . . well, he didn't have any recommendations for that.

Our patrol was approximately three hundred meters northwest of where we were supposed to have gone in, so it would not take us long to get back on track once we cleared the minefield.

Skillfully, Closson led the team out of the minefield by guiding us through a shallow, washed-out gully that had been cut through the clearing by the torrential monsoon runoff. An added benefit of moving down the narrow gully was that it ran in the general direction of Dong Ap Bia, the mountain that made up the southern and western parts of our recon zone.

We eventually reached the edge of the jungle and knew we were finally out of danger from the mines. We stopped to catch our breath under the protection of the double canopy that ringed the clearing. Ahead of us lay a dark, foreboding jungle that reeked of danger and death—and of the enemy.

For the first time since we'd inserted we were able to check our maps to orient ourselves. We quickly discovered that we were less than four hundred meters from the Laotian border. It was a bad place to be running ops, even without unplanned, unanticipated problems. And on this patrol there were plenty of both.

Ahead of us to the southwest the ground began to rise in a long, steady gradient that eventually became the east face of Dong Ap Bia. The maps, if they were correct, indicated that halfway up the mountain the contour lines began to draw very close together. This meant we would have to negotiate some pretty steep terrain over the next three days in the field. Our mission was to scout the east and southeast faces of Dong Ap Bia to determine if the area was supporting an NVA base area.

As darkness began to fall that first night in the jungle, we moved into heavy cover and set up a night defense perimeter, only to discover immediately that we were unable to raise the radio relay team across the valley on Fire Support Base Blaze. Since our patrol was still pretty close to its original insertion point, putting a little more distance between ourselves and the LZ would be a wise move anyway. Closson decided to ascend the slope another forty or fifty meters, then set up again just off the crest of a short secondary ridgeline that rose up gradually and tied into Dong Ap Bia. We hoped the move would provide us with enough elevation to reestablish radio contact with the relay team, and put us a little farther away from our initial insertion point, just in case the enemy sent out patrols to see what had brought an American helicopter so close to their mountains.

Chambers took the point and moved directly uphill. Within twenty meters he encountered a heavily used high-speed trail and signaled for the team to halt in place. The bare earth on the trail was free of leaves and forest debris and was still damp from recent showers. It clearly showed the outline of numerous enemy footprints. We'd hit the jackpot!

The trail appeared to emanate from somewhere down on the valley floor, and ran upward toward the crest of Dong Ap Bia. To cross the trail and continue uphill in the growing darkness would be placing the team in jeopardy, especially since no one knew what lay ahead of us.

Closson signaled for Chambers to back off the trail and move the patrol back down away from the crest of the ridge. He wanted us to locate a suitable NDP close enough to the trail to monitor enemy traffic, yet far enough away to avoid detection.

Twenty meters off the crest Chambers located a cluster of large boulders sitting among a stand of forest giants interspersed with oversize, broadleaf jungle vegetation. It was an excellent spot for a night laager with plenty of cover and concealment. Closson nodded for his point man to move the team into the thick cover. It was close enough to the trail for us to hear anyone passing by in the night. If we were forced to escape and evade, the floor of the valley with its numerous clearings was no more than a couple hundred meters below us.

While the patrol set up security, Rucker tried once again to establish commo with the relay team on Fire Support Base Blaze, this time with more success. The signal was weak, but we had commo. With the skill of a seasoned professional, Rucker quickly rigged a field-expedient wire antenna, stretched it through the branches above our perimeter, improving the radio signal dramatically. With the patrol's link to survival restored, every man on the team breathed a little easier. However, the secondary radio seemed to be malfunctioning. Rucker couldn't make radio contact with the artillery fire control director on Blaze at all.

Shortly after 2100 hours the first NVA unit passed by on the trail above us. They were moving up the ridge toward the crest of Dong Ap Bia. We estimated the size of the group at twenty to thirty. The NVA soldiers were moving slowly and making very little noise. This worried Closson more than he would admit, and he put the team on fifty percent alert for the remainder of the night.

A second group of NVA, approximately the same size as the first, passed through an hour and a half later. Then, a little after midnight, a gasoline generator kicked on three to four hundred meters up the mountain from our position. It ran continuously until nearly 0300 hours, when it shut down for the remainder of the night.

A third group of enemy soldiers climbed up the trail and passed by our location at sunrise. Impressed with the high level of enemy activity on the trail above us, Closson decided to move the team two hundred meters farther up the mountain and establish a new observation post overlooking the trail.

We moved out a short time later, going slowly and paralleling the trail twenty meters back in the double canopy. Less than 150 meters away, the terrain forced us to choose between crossing the trail and backtracking to where we'd started. The trail ran directly along the gently rising ridge, apparently continuing that way all the way to the top. The face of the ridge we were traversing had become too steep for us to continue on without moving closer to the trail. Closson decided to lead us across the trail and set up an OP on the wider, more level left flank of the ridge. This would in effect put us on a direct line-of-sight bearing to Fire Support Base Blaze, perhaps removing any need for a field-expedient antenna. It would also put us almost directly above our designated extraction point on the fourth and final day of the mission.

Closson sent Chambers and Sours up ahead to scout the trail and locate a suitable crossing. When the two Rangers returned ten minutes later, they reported that they had found a good spot to cross where the cover was thick on both sides.

We moved up slowly, and stopping first to look and listen, we crossed the trail in pairs. Once on the other side, the team set up a hasty defensive position twenty meters back from the trail on the military crest of the ridge. We waited fifteen minutes to determine if our crossing had attracted anyone's attention. It hadn't. Cautiously, we rose to our feet and moved back from the trail.

Rucker was soon in touch with the relay team on Blaze. His smile indicated that our commo problems had been solved. However, the secondary radio that Hillman carried was still not functioning. Rucker couldn't get anyone to answer when he called for a commo check.

For the remainder of the second day we watched the trail and listened for sounds of enemy activity on the mountain above us, but we saw and heard nothing. The NVA appeared to be reserving their activities until the hours of darkness.

At 1530 hours the sounds of chopping and hammering drifted down to us from high up on the mountain. The noise seemed to emanate from the same general area where the generator had been running the night before. Thirty minutes later dark, ominous clouds moved in from the west, and we soon found ourselves sitting in the middle of a brief but fierce thunderstorm. Heavy rains drenched us as lightning flashed all around. Thirty minutes after it began it was all over, just in time to reveal the last glimpse of the day's sun dropping behind the crest of

Dong Ap Bia. Without the sun's warmth to dry us, we would be spending a cold, wet, miserable night in the jungle.

The next morning Closson decided to move the team farther up the side of the mountain. He told us that he wanted to find out exactly what the enemy was up to. This caused a serious disagreement between Closson and the other four senior Rangers on the patrol. We argued that we already "knew" what the enemy was doing up on Dong Ap Bia, and trying to get close enough to eyeball their activities wouldn't accomplish anything more than getting everyone killed. Besides, my month-old premonition was still firmly implanted somewhere in the back of each of our minds.

To make matters even worse for Closson, I absolutely refused to go any farther up the mountain, suggesting that he continue on his own if he had to see what was up there. Closson, realizing that he was losing control of his team and seeing that my noncompliance was the cause, threatened to see that I was court-martialed upon our return. This was a bad mistake! I sneered and told him that if we went up to the top of that mountain there would be no one left alive to court-martial. Sours, Rucker, and Chambers agreed with my logic. Closson was on his own.

Hillman, the new Ranger, stayed out of the conversation, but it was obvious from the apprehension on his handsome young face that he, too, didn't want to go any farther up that mountain. Finally Closson relented, deciding for the sake of team integrity to rescind his orders and his threats.

Our patrol remained in place, and that day we spotted two more NVA units heading up the mountain. The enemy foot traffic had all been moving toward the crest of Dong Ap Bia. Whatever was going on up there must have been important, because no one was coming back down from the mountain.

Again at 1600 hours on the third day, a massive thunderstorm struck, moving in from Laos, and quickly soaked us for the second day in a row as we sat huddled under the double canopy jungle on the side of the ridge. It would be our second night in a row fighting off the bone-chilling prospects of hypothermia.

We remained at the same site for the next two nights, something that was not in the Ranger SOP. But the circumstances called for unusual measures, and moving around on the side of a mountain that was teeming with large numbers of NVA soldiers was nothing but a buggery waiting to happen. After this latest thunderstorm, Closson's suggestion to at least move to another OP site also met with stiff resistance from each of us. By that time we wanted only to get through the final day of the mission and get out of the area.

That night around midnight, as we struggled in vain to stay warm, the NVA generator came to life once again. It ran continuously until 0300, then shut down for the rest of the night. There was no indication that enemy troops were using the trail that night, but Closson posted two-man guard shifts just to be safe. For a change he got no argument from us.

We awoke wet and chilled to the bone, but it was with the knowledge that it was our last day on the patrol. We neither saw nor heard traffic on the trail above us during the day, but on two occasions we could clearly hear more pounding and hammering coming from up on the mountain. And for the first time we also heard what sounded like someone operating a chain saw. Unless the enemy was conducting "shop" classes, there was some very intensive construction work going on less than four hundred meters from our OP.

At 1500 hours Rucker radioed in a sit rep and reported that our patrol would be at its PZ (pickup zone) at 1800 hours. We would be going out on the same LZ that we were supposed to have used on our insertion four days earlier. It was only about three to four hundred meters below our present position. Unless we ran into some unforeseen difficulties, it would take us less than an hour moving downhill to reach the site.

A few minutes before 1600 hours we once again watched the storm clouds gathering over the top of Dong Ap Bia. By then we knew that in a matter of minutes the routine daily tempest would break over us once again, but this time we really didn't care. As a matter of fact, we looked forward to it. When it was over we were going to be getting out, which is all that mattered to any of us. Apparently, my premonition was not going to come true. It was one time that I didn't mind being made the fool. All we had to do was to ride out the storm and then move down the side of the ridge to the PZ. We would be wet, for sure, but a least we would be alive and back at Camp Eagle by that evening. This meant a hot shower, warm food, and a dry bed. And for Sours, Rucker, and myself, it meant a permanent stand-down until we DEROS'd. So let it rain!

And rain it did! The skies opened up with an uncontrolled vengeance, soaking us and our equipment in a matter of seconds. It was as if the storms we'd faced the previous two evenings had been only scrimmages in preparation for this, the real game. The lightning flashed all around us with an intensity none of us had ever experienced before. The thunder was continuous and deafening, and this time the rain came down mixed with marble-size hail that pelted us with bruising force. But it was only temporary discomfort. Just as before, twenty minutes into the storm it began to show signs of breaking up.

Closson whispered to Rucker between crashes of thunder, "Call in a sit rep and tell them we're preparing to move out toward the PZ." Rucker smiled, then nodded and lifted the handset to his ear. When the RTO keyed the send button, the world exploded around us. A tremendous flash, followed a microsecond later by a powerful, concussive blast of smoke and shredded jungle debris, enveloped us. If this was hell, we were in it!

I awoke sometime later not knowing where in the hell I was. There were no sounds around me but the soft, steady dripping of raindrops onto the forest floor. I was having a difficult time breathing and my mouth was full of mud, shredded leaves, and twigs. I tried to get up but nothing seemed to work except my best intentions. My body—if it was still my body—had taken a long sabbatical. I fought back the panic I felt welling up inside me. I knew I had to be hurt really bad, but there was no pain to assure me that I was right ... and just about then I needed real badly to be right about something.

Reaching back with my right hand, I tried to feel my legs. It was an effort that required my total concentration. I remember feeling a rush of relief that my right arm was functioning. But the relief ended quickly when my hand squeezed someone else's leg where mine should have been.

I could tell that there was a leg there because I could feel it with my hand, but there was no simultaneous sympathetic response in the leg. This couldn't be happening to me!

I squeezed the muscle beneath my hand a second time, only to sense that it was mushy and had the consistency of warm Jell-O. It was enough for me. For the first time I knew that I was paralyzed and my legs were gone. The premonition had come true after all. I was a dead man waiting for confirmation.

I heard a noise down the hillside from where I lay. It had to be the enemy looking for me. It was almost a relief, knowing they were coming. I knew they would finish the job because the enemy wouldn't have much use for an American POW who had to be carried. I closed my eyes and waited for the bullet to tear into the back of my head.

"Linderer . . . hey, man, are you okay?"

Jesus Christ, it was Chambers! He crawled up alongside me and lifted my head out of the shallow pool of water it lay in.

"Leave me alone, Larry. I'm all busted up. I don't want to go home like this."

"Hang in there, man. I'll get some help. You'll make it," he said as I struggled to speed up my death.

While I lay there feeling sorry for myself, Chambers crawled off to my rear. It was only then that I realized that his legs were also paralyzed. What in the name of hell had we been hit by?

When the cloud of black smoke had finally dissipated, the team's previously compact defense perimeter located just off the military crest of the ridge was gone. Most of our rucksacks, weapons, and equipment had simply vanished. The ground around our perimeter was smoking as if it were ready to burst into flames at any moment.

Rucker sat next to his ruined radio, crying softly in shock and confusion. He was staring wide-eyed at his blackened, numbed hand still gripping the smoking radio handset.

Closson struggled to make it to his feet, but was wobbling back and forth like a drunken penguin, the left side of his body paralyzed. He was distant, unable to speak intelligibly, and was totally oblivious to the present condition of his team or of himself.

Hillman, the only other Ranger still inside the team's

perimeter, was miraculously uninjured by the blast. He now
stood back in shock and bewilderment as he watched the two
veteran Ranger NCOs acting like escapees from the B ward of
a state mental hospital. To make matters even worse, there was
no sign at all of the three remaining Rangers. It was almost as
if the ground had opened up and swallowed them.

Then Hillman spotted Sergeant Sours struggling up the side
of the ridge, trying to reach the perimeter. Holding his right
arm cradled against his body, he was in obvious pain. Several
minutes passed before Chambers, too, crawled back in from
somewhere out on the right flank of the perimeter. He was
unable to use his legs, but otherwise seemed in control of his
faculties. He shouted that Linderer was fifty feet back behind
him, paralyzed from the chest down and in bad shape.

What the hell had happened? What had gone wrong? Had
we been ambushed? Artillery? A claymore? Whatever hit us
had destroyed our ability to defend ourselves; there were only
three weapons still inside the perimeter, and one of those was
damaged beyond repair. And even if we'd still had all the
weapons, only the new man, Spec 4 Marvin Hillman, could
have used them to defend the team. And at that moment Spec 4
Marvin Hillman was still searching for someone who could tell
him what to do next.

Sours managed to gather enough of his wits about him to go
back out with Chambers and drag me back into the perimeter.
I knew that I looked bad, covered in mud and unable to move
from the chest down. Hell, I felt bad, at least that part of me that
could still feel. When Sours and Chambers reached me, I
demanded that they leave me alone to die in peace. I told them
that I didn't want to live all busted up the way I was. But the
two injured Rangers ignored my ramblings and Sours dragged
me back into the perimeter.

Those of us—not me!—who still had some of our wits, tried
to restore order to the situation, but without the ability to
defend ourselves or our teammates, or even to communicate
with the radio relay team on Fire Support Base Blaze, even that
attempt seemed useless.

Confused and babbling incoherently, Rucker was still
moaning and staring at his hand. Whatever hit us had totally

destroyed the primary radio and the handset. From the amount of damage and destruction around us, it appeared that something or someone had set off all five of our claymore mines, sending five very powerful, concussive back blasts hurtling into our tiny perimeter. The only thing as bad as getting caught in front of a claymore is getting caught behind one.

Not one of us was prepared to resist an enemy assault, so anyone who could still function at all did so as if there would be no follow-up assault. It was almost like "time out—at least until we figure out what the hell happened here." Not a very realistic attitude, considering the circumstances, but for the moment it was all we could do.

Begging Closson to tell him what had happened, Rucker finally began to come around. But Closson couldn't or wouldn't answer. Sours interrupted the injured RTO and told him to get on the radio and call for a medevac. Rucker answered in the negative, reaffirming that the primary radio had been destroyed.

Hillman, who had been carrying the artillery radio, heard this and hurriedly brought his rucksack over to Rucker. But the senior RTO only shook his head—the artillery radio hadn't functioned properly from the time we'd inserted four days ago. But right then it had a much better chance of reaching help than the melted PRC-25 that lay smoking on the ground next to him. Using his uninjured left hand, Rucker adjusted the frequency to the radio relay net on Blaze. When he keyed the talk button on the handset and called for the relay team, he was shocked to hear them come back loud and clear. Quickly, he gave them our situation report, then requested an immediate medevac and a reaction force. He told them that we were in very bad trouble, and if we didn't get some help immediately, we weren't going to make it off the mountain.

Fortunately for us, a medevac aircraft from the 326th Medical Battalion, Eagle Dustoff, was already on a low priority mission northeast of the Ashau. When the pilot intercepted our distress call, he radioed that he was only ten minutes out and would make the pickup. The Eagle Dustoff pilot knew that his aircraft could reach us thirty minutes before the nearest reaction force could.

Sours and Chambers, who was just beginning to recover the use of his legs, began to look around for an opening in the overhead cover large enough to accommodate a jungle penetrator. The nearest one was right over our perimeter. The same explosion that had caused so much damage had also cleared out much of the jungle canopy over our position.

Soon the medevac helicopter could be heard coming in across the valley. The pilot requested that we mark our location, and Sours tossed out a smoke grenade that he'd retrieved from Hillman's rucksack—the only one that survived the blast.

At about that same time, Captain Cordona arrived on the scene in his C&C aircraft, a 2/17th Cav LOH, that had flown out to the valley ahead of the extraction aircraft. When the pilot saw the small opening he immediately dropped the scout helicopter down into it, chopping away some of the remaining vegetation with his rotor blades. A dangerous maneuver, but it worked well enough to allow the medevac access to the Ranger team below. Satisfied that he had done all he could, the scout ship pilot lifted up out of the hole and moved out of the way of the waiting medevac.

The Huey worked its way in over the narrow opening in the trees and came to a hover sixty feet above us. Within seconds a metal recovery basket was lowered on a cable. The crew chief leaned out over the edge of the cabin floor and grabbed the cable in an attempt to guide the basket around some damaged trees still protruding over our perimeter. The basket kept fouling on a single, jagged tree that jutted up out of our NDP, and try as he could, the crew chief couldn't maneuver the basket past that leaning piece of kindling.

Chambers and Sours both attempted to push the tree on over the edge of the ridge, but their efforts proved useless. It would give a little, but wouldn't break free of its grip on the mountain. Suddenly, still suffering strokelike symptoms to the left side of his body, Closson started hobbling down the side of the ridge, picking up speed as he went. As he reached the tree, he threw all of his weight against it. For a moment nothing happened, then slowly, ever so slowly, the tree began to give, until finally it groaned, cracked, groaned again, then broke free and toppled slowly over the side of the ridge.

With the tree out of the way, the medevac crew chief was able to lower the body basket to the ground. It seemed like an hour before Sours and Chambers rolled me into the litter and strapped me down. Then Sours stepped back and signaled the crew chief to hoist me up.

Closson went up next in the basket, then Hillman and Rucker rode the jungle penetrator up together. Sours and Chambers both expected to be left behind by the overloaded medevac, but were surprised when the penetrator once again started down for them. The crew chief fed the cable out over the edge of the cabin floor and held out two fingers.

The two Rangers quickly straddled the folding metal legs on the penetrator and, facing each other, signaled that they were ready to be hoisted up. The sixty-foot ride to the helicopter seemed to take forever. With the added weight of the last two Rangers, the aircraft commander was beginning to experience difficulty maintaining his hover.

Suddenly, just as the crew chief was pulling Sours and Chambers into the safety of the open cabin, shots rang out from up the ridge near the trail. A party of NVA soldiers had arrived on the scene. They had finally decided to come down to investigate all the activity.

As the pilot dropped the nose of his aircraft to pick up forward airspeed, several enemy soldiers broke into our abandoned position and opened fire at the departing helicopter. Looking skyward in frustrated disappointment, they fired several long bursts into the air. They had been only seconds away from catching our "dysfunctional" patrol on the ground.

At the 85th Evac Hospital chopper pad at Phu Bai, several gurneys and a large number of U.S. Army medics, doctors, and nurses were on hand when the medevac landed. Sours, Closson, Rucker, Chambers, and I were triaged, then wheeled into surgery for closer medical analysis. In spite of the gravity of our symptoms, all five of us recovered within five days. I was the most seriously injured and the last to be discharged—just in time to catch my R&R flight to Honolulu. The partial paralysis suffered by five of the six Rangers on the patrol was later determined to have been caused by a combination of concussion resulting from the back blasts of five claymore mines and the detonation of a single concussion grenade that had exploded in the side pocket of the rucksack I'd been sitting on. Of course the lightning strike that exploded Rucker's radio, melted the handset, and discriminately set off the claymores and the concussion grenade without detonating any of our fragmentation or white phosphorous grenades, probably would have caused its own share of injuries without help from the military pyrotechnics.

Ranger Ron Rucker would never forget who answered his radio transmission that day. He learned that lightning, dominant terrain features, and whip antennas can combine to produce a deadly reaction. And my premonition? Well, needless to say, it didn't come true, but it did prove that horseshoes and hand grenades are not the only things where "close counts."

8

AIRBORNE
RANGER

L CO

75TH INF

The Cost of Being a Warrior

It must have been disheartening to serve in a Ranger company in a noncombatant role, watching your friends going out on one dangerous patrol after another while you remained behind in the rear. For some Rangers it caused a personal crisis that could only be resolved by getting on a team and going out in the bush even for a single mission. At least then you would be able to tell your comrades, your friends, your relatives—even yourself—that you had what it took to be a Ranger. Sergeant Keith Hammond was just such a soldier, and this is his story.

On May 1, 1969, Sergeant Kenn Miller, a veteran Lima Company team leader, was given a warning order for a reconnaissance mission into the southern end of the Ashau Valley. The RZ was in an extremely "hot" area. During the briefing, Miller was informed that during the previous year a CCN SOG team staging out of FOB 1 and a recon team from Project Delta had both disappeared without trace in the same general area. Each team had failed to make a scheduled sit rep and was never heard from again. Neither team had reported anything unusual during its previous sit rep. Efforts were made by air and ground to recover the two recon teams, but no trace was ever found. Heavy enemy activity in the area prevented a more thorough search. Their disappearance remained a mystery.

111

Miller's long range reconnaissance patrol was instructed to be on the lookout for evidence that might indicate what had happened to the two lost patrols. Miller was given their last known coordinates, but not the details of either team's proposed route of march.

When Miller and his ATL, Sergeant Bob Dearing, went out on their overflight that morning, they discovered that the terrain in the area of their mission was extremely mountainous, but their recon zone was in a dogleg valley with a wide, slow-moving stream. The valley looked like a good place to find an enemy base camp. The wide, shallow stream was east of and just outside Miller's RZ. There was a lot of double canopy in the valley, but there were also a number of large open areas with tall grass and pockets of thick timber along the lower slopes of the ridgelines. A large amount of triple canopy jungle clogged the north-south leg of the valley, but the northwest-southeast section was a vast sea of tall elephant grass broken only occasionally by an isolated, heavily forested island.

Miller's primary mission was reconnaissance, to ascertain if NVA units were homesteading that part of the valley. But at the premission briefing he was also assigned the secondary mission of trying to snatch a prisoner. A major from G-2 promised a pallet of beer and a case of whiskey if the team came out with a POW. He told them that Division would very much like to get its hands on a prisoner from that specific area, one who could possibly shed some light on what had happened to the two missing recon teams. There were still a lot of people down at Danang and in Nha Trang who wanted to know what had happened to them.

The major issued the team a newly developed Starlight scope, much smaller than the heavy, awkward devices previously used. He also produced a half-dozen recently designed, fully collapsible gas masks that were specifically useful against CS gas. When Miller asked the reason for the gas masks, the major was quick to suggest that the team consider using CS gas to disable the enemy soldier they selected for capture. Miller thought the idea was ridiculous, but filed it in the back of his mind for future recall.

After the overflight, Miller's ATL made the comment that a

large portion of the valley appeared to have been burned off in earlier years. Miller agreed, but he'd seen something else, something that disturbed him greatly—there was almost a total absence of bomb craters or artillery impacts anywhere in the recon zone, that is, except for a few old ones up on the secondary ridgeline the team was inserting into. It was obvious to Miller that this area had been selected as a "no fire zone" by the U.S. military. Why?

The mission was scheduled to go in on the morning of May 3, 1969. However, Miller was still short a man until Sergeant Keith Hammond volunteered to go out with the team. Hammond was from a well-to-do Massachusetts family and had a college degree. He had never been assigned to a team; instead he'd worked in the TOC, drove the CO's jeep, and had most recently managed the Ranger Lounge. His experience in the field had been limited to a couple of humbug missions outside the wire that he'd been allowed to accompany to get his feet wet and to pick up a little bragging time.

Miller liked Hammond—everybody did—but he knew that Hammond was a "Remington Ranger," and he didn't have the background or the adventurous streak it took to make an effective long range patroller. But Hammond had watched too many of his comrades return from one "hot" patrol after another, and the thought that in his own eyes he somehow didn't quite measure up to them was enough to drive him to find a spot on a team.

Hammond knew that he had to fulfill his own destiny, to complete his right of passage into manhood, and at that point in his tour nothing else mattered to him. Against his better judgement, Miller agreed to let him join the team as the sixth man.

The team's insertion was scheduled at first light on the morning of May 3, but it managed to get in four hours late, an auspicious start for such a high risk mission! As the helicopter approached the low-lying ridge where the team's LZ was located, Miller spotted smoke rising from two locations in the surrounding jungle. Since Division reported that a number of heavy thunderstorms had occurred in the AO during the night, Miller was pretty certain he wasn't looking at the early stages of a forest fire. No, the patrol definitely had company waiting below them in their recon zone—company who wouldn't take kindly to a six-man Ranger team dropping in without an invitation.

A half-dozen Rangers dropped from the aircraft while it was still above the ground. Heading for a patch of jungle less than twenty meters to the south, they sprinted across the lightly cratered clearing. When they reached it, they crawled another twenty meters into the trees to lay dog while they watched and listened.

Satisfied that the NVA had not spotted their insertion, Miller moved the team down the slope and immediately discovered a large, complex trail network, the likes of which he'd never seen before. The majority of the trails ran parallel to each other and to the crest of the ridge, but a number of other footpaths dropped off the side of the ridge and intersected with the lateral trails paralleling the crest.

There was very little cover in which the exposed Rangers could conceal themselves so they kept moving down the slope. Two hundred meters from the LZ, sitting back in the trees just off the intersection of three main trails, they ran into a half-dozen long-abandoned hooches. The Rangers hurriedly searched through the hooches, snapped a few photographs, then continued downslope.

They hadn't gotten very far before they hit another high-speed trail, one covered with a lot of fresh sign. Sensing danger, Miller pulled the team off into some thick cover nearby, then sent Hammond with Dearing, his point man, to scout the trail. They returned after only a few minutes, saying they'd just discovered a fresh cache.

Miller instructed the two Rangers to lead the team back down to the cache site and set up security around it. While four of his teammates watched the surrounding jungle, Miller and Dearing began to dig in the fresh, loose dirt at the cache. They soon uncovered a rough wooden coffin that, from the condition of the ground, appeared as if it had just been buried. However, the coffin itself was old. Miller checked it for booby traps, then slowly lifted the lid. Inside they found the skeleton of a man, lying in a bed of black mud. There appeared to be nothing else in the coffin, nor for that matter in the grave. Miller backed off a few paces and took a picture of the macabre scene, then he and Dearing hurriedly filled in the grave, trying to leave it as close as possible to how they'd found it.

The patrol dropped off the ridge, crossing several heavily used trails. They began to encounter a number of well-maintained clearings alongside some of the trails, each one large enough to accommodate a full platoon in an overnight laager. The large number of trails indicated a large enemy presence in the area. It was enough for Miller. He pulled his Rangers into some heavy cover and spent the remainder of the day monitoring a major trail intersection farther down the ridge. The patrol remained hidden beneath the double canopy just above the trail junction, but farther down the slope the trees gave way to an area choked with elephant grass and low brush.

They sighted nothing of the enemy during the remainder of the day. That night they elected to crawl a short distance away into a very dense thicket, where they waited for the NVA to come looking for them. Amazingly, they were left alone.

The next morning they remained in their NDP until almost noon, fearing that the NVA, knowing their patrol was in the area, had set up ambushes nearby and was lying in wait for the Rangers to move. When nothing had happened by midday, Miller decided to lead the team out of hiding and bring them down through the jungle to where the trees ended and the open grasslands began.

As soon as they hit the grass they ran into a hard-packed high-speed trail that was the closest thing any of them had seen to an enemy interstate highway. It was exactly what they were looking for: an ideal spot to snatch an enemy soldier and call for a quick extraction. Miller signaled the rest of his team to quickly set up an OP back in the trees, while he and Dearing rigged a number of CS grenades with electric detonators out along the trail. Within minutes the six Rangers were out of sight, watching and waiting for someone to come diddy boppin' down the trail.

An hour went by with no sign of the enemy, then the Rangers heard someone singing in Vietnamese. They soon spotted a single NVA soldier dressed in OD fatigues coming down the trail directly at them. He was alone, unarmed, and appeared totally oblivious to the danger that awaited ahead. To make the situation even more inviting, the enemy soldier was carrying a large canvas satchel slung over his shoulder. He was obviously a courier, and an enemy courier meant hard intel—documents, maps, orders, unit identification. It was the perfect snatch situation, and Miller, despite his own nervousness, smiled as he played out the coming snatch over and over in his mind. The Ranger team leader signaled his teammates to put on their gas masks and prepare to make the grab.

Miller blew the CS grenades just as the enemy soldier walked in front of the hidden team. Dearing and Glasser immediately leaped over the cover and landed on the trail, expecting to find a gagging and incapacitated NVA soldier groveling on his knees in the middle of the path. What they encountered was an empty trail, the terrified enemy soldier sprinting back down it the way he'd come as fast as his legs could carry him. Over his shoulder the canvas satchel was flapping in the wind. To make matters even worse, every time the terrified courier stopped choking, he began to scream for help at the top of his lungs.

Realizing they were not going to catch him before he reached North Vietnam, Dearing and Glasser decided to take a few potshots at him in the hope of slowing him down enough to make continued pursuit feasible. The two Rangers opened fire at the rapidly disappearing NVA soldier, and one of them managed to wing him. However, the impact of the bullet only succeeded in making him increase his speed until he disappeared around a bend in the trail.

Miller was royally incensed. Somebody back at Division had given them some bad info. The CS gas had not worked as stated. Instead of immediately immobilizing the NVA soldier, it apparently gave him an adrenaline rush, inspiring him to new heights in long distance sprinting. By now he was traveling across the Ashau Valley heading west at somewhere in the neighborhood of Mach 4, and undoubtedly announcing the team's presence to every NVA within a three day march.

Within seconds the Rangers heard someone yelling to the speeding courier from farther down the trail. Miller knew then that the party was over. He gave the signal to blow the claymores and E&E in the opposite direction. Within a few short minutes the team had put a healthy two hundred meters between themselves and the ambush location. Not wanting to remain on the high-speed any longer than necessary, Miller swung the team into heavy cover off the side of the trail. They were safe for the moment, but the team leader had for the first time realized that the weather was changing—and it was changing for the worse.

Heavy clouds were rapidly rolling in from the west. His mission compromised, Miller radioed for an immediate emergency extraction from the team's alternate insertion LZ. The X-ray (radio relay) team set up on a distant firebase picked up the transmission and radioed the patrol's request to Captain Lannie Cardona, the company CO, back at Camp Eagle. Miller was amazed and outraged when he heard the Ranger company commanding officer call back to the X-ray team and tell them to pass the message that the patrol was to forget the extraction and continue the mission. To make matters even worse, he wanted Miller to "develop the situation." It was not the message the patrol had been waiting to hear. Control of the immediate situation had just passed over to the NVA.

Miller decided that no matter what Captain Cardona wanted, he wasn't "developing" anything. Without a moment's hesitation the six Rangers were busting brush heading for their alternate LZ. But the weather broke even before they could reach the clearing, the worst rainstorm Miller had witnessed in his two and a half tours in Vietnam. The sky grew dark and the rain came down so hard that he didn't know whether to shit or give thanks. The Rangers could not see or hear anything farther away than the ends of their arms, so Miller shouted for them to do the only thing that made sense—crawl into the nearest heavy cover and hide.

They spent a miserable night in a wagon-wheel perimeter hidden in a patch of brush between two high-speed trails. The foul weather soon knocked out their commo and dropped the temperature so far down the scale that they nearly froze to death waiting for morning to arrive. Miller later said they had to go into hypothermia so they could shake hard enough just to get warm.

During the night, between showers, enemy soldiers walked up and down the trails with flashlights looking for the recon team. A couple of the Rangers thought they heard dogs. No one slept a wink.

Finally, during the first hour of daylight, the rain slacked off and the team's commo was restored, albeit weakly. Miller immediately reported what had transpired since his last transmission the night before. Surprisingly, Captain Cardona instructed them to move directly to their extraction point for an emergency pickup.

The Rangers moved out immediately and found boot prints everywhere in the deep mud around their position. However, they didn't see anyone around and they didn't think anyone had yet spotted them, but that was nothing any of the Rangers would put money on.

When the extraction aircraft arrived over the small PZ, Dearing quickly popped a smoke grenade to mark the team's location. Miller saw Staff Sergeant Steve Miners, the Ranger NCO flying bellyman, peering down from the open cabin ready to kick out the ladder. Miller swore softly under his breath. He hated ladder extractions. The rungs were too far apart so it was difficult for a fully laden Ranger to climb the forty to sixty feet to reach the aircraft, and it also kept the team members and the helicopter fully exposed to enemy fire for an extended period of time. But with large numbers of enemy soldiers maneuvering all around the patrol, they were unable to move across country to a safer PZ.

The tall grass and underbrush were whipping around madly in the rotor wash of the Huey as the Rangers began to climb upward to safety. Miller and Dearing remained behind on the ground to stabilize the ladder as their comrades struggled to reach the open bay of the hovering aircraft. Suddenly, Miller heard the sounds of gunfire coming from behind them. Dearing screamed for Miller to start up the ladder, volunteering to anchor it and go up last. There wasn't time to argue the issue so Miller began climbing. Just as he reached the top and was ready to scramble into the cabin, the door gunner signaled for him to get off the ladder. The Ranger team leader couldn't quite understand what the hell the door gunner meant, but he knew that he wasn't about to turn around and climb back down that ladder. Miller reasoned that the door gunner had either just taken a head wound or the man was totally nuts.

Suddenly, the aircraft began to spin, rotating around on its own shaft. The extreme midday heat and the overloading of the helicopter had combined to cause the pilot to lose directional control; in effect, he simply ran out of tail rotor pedal. This caused the Huey to go into such a rapid spin that the end of the ladder with Dearing still hanging on to it was nearly even with the cabin floor of the aircraft.

The Rangers were in big trouble. And as the helicopter spun into the hillside and began rolling down the slope, they also realized that they were about to die.

Unknown to Miller and the rest of the team, Hammond had leaped from the cabin on the uphill side of the aircraft just as it corkscrewed into the ground. The spinning main rotor blade immediately caught him across the top of the head. Glasser and the other two patrol members on board with Hammond had also jumped, but from the opposite side of the aircraft. They had somehow avoided the helicopter as it began to roll over them. Miller, Miners, and the aircraft crew were still inside the helicopter as the Huey continued its sickening roll downhill. Dearing, outside the aircraft on the bottom of the ladder, had been thrown free.

Miller awoke sometime later. His first thought was, I don't hear the helicopter anymore. Then the image of the Huey bouncing and rolling down the hill came rushing back. He stood up slowly, trying to regain his senses. He could tell that he was standing alone on a slope. His rucksack and weapon were gone and he had a sharp, stabbing pain in his hand. He looked down. A jagged piece of metal was sticking through his palm. Miller wondered why it didn't hurt worse than it did, but quickly forgot about pain when he looked up and spotted the wrecked Huey lying on its side uphill from his position.

He started climbing but frequently dropped to his hands and knees. A short distance up the slope he discovered his rucksack and the now useless Starlight scope. But he couldn't find his CAR-15.

Miller climbed a little higher, stopping briefly at a tiny trickle of water running down the hillside to wash the dirt from his face. Just as he started to cup his hands under the flow, he realized that it wasn't water but chopper fuel from the wrecked aircraft.

Miller knew he had to locate the rest of his team. He was certain that Dearing had been crushed when the helicopter crashed to earth, but if he himself had survived the crash, then maybe some of the others had, too.

Just as he reached a level area fifty meters below the wreckage, he spotted Dearing up ahead near the PZ. The two NCOs quickly linked up then turned and headed back to the wreckage. Ten meters away they stumbled across Hammond's body, which was nearly hidden from view in the tall grass. There was little doubt that he was dead. The top of his head had been lopped off by the wildly spinning main rotor blade.

Miller was crushed. One lousy mission and Hammond was gone. He had been too short to go out on a real patrol. But he wouldn't listen and now he was dead. There was nothing Miller could do about it. He knew he should have kept Hammond off the team, but he hadn't, and now the guilt was staring him straight in the face.

While the distraught team leader remained with the dead Ranger's body for a few more moments, Dearing searched the grass around the PZ, hoping to find Hammond's rucksack and weapon. No joy.

Finally, Miller rejoined Dearing, and they climbed higher up the ridge until they reached a small box draw. There they found the slick pilot—an aviation captain—running back and forth stammering incoherently and blaming the Rangers for his wrecked aircraft. When he began shouting orders that didn't make a lot of sense, Miller pulled out his pistol and shoved it into the officer's face. After the captain had gotten a grip on himself, Miller informed him that he was in control on the ground, not the pilot. This seemed to work and the officer began to calm down.

Miller suddenly spotted the peter pilot and the door gunners sitting dazed on the ground outside the wreckage. That they had survived the crash at all seemed a miracle, but it would be a long while before they recovered enough to function again. There was no time to wait. Miller and Dearing crawled into the wreckage and quickly recovered the SOIs, the radios, the M-60s, and several cans of ammo. The NVA would be moving in on the crash site as soon as they got organized, and the Rangers and air crew would have to be in a position to defend themselves if they wanted to survive.

Miller heard something overhead and looked up to see a Cobra gunship diving to make a gun run. With the Rangers and the air crew still scattered around the crash site, he knew they were in imminent danger of being hit by friendly fire.

Miller grabbed one of the salvaged radios and got Captain Cardona on the horn. He told him they needed several Hueys equipped with Maguire rigs. Cardona came back on the push and babbled something about there not being any helicopters in all of I Corps equipped with Maguire rigs. It was going to be a long time before the men on the ground got any help.

Captain Cardona, flying high overhead in the Command & Control helicopter, was having his own problems. When the extraction aircraft had gone down, the officer had flipped out. He grabbed the radio handset and began calling for mede-vacs, gunships, and extraction ships but without any plan of action. The LOH scout pilot, Warrant Officer Roger Barnard of A Troop 2/17th Cav, tried to get the Ranger officer off the net, but the shaken captain absolutely refused. Realizing that they weren't doing the downed air crew and the Ranger patrol any good, Barnard left the scene of the crash and flew across the valley to Fire Support Base Rifle. Slamming the tiny scout helicopter down, the pilot got out and walked around to Cardona's side of the aircraft. He reached in and unbuckled the officer's seat belt, then grabbed him and tossed him out on the ground. An argument ensued with Cardona threatening to court-martial the young warrant officer. In spite of the threats, Barnard got Cardona under control, the two men got back into the aircraft and flew back out to the crash site.

Back at the crash site the survivors suddenly found them-selves alone. The Cobra had to return to Camp Eagle to rearm, and the C&C aircraft had already departed without warning. Things looked desperate on the ground. Miller heard NVA sol-diers moving around above them. He radioed the relay team on

FSB Blaze and told them that if they didn't get some help out to them soon, they were going to be overrun.

While waiting for help, Miller and two of the Rangers went down the slope to recover Hammond's body. By the time they returned to the perimeter, the CO's C&C ship was back over them. Miller radioed Captain Cardona for permission to destroy the wrecked Huey, and was told that the CO wouldn't accept the word of the team leader or the pilot that the aircraft was beyond salvage. He added that he would have to get permission from a general officer to authorize the destruction of the wrecked slick.

Miller could only shake his head at that bit of insanity. Either the Rangers destroyed the ship or the NVA were going to get it.

Finally, a medevac from Eagle Dustoff arrived on the scene and moved in to hover over the tiny perimeter. A hot mike on the medevac ship prevented Miller from talking directly with the medevac pilot, forcing him to relay his transmissions through the relay team on FSB Blaze. Suddenly, Miller saw the aircraft taking hits in its underbelly and notified the pilot that he was taking fire. The aircraft commander radioed back that he was aware of it but he wasn't leaving without picking up the dead Ranger and any other casualties on the team.

They quickly extracted Hammond's body, and the medevac pilot wanted to know if they had any wounded. Miller had already pulled the shrapnel from his hand and slapped a bandage over the jagged wound. He was sorely tempted to go out as a casualty, but the temptation passed as quickly as it came. Instead he radioed a message thanking the pilot and sent him on his way.

An hour and a half later another 2/17th Cav slick arrived at the wreck site with Ranger Sergeant Larry Chambers flying belly-man. The aircraft was equipped with a ladder which failed to reach the ground. Miller instructed the crew from the downed helicopter to climb up on the nose of their aircraft and leap for the end of the ladder. He never believed they would make it, but all four were soon scrambling up the rungs! Unfortunately, each of them ran out of gas long before he reached the deceptive safety of the cabin. Sergeant Chambers was forced to come partway down the ladder to help each man finish his climb and move into the aircraft.

During the entire rescue operation the pilot was boxed in between the slope and the surrounding trees. It took supreme effort on his part to hold the aircraft steady while Chambers struggled to get the air crew aboard. Then four of the Rangers ascended the ladder, leaving only Miller and his radio operator, Spec 4 Marvel McCann, still on the ground. The pilot radioed the Ranger team leader then and told him that he would have to come back for him and his RTO; his aircraft was overloaded, and he was already concerned about reaching the nearest firebase safely.

The Cobra gunship had shown up again during the extraction effort. It made a few gun runs, took some heavy ground-fire, and then flew off to the northwest, followed close behind by Captain Cardona in the C&C ship. Miller never saw either one of them again.

As the sounds of the departing aircraft faded in the distance, Miller and McCann hid themselves as best they could. Between them they had a pistol, an M-79, and somebody's M-16 with which to defend themselves. Each Ranger had a PRC-25 radio.

It had been nearly six hours since the slick had gone down, and Miller could see the usual afternoon thunderstorms moving in out of Laos. The black, rolling clouds were a pilot's nightmare, and Miller knew that the extraction slick would not return in time. He looked at McCann and saw that his RTO also knew the score. The helicopters would not be coming out before dawn, and for the two Rangers this meant a night in the bush alone. Neither man expected to be alive by the next morning.

Suddenly, McCann spotted the tiny dot of a helicopter racing ahead of the onrushing storm front. The Huey reached them while the storm was less than three miles away and closing fast. It was Chambers again, and Miller was never so glad to see anyone in his life. The slick took up a position above the nose of the wrecked aircraft and held its hover as Chambers helped Miller and McCann aboard.

As they were departing the AO, they spotted an F-4 Phantom fast-mover tearing down the valley. He dove in and put a five-hundred-pound iron bomb on the crash site, destroying the Huey in place. Some general somewhere had finally decided to allow the good guys to destroy the wrecked Huey, and the job had been quickly completed with a flourish.

When the aircraft set down at Camp Eagle, Chambers told Miller and McCann that the pilot of the pickup ship had reported what was going down just as the aircraft was lifting them out. Through his nose bubble he'd spotted a large number of NVA swarming all over the slope the two Rangers had just come off. Chambers said that it was almost as if they had been waiting for everyone to leave. Miller wiped his brow and stated that he hoped the fast-mover had gotten them all. It had been too close a call.

9

A Hero's Death

A couple of days later two more L Company long range patrols were inserted not far from where Hammond had been killed. The patrols, one under the command of Sergeant Ray Zoschak and the other led by Sergeant Ron Reynolds, were operating in adjoining recon zones in the foothills along the edge of the valley. The two teams had gone in one behind the other at first light on May 7. They had each located heavily used high-speed trails shortly after moving away from their LZs.

The patrols moved cautiously, even more alert than normal. Prior to the mission, they were briefed to be on the lookout for the remains of a pair of SOG recon teams that had disappeared in the same general area earlier in the year. This, and the fact that Sergeant Kenn Miller's team had gotten itself into a ball-buster not five klicks away two days before and had lost a man killed . . . well, it was enough to shut down anyone's sphincter.

On the second day of the mission Reynolds's team, paralleling a trail, patrolled right into the middle of an abandoned enemy base camp. There were well-camouflaged bunkers and hooches everywhere, but no sign of the camp's occupants.

With their hearts in their throats, Reynolds's team eased into the NVA compound and began checking out the structures. It was obvious that the camp had been occupied by the enemy in the very recent past. The Rangers found NVA uniforms spread over the surrounding bushes, where they had been put out to dry. They were still damp. The embers in the cooking fires were still smoking.

Reynolds immediately realized that he was in a precarious position. The camp was large enough to house a reinforced NVA company, and from what the Rangers could see, there were no vacancies anywhere. Unlike most people who suddenly find themselves in the middle of a large enemy encampment with the distinct likelihood that the enemy could return at any moment, the tall NCO from Texas never panicked. Instead he calmly backed his team up to the edge of the base camp and set them up in a tight defensive perimeter while he radioed news of their discovery to the radio relay team set up on a firebase twelve klicks to their northeast. While Reynolds was waiting for his transmission to be relayed to the Ranger TOC back at Camp Eagle, he thought he heard noises on the other side of the enemy encampment. He was still listening when the message came back from Captain Cardona for him to lay dog until Zoschak's team could get there to reinforce him. When Reynolds came back and asked for an ETA, he was told that the other Ranger patrol was "only" four klicks away and would be there in two to three hours. Reynolds doubted that was likely, however he had little choice but to wait. He was sitting on a major find and couldn't understand why the CO wanted to develop the situation without sending in a line unit to reinforce the team. But he knew that line companies often had a way of stealing all the credit for themselves, and Captain Cardona probably wanted to make sure that he got some of the credit this time. The only problem was that Captain Cardona wasn't sitting out on top of an enemy base camp, as he and his teammates were. If he had been, he might have felt differently about the entire situation.

Early in the afternoon, Reynolds picked up a transmission from Zoschak's team on the radio. Zo reported that they were getting close and said he wanted to make sure that Reynolds's team didn't fire them up when they came in. The two team leaders maintained unbroken commo with each other until the link-up was successfully completed.

After Zoschak saw the size of the base camp and all the fresh enemy sign, he quickly suggested that they move to a more defensible location and call in for a company-size reaction force—no matter what the CO wanted. Reynolds agreed, and the two teams were soon ready to move out of the NVA base camp.

Sergeant Reynolds took point himself and was just starting to lead the combined patrol out of the enemy camp, when an NVA column suddenly appeared at the edge of the jungle on the far side of the encampment. Reynolds saw them at exactly the same moment they spotted him. He had no choice but to open fire on their point element. He hit at least two of them. But the NVA reacted quickly. Within seconds a heavy volume of enemy small-arms fire was chewing up the cover around the Rangers, driving them back into the trees. Reynolds remained behind and continued to put down a heavy volume of suppressive fire, but his one weapon was no match for what was being thrown at him. Hit in the chest by an AK-47 round, the big Ranger team leader was driven backward. Mortally wounded, he stayed on his feet and continued shooting, emptying two more magazines on full automatic at the enemy soldiers before his knees finally buckled and he collapsed to the ground. Spec 4 George Thomas and two other Rangers were also wounded in the exchange of fire. The NVA, believing they'd walked into an ambush, turned and fled back into the jungle.

Soon, a medevac helicopter from Eagle Dustoff, escorted by a pair of Cobras, arrived on station and moved in to hover overhead. The Rangers marked their location with a smoke grenade, and a recovery litter was lowered to the ground. But it was already too late. Sergeant Ron Reynolds had died on the ground. His grieving teammates carried his body over to the steel litter and strapped it in. While the gunships flashed back and forth trying to locate the enemy, the medevac crew chief winched Reynolds's body slowly into the aircraft, followed by the three wounded Rangers. With the dead and wounded on board, the Huey turned and headed back to Graves Registration and 85th Evac.

A short time later Captain Cardona arrived above the team in his C&C aircraft accompanied by a pair of slicks and two more

Cobra gunships. Just before dark the remaining eight Rangers were extracted from the enemy base camp and returned to Camp Eagle. An hour later an air strike dealt with the NVA stronghold.

Sergeant Ron Reynolds had been a very popular team leader in the company. He had transferred into the unit from the Division Pathfinder detachment nearly a year before, when L Company was still F Company, 58th Infantry (LRP). He had extended his tour for six months to get an early out. He spent his extension leave at home with his parents and sisters, but something didn't seem right, either to him or his family. When he climbed aboard the commercial flight to return to Vietnam for his final six months in-country, his mother reported that Ron never turned back around to wave when he reached the top of the loading platform, as he always had before. She knew then that something was seriously wrong. The posthumous Silver Star was a poor substitute for her only son.

The NVA had killed three L Company Rangers in two short weeks.

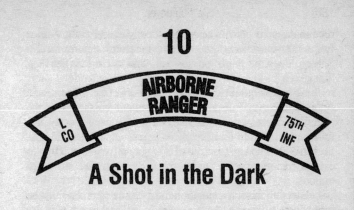

10

A Shot in the Dark

Leadership is a critical factor in any military operation. It is often the difference between success and failure. When a strong leader falls in battle, the outcome of that battle rises or falls in direct proportion to how quickly and how well a junior leader stands in to fill the command void.

In the heat of battle, an infantry company that loses its commander hopefully sees a junior officer or a seasoned NCO step forward to take over the reins of command within minutes. If this does not occur, pandemonium—followed by defeat—is typically the outcome. But a six-man reconnaissance patrol in the same situation has only seconds to replace a fallen team leader and continue the fight. The paucity of time requires an instantaneous response from the next individual in the chain of command. It is an ability not taught in service academies, officer candidate schools, or NCO courses; it is not acquired through command experience; and it is certainly not genetically or chemically engineered. The ability to move forward without breaking stride and take command of a leaderless recon team fighting for its life derives from the very nature of the command—the team.

The recon team is usually a highly trained group of volunteers brought together to accomplish specific types of missions. The key phrase here is "highly trained." Long range reconnaissance patrols operating deep behind enemy lines frequently find themselves face-to-face with enemy forces. Seldom does the patrol possess an edge in battle other than that given by the element of surprise—a tremendous short term asset that quickly, however, loses its effectiveness.

In nearly every instance of inadvertent contact with the enemy, the small reconnaissance patrol finds itself grossly outnumbered, far from reinforcement or rescue, and deep in hostile territory. The key to survival is to stay alive long enough to escape, be reinforced, or be rescued. There are no other options.

Leadership in such a situation must be strong and it must be immediate. When it ceases to function, either through casualty or command breakdown, the speed at which this role is assumed by someone else determines the ability of the team to survive. That is why reconnaissance teams drilled continually, each man training at various positions on the patrol. Immediate action drills, patrol movement drills, artillery support drills, close air support drills, escape and evasion drills, were all designed to eliminate surprise in the field. Running the drills from different positions on the team not only instilled self-confidence among the members of the team, but also established the individual's ability and the self-assurance that was necessary to take command in a crisis situation.

Not surprisingly, the history of the Lurp/Rangers of the 101st Airborne Division in Vietnam has numerous examples of patrols losing team leaders in the midst of heavy contact, only to be saved when another team member stepped forward to take command. This is the story of just one of those patrols.

Ranger Team 1-3, led by Sergeant William Travis Marcy, received a warning order on May 19, 1969. Marcy, the son of a U.S. Navy admiral, was ordered to insert his team at first light the following morning on a prominent terrain feature just south of Fire Support Base Rakkassan. The rugged mountains in the area overlooked the rolling piedmont to the east and the Song Bo Valley to the south. The 6th and 7th NVA regiments were reportedly based somewhere back in the mountains west of the team's AO, and elements of both units were suspected of occupying positions along the rim of mountains overlooking Camp

Evans and LZ Sally, at which they frequently launched rocket and sapper attacks and engaged in running food supplies up the Song Bo to their camps.

Marcy's mission was to spend five days monitoring a four-grid-square AO along the rocket belt to determine if the enemy was using the area, and if so, to discover what they were doing there. It was a typical long range recon mission, and Marcy's team was good. His ATL, Spec 4 Frank Anderson, had just returned from MACV Recondo School at Nha Trang and had six months of patrolling to his credit. Anderson was also tapped for the role of senior RTO—a position at which he was exceptionally adept.

The team's point was shared by Spec 4 Bill McCabe, a full-blooded Navajo who hadn't forgotten the ways of his ancestors, and Spec 4 John "Sonny" Sontag, a recent transfer to the Rangers who liked to carry an M-60 on recon patrols. McCabe was excellent in the field, and like Anderson, had six months of patrolling under his belt. Sonny Sontag had just come to the Rangers, but he had seven months combat time down in III Corps with Echo Company 3/506th—the 101st Airborne Division's "bastard" battalion. Echo Company, originally a recon unit, had become a full-fledged long range patrol company, so the transfer to the Division Ranger company was little more than a change in scenery for Sontag.

Spec 4 Dan Croker, a blond, baby-faced California surfer type, walked the tailgunner slot. He, too, had joined the Rangers six months earlier, coming into the unit along with Anderson and McCabe when it was still F Company, 58th Infantry (LRP).

The final member of the patrol was a newly arrived PFC by the name of Ernest Brown. "Brown Dog," a well-built black paratrooper from southern Georgia, was an outstanding amateur pugilist who always enjoyed "going a few rounds" with the other accomplished boxers in the Ranger company.

The team inserted at first light on May 20, going into a small clearing on a high knob surrounded by single canopy vegetation. The team immediately moved off the LZ and lay dog for fifteen minutes in the heavy brush surrounding the clearing, watching and listening. Satisfied that they were alone and undetected, Marcy brought the team up a slight rise to a nearby mountaintop. They immediately discovered a minor high-speed trail running into the triple canopy jungle that covered the ridgeline sloping down from the opposite side of the mountain.

Marcy moved the team into the heavy undergrowth twenty meters back from the trail. He ordered McCabe to take point and to parallel the trail, staying ten to twenty meters back in the triple canopy.

The team moved slowly, covering only a couple of klicks by late evening. Just before dark McCabe began complaining of nausea and chills. Marcy felt his head. His point man was burning up with fever. The team leader suspected it to be a bout of malaria, and knew that McCabe would not be able to go on. Marcy decided that under the circumstances he would have to abort the mission. But first, in order to medevac the stricken Ranger, the team would have to get out from under the unbroken triple canopy jungle they were in. Marcy's intentions were to return to Camp Eagle, pick up a replacement for McCabe, then reinsert the patrol into another part of the AO the following morning.

The team's secondary LZ was nearly three klicks ahead, down in the valley of the Song Bo. It was nearly dark, and Marcy didn't want to attempt moving three thousand meters under triple canopy at night. So, against his own better judgement and Ranger SOP of "never going back the same way you came in," Marcy decided to return to the original insertion LZ just over the crest of the mountain to their rear. The distance was definitely shorter, they were already familiar with the terrain, and they hadn't seen any fresh sign of enemy activity on the way down from the LZ, so Marcy figured there was slim chance that they would encounter them now. The Ranger patrol leader then instructed his teammates to return to their original LZ by the quickest means possible—over the enemy high-speed trail that ran down the crest of the ridge.

It was fully dark when the patrol finally reached the edge of the LZ. Marcy sent Sontag on a point reconnaissance to check out the area for any signs of the enemy, and also to locate and secure a hiding place for the team. The Ranger point man circled the clearing, found no indication the NVA had been there since the team's insertion, and discovered a cluster of large boulders choked with single canopy vegetation twenty meters back from the LZ that would provide a good spot to lay up until the extraction aircraft arrived. There was plenty of cover and concealment, and it was close enough to the LZ that the Rangers could keep an eye on it.

When Anderson attempted to call in a sit rep to the Ranger TOC back at Camp Eagle, to notify his commander that the team had arrived at the LZ and was requesting a medevac and an extraction, the primary radio that had worked well during the day now no longer worked at all.

Right after the team had set up security in the rocks, Sontag whispered that he thought he heard something on the other side of the LZ. The patrol froze in place and listened breathlessly for perhaps thirty full minutes, but heard nothing out of the ordinary. Marcy finally decided that the new man had been imagining things.

Anderson was still unable to get his primary radio working, so Marcy took the secondary radio from Brown and turned the frequency to the primary setting. For some reason, he was still unable to establish radio communication with Camp Eagle.

In a whisper, Marcy ordered the team to stay where they were. He was going to try to transmit from outside their perimeter because he believed the trees and boulders might be blocking the radio transmissions.

Marcy took Sontag with him as security and moved twenty meters into the middle of the LZ, hoping to get better reception for the radio antenna. Sontag had traded his M-60 for McCabe's lighter M-16. The two Rangers had just gotten set up in the center of the clearing and were preparing to call for extraction when they detected movement behind them, directly downhill from their position and along their original line of march. Seconds later they heard muffled voices back in the brush. They realized immediately that the enemy had followed their patrol back to the LZ.

Marcy and Sontag remained frozen out in the open, afraid to move a muscle. But within seconds the sounds of enemy soldiers chattering and moving around in the brush on the edge of the clearing got too close for comfort. Marcy decided the only thing they could do was leave their radio behind and try to make it back to the rest of the team still hidden among the rocks on the far side of the LZ.

On Marcy's silent signal, the two Rangers leaped to their feet and sprinted across the clearing. Just as they reached the rocks and began to dive headlong into the protection they offered, shots rang out from across the clearing. It sounded as if two or three of the enemy soldiers had opened up on full automatic while a couple of others were firing single, spaced shots. Sontag landed and rolled between two boulders, safe from the enemy fire. But Anderson heard Marcy cry out and saw him roll over on his back. When he reached the team leader's side, the Ranger was gritting his teeth and moaning in pain. He arched his back once, rolled his eyes back in his head, and then died. It was that quick. There was nothing Anderson could do. Marcy had taken a single enemy round in the lower right quadrant of his back, probably hitting a kidney.

Immediately, Anderson realized that he was now in charge of the patrol. Unsure of the size of the enemy forces facing them, he knew that if the Rangers fired their weapons, it would only give away their position. He ordered the rest of the team to avoid using their personal weapons unless absolutely necessary. Instead, he instructed them to pitch grenades into the trees on the opposite side of the clearing. The five Rangers then engaged the enemy soldiers with frags, driving them back away from the LZ.

Suddenly, the Ranger ATL realized that Marcy had left their only working radio out in the center of the LZ. Grabbing his weapon, Anderson darted out to the middle of the clearing, snatched up the radio and sprinted for the safety of the rocks. Miraculously, the enemy soldiers held their fire.

Back in the perimeter, Anderson took the radio handset and began trying to make contact with their TOC. Finally, he got a weak response from the NCO on radio watch in the Ranger rear. Anderson immediately gave the team's coordinates, reported they were in contact and that their "Six" was KIA. He called for an emergency extraction.

Thirty minutes later Cobra gunships arrived overhead. Coming up on the command net, the lead aircraft identified himself as "Condor 1-2" and requested that the team mark its position. Anderson quickly tied a strobe light to the whip antenna on the primary radio and turned it on. The lead ship from the 2/17th Cav came in close and began working over the opposite side of the LZ with accurate minigun fire. As the two Cobras worked away from the Ranger team's perimeter, they switched their suppressive fire from minigun to 40mm cannon, tearing into the jungle on the far side of the clearing.

Two hours later the distant sounds of Huey slicks announced the arrival of the 2/17th Cav's reaction force. It was nearly 2100 hours when the platoon of "Blues" landed on the clearing and linked up with the team. Their orders were to secure the LZ and hold it until dawn. The aero-rifle troopers quickly expanded the Rangers' tiny perimeter, setting up security positions all around the clearing.

Anderson didn't want to see Marcy's body lying uncovered and unattended out in the open, so he asked the Blues' commander if any of his soldiers had a poncho. The lieutenant checked with his men but came up empty-handed. Undaunted, Anderson dug into his rucksack, retrieving his own poncho liner and an extra spool of claymore wire he always carried with him. He then went over to where Marcy's body lay amid the boulders. Checking the fallen Ranger's pockets, Anderson retrieved his map, SOI code book, and a number of other personal items, then secured them along with his weapon, rucksack, and web gear. Then the Ranger assistant team leader gently rolled Marcy's body in the poncho and wrapped it securely with the claymore wire. With Sergeant Bill Marcy's body thus cared for, Spec 4 Anderson and the infantry platoon leader spent the remainder of the night in the center of the clearing directing artillery fire from LZ Sally and Camp Evans onto suspected enemy positions outside their perimeter.

At first light the next morning, the Blues' commander sent out a ten-man security patrol to sweep the immediate area around the LZ. Returning a short time later, they reported finding plenty of fresh sign on the trail at the edge of the jungle but no indication that the NVA were still in the area.

At 0700 hours a single Cav slick arrived at the LZ and picked up the entire Ranger patrol and the body of the slain team leader. The short trip back to Camp Eagle was a somber one. The aircraft detoured briefly to land at Phu Bai to drop off Bill Marcy's body at Graves Registration. Lima Company had lost a popular and outstanding team leader, and the Rangers had lost a comrade and a good friend. In a three-week period the unit had lost four Rangers—three of them team leaders.

For his courage under fire, Bill Marcy, the admiral's son, would receive the Silver Star medal posthumously. Spec 4 Frank Anderson's quick assumption of leadership in a combat situation had resulted in the patrol's survival and its success in dealing with an enemy element of unknown size. Anderson's conduct after Marcy's death earned him the gratitude of his teammates and an Army Commendation medal with V device. It wasn't enough for what he'd accomplished.

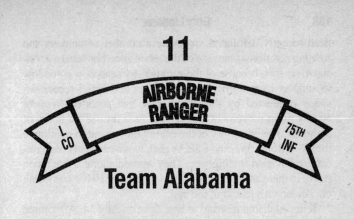

11

Team Alabama

Perhaps one of the most intimidating weapons in the enemy's arsenal during the Vietnam War was the 122mm rocket. Indiscriminate in its target selection, the "flying stovepipe" was employed by the VC and NVA more as a terror weapon than a tactical one. Often launched against U.S. forces basking in the relative safety of battalion-, brigade-, and division-size base camps, it was not an easy weapon to defend against.

Although the weapon's actual toll in lives and property damage was minimal, the ability of the enemy to launch remote strikes of such a potentially devastating nature was a constant source of fear and apprehension for every U.S. soldier not out in the field. When the enemy's rockets were discovered prior to their deployment, it was always a source of joy and satisfaction for those who would likely fall under their "rain" of terror. In the hot summer of 1969, a Lima Company long range patrol discovered a sizable cache, thirty-two deadly 122mm rockets on the edge of the rocket belt that lay to the west of the Hue/Phu Bai/Camp Eagle military complex in central I Corps. This is how it happened.

On July 13, 1969, Ranger team leader and newly promoted Sergeant Frank Anderson received a warning order for a five-day reconnaissance mission in the area of Fire Support Base Veghel northeast of Route 547. Much of the team's AO had been recently defoliated, exposing a number of bunkers and fighting positions. One side of the recon zone bordered a good-size river that, because of the summer dry season, was too low to support river traffic. Sniffer reports and aerial reconnaissance conducted by the 2/17th Cav had reported frequent enemy troop movement through the area during the hours of darkness. The proximity of the enemy movement in relation to the river, Route 547, and FSB Veghel, was a cause of great concern to Division Intelligence. They wanted a long range recon patrol in there as quickly as possible to find out what was going on. Anderson's team got the nod.

Team Alabama inserted at first light on July 14. After three days of intense patrolling they had discovered a number of fighting positions and several trails—but all the enemy signs were several months old. They spent three long nights monitoring different trail intersections, but there was no indication that the enemy was using any of them or that the NVA were even in the area.

The Rangers had gone out on the patrol carrying nearly three gallons of water each. Anderson had overloaded himself with thirteen quarts of water, but by first light on the morning of the fourth day of the patrol nearly everyone was on his last canteen. The dry heat and lack of rainfall had turned the jungle into a sauna, forcing the patrol to consume a large quantity of salt tablets and drink water at an alarming rate. With two more days of intense patrolling yet ahead of them, Anderson decided to move down out of the hills to the river valley on the west side of their recon zone.

Knowing that any enemy soldiers in the area would be close to water, Anderson led the team in a wide circling movement, approaching the river through an area of dense, heavy undergrowth. Although the river was normally wide and deep, the summer dry season had reduced it to a series of deeper pools connected by a shallow, slow-moving trickle of water. The team had moved out at 0700 and by mid-morning had reached the river. Locating a spot where the cover ran all the way to the bank, Anderson sent two men down to the water to fill their canteens. He spread out the remainder of the team in the thick brush ten meters back, but where they could still watch up and down the river and observe both shores at the same time.

After the two Rangers had returned with the full canteens, Anderson decided to spend the next few hours monitoring the river. An old trail ran along the water, and even though it didn't appear to have been used recently, its proximity to the river made it the most likely place the Rangers had yet found to locate the enemy.

Anderson pulled back away from the river and moved his team fifteen meters upstream. Just ahead of them and a little higher up the bank, they spotted a cave entrance in the limestone bluff. Closer inspection showed the cave to be little more than a shallow grotto worn in the cliff face by countless years of heavy currents washing against the bank during the rainy seasons. But something told Anderson to check it out anyway. Setting up security around the mouth of the grotto, Anderson and his RTO entered the shallow cave and soon discovered that they had not been the first humans inside. In the back of the grotto, sitting on a sheet of canvas, were a number of dismantled 122mm rockets. In the shadows at the rear of the cave, Anderson counted thirty-two rockets, propellants in one pile, warheads in another, and fuses in a third. By their condition, the rockets had been in the cave at least two to three months, probably brought in by sampan sometime during the end of the rainy season.

Anderson and his teammates were excited. This was an accomplishment few long range recon patrols could claim. Thirty-two 122mm rockets could do a lot of damage to a forward combat base like Camp Eagle.

When Anderson radioed in their discovery, they were told to recover four complete rockets and prepare the rest for destruction. The four would be neutered then placed on display at Division Headquarters. Division would send in a full infantry company in the morning with an attached engineer team to blow the cache. The Rangers were ordered to secure the area and remain overnight.

Anderson had a difficult time accepting this final instruction from Division HQ. He understood their delight in the Rangers' discovery, but he had a real problem with securing a valuable enemy weapons cache with a lightly armed six-man long range patrol. The local NVA commander was surely aware of the cache, and although it had been untouched for a period of time, one never knew for certain just how often an NVA patrol dropped by just to check things out. Anderson didn't want to be setting up housekeeping in someone else's house on the night they returned home. It was not the militarily correct thing to do.

As the commander on the ground, Anderson decided to do the militarily expedient thing—leave the cache alone overnight while he pulled back a few meters into the thickest cover he could find. The Rangers would be able to keep their collective eye on the site without all the nasty possibilities of being caught sleeping in Papa Bear's bed.

The patrol found an incredibly tight thicket twenty meters upstream from the cave, crawled into it, and set up in a wagon-wheel perimeter with their feet touching in the center. During the night Anderson called in frequent H&I fire all around the patrol's position. If Mr. Charles had picked this particular night to run his trap line, he would have to do it with extreme caution.

At first light the next morning, true to its word, Division HQ combat-assaulted an entire infantry company onto a sandbar two hundred meters downstream from the cave. With them were two engineers from the 326th Engineer Battalion. The two EOD (explosive ordnance disposal) soldiers had brought enough C-4 explosives, blasting caps, and det cord to relocate Fire Support Base Veghel a full klick to the east. With enough air cover to establish air superiority over Hanoi, the grunts moved upstream and linked up with Anderson's patrol. Then the combined elements moved in to secure the area around the cache.

In short order one full platoon of grunts removed four of the 122s to the sandbar for evacuation. The remainder of the rockets were piled in a clearing not far from the cave. After the engineers did their thing setting multiple charges over, under, and around the huge stack of enemy rockets, everyone *di di*'d (ran) 150 meters and took shelter.

The blast was quite magnificent; the engineers had placed

the charges in such a way that the rockets' propellants and warheads would consume themselves completely in the explosion.

After the smoke cleared and the debris had settled, an infantry squad returned to the crater to make certain there were no usable parts left behind for the enemy. Satisfied that the engineers knew their stuff, the grunts returned to the sandbar and reported the mission completed.

Anderson's team was extracted shortly afterward and returned to Camp Eagle to receive the thanks and congratulations of a grateful division staff—which now had four "safe" 122mm ChiCom rockets sitting outside Division Headquarters.

12

AIRBORNE RANGER

L CO

75TH INF

Team Norway

At 1000 hours on the morning of October 19, 1969, Recon Team 2-4, the Bushwackers (call sign "Norway"), inserted into the Tennessee Valley northwest of Camp Eagle. Ably led by team leader Sergeant Dennis Karalow, their mission was to determine if there were NVA units using the valley as a staging area for attacks on Camp Evans and LZ Sally.

The team's point man, Sergeant Andy Ransom, soon discovered a well-used, high-speed trail just off the LZ. Leading the patrol away from its initial insertion point, Ransom followed the trail uphill for two to three hundred meters, moving cautiously and stopping frequently to listen for sounds that would indicate the presence of the enemy.

The patrol was being extra cautious on this mission, and not just because of the "bad" area they were reconning. Their Senior RTO, Corporal Frank Johnson, while taking in an open air movie at the 2/17th Cav compound, had lost a lucky gold cross and felt that was an omen of evil things to come. Everyone on the team was aware of this recent catastrophe, and though most of them were not the least bit superstitious, they were taking no unnecessary risks.

At noon the patrol halted, moving off the trail five to six meters and setting up security in the center of some very thick cover. Karalow gave the word to chow down in shifts of two, and whispered for his assistant team leader, Sergeant Ed Drozd, to take take up a security position behind a large tree out near the trail.

Twenty minutes later the entire team froze in place when they heard Vietnamese voices laughing and talking above them, just off the trail. Sergeant Karalow and Corporal Johnson slowly rose from their positions in the brush to scan the area where the voices appeared to be coming from. They immediately spotted three NVA soldiers, sitting off to the side of the trail just above the spot where the Rangers lay hidden in the thick underbrush. The NVA appeared to be eating a meal and seemed unaware of the American patrol hiding nearby. The Ranger recon team had managed to patrol within twenty meters of the resting NVA without realizing they were there. Fortunately for the Rangers, the three enemy soldiers were too busy satisfying their hunger to pay attention to anyone else on the trail.

Sergeant Karalow eased slowly back into the cover, where he conferred briefly with Johnson about the team's options. Johnson, always a little more gung ho than most, suggested that they go for a prisoner. Karalow quickly agreed and ordered his RTO to get on the radio to alert the TOC that they were about to attempt a prisoner snatch and to request immediate backup. Due to the close proximity of the enemy soldiers, Johnson was forced to whisper the message and had a difficult time getting his transmission through. Finally, with the help of another recon team that relayed the transmission, he was able to get his message across to the Rangers manning the TOC back at Camp Eagle.

Suddenly, the three NVA stood up and began moving in the team's direction. Karalow and Johnson, both down on their knees in the brush planning the snatch, were unaware that the NVA were now on the move. The lead enemy soldier was nearly five meters out in front of his companions when Sergeant Drozd, still kneeling behind the tree next to the trail, opened fire on him. The rest of the Ranger team were unable to see the assistant team leader or the NVA through the dense underbrush. Not sure of what had just happened out on the trail, Johnson and Karalow leaped to their feet to move to

Drozd's support, while Sergeant Andy Ransom, PFC Mike Lytle, and Spec. John Stope remained behind to cover their own areas of responsibility.

At the same time, the remaining two North Vietnamese Army soldiers, now fully aware of the Americans' location, opened fire from farther up the trail, narrowly missing Johnson. The brief but heavy volume of enemy fire forced Johnson and Karalow to the ground. But seconds later both Rangers were back up on their knees pitching fragmentation grenades at the enemy, wounding both NVA.

While the RTO called in the contact, Sergeant Karalow leaped to his feet and began firing his CAR-15 on full auto, spraying the area where the enemy soldiers had disappeared. As Karalow stopped to change magazines, the wounded NVA soldiers broke contact and retreated up the trail, disappearing quickly into the jungle.

With the firefight apparently over, Karalow and Johnson moved up to Drozd's location. He was still kneeling behind the tree at the edge of the trail, keeping a watchful eye on a dead NVA soldier. Without taking his gaze from the body, Drozd reported to his team leader that he'd heard the enemy soldiers talking somewhere up above them. Uncertain as to what they were doing, Drozd had continued to monitor the trail, paying particular attention to the direction the voices were coming from. Suddenly, the enemy point man appeared on the trail and walked right up to him. Drozd had no choice but to open fire, putting three rounds through the NVA soldier's head. No one else on the patrol had witnessed the developing situation because of the heavy underbrush.

Checking the body and the area from where the remaining two NVA had opened fire, the Rangers recovered an AK-47 assault rifle, along with two fifty-pound bags of rice, one of which also contained a substantial amount of Vietnamese piasters and a number of military documents. Evidently, the three enemy soldiers were on their way to a nearby unit with supplies and payroll when their journey was cut short.

After sweeping the area, the team pulled back and called in an air strike on the hilltop, just in case there happened to be more NVA behind the three that had walked up on the Rangers.

Soon a flight of F-4 Phantoms arrived overhead, dropping napalm canisters on the high ground above the team, turning the crest of the hill into a raging inferno.

As the jellied gas burned itself out, a ready reaction force from the Blues of the 2/17th Cavalry arrived along with a canine tracker team. The Blues went on line and swept the scene of the firefight, then moved up to the top of the hill to the area burned by the napalm. With the help of the dog, they located two blood trails, but were unable to find the bodies.

Back at the LZ, one of the Blues saw blood running down Johnson's arm and pointed it out to him. Johnson, dropping his ruck and web gear, removed his shirt to discover that he had a small piece of shrapnel embedded in his shoulder. Carefully, he removed the metal sliver, grinned, and announced that it was nothing. Team 2-4 and the Blues were extracted thirty minutes later without incident.

The next day Team 2-4 and the Blues went back into the same AO. Sergeant Ransom was to depart later that day to attend MACV Recondo School at Nha Trang, and he was replaced by Staff Sergeant James Salter.

After running a short combat patrol back up to the site of the previous day's battle, the Blues returned once again to the LZ and were lifted out by helicopter. However, the six-man Ranger patrol remained behind, waiting in ambush along the trail. They would be ready in case the NVA sent scouts down to the LZ to check out the recent activity. After an uneventful night in the bush waiting for the enemy to show up, the ambush team was extracted early the next morning.

The "stay behind" ambush was a tactic used more frequently by the Rangers in the coming months. Sometimes very effective, its increased use would soon alert the observant NVA to expect such tactics. That would result in a large number of Ranger casualties later in the war.

13

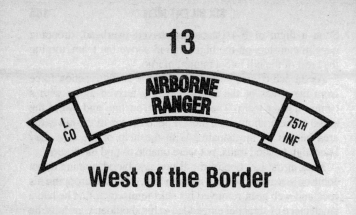

AIRBORNE
RANGER

L
CO

75TH
INF

West of the Border

There are a lot of stories of U.S. long range recon patrols, in addition to those from SOG, operating in Laos and Cambodia. Most of them are just that—stories. But some of them have been substantiated, and others, though officially unproven, have enough eyewitness testimony to confirm that at least the participants believed they were someplace they didn't belong—and really didn't want to be.

On October 20, 1969, Sergeant Frank Anderson's team got a warning order for a mission far out in the western expanses of the 101st Airborne Division's Area of Operations. Their mission was to locate the route of march of enemy replacements being fed into South Vietnam to rebuild the 5th NVA Regiment, which was operating somewhere in the southwestern Ashau Valley. Led by the notorious Colonel Mot, the 5th NVA Regiment had been a poison thorn in the side of the 101st Airborne Division for nearly two years. Repeatedly bloodied by elements of the division, remnants of the 5th always managed to regroup under Mot's able leadership and quickly reappear to strike again.

The most disturbing thing about this particular mission was that the border indexes on the AO map didn't match any maps the Rangers had ever used before. As a matter of fact, the map of the team's RZ didn't have any names or terrain feature that rang anyone's chimes.

Nothing unusual happened at the briefing except that the operations officer who conducted it told the Rangers that they would be carrying a newly developed AM radio and a single PRC-25, instead of the usual two PRC-25s. In addition, the patrol leader would be issued a URC-10 emergency survival radio, which was good only for transmitting to aircraft passing overhead. Finally, the team's normal SOP for sit reps had been slightly modified. Normally, a long range reconnaissance patrol was to transmit a minimum of four to six scheduled sit reps per day, more if the area or the situation merited it. But on this patrol the team had been assigned only two daily sit reps—one at first light and one at last light. These patrol requirements were very unusual.

The first-light insertion on October 22 went in without an overflight. This bothered Sergeant Anderson almost as much as the one-hour chopper flight to the team's AO. To make matters even worse, none of the Rangers failed to notice that their insertion aircraft had continued flying west on a 270-degree azimuth even after they passed over the Ashau Valley. It didn't take a master's degree in geography with a minor in cartography to tell Anderson and his teammates that they had probably brought along the wrong passports.

The five-man team went in on a tiny clearing on the tip of a finger ridge nestled amid towering mountains. It was rugged country and practically devoid of the normal bomb and artillery craters so plentiful in the Ashau. Anderson's patrol got off the LZ as quickly as it could and immediately found itself in triple canopy jungle with multiple layers of lush ground cover.

The patrol spent the first two days of the four-day mission slipping around the mountains looking for traces of the NVA replacements. But there was no indication that anything other than a few wild animals had ever set foot in the AO.

The team experienced commo problems from the very onset of the mission. The PRC-25 was only capable of intrapatrol commo, and the new AM radio, which operated on two batteries instead of one and was heavier than the PRC-25, was also having a difficult time reaching the radio relay team—wherever it was.

On the third day, Murphy's Law took effect to relieve the boredom. In the midst of the monsoon season, the weather changed for the worse. Thick, dark clouds rolled in from the west, and the patrol was soon immersed in a driving downpour.

The Rangers had moved into an area of double canopy jungle the evening before and set up an NDP on the crest of a wooded knoll. Except for a large number of fallen trees, there was little to no ground cover under the forest. With a swing set or two, a drinking fountain, and some horseshoe pits, the area would have made a great city park.

In the middle of the storm, Anderson ordered his Senior RTO to set up the field-expedient wire antenna for the AM radio so the patrol could make its scheduled first-light sit rep. They completed transmitting and were busy putting away the antenna wire when a column of NVA soldiers suddenly materialized out of the driving rain no more than ten meters from the nearest Ranger.

The enemy platoon had been climbing up the steep side of the knoll, moving in a wedge-shaped formation with a point element out front and flankers to the sides. They were moving fast in the heavy rain, almost as if they were trying to reach shelter somewhere nearby. The NVA were wearing pith helmets, khaki uniforms, and rucksacks, and were carrying their weapons at port arms. However, their initial shock at seeing a five-man Ranger team strewn across their path didn't keep them from responding. The NVA point man opened up immediately, hitting Anderson and another Ranger in the back and wounding a third in the lower leg.

The Rangers responded a split second later, dropping five or six NVA in the front of the column before they could react or retreat. Anderson himself put at least three of them down with a long eighteen-round burst. The remainder of the NVA recoiled and fell back beyond the military crest of the knoll to regroup. They had been just as surprised as the Rangers and needed time to lick their wounds, assess the situation, and react properly.

Up on the knoll the Rangers were doing exactly the same.

High on the back near his shoulder, Anderson's wound was painful, but fortunately, a grazing wound. It would not keep him from performing his duties. The patrol's rear security man, PFC Whitledge, had not been so lucky. Leaning against a fallen log directly in the path of the NVA patrol, he'd been the first Ranger to get hit. A single round had blown out a large piece of his left calf, breaking both bones on the way through. The wound was serious, but the tough young Ranger kept his cool and returned fire immediately, nailing the NVA who had shot him, then dropping the soldier directly behind him.

The third Ranger hit was the RTO. Like Anderson, he'd taken a round in the back. Unlike Anderson, his round had gone in just above the right kidney and exited through the Ranger's shoulder joint, puncturing a lung on the way out. With sixty percent of the recon patrol wounded in the opening seconds of the battle, the odds for their survival seemed lower than a private's base pay.

Anderson knew that if the enemy was at all savvy, they were preparing to fire and maneuver against the team. He ordered those Rangers who could to toss frags over the edge of the knoll. The grenades detonated among the NVA just as they were beginning to move back up to the military crest of the knoll, once again breaking up their plans. This gave the Rangers time to act.

With the RTO out of action and the team's next scheduled sit rep twelve hours away, Anderson suddenly remembered the URC-10 in the cargo pocket of his pants. He reached down with his good arm and extracted the small rectangular survival radio, praying that the unfamiliar radio still worked. He quickly transmitted a message identifying the sender as Ranger Team 1-3, stating that he had casualties. He gave the team's six-digit coordinates, the frequency for the Ranger TOC, and asked the receiver to alert that station. He repeated the message four more times, then set the beeper device on the transmitter.

Two hours later a single C-130 flew over the patrol's location and picked up their emergency transmission. The pilot quickly put out a call for help, and alerted the Ranger TOC that it had a patrol in trouble.

Two more hours passed before the Ranger patrol heard the

distinctive sounds of Huey helicopters heading their way. The NVA had been quiet for the past four hours, but Anderson knew they were still out there. He suspected they were waiting for reinforcements and the coming of darkness before moving against the team. Their first effort had already proven too costly.

A pair of slicks from A Company, 158th Aviation Battalion, "The Phoenix," had arrived from Camp Evans. The lead ship was flown by the battalion commander, a lieutenant colonel, and was equipped with three Maguire rigs. Unfortunately, the two slicks were a long way from home and without gunship support. Anderson realized that they were probably flying into a trap, and not knowing their frequencies, had no way to warn them to abort. Suddenly, the aircraft commander of the lead ship came in over the team's PRC-25. He told Anderson to pop a smoke grenade. The Ranger team leader complied, and soon the slick pilot had the team's position pinpointed in the double canopy.

When the lead aircraft moved in to hover directly over the team, the enemy hiding back beyond the military crest of the knoll opened fire. Immediately the second Huey moved in and took up position to one side of the rescue ship and began suppressing the enemy small-arms fire with its two M-60s. While the slick-turned-gunship held the NVA at bay, the crew chief on the lead aircraft kicked out the Maguire rigs directly over Anderson's patrol.

Down on the ground, Anderson helped Whitledge and his nearly unconscious RTO into two of the rigs. He then decided that one of the two Rangers who had not been hit would have to go out with the two wounded men to stabilize them in their rigs. Anderson and the remaining Ranger would stay behind and wait for the second lift. He knew it would be almost completely dark before the slicks returned and doubted that either one of them would still be alive by then.

The lead aircraft took several hits while lifting out with the first three Rangers. The courageous pilot knew that the two men left behind would never survive until he could drop off his load at Evans, refuel, and get back out to the AO, so he did the only thing he could think of. He flew approximately five klicks to the east, where he found an abandoned crop field and lowered the three Rangers to the ground. He set down beside them and, as his door gunner and crew chief recoiled the Maguire rigs, he yelled for the three Rangers to find a place to hide until he returned.

Anderson was surprised when two more Hueys arrived overhead so soon. He watched as two Maguire rigs dropped through the trees and landed inside their tiny perimeter. His companion helped him into the loop at the bottom of one of the ropes, then turned and climbed into the remaining rig.

Anderson signaled that they were ready to go. He dreaded leaving the team's equipment and radios behind, but there had been no opportunity to destroy it and there was nothing he could do about it at the moment. Right then, their lives seemed more important than a bunch of easily replaceable gear.

The aircraft commander of the lead Huey began to slowly lift his ship straight up and out of the LZ. Immediately, the aircraft took hits from enemy small arms fired from the surrounding jungle. Once again the second Huey maneuvered alongside and began laying down a heavy suppressive fire with its two M-60s.

At the ends of the ropes the two Rangers were expecting at any moment to be shot off the Maguire rigs. Miraculously, the enemy soldiers hidden in the trees below seemed to be concentrating their fire on the helicopters, totally ignoring the two Rangers dangling helplessly beneath.

Suddenly, Anderson found himself hung up on a large limb. With his injured shoulder, he was unable to push himself away from the tree and was in immediate danger of being stripped out of his seat by the strain of the aircraft attempting to drag the rigs through the trees. Just in time the pilot realized what was happening below him and lowered the aircraft just enough for Anderson to free himself. When the Ranger team leader was once again out in the open, he signaled the pilot to continue the lift, but he lost his balance and nearly fell out of the rig when the aircraft commander brought the Huey straight up in a rapid, nearly vertical climb. Then they were above the jungle and away from the area.

The Phoenix bird set down minutes later in an overgrown

field at the foot of a tall mountain. Anderson and his fellow Ranger freed themselves from their Maguire rigs and started for the helicopter, only to see their three comrades moving slowly toward them from a nearby thicket. Realizing for the first time what had transpired, Anderson nodded his approval to the pilot as he joined his four teammates and quickly climbed aboard the helicopter. They were soon on their way back to the rear.

Low on fuel, the two shot-up Hueys finally set down at Camp Evans. The two badly wounded Rangers were removed from the aircraft and taken directly to the base field hospital to have their wounds treated. There they would be stabilized for a future medevac flight down to the 22nd Surgical Hospital at Phu Bai.

Anderson and the two remaining Rangers stayed on board as the Phoenix aircraft refueled then flew them directly to the 22nd Surg. There, they were checked out thoroughly to make certain they hadn't sustained any wounds they were unaware of. Meanwhile, the Ranger company was informed of their arrival by land line and a truck sent to return them to the Ranger compound.

A few days later Anderson received word from his company commander, Captain Robert Guy, that the 158th Aviation Battalion commander had called him to find out how the five Rangers had fared. Anderson had missed his one opportunity to thank the courageous pilots and their crews. If not for them, he and his teammates would never have gotten out of the jungle alive.

Sergeant Frank Anderson and his two Ranger teammates soon returned to the company to continue running patrols. Whitledge and the RTO were sent back to the States to recover from their wounds. Their war was over.

14

AIRBORNE RANGER
L CO
75TH INF

With Their Backs to a River

Just after the morning formation on October 23, 1969, a warning order arrived at Lima Company's Tactical Operations Center from Division G-3 for a reconnaissance mission into the mountains behind Nui Ke ("Ke Mountain"). Sergeant Dave Bennett's Ranger Team Excalibur was assigned to conduct the patrol.

Dave Bennett was a veteran Ranger team leader who was just beginning a six-month extension after having served a full year, through the transition from F Company, 58th (LRP), to L Company, 75th (Ranger). Bennett and his assistant team leader, Staff Sergeant James "Lobo" Bates, hurried to the briefing at the company TOC. Captain Robert Guy, the Ranger company CO, conducted the premission briefing, informing the two Ranger NCOs that their team would be going in to patrol a recon zone about six klicks west of Nui Ke.

The valleys and ridgelines around Nui Ke had been extensively worked during the past eighteen months by the 101st Airborne's LRPs and Rangers. Dominating the narrow "rocket belt," where the NVA frequently launched its 122mm "block-busters" at Hue, Phu Bai, and Camp Eagle, Nui Ke stood as a constant reminder of the enemy's presence in the Screaming Eagle AO. Over the past year and a half missions into the rocket belt had resulted in a score of contacts, and a large number of close calls. With few exceptions, every time a long range patrol was inserted into the area, the NVA had been there.

This time G-2 had come up with new intelligence indicating that an enemy build-up was occurring in the mountains behind Nui Ke. The particular unit involved was said to be the company's old nemesis, the 5th NVA Regiment. Recently a number of positive "sniffer" (sensors that recognized human odors) contacts substantiated that "someone" was out there . . . and in large numbers. When the NVA moved so close to Hue/Phu Bai/Camp Eagle, it usually meant that an enemy offensive was in the making, or at the very least the area's civilian/military complexes were in for another pasting from NVA rockets. Either way it spelled trouble for the South Vietnamese and their American allies. And the only way to counter this type of trouble was to stop it early, right where it began.

Division G-2 wanted a Lima Company long range patrol to slip into the area to determine just what was causing the sensor readings. Sergeant Dave Bennett was more concerned than normal when Team Excalibur got the nod for the patrol. At the time, he was two men short of a full six-man reconnaissance team. Not that this made any difference to Bennett; four-man patrols had been used before in the company, and were even preferred by some who believed they were a lot quieter than ordinary six-man patrols. However, when the proverbial shit hit the proverbial fan—and that could happen very quickly in the rocket belt—two extra weapons might be the difference between coming out alive and not coming out at all. But then, that's why young buck sergeants traditionally weren't the ones who made the "big" decisions.

To make things even a little more spicy, Bennett was informed that his team would go in at last light on the twenty-fifth. Last-light insertions, though very effective, were always a little riskier than first-light insertions because a team compromised at last light usually meant a night extraction under fire, or at the very least, escape and evasion through pitch-black jungle, either of which can make your life insurance agent a very unhappy camper.

With the mission plans finalized and everyone briefed, Bennett made the decision to walk point himself during the patrol. He assigned PFC Mike Lytle to walk his "slack" while carrying the primary radio. Sergeant Bob Stein would occupy the third slot and carry the artillery radio, and Sergeant Jim Bates would bring up the rear. In addition to the two main PRC-25s, Bennett and Bates would also carry small squad radios. That way everyone on the team could communicate with someone should they get separated on E&E routes.

The overflight on the morning of the twenty-fourth confirmed Bennett's original suspicions that the AO was composed of the same steep jungle-covered mountainous terrain that ran throughout the entire area. However, he was pleased that the thick double canopy did appear to open up into a fifty-meter-wide belt of sparse scrub vegetation along both sides of the Khe Dau River, which ran through the middle of the RZ.

The river was a plus for the team. It meant that water wouldn't be a problem during the patrol, and that the four Rangers would be able to leave behind the large collapsible canteens they usually carried in their rucks. Without the added weight of all that extra water, the four-man team would be able to hump more ammo. With only four men, the extra ammo could come in handy in case they made contact with an enemy unit.

Bennett selected a small clearing as the team's primary LZ. It was located on a narrow secondary ridge that rose slowly away from the river until it connected with a major ridgeline that crossed the team's RZ. Bennett knew that because of the exceptionally dense vegetation covering the high ground, it would be extremely difficult for NVA troops in the immediate area of the insertion to observe exactly where the Huey slick dropped off the patrol.

On the evening of the twenty-fifth, Team Excalibur went in during that brief window of opportunity between dusk and full darkness when shadow and shade begin to merge into night. The slick flared briefly over the LZ as the four Rangers dropped from the skids and disappeared into the trees at the edge of the clearing. In the heavy cover off the LZ, they remained frozen for a full fifteen minutes while the jungle slowly forgave, then forgot, their rude interruption. Finally, satisfied that the insertion was cold and they were alone on the small ridge, Bennett took the handset from Lytle's radio and called in a negative sit rep to the choppers circling off in the distance and got a commo check from the relay team set up on Firebase Birmingham, seven long klicks to the north.

With full darkness only minutes away, the team moved silently away from the LZ, heading down toward the river below. Bennett knew that if there were any major trails in their recon zone, they would likely be on the level, more open ground near the water. He also realized that it was dangerous breaking brush and covering ground at night, but he'd learned the hard way that it was even more dangerous remaining too long in the vicinity of an LZ.

Team Excalibur moved cautiously downhill through the heavy jungle, stopping every few minutes to wait and to listen. When they had covered a hundred or so meters, Bennett located some dense cover just off their line of movement and led the patrol into the center of it. It was a good spot to laager up, but Bennett was worried. Coming down off the ridge, his patrol had made a lot more noise than he liked, but it couldn't be helped. However, just to be on the safe side, he had instructed Bates to take extra precautions in sterilizing their back trail.

While Bennett called in the team's location, Bates and Stein quietly moved outside the thicket to set out four claymores, strategically located to cover their tiny perimeter. With this accomplished, the four Rangers pulled back into the heavy brush, setting up in a tight square. The team leader whispered instructions that everyone would be on full alert until midnight, then each man would stand a one and a half hour guard shift, the last one ending at 0600 hours.

The early part of the evening proved uneventful, with the four Rangers listening intently as the normal sounds of the night returned to reassure them that no one was in the neighborhood searching for them. At 2400 hours Bates took the first guard shift, sitting there in the darkness, alert, until he turned it over to Lytle at 0130. Lytle gently shook Stein awake at 0300 and told him that he'd heard nothing unusual.

It was 0330 hours when Stein shook Bennett awake, whispering that they had movement on the ridge above them and more to their south near the river. Bennett shook off the last vestiges of sleep, cupped his hands behind his ears, to amplify the sounds to his front, and listened. It wasn't long before he picked up the hushed sounds of several voices talking quietly—and they weren't using English. He cocked his head to the side, angling it toward the river down below. He immediately heard the same thing in that direction. The enemy was out there and they were close.

Now fully alert, the two Rangers gently woke their teammates. Bennett moved to the radio and contacted the relay team on Birmingham to report the news that enemy troops were nearby and that the situation did not look promising. The X-ray team immediately relayed this information to Captain Guy back at the company TOC. After a short pause, the Ranger CO radioed back that the team should lay low and remain on full alert for the rest of the night. He promised that he would be in the air with support at first light.

After a stressful night, dawn finally began to break on the morning of the twenty-sixth. True to his promise, Captain Guy was there in his C&C ship, and had thoughtfully brought along a "Pink Team" to handle any emergencies that might arise. The LOH scout helicopter ("white") and the pair of deadly Cobra gunships ("red") from the 2/17th Cav orbited off in the distance, ready to respond.

Bennett radioed Captain Guy that the enemy movement around them had quieted down somewhat shortly before daylight. But he suspected that the enemy soldiers might still be in the vicinity, waiting for the patrol to come out of hiding.

Bennett had decided to continue moving south in the direction of the river. It was where they'd heard muffled voices during the night, but except for their LZ, it was the only open ground in their AO if they had to come out in a hurry.

After recovering their claymores, the four Rangers moved out cautiously in patrol file, five meters apart. They took their time coming down off the ridge, making certain that they made no unnecessary noise. Fifty meters from their night defense perimeter, they suddenly broke out of the underbrush and found themselves looking down on a high-speed trail, six feet wide.

Plenty of fresh sign, running in both directions, showed that the route had seen recent heavy use by enemy troops. As far as Bennett could see in either direction, the overhead canopy had been pulled together and tied off to conceal the trail from the air.

When Bennett reported the discovery of the trail, its location, condition, and direction, Captain Guy suggested that the patrol back away from the trail and lay low while he took the Pink Team to Firebase Birmingham to refuel.

As soon as the helicopters had departed the area, the sounds of enemy movement above and behind them began once again, but this time in earnest. The NVA were talking openly, occasionally shouting back and forth at each other. Bennett was certain the enemy soldiers now had a fairly good idea of where the team was holed up. It was apparent they were maneuvering in to flush the Rangers from hiding before the helicopters could return.

Bates sensed it, too. He quickly exchanged glances with Bennett then whispered, "We got to get the hell out of here."

Bennett nodded and motioned for everyone to follow him, then signaled for them to move as quietly as possible and stay close together. Their survival might depend on what happened in the next five minutes.

The patrol turned and headed away from the sounds of the enemy. As the Rangers moved out, the noises behind and above them increased noticeably, indicating that the NVA were close enough to observe the patrol.

Bennett soon realized that the NVA soldiers had gotten on line, stretching from the ridgeline above them all the way down to the river. They were moving slowly, maneuvering toward the team, making a lot of unnecessary noise, apparently trying to drive the Americans farther up the valley. Bennett concluded they must have a good reason for doing so.

The Ranger team leader halted the team just long enough to switch rucks with Lytle so he could handle the radio as they moved. Keeping the young RTO on an umbilical cord only served to prevent him from acting independently. With only four players on his team, Bennett could ill afford to have two of them tied together.

Sacrificing noise discipline for speed, they continued busting through the waist- to head-high brush. Bennett radioed the X-ray team on Birmingham and asked for an emergency extraction. Captain Guy, back on the net again, radioed that help was on the way.

The four Rangers—massive doses of adrenaline pumping through their systems—forgot about the heavy rucksacks they were carrying on their backs. The only thing that mattered to them was putting more space between themselves and the pursuing NVA. If they failed to outdistance them, the enemy would overrun them in seconds.

Suddenly, Bates opened up from the rear of the team, at the same time screaming, *"Got visual—They're all over the place!"* AK-47 fire erupted behind the team. The trees overhead exploded with the impact of the enemy rounds. The NVA were firing high, but it wouldn't take them long to realize their error and adjust their fire.

With only four men at his disposal, Bennett knew it was pointless to try holing up and fighting it out. Rangers fought like tigers when they were cornered, but even tigers know when to cut and run. There were just too damned many NVA, and they controlled the high ground above the team. No, it was definitely time to escape and evade.

Bennett broke brush, heading toward the high-speed trail down along the edge of the river. It was a dangerous move, but the team was rapidly running out of good choices. If the NVA got to the high-speed trail first, they would overtake the patrol and cut them off in a matter of minutes.

About this time the C&C ship came back on station and Captain Guy radioed the team, wanting to know where they were so he could direct the Pink Team in to support them; he couldn't see the team under the single/double canopy, and Bennett didn't have time to stop and fix his position. Finally, by instructing his pilot to fly grids back and forth over the valley, Captain Guy spotted the team when they flew directly over its position.

Bennett looked up as he ran and screamed into the handset, *"Mark! You just passed over my position."*

As the scout ship slowed to come around again, it seemed like every enemy weapon in the valley and dozens more up on the ridge shifted fire to the tiny chopper. Bennett heard the pilot scream over the radio, *"Jesus Christ, they're everywhere!"*

Seconds later the Ranger patrol reached the "red-ball," just as the first Cobra gunship began its run, firing up the trail behind the team. The Rangers heard the NVA screaming and shouting as the Cobra's miniguns turned the single canopy vegetation to mulch. Bennett chanced a quick glance over his shoulder to make sure no one had been hit, then sprinted north down the trail away from their pursuers. Between the deadly Cobra gun runs, the Rangers heard the enemy soldiers shouting as they tried to reorganize their forces and continue their pursuit.

Then Captain Guy was back on the air, informing Bennett that he had just located a suitable LZ only two hundred meters ahead. He also reported that additional Cobras and the patrol's lift ships were now on station and waiting to extract the team.

The LOH darted in again and again to mark the Ranger team's location as they fled the NVA. This permitted the Cobra gunships to make repeated runs over the Rangers' heads, keeping the nearest enemy soldiers off their backs. Then suddenly, seventy-five meters to their front, all hell broke loose. An attacking Cobra had drawn a heavy volume of small-arms fire from the jungle directly ahead of the team, confirming what Bennett had suspected: the NVA behind them had not been chasing the patrol, they were driving it into an ambush. Fortunately for Bennett and his teammates, the waiting NVA weren't disciplined enough to pass up an opportunity to bring down a Cobra. Their excitement and lack of professionalism had warned the team.

Bennett screamed for his men to get down. With NVA to their front, rear, and above them, there was no place left to run. They were boxed in on three sides and the only option left to them was to the east—the river. Then, without waiting for the command to run, all four Rangers leaped to their feet and dashed for the blue line a long, long, fifteen meters away. None of them knew what they would do when they got there, nor did they really care.

The Rangers' hopes of escape were dashed when they reached the edge of the river. There before them raged a roaring torrent twenty-five meters across. The recent rains had swelled the river. Bennett glanced over his shoulder, then back again at the water. He knew that only certain death awaited his team on this side of the river. Despite the danger presented by the river, crossing it was their only chance for survival.

The four Rangers huddled next to the water as the team leader got on the radio and reported to Captain Guy that there was an NVA ambush set up between the team's location and their extraction LZ. Bennett explained that his team was trapped and they were going to attempt to swim the river. He requested the CO to locate a new LZ on the other side—just in case they made it across.

Heavy firing broke out behind them as the enemy maneuvered to close in on the trapped Rangers. The Cobra gunships were effective, but they were forcing the NVA soldiers to move in on the Ranger team, rather than wait for it. The NVA were trying to snuggle up as close as possible to avoid the Cobras' rocket and minigun runs.

Bennett yelled for the ATL, Bates, to get the team across the river, then turned back to cover them. Still wearing their rucks and LBE, hanging onto their weapons, the three Rangers leaped into the raging water. Bennett remained behind on the shore, putting out as much firepower as one man could manage. Stopping to change magazines, he cast a quick glance back over his shoulder at the river. They were gone. He panicked for a single, brief moment, until he saw two heads break the surface at midstream and strike out for the far shore. Bennett, now locked and fully loaded again, returned to putting down covering fire for his teammates. That he still had the river to face with no one covering his backside had not yet crossed his mind.

Trying desperately to break the enemy's back, the gunships were now making runs from all directions. As Bennett stopped once again to reload, he looked back across the river and saw Bates and Stein struggling up the opposite bank. He watched as they crawled behind some large boulders and dropped out of sight.

Just as he turned back to fire, well-placed NVA rounds began kicking up dirt at his feet. Then a large explosion erupted just to his front, knocking him backward into the shallow water at the edge of the river. Stunned and fighting for air, the Ranger team leader struggled against the current and the weight of his gear to reach the surface. Finally, his lungs nearly bursting, he broke free of the water, pulled himself to shore, and crawled back up the bank on his hands and knees. Miraculously, he still had his weapon. With the NVA closing in, he raised the CAR-15 to his shoulder and pulled the trigger, only to have the chamber explode in his face. Either an enemy round had damaged the weapon or river water in the barrel had caused the malfunction. He was now unarmed and on the wrong side of the blue line, with a large number of very angry enemy soldiers closing in for the kill. There would never be a better time to get out of Dodge.

Slinging his now useless weapon over his head, Bennett turned and jumped into the current, immediately sinking ten to fifteen feet to the bottom. The water was so cold it took his breath away.

Bennett squatted, then pushed hard off the bottom in a vain attempt to reach the surface, but it was useless—like a heavy anchor, the NCO's rucksack, LBE, and weapon were holding him down.

Like all Rangers, he'd been taught to hang onto his equipment and his weapon no matter what the cost, and that belief had saved his life on more than one occasion, but this time to do so would mean death. Wasting no more time in idle thought, he struggled to remove the CAR-15 slung over his neck, then Lytle's ruck, and finally his own web gear. Breaking free of the dead weight, he kicked off from the bottom of the river and made his way to the surface.

Coughing and gasping for air, Bennett struck out for a large tree stump jutting just above the surface of the river. Growing up along the Pacific rim and spending his youth riding surfboards down southern California breakers had prepared the young Ranger for this moment. Maintaining his position against the raging current, he gained ground on the stump, moving ever closer.

When he finally reached it, he grabbed hold then looked back across the river for his teammates. He soon spotted Bates and Stein still crouched behind some large boulders on the opposite shore, but he couldn't see Lytle anywhere.

By now the sounds of battle had died down to a few scattered bursts of small-arms fire, as the Cobras continued their devastating runs against the enemy soldiers. Unable to do anything more than hide, the NVA were no match for the deadly gunships. The Cobras had taken a horrible toll from them.

Bennett was still in a bad spot, cut off from everyone else, on the wrong side of the river and without weapon or commo, but his safety was no longer the top tune on his hit parade. The Ranger team leader was already trying to resolve the issue of his failure to protect his team. He began to ask himself what he could have done to prevent this. But the urgency of the situation didn't allow him time to dwell on it for long. Hopefully, he thought, there'll be opportunity to sort it all out later.

Bennett had to get his team back together, and he couldn't accomplish that from this side of the river. Leaving the stump, he jumped back into the water and struck out for the opposite shore, but the current was too strong. Before he realized what was happening, the current had sucked him around a bend in the river and had shoved him back toward the shore he'd just left.

He turned and swam for it, even though it was on the wrong side. Anything was better than drowning. With the last of his strength, Bennett finally reached the near shore and pulled himself onto the rocks. He was finished for the moment—out of gas. If the enemy had spotted him struggling ashore, they would soon be swarming all over him.

Waiting several minutes until he had recovered enough strength, Bennett crawled over the rocks to a nearby sandbar. Taking a foolish chance, he stood up and yelled across the river at Bates and Stein, "Where's Lytle?"

Over the steady roar of the current, Bates cupped his hands to his mouth and hollered back, "Lost him crossing the river!"

Bennett then waved his arms to attract the attention of the C&C ship hovering a hundred meters away. It soon spotted him, came across and landed on the sandbar. Captain Guy jumped out and ran over to where his young team leader stood, telling him that a reaction force of Blues from the 2/17th Cav was on the way. Bennett dropped his head in resignation. He knew that for Lytle the help was too late.

A short time later seven slicks settled in from the east, circled the river, then dropped in to let off the aero-rifle platoon on the sandbar. The Blues quickly scattered across the spit, moving to set up a half-moon perimeter around the C&C ship facing out toward the nearby jungle. With the perimeter secured for the moment, Captain Guy sent the scout helicopter across the river to pick up Bates and Stein.

Apparently, the surviving NVA had pulled back away from the river after realizing that help was on the way. Of course, the sight of four Cobra gunships alone can be a pretty disheartening experience. But for whatever reason, the NVA were gone.

With the survivors of the patrol back together once again, Captain Guy went over to his helicopter and radioed the pilot of the LOH, asking him to work the river to try to locate Lytle's body. In the dingy, swirling water, there wasn't much hope for a recovery, but the Ranger CO had to try.

The small scout ship immediately swung far out over the river and began to make slow, deliberate passes back and forth across the current. Suddenly, downstream near the far end of the sandbar, the door gunner leaned out and pointed straight down beneath the hovering aircraft. He'd just spotted Lytle's body submerged in ten to fifteen feet of water, snagged on a pile of tree roots and flood debris.

The LOH pilot got a fix on the body, moved back up the river, landed on the sandbar and shut down its engine. The Cobras continued patrolling the hills above the river, but were no longer firing. Bennett took advantage of the relative silence to have a quick conference with Captain Guy, the LOH pilot, and the platoon sergeant of the Blues to determine how they could best recover Lytle's body.

While they were conversing, one of the Cav troopers stripped off his gear and entered the river above the spot where Lytle's body lay wedged in the current. He made a valiant effort to swim out in the river to the snag, but the current was too swift for him to make it. The soldier quickly turned around and came back.

Bennett grabbed a coil of rappelling rope from Captain Guy's C&C ship, tossed the loose end to the LOH pilot and asked him to fly it over to the opposite shore. When the aircraft reached the far side, the ship's gunner got out and secured the rope to a large boulder. The LOH returned to the sandbar, where Bennett and Bates quickly fastened the other end of the rope to the skid of the C&C ship. One of the slick's door gunners then fastened another section of rope to himself and secured it to the lifeline now spanning the river. Hauling himself hand over hand to where Lytle's corpse lay submerged, he dove beneath the water. Thirty seconds later he returned to the surface without Lytle's body. Several more times the crewman dove, but was still unable to recover the body. Gasping for breath, he shouted that the current was too strong and was holding the body tight against the debris.

Then Bennett stripped, dove into the river and swam across to the crewman. Between them, they managed to pry Lytle's body from the debris. Gasping for air, the two soldiers brought it to the surface and swam with it back across the river to the sandbar.

When they got Lytle's body up on the rocks, Bennett dropped to his knees and tried desperately to revive him with mouth-to-mouth resuscitation. Captain Guy finally brought a halt to his efforts when he draped his arm around the young team leader's shoulders and said, "It's over, Dave."

Bennett stood up, tears welling up in his eyes. He could no longer hold back the emotions that now came flooding out. He felt he was responsible for the death of a teammate. If he'd only done things differently, Lytle might still be alive!

Captain Guy stepped back and ordered a number of the Blues to put Lytle's body aboard his C&C ship. Reluctantly, one of them bent over and grabbed the dead Ranger's stiff form around the shoulders, while another grabbed a boot. They began dragging him across the sandbar toward the waiting helicopter. Handling the body like a piece of luggage, the two soldiers banged the dead Ranger's head along the rocks.

Bennett came unglued. Still naked, he sprinted across the

sandbar and shoved the two surprised troopers roughly to one side. Without a word he squatted down in the sand, lifted Lytle's lifeless body in his arms, and carried him the rest of the way to the waiting helicopter. Gently, Bennett slid the corpse of his dead teammate across the floor of the cabin feet first, taking special care that Lytle's head took no more abuse.

Looking on from the side, Bates and Stein handed Bennett his clothes then climbed silently into the waiting slick. For the first time since they had hit the river, the four Rangers were together again. No one said a word—no one had to. The Huey rose from the sandbar and returned to Camp Eagle.

Back at the company area, Bennett wrote a long letter to Mike Lytle's parents, telling them what had happened out in the jungle that day. They had a right to know how their son had died. Bates and Stein stayed away from him. They had enough sense to leave the grieving team leader alone with his thoughts for a while. They knew what he was going through, and there was nothing they could say or do to console him.

15

AIRBORNE
RANGER

L
CO

75TH
INF

Team Opel

The primary mission of most long range patrols during the Vietnam War was covert reconnaissance. Success meant getting in, gathering intelligence, and getting back out again without being detected. But once in a while the enemy got lucky and managed to trap a long range reconnaissance patrol deep in hostile territory. It was then that the enemy found out how ferociously Rangers could fight. Cornered, with their backs to a wall and no place to run, the recon teams fought like wildcats.

One such mission began on January 12, 1970, in the middle of the winter monsoon season. The weather had been miserable for nearly two months, with almost continual rain, overcast, and heavy ground fog. L Company had sent out a few patrols during occasional breaks in the weather, but two to three clear days in a row were becoming as scarce as in-country R&Rs.

Ranger Staff Sergeant James "Lobo" Bates, veteran team leader of Team Opel, received a warning order on January ninth to lead a ten-man heavy team into a recon zone in the northwest corner of Quang Tri Province. Searching for an NVA training base that Division Intelligence had placed in the vicinity, the company had been working that area for a month. G-2 knew it was out there from a combination of agent reports,

POWs, and captured enemy documents, but LRPs had not yet managed to locate the base—probably because they were all making contact on the first or second days of their patrols. It's tough trying to find Easter eggs when you're up to your ass in man-eating rabbits!

The terrain in the patrol's AO consisted of rugged, jungle-covered mountains, broken only on the lower slopes and in the valleys by vast fields of nearly impassable elephant grass. It was tough country to find your way out of, and an even tougher place to locate someone else who was trying not to be found.

Staff Sergeant Jim Bates's ten-man team consisted of himself as team leader; Staff Sergeant Joe Stauffer as ATL; Spec 4s David "the Hawk" Weeks and Calvin "the Kid" Dunkle as senior scouts; scout/observers Spec 4s Dave "Canadian" Hazelton and Mark Martin; patrol medic Spec 5 John Fowler; Senior RTO Spec 4 Mike "Gringo" Blinston; Junior RTO PFC Robert Raller; and a Kit Carson scout—Vo Can Sau.

It was a veteran team, one of the best combinations of skill and experience the company could put together. Their mission order read that they were to get into the AO, grab two or three prisoners, and then get out. They were scheduled to go in on January 10, but the weather had failed to cooperate. Every rain-soaked day was the same routine—wake up, grab gear, move to the acid pad . . . and wait. And every day the mission was canceled.

Finally, in the middle of the afternoon on January twelfth the weather broke just long enough to encourage the Merlins up at Division to give the mission the green light. Team Opel saddled up, the helicopters cranked up, and nine Rangers and their trusty Kit Carson scout clammed up as they climbed aboard. But something was wrong with the home team. The usual premission banter and joking around was missing, and no one gave a thumbs-up to the Rangers who had come down to the chopper pad to see them off. Already the mission didn't feel right, and the Rangers weren't even off the ground yet.

The LZ was on a small finger running down from a main ridgeline. The narrow finger was covered with dense elephant grass about seven feet high, and sloped gently up toward the ridgeline. But before it actually reached the main ridge, it doglegged to the right and ran parallel to the ridgeline. Between the finger and the main ridge lay a deep cut, or gorge. As the finger ran onward, it continued rising, until it culminated on a small hilltop covered with trees.

The two Hueys dropped the patrol off in the middle of the LZ then skipped across the valley, occasionally dropping down again to make a false insertion. But back in the LZ, none of the Rangers suspected for a moment that the enemy had been fooled by the sleight of hand. This was confirmed a short time later when the patrol found a large number of fighting positions located along the finger, not far from the LZ. The bunkers and spider holes were new and arranged in an excellent configuration for ambush.

The patrol moved on the finger as long as it could, but when it finally hooked to the right, parallel to the main ridgeline, Spec 4 Weeks, at point, saw seventy-five to a hundred NVA soldiers busily working on bunkers and defensive positions just below the military crest of the main ridgeline. There was no way the enemy troops could have missed seeing the team's insertion; it had gone down right under their noses, and unless it was some kind of ROTC company from the Hanoi Institute for the Blind, Deaf, and Dumb, the NVA milling about on the neighboring terrain feature knew for certain they had visitors coming up the finger.

The members of the patrol fought a nearly uncontrollable urge to bunch up in the tall grass when they first spotted the enemy soldiers on the ridge above. It was obvious that the NVA were pretending they had not seen the Americans arrive on the LZ.

The Rangers continued to parallel the main ridge, hoping to pass the enemy without drawing fire. Weeks was out on point, with Dunkle at his slack, then the Kit Carson scout, Bates, Blinston, Hazelton, Fowler, Raller, Stauffer, and Martin walking tailgunner.

Except for their Kit Carson scout, most of the Rangers seemed almost relieved knowing where the enemy was. It certainly made finding them a lot easier. They only hoped that the NVA soldiers up on the ridge were not experiencing the same kind of relief knowing that they grossly outnumbered the small group of American soldiers quietly slipping through the elephant grass below.

The Ranger patrol finally climbed the rise at the end of the finger and moved into the tree line on the top of the hill. It wasn't much of a place, really, measuring no more than twenty to twenty-five feet in diameter. And to make matters even worse, between the Rangers and the NVA on the opposite ridge there was a shallow saddle, just wide enough to accommodate a large number of enemy soldiers if they wanted to cross the gorge without a lot of unnecessary climbing. Extending from the right side of the saddle was a gentle slope that dropped down into a small valley, then rose up again to meet another ascending finger that tied back into the primary ridge. A well-used, high-speed trail ran down from the hilltop where the Rangers lay hidden. About ten feet from the crest it forked, forming a Y that ran off through the brush down each flank of the saddle. The shaft of the Y ended right where the Rangers had set up their perimeter. The trail seemed to serve as a signpost pointing directly to the Rangers. However, it couldn't detract from the fact that the hilltop was the best defensive position in the area and made an excellent OP from which to spy on the NVA on the opposite ridge.

Protected by a fallen tree, Weeks set up high on the left side of the trail. From there he was able to observe anyone attempting to come up either of the two trails that flanked the saddle. Hazelton had set up to Weeks's right, then the KC scout, Stauffer, Dunkle, Raller, Martin, Blinston, and Fowler. With the radio, Bates took up a command and control position in the center of the perimeter.

As it began to grow dark, a number of the Rangers slipped outside the tiny perimeter to set up a defensive outer ring of claymore mines. Finished with the task, they soon settled down to get as comfortable as possible in their overnight positions. A few of them ate an evening meal of cold LRRP rations or snacked on something light to take the edge off their hunger. The patrol's Kit Carson scout, Vo Can Sau, an ex-NVA lieutenant with seventeen years service on the wrong side of the wire, lit up a cigarette and started to smoke. Suddenly, he dropped it on the ground, stomped it out and went for his rifle.

Unable to converse in English, the scout turned and attempted to communicate with Sergeant Bates by means of a series of prearranged hand signals.

Bates, not quite certain he was comprehending what the scout was trying to say, whispered, "Beaucoup NVA?"

Vo Can Sau nodded his head vigorously and repeated, "Beaucoup NVA."

It was confirmation of what Bates had been expecting ever since the patrol had reached the hilltop.

But when nothing happened over the next sixty minutes, Bates came to the conclusion that the KC scout had been wrong. He assigned two Rangers to pull security detail and whispered for the rest of the patrol to try to grab a little shut-eye. But keying on Sau's continued anxiety, no one was able to sleep.

About 2100 hours the Rangers heard an engine, probably a generator, start up in the valley to the south of the patrol. A short time later lights were flickering dimly through the trees no more than fifty to a hundred meters away. Suddenly, both the patrol's radios simultaneously went dead. Sitting in the jungle without commo within fifty meters of an enemy encampment was unnerving.

Thirty minutes passed before Weeks signaled that he thought he'd heard something out on the trail to their immediate front. Soon the others heard it, too, a faint scuffling noise as if someone was trying very hard to be quiet but not quite succeeding. Seconds later, down in the valley below them, the generator kicked off and the lights blinked out. Something major was about to happen.

The air around the patrol suddenly seemed to grow heavy, almost as if some spectral presence had descended upon them. The Rangers grabbed their knives, claymore clackers, and frags and waited for the attack. Sergeant Bates had already ordered that no one should use his weapon, warning that the muzzle flashes would only give their positions away.

A few minutes later a lone plane flew over, flying from west to east. The Rangers listened as the sounds of the aircraft faded in the distance. Three minutes later the generator started back up and the lights came on again. This sequence repeated itself several more times during the early part of the evening every time a plane passed over the area. To the surprise of the Rangers, the enemy appeared to have an excellent aircraft early warning system.

Around 2130 hours the sounds of movement around the team intensified. There was no longer any doubt among the Rangers that the noises they'd been hearing were enemy troops maneuvering into position for an assault on their perimeter. They knew they were going to be in for a very long night.

Soon the NVA began beating bamboo sticks against the stocks of their weapons, both to signal each other and to get the Americans to give away their positions. Other soldiers began talking aloud and calling out to each other as they maneuvered around the hilltop. Some of the NVA even began shining flashlights back and forth through the brush to locate the patrol. This activity continued for nearly an hour and a half as the enemy tried to flush the Rangers or keep them on edge.

Knowing that they would need their rest before the night was over, but forced to respond to the increasing enemy presence around them, Bates silently passed the word for the patrol to go on fifty percent alert. Of course, by this time none of the Rangers was able to sleep; no one wanted to waste two or three minutes trying to wake up and clear his head before defending himself. There wouldn't be enough time for that. By 2200 hours they knew they were surrounded.

Several times during the night the Rangers lost commo, then just as suddenly as it had stopped, it would start up again. For all practical purposes the patrol was entirely on its own without support from the rear. It wasn't a new experience for the Rangers; many patrols out on the fringe often lost commo.

Just before midnight, an NVA soldier suddenly walked up the trail shining a flashlight just ahead of him on the ground. He stopped about five feet from Weeks and Hazelton. The enemy soldier was much larger than the average Vietnamese; Weeks estimated that the man was five-ten to -eleven and weighed close to 170 pounds. Hazelton covered the NVA with his weapon while Weeks prepared to take him out with the large Buck knife he carried on patrol.

Suddenly, the man shined the beam of his flashlight directly on Hazelton. Seconds later he shifted it over to Weeks. A big smile spread across the NVA soldier's face, practically unnerving Hazelton. It didn't do much for Weeks, either.

Weeks was just preparing to launch himself at the NVA soldier as he stood there grinning stupidly, when two things intervened to stop him. First, Sergeant Bates gently put his hand on Weeks's leg to stop him, and second, the enemy soldier suddenly turned on his heel and walked slowly away. Not once did he increase his stride or even look back over his shoulder. He was one cool character!

There was no doubt about it anymore. The team had been made, and the enemy now knew right where they were hiding. The pucker factor among the ten soldiers trapped on top of that little hill went off the charts.

Fifteen to twenty minutes after the NVA soldier departed, the Rangers smelled marijuana smoke drifting uphill from the saddle. Apparently the enemy soldiers were getting a quick buzz on to build up their confidence prior to attacking the patrol.

Silently, each Ranger slowly and deliberately set out frags in front of his position and laid out extra magazines for his weapon to his right. There would be no time for searching through rucksacks and ammo pouches in the heat and confusion of a firefight. Weeks stuck his Buck knife in the ground to his right and jacked a round into the chamber of his 9mm pistol. Every man on the tiny hilltop was making the same final preparations for battle.

At midnight the enemy decided it was time to close in on the Rangers' positions on the hill. Dunkle and Weeks heard them coming and wanted to go out to meet them with their knives. Bates quickly nixed the idea. But for some reason the enemy changed their plan at the last minute and remained below the crest of the hill.

Mysteriously, just before dawn the patrol's radio came back up on the air, and they had commo once again. Bates quickly radioed the relay element and explained what had transpired during the past six hours. Without ceremony he told them that the patrol was now surrounded and in immediate danger of being overrun by a vastly superior enemy force. He warned that the patrol's location was currently socked in by thick

ground fog and dense overhead cloud cover, but that he still
needed slicks and gunships immediately if the team was going
to survive. The relay team's response was far from promising.

Back at Camp Eagle Captain Guy had just arrived at
Division HQ to report that he'd lost contact with Team Opel
during the night, but that they had reported in minutes before,
requesting immediate extraction. General John Wright, commanding general of the 101st Airborne Division, listened to the
news of Opel's imminent peril with deep concern. However,
after Captain Guy had finished his briefing and requested
immediate help, General Wright confided that he had better be
ready to write off the patrol. Because of the weather and the
patrol's immediate peril, he didn't feel that Team Opel was
going to make it back. With the exception of A Troop, all units
of the 2/17th Cav were standing down at Camp Eagle, a full
hour's flight away, so there wasn't any help close enough to
reach the surrounded patrol in time. At its home base at Quang
Tri, A Troop was twenty minutes away, but for the Rangers of
Team Opel, twenty minutes away was still twenty minutes too
long. They needed help immediately.

Thankfully, L Company First Sergeant Bob Gilbert had been
a step ahead of everyone else. When he discovered during the
early morning hours that Team Opel had failed to make
two scheduled sit reps, he got on the land line and woke an old
buddy of his, Master Sergeant Thomson, the operations
NCOIC for the 4th Battalion, 77th Aerial Rocket Artillery, a
heavy gunship battalion. Its Charlie Battery was flying out of
LZ Sally, north of Camp Eagle. The battalion's Cobras were
each armed with six dozen 2.75 in. rockets, a load that could
bring mountains of grief upon any enemy force insane enough
to get caught on the wrong side of their gunsights. For months
Thomson had been begging Gilbert to let his unit fly support
for the Rangers. Now, in this moment of extreme crisis, Top
Gilbert was ready to comply. He quickly apprised Master
Sergeant Thomson of the situation with his Ranger patrol up
north in Quang Tri Province. Thomson wrote down all of the
pertinent information, then told him he would take care of
the problem.

Against orders, and probably every military regulation in the

book, Thomson ordered Charlie Battery into the air. Before
General Wright had time to cancel the lease on Team Opel,
Charlie Battery, 4th Battalion, 77th ARA, had a hunter/killer
team of two Cobras on station, just outside Team Opel's AO.
Three more hunter/killer teams were on a two- to four- to six-
minute standby alert back at LZ Sally. The program was
that when the shit hit the fan at Team Opel's location, the
hunter/killer team would suddenly come up on the Ranger
push and say, "Hey, we were just passing by. Do you guys need
any assistance?" Master Sergeant Thomson's plan was slick,
real slick—and "highly irregular"—but before the day was
over it would save the lives of nine U.S. Army Rangers and
their loyal Kit Carson scout.

At about 0700 a slight morning breeze began to clear out
the dense fog. Back at Team Opel's perimeter, Weeks spotted
an NVA soldier on one of the side trails down near the saddle.
Seconds later all of the Rangers were seeing enemy soldiers
moving everywhere. The Rangers soon detected heavy movement on three sides of their tiny perimeter. The only direction
apparently free of NVA soldiers was the side of the hill facing
their LZ. Bates radioed this information back to Captain Guy,
asking for instructions. Guy came up on the team's push and
ordered them to blow their claymores, then E&E down to
the LZ.

Suspecting a trap, Bates took a quick vote among his
Rangers, asking them if they wanted to E&E to the LZ, or
stand where they were and go down fighting. With little wasted
discussion among them, the Rangers decided that the hilltop
was as good a place to die as any other; to a man they opted to
stay put where they were.

A short time later, Spec 4 Martin, pulling security over the
team's escape route down to the LZ, yanked lightly on his claymore wire to test it and discovered that it had been cut sometime during the night. He passed the word around the tiny
perimeter to let his comrades know that they had made the
right choice deciding to stay put. The NVA had them set up for
an ambush. They were silently waiting below for the patrol to
peel off the hilltop in a break for the LZ.

About 0900 hours dogs began barking from the direction of

the enemy's generator. Dunkle then saw an NVA soldier rise up out of some nearby cover with a fragmentation grenade in his hand. Dunkle fired a single shot just as the enemy soldier started to throw the grenade, dropping him. Seconds later the frag exploded. It was time to rock 'n' roll.

For the next few minutes no one was able to do anything but take care of his immediate front. Enough enemy targets were popping up downrange to keep everyone hopping; dozens of enemy troops were charging up the two trails that converged at their immediate front.

Weeks, firing single shots, put a round in the chest of the NVA soldier in the lead, but the man continued coming even as the second and third rounds struck his body; Weeks's fourth round was to the head and that put him down for good. Relieved, Weeks glanced back at Bates, who shrugged and continued firing. There was no shortage of enemy soldiers and no time for reflection.

Bates got on the horn and completed his prearranged "spontaneous" conversation with the hunter/killer team from Charlie Battery, 4th Battalion, 77th ARA. The flyboys were in the neighborhood on a routine patrol (just as they'd promised) and were looking for targets of opportunity. Team Opel just happened to be up to its neck in targets of opportunity, and invited the Cobras to join the party.

An exploding grenade inside the Ranger perimeter peppered Weeks, Bates, and Hazelton with shrapnel, but not seriously enough to knock any of them out of the fight. While Bates stopped to slap a dressing on his wounds, Weeks snatched up the radio handset and placed it to his ear just in time to hear the first Cobra pilot announce, "I'm coming up on your location. You've got little people everywhere! What do you want me to do with all this ordnance?"

Weeks told him, "Bring it on in."

The Cobra pilot immediately walked a stream of deadly minigun fire right up the trail toward the Rangers' tiny perimeter. He stopped it ten feet away from Weeks and Hazelton. As the Cobra shot past directly over the heads of the stunned Rangers, the pilot asked over the radio, "Are you okay?"

Weeks responded quickly, "Yes. Do it again. I'll tell you when to stop."

The firefight lasted for nearly two hours before a reaction force of Blues from the 2/17th Cav arrived at the Ranger patrol's original LZ. Twenty minutes later they were blasting their way through the enemy ambush. Without stopping to count bodies, they fought their way up the slope toward the Rangers' perimeter. But the officer in command of the Blues nearly got his Kit Carson scout killed when he sent him out on point to link up with the Rangers. The only thing that saved him was Ranger Martin's cool head. Low on ammo, when Martin saw the Vietnamese soldier suddenly break through the brush nearby, he took time to aim in order to make one shot count. The Kit Carson signaled Martin to hold up just before he fired.

The Blues had taken a lot of small-arms fire on their way up to the Rangers' location, but when the two U.S. elements managed to link up, the enemy quickly realized the battle was over and pulled out. The Blues had arrived just in time. The Rangers on the hilltop were out of frags and down to a few rounds of ammo apiece. Weeks had his Buck knife and two rounds left in his 9mm Browning—the last one with his name on it.

After the Blues had secured the area, their commander sent out a three-man patrol to check out the enemy bodies. They went outside the perimeter about fifteen feet, stood there looking all about, then turned around and came back. They walked up to the lieutenant in charge and told him they weren't going out there again because all they could see was blood and bodies everywhere.

The Rangers rose stiffly from their cramped positions, some still visibly shaking from the long battle and the even longer night. Bates ordered them to pick up their claymores and prepare to move down to the LZ for extraction.

When the Rangers went out to disarm their claymores, they made a sobering discovery. Although nearly all of them had been awake during the night, three of the eight claymores had had their wires cut, two of their blasting caps were stolen, and a fourth claymore was turned around to face the Ranger perimeter. If Team Opel had attempted to detonate its claymores as their CO had advised, they would likely have suffered tremendous casualties.

When they were on their way back down to the landing zone a short time later, the Rangers spotted a superbly camouflaged enemy bunker they had somehow missed earlier. It overlooked the exact route they'd taken the evening before when they began to climb the slope to the hilltop. From that vantage point the enemy had likely watched Team Opel enter the area.

If the NVA had been on to them from the beginning, why hadn't they attacked earlier? The Rangers could only speculate that an enemy scout had witnessed their arrival, and by the time he reported in, it was already too dark to respond. The enemy had actually attempted to locate the Ranger patrol during the night but had not been successful in time to carry out an attack before dawn. Again, maybe the NVA were worried that an attack would tip off the Americans to the presence of their base camp. There was also the possibility that the NVA had attempted to lure the Rangers into a massive ambush in order to kill them all quickly before they could get out a call for help. If that was their plan, it had failed when the Rangers decided to stay put on the high ground and fight it out. It was a decision the enemy force could hardly have anticipated.

Top Gilbert was waiting at the acid pad for the team to return from the patrol. When they disembarked from the two Hueys, he had cold Cokes waiting for them. Bates and Weeks knew that if not for Top Gilbert's foresight and ingenuity, they would probably all have been lying dead on the hilltop. He was a tough taskmaster, but when you were up to your ass in alligators, Top Gilbert always showed up to pull your buns out of their jaws.

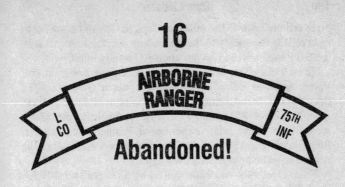

16

Abandoned!

The unspoken fear of any reconnaissance team is to be written off, accidentally left behind, or abandoned while on patrol. In the U.S. Army in Vietnam any of those was a very rare occurrence. Usually, every effort was made to recover a patrol, even if only the bodies were brought out. Many millions of dollars were expended to recover American recon personnel trapped behind enemy lines, and often with the added cost of additional lives lost in the rescue effort. But the total commitment to retrieval represented the extremely high value placed upon our special operations soldiers, not only by their own comrades, but also by the military leaders who commanded them. American soldiers were not supposed to be "expendable," a deciding factor that made young eighteen- and nineteen-year-old boys volunteer to go out repeatedly in small teams. But too often proper support is a tenet that politicians forget when the fighting is over.

On January 22, 1970, Team 1-5, call sign "Polar Bear," and Team 2-5, call sign "Opel," received a warning order for a ten-man heavy team reconnaissance mission and prisoner snatch in Recon Zone Donna, deep in the mountains east of the Ashau Valley. The area was so hot with enemy activity that the briefing officer had to erase red pencil marks on the map just to be able to read the terrain features. Because of the extremely heavy enemy activity in the vicinity of the RZ, there was to be no overflight prior to the mission; Captain Guy did not want to risk alerting the enemy to the impending operation. As a result, the ten Rangers would go into their AO totally blind.

Team Polar Bear was led by veteran Staff Sergeant Jeff Paige, and was made up of Sergeant Leroy Suko as ATL; Spec 4 Joel Conrad, senior scout and point man; Spec 4 David Annelli, Junior RTO; and PFC Britton Buehrig, the junior scout. Like many other experienced Ranger team leaders, Paige knew the value of having commo on hand when he needed it, so he humped his own radio.

Team Opel, too, was commanded by an experienced NCO. Staff Sergeant James "Lobo" Bates, better known to his fellow Rangers as "Contact Bates," was a survivor of a number of hairy missions, but by a combination of skill and luck, he had always managed to come out unscathed. His team was made up of Spec 4 Mark Martin, ATL; Spec 4 Dave Hazelton, senior scout; Spec 4 Larry Fout, Senior RTO; and Spec 4 Jimmy Shepherd, junior scout.

At 1500 hours on January 24, the two Ranger teams headed west toward the mountains from Camp Eagle in two Huey slicks. The mission plan called for the two teams to go in on the same LZ, but First Lieutenant David Ohle, the Ranger company's operations officer, who was flying bellyman in the second slick, decided at the last minute to insert the teams two hundred meters apart in separate LZs. After they reached the ground he wanted them to patrol toward each other until they effected a link-up.

The slicks came in fast, dropping quickly below the crests of the surrounding ridgelines. Team Polar Bear was inserted on its proper LZ, but in the confusion of the last minute change in plans, the pilot of Team Opel's lift ship set his five passengers down in the wrong LZ, nearly two hundred meters east of Team Polar Bear.

Captain Guy, flying high overhead in the C&C chopper, broadcast the message that the teams were in. Staff Sergeant Paige, still expecting Opel to show up on his LZ, radioed back that both teams were "not" in. Paige had already pulled his team off the brush-covered clearing and set them up in a tight circle to cover the expected arrival of Team Opel. When Opel failed to show, Paige couldn't understand what had happened until Captain Guy convinced him that Opel had gone in at the same elevation, but had ended up in a grass-choked LZ some distance away.

The teams soon established radio contact with each other and the C&C ship. It was decided that each ground element would lay out a signal panel to mark its location, then the C&C ship would fix the teams' positions and give them bearings to enable them to move toward a quick link-up. When this was finally accomplished, Paige radioed Bates to stay where he was while Polar Bear moved toward him. He thought that would be safer than having both teams moving toward each other.

Less than twenty meters out of their LZ, Polar Bear's point man suddenly stopped and threw up his arm, signaling that he'd seen or heard something to his immediate front. While the team was frozen, the Rangers began to hear the sounds of heavy movement in the brush all around their position. It seemed to be coming from three different directions at once, and there was little doubt that the sounds were those of men moving through heavy cover.

Paige realized immediately that they were in big trouble; within minutes of their insertion a large number of enemy soldiers were already out in force looking for them. This implied the presence of a large enemy base camp in close proximity to their LZ.

Cautiously, Sergeant Paige circled his teammates into a tight 360-degree defensive perimeter to wait out the events that were beginning to unfold around him. He quietly informed Captain Guy, who was still circling on station in the C&C ship, of their situation. That accomplished, Paige cupped his hands to his ears and tried to pinpoint the locations of the enemy troops. After a few minutes the sounds of movement began to fade away. That didn't make a lot of sense to Paige, but he wasn't going to pass up the opportunity to make a second attempt to reach Team Opel. Once again he began to maneuver his team toward Opel's position.

As a precaution, he contacted Bates again to let him know that Polar Bear was coming in. It was only then that Bates reported that he was laying low because he, too, had movement in the dense underbrush all around his LZ. Now the alarm bells were going off in the minds of both team leaders. The NVA soldiers had their shit together; the next hour was going to spell life or death to the two Ranger teams.

As if to confirm the growing peril closing in on the two teams, the pilots flying the insertion ships radioed that they had spotted a large number of enemy soldiers moving rapidly in the direction of each team's location coming in from the west.

Paige again held up his team and whispered for them to take up defensive positions. Several long, terrifying minutes passed before they heard nearby gunfire from the vicinity of Team Opel. Paige waited a few minutes then radioed Bates to find out what had happened. Bates reported that one of his teammates had observed two NVA soldiers standing near a small creek fifty meters away. But the enemy troops had spotted him at the same time and opened fire, wounding one of the Rangers with shrapnel from an RPG round. The rest of the team had immediately returned fire but with unknown results.

With Opel now compromised and in major trouble, Team Polar Bear immediately went to ground, establishing a circular perimeter in the heavy cover around them. Minutes later Polar Bear began reporting movement. The enemy was moving back in on Paige's patrol and soon began signaling to each other with single carbine shots. A short time later the NVA began sweeping through the brush, clacking bamboo sticks together in an effort to stay on line as they hunted for Team Polar Bear.

Team Opel radioed the C&C aircraft that they were pinned down in a shallow gully, taking sporadic small-arms fire from two sides. Their wounded man was not seriously hit, but the enemy was too close for them to maneuver to higher ground.

Overhead, Captain Guy decided to extract both teams. Team Opel, in immediate danger of being overrun, would have to come out first. Paige acknowledged this and stated that he would keep Polar Bear in place until Opel was out. The veteran team leader then turned to his teammates and instructed them not to fire their weapons unless they were spotted and engaged by the enemy. Two teams in contact at the same time would be disastrous to the rescue effort.

It was 1905 hours and beginning to grow dark when the

Huey slick came in low to pick up Team Opel. It turned out to be a running extraction with the helicopter never quite coming to a complete hover. In spite of a brace of Cobra gunships firing miniguns and 2.75 in. rockets, while pulling the trapped Rangers out of the LZ the extraction slick still took seventeen hits from an estimated twenty to thirty NVA.

As soon as the C&C aircraft reported that Opel was safe, Paige decided to make for higher ground. There was still a lot of enemy movement on three sides of the team, most of it less than thirty meters away, but the patrol was too far from its original LZ to try to return to it. Their best chance of survival was to reach the high ground and extract by Maguire rig.

The NVA were now yelling and shouting in an effort to rattle the Rangers into giving away their positions. But Paige had seen that technique used before. Whispering softly to his comrades to hold their fire, he ordered the five Rangers to continue moving up the slope.

Suddenly, Paige saw Buehrig lift his weapon and aim at an NVA soldier standing in an opening twenty-five meters downhill from their position. Since the NVA soldier had not yet spotted the Rangers, Paige signaled for Buehrig to hold his fire. Buehrig nodded and slowly crouched out of sight in the brush.

At that moment the Cobra pilots radioed that they were out of ammo and heading back to Phu Bai to rearm. They told the Rangers that two other gunships were less than fifteen minutes out.

Paige, a veteran of two combat tours with the 1/327th's famed Tiger Force, knew that the NVA would move quickly to capitalize on the absence of friendly air support. Fifteen minutes without air cover could well mean the end of Team Polar Bear. Paige radioed the Cobras and asked if they could hang around until the other ARA team arrived on station. The lead pilot, understanding the danger their departure would present to the Rangers, radioed back that he would make dry gun runs to keep the enemy's heads down until more help arrived.

During the next three hours a host of American helicopters arrived and departed the AO. When night descended, flare ships kept the area under constant illumination, while Cobra gunships chewed the surrounding countryside to a pulp. But the enemy seemed undaunted by the massive support effort, to the extent that they boldly attempted to shoot down the descending parachute flares. And each time a slick moved in to extract the team, enemy small-arms fire erupted from a number of locations to drive it away. Then thick cloud cover began moving in from across the border in Laos. This was a common occurrence in the Ashau Valley. Sergeant Paige became certain that if he didn't get his team out soon, there would be no rescue until the next day. And the next day would be more than a lifetime away.

At 2245 things were beginning to go sour. The cloud cover was dropping and the enemy ground fire was picking up. The ceiling was then less than two hundred feet, and with the large number of U.S. Army helicopters circling the area, open sky was becoming a pretty rare commodity. Something positive had to happen quickly or Ranger Team Polar Bear would be doomed.

On the ground Sergeant Paige was considering his options. For the first time, an attempt at cross-country escape and evasion was being given consideration. It was not a thought he relished. To split up the team and individually attempt to break through the enemy positions was a formula for disaster. But it was much better than being surrounded at night by an overpowering enemy force, and especially without the benefit of close air support.

At 2300 hours Division ordered the mission aborted. All helicopters involved with the rescue attempt were ordered to return to Phu Bai immediately. With the weather closing in and enemy resolve increasing, no further attempts were to be made to pull out Team Polar Bear until the next morning.

Paige listened to the order over the radio and momentarily fought back the urge to transmit a panicked plea for help, but he knew that there was little that God, the commanding general, or anyone else could do about his team's situation. If the helicopters remained on station much longer, they would have been flying blind. With a feeling of resignation, Paige accepted the news that rescue efforts were to be abandoned. Besides, he had already begun to suspect that the extraction effort was playing out. He did not blame anyone in particular, but the

Platoon Sergeant Richard "Bernie" Burnell—a legend in his own time, February 1969. (Author's collection)

Sgt. Kenn Miller and WO Barry Schreiber after a "hot" ladder extraction in February 1969. (Author's collection)

Left to right: L Company Rangers Gary Linderer, Ray Zoschak, and Jim Schwartz, February 1969. (Author's collection)

Ranger S.Sgt. "Contact" Johnson flying bellyman on a patrol insertion in March 1969. (Author's collection)

First platoon "heavy team" after a mission near Leech Island, April 1969. (Basil Leussis collection)

Sgt. Larry Closson, left, and Sgt. Gary Linderer seconds before being struck by lightning on the side of Hamburger Hill in the Ashau Valley, April 23, 1969. (Author's collection)

First Lieutenant Owen "OD" Williams and S.Sgt. Ron Reynolds. Reynolds was KIA in May 1969. (Author's collection)

Sgt. Keith Hammond, KIA May 1969. (Author's collection)

Ranger patrol on a training mission. Sgt. Bill Marcy (on radio) was KIA in May 1969. (Basil Leussis collection)

Sgt. Kenn Miller flashes a mirror to mark his position while RTO Spec 4 Marvel McCann makes radio contact in May 1969. (Author's collection)

Set up in a night defense perimeter, 1970. (Ray Price collection)

L Company 1st Sgt. Neal Gentry and commanding officer
Capt. David Ohle at the entrance to the Company Tactical
Operations Center in 1970. (Ray Price collection)

L Company Ranger
checking NVA structure
deep in the jungle
somewhere in northern I
Corps in 1971. (Ray Price
collection)

L Company Ranger clearing an enemy bunker somewhere in northern I Corps in 1971. (Ray Price collection)

Sgt. Herman Brown receiving the Distinguished Service Cross in 1971. (Ray Price collection)

A four-man wiretap team after a harrowing mission in the Ashau Valley in mid-1971. Left to right: 1st Lt. James Smith, Sgt. Harold Kaiama, S.Sgt. Jim Bates, and Sgt. Ray Price. (Ray Price collection)

Spec 4 Antonelli of Team Polar Bear "packing heavy" for a mission in 1970. (Jeff Paige collection)

Company commander Capt. Robert Guy (with beer) relaxing with his Rangers in 1970. Fraternization was not frowned upon in the Rangers. (Jeff Paige collection)

Ranger team leaders S.Sgt.s Jim "Lobo" Bates and Jeff "Pengun" Paige (in T-shirts), enjoying a beer with their teammates between missions. (Jeff Paige collection)

Shot from the chase ship of a Huey slick approaching an LZ along the Song Bo in 1969. (Author's collection)

prospect of being deserted in the face of the enemy was difficult to accept.

When Paige finally summoned the courage to inform the rest of his teammates of their predicament, no one panicked. His pride in their courage was unbounded. In the face of the devastating realization that they would soon be on their own at night, surrounded in the middle of "Indian country," his Rangers were still the consummate professionals.

To attempt a breakout, Paige decided to divide the team into two separate elements. Annelli, Conrad, and Suko would move out first, while he and Buehrig would follow their own E&E route a few minutes behind them. Buehrig was the "cherry" on the team, so Paige decided to keep with him. The odds of everyone making it out of the trap were remote, but their chances of survival were totally nonexistent if they remained where they were for the rest of the night.

Sergeant Paige sent Suko and Annelli on a close-in scout outside the team's defense perimeter to determine if there were any open escape routes through the enemy forces moving in the brush around them. The two Rangers crawled out about forty to fifty meters before returning. Suko reported that there were enemy soldiers everywhere to their north. Annelli stated that there seemed to be no movement at all to the east, at least out as far as he had dared to venture. Armed with this new information, Paige decided to escape and evade to the east. At least it was in the general direction of friendly forces, albeit over twenty klicks away.

The team leader radioed Captain Guy that Polar Bear understood what was happening and gave the C&C the azimuth for their E&E route. At least the rescue force the next morning would know where to look for survivors . . . or bodies.

Suddenly, the pilot of Banshee 5-4, an orbiting Huey rigged for command and control, radioed that he was going to make one final effort to extract the team. "Mark your position, we'll try to come in and get you out."

Immediately, a command voice broke in on the transmission and said, "Banshee 5-4, you are ordered to abort the mission."

Banshee 5-4's immediate response was classic, and gave heart to the trapped Rangers, "Get off the net, we're coming in."

Paige, searching for a way to signal the chopper without marking his location for every NVA soldier in the vicinity, grabbed Buehrig's M-79. He broke the grenade launcher open and shoved his strobe light into the chamber, then wrapped a "dew rag" over the end of the barrel to suppress the bright flash of the strobe light. When he was finished, he radioed Banshee 5-4 and told him to look for the flashing light. Banshee 5-4, still a good distance out from the team's location began moving toward them. Finally, Paige heard the pilot acknowledge that he had their signal in sight.

Soon the Rangers could hear the blacked-out Huey making its final approach. It seemed to take forever. Paige quickly shifted positions in an effort to get his teammates ready to make a dash for the helicopter, only to have Banshee 5-4 radio, *"Point it at me . . . Point it at me."*

Then Paige saw the running lights turned on in the blacked-out Huey. It was coming in slowly, directly at the team. The pilot radioed one final time, telling the Ranger team leader to have one of his men get in each of the two transmission wells with his door gunners. The other three team members were to squeeze into the cabin. Paige acknowledged the transmission and turned to instruct his teammates what they were to do.

Escorted by a Cobra gunship on each flank, Banshee 5-4 maneuvered carefully in over the LZ. It was forced to hover six to seven feet above the ground due to the very real danger of a blade strike in the surrounding vegetation.

As the Huey came to a stationary hover, Conrad, Buehrig, and Annelli broke out of the brush and made a mad dash for the skids, while Suko and Paige held back to cover them. Suddenly, a ChiCom grenade exploded among the three Rangers running for the helicopter, wounding Buehrig in the chest. The wound was superficial, barely slowing down the young Ranger as he pulled himself up into the waiting aircraft.

When the first three Rangers were safely inside, Suko and Paige rose from cover and sprinted for the ship. When they reached the skids the six-two team leader got under the shorter Suko and hoisted him toward the waiting hands of Annelli and Conrad, who pulled him inside. Looking around to make sure no one else was still on the ground, Paige slung his weapon and was getting ready to leap for the skids when an M-16 fell from the open cabin of the hovering helicopter, narrowly missing him. Quickly, he reached down, snatched up the weapon and tossed it back up into the open cabin, then jumped for the skids. With the help of two of his men, Paige was soon sprawled on his stomach across the cabin floor of the helicopter.

The aircraft commander of Banshee 5-4 wasted little time getting out of the LZ. Because of the surrounding darkness and the height of the vegetation, the courageous pilot was forced to rise straight up until he gained enough altitude to maneuver. Then he dropped his nose to pick up forward airspeed and shot out of there like the hounds of hell were chewing at his tail boom.

During the rescue operation muzzle flashes from a multitude of enemy weapons lit up the hillside all around them, as tracers crisscrossed back and forth through their tiny airspace. It was a miracle that the aircraft received no hits.

When Banshee 5-4 landed on the acid pad at Camp Eagle, the entire company had turned out to welcome Team Polar Bear back from the dead. Most of the Rangers had been listening on the radio at the company TOC when it was decided to abort the rescue mission and abandon the team. Each of them must have wondered at that moment how he would have felt if he had been on the ground with Polar Bear. When the word had finally come in that Banshee 5-4 was attempting a final rescue effort, every Ranger held his breath. Then the radio went dead during the height of the extraction. But minutes later the gathered Rangers heard the pilot say, "They're out."

Word that Polar Bear was safe brought uncontrolled cheering from the recon men crowded inside the TOC. The good news quickly flashed through the company area. The Rangers were ecstatic. At the last minute five of their comrades had been pulled from the hands of the enemy.

A mission had come to an end, but there would be no rest for the weary Rangers. The next day Team Polar Bear was briefed for yet another mission. This time they would be going out in the evening to beef up a radio relay team in the vicinity of their previous night's contact.

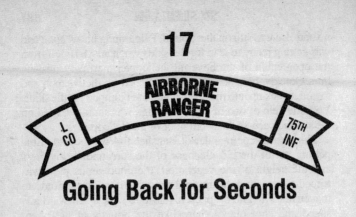

17

Going Back for Seconds

Ranger Sergeant Riley Cox was a true warrior and a loyal teammate, but above all he was a survivor. Severely wounded in the stomach, arm, and neck on a November 20, 1968, heavy team mission with F Company, 58th Infantry (LRP), Cox returned to the unit, now L Company, 75th Infantry (Ranger), nearly a year later in the fall of 1969. To accomplish this feat, Cox had to convince a number of Army doctors that he had fully recovered from his wounds and was ready to return to active duty. But he had not fully recovered—no one fully recovers from the kinds of wounds that Cox had sustained. During his drawn-out year in a military hospital he had learned to accept the physical pain. It was infinitely better than the emotional pain he had experienced dealing with the fact that he still had buddies fighting and dying back in South Vietnam while he lay mending in a stateside hospital.

Cox's F Company had been deactivated on February 1, 1969, then immediately reactivated as L Company, 75th Infantry (Ranger). But nothing had changed at all—nothing, that is, except the name. It was still the same kind of people, pulling the same kind of missions, and Riley Cox needed to be a part of it.

In early January 1970, Riley Cox found himself a member of a twelve-man heavy team on a reconnaissance mission deep into the rugged mountains west of Quang Tri. The Rangers were not going in "heavy" because bigger teams were quieter—they were going in "heavy" because in the "real bad areas" twelve men can last longer in a firefight than six. And this AO was one of those "real bad areas."

It was still the middle of the annual monsoon season in northern I Corps, and there was always the danger of a long range patrol getting socked in and forced to remain on the ground until the weather turned better. This possibility forced the Rangers to carry spare batteries and extra food, and for those who anticipated the worst—plenty of additional ammunition.

Inclement weather also meant little or no tactical air support, and for the small, lightly armed long range reconnaissance patrols, air support was often the only difference between living and dying.

The 2/17th Cav was flying slicks and gunships in direct support of Lima Company. They knew that the Rangers put their lives on the line every time they jumped off a skid. The pilots and crewmen respected the Rangers and they frequently put aside caution and common sense to do what was necessary to recover the young warriors.

The teams of Sergeants Vance and Chapman were combined to make up the heavy team. Sergeant Kline was Vance's assistant team leader and Cox was Chapman's ATL. They were to conduct a routine LRRP deep into the mountains where an NVA battalion was suspected to be operating.

The initial insertion went smoothly, but instead of both teams going in on a single LZ, as originally planned, Vance's team was dropped in low on the side of a primary ridgeline, and Chapman's team was inserted higher up on the same ridgeline, but just off the crest.

After the two teams lay dog for nearly twenty minutes, they broke radio silence long enough to establish contact with each other. The two team leaders then decided to move their teams toward each other to effect a quick link-up. Until they managed to accomplish this maneuver, they would not be able to carry out their mission.

Almost immediately upon moving out, Chapman's team

hit a "red-ball"—a heavily used high-speed trail. Fresh footprints were pressed deeply into the soft surface of the trail.
Rainwater from a recent downpour had not yet seeped back
into the tracks. There were also a number of trail markers
along the side of the red-ball. Just off the left flank of the
ridgeline there was a large, fairly open clearing. The high-
speed trail crossed the clearing then disappeared into the
triple canopy just ahead.

After making certain there were no enemy troops on the
trail, Chapman's team quickly crossed it and linked up with
Vance's team coming up the ridge. The combined teams then
moved quickly into some heavy cover and set up security.
Vance called in a sit rep to report that the two teams had linked
up and discovered a trail.

Captain Guy, still on station in the C&C aircraft a few miles
away, radioed instructions for the patrol to take Vance's Kit
Carson scout back to check out the trail markers, in the hope
that he would be able to read them and understand what they
meant.

Cox was nervous. When he spotted the footprints and
noticed that they had not yet filled with rainwater, he immediately straightened the pins on his grenades and took a couple of
bandoleers of ammunition from the top of his rucksack. Two of
the newer Rangers on the team asked Cox what he was doing.
He told them that the enemy was close and he was getting
ready.

Vance and Kline moved over to where Cox was standing
and asked him to go back with them and the Kit Carson scout
to check out the trail markers. He complied, but not without
expressing his reservations. As the four men neared the spot in
the trail, Cox got a weird feeling and held back. During the
entire trip back to the trail markings the Kit Carson scout kept
whispering, "Beaucoup VC! Beaucoup VC!" But only Cox
seemed to be paying any attention to him.

When they finally reached the trail markers, Vance looked
back over his shoulder and motioned for Cox to move up to
join them. Just then Cox froze; Vance's eyes shifted to the right
and his lower jaw dropped.

Suddenly, Cox caught sight of movement out of the corner

of his eye. He instinctively turned and sprayed the area with his M-16, then put out a quick frag before stopping to change magazines. When the grenade went off, all hell broke loose. Unseen by any of the Rangers or the Kit Carson scout, an NVA unit had moved up behind the team. When Cox opened up and tossed out the frag, the enemy force reacted by immediately swinging on line and assaulting the Rangers' position.

AK rounds ripped through the foliage around them as another grenade exploded among the enemy soldiers. The NVA were taking casualties, lots of casualties, but it didn't seem to slow them. They were still coming.

Then from back up the trail the rest of the Rangers opened up. Spec 4 Ralph Holloway, carrying an M-60 with a hundred-round belt already in the feed tray, put down an initial heavy burst that chewed up the jungle around the assaulting NVA. At such close range the machine gun broke up the attack and sent the surviving enemy soldiers reeling back into the trees.

Vance and Kline turned to Cox and asked him what they should do. Cox answered quickly, "Put some frags up the ridge and some more down below, and then let's get back to the rest of the team." Vance nodded in agreement, then ordered the Rangers and the Kit Carson scout to start chucking fragmentation grenades. In the exchange of fire that followed, Holloway took an AK round through the arm just as he released his last grenade. It was not a life-threatening wound, but Holloway was out of the fight and in a lot of pain, and needed to be evacuated at the first opportunity.

After the two Ranger elements had successfully joined up again, Vance grabbed the radio and requested a medevac. He also called for and directed air strikes on the enemy forces occupying the ridgeline above them. While they were waiting for the Eagle Dustoff aircraft to arrive, the team detected the sounds of more enemy soldiers moving up below them. The Rangers responded immediately by putting out a large number of fragmentation grenades to keep the enemy at bay. It worked, and the movement quickly ceased.

When the medevac arrived and lifted Holloway out, the accompanying Cobra gunships reported that they were taking heavy ground fire. In light of the fact that the enemy was still in an offensive frame of mind, Captain Guy decided to extract both teams at that time. His Rangers had stirred up enough hornets for one day.

As the Rangers moved into heavy cover to await the arrival of the lift ships, the enemy fire began to die off. Cobra gunships prowled overhead, anxiously waiting for the NVA's next move. A few Rangers took the opportunity to light up long awaited cigarettes. Patrol discipline was no longer necessary, since the enemy had a good idea where the Americans were located.

Cox, a nonsmoker, passed on the cigarettes. However, a longtime fan of the culinary arts, he decided that his appetite could use some care. He dropped to his knees, broke out a Lurp ration and began to chow down with relish. Cox had never met a Lurp ration he didn't like. As he was joyfully finishing his meal, he glanced at his watch to see how much longer it would be before the helicopters arrived, only to discover that a narrow rivulet of blood was running down his right arm. A closer look revealed that sometime during the battle a small piece of shrapnel had gouged a deep furrow along his wrist right next to his metal watchband.

"Hey," he announced, more in surprise than in pain, "I've been hit!"

Suddenly worried about their veteran comrade, Chapman and Vance moved over to take a look at Cox's wound. They were relieved that it wasn't really serious, but decided to be safe and medevac him out of the LZ anyway. Cox didn't want to go, but the two team leaders had decided that since the C&C was going to pull out both teams anyway, Cox might as well get an early out from the bush.

The medevac arrived soon, lowered a penetrator and hoisted Cox out of the jungle. Twenty minutes later the aircraft dropped him off at the surgical evacuation hospital at Quang Tri where Army doctors soon had him stitched up and ready to go again. Cox flagged down a ride back to Camp Eagle on a "Phoenix" bird from the 158th Aviation Battalion that was getting ready to return to Camp Evans after spending a full week up at Quang Tri flying for CCN (Command & Control North) teams running missions on both sides of the border.

When Cox finally arrived back at Camp Eagle, his

fellow Rangers seemed almost surprised to see him again. The remainder of the two teams had already returned and broken the news of Cox's and Holloway's wounds. Most of his comrades had expressed their concern that it had been Cox's drinking hand that had gotten hit. But the burly Ranger was quick to ease their worries. He nodded his head wisely, and pointed out to them that he'd been with the Lurps in '68, and while he was there had learned how to drink beer with either hand—like a real man.

18

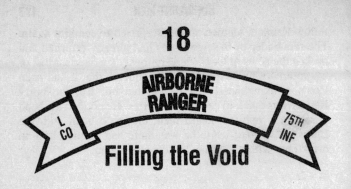

AIRBORNE RANGER

L CO

75TH INF

Filling the Void

During the Vietnam War, U.S. Army Rangers were trained to fill any role on the team that circumstances called for. If the team leader or assistant team leader went down, there was always that assurance that someone could step up to take over the leadership role on the patrol.

On January 8, 1970, Staff Sergeant James Salter received a warning order for an operation deep in the mountains west of Quang Tri. It was scheduled to be a simple three-day reconnaissance patrol to locate NVA units suspected of moving into the area in preparation for Tet attacks against Quang Tri City. This was on the back side of the winter monsoon and the weather was still nasty and unpredictable.

Captain Guy spent the better part of two days in the C&C ship flying high above the general patrol area in an attempt to insert the team, but each time he located a brief window or opening in the fog and low overcast, it quickly closed up before the team could infiltrate. Finally, late in the morning on January 11, Captain Guy radioed the helicopters sitting on pad alert at Quang Tri to "crank 'em up."

Back at the strip, Sergeants Salter and Jones got their team together in a hurry and climbed aboard the waiting slick. The two NCOs, both stateside shake 'n' bakes," were taking out a team of cherries—new guys who hadn't yet had their innocence shattered by an AK-47 round or an RPG rocket buzzing by their ears. Salter had been around for a while, but Jones was going out on his very first patrol.

Sergeant Riley Cox, an experienced second tour Ranger, had recently been assigned to Salter's team, but he'd been wounded a few days before and was still suffering from a serious bout of immersion foot. Captain Guy and First Sergeant William Unzicker didn't like sending the team out with only a single veteran on board, but they had just lost a large number of veteran Rangers to DEROS (rotation to the U.S. at the end of an assignment to Vietnam), causing a major shortage of experienced men.

The single Huey slick had already completed several false insertions when it suddenly plunged from its flight path, then flared out seconds later directly over the long range patrol's designated LZ. The six Rangers dropped quickly to the ground, only to discover to their horror that they had inserted into the center of an enemy bunker complex. This unexpected revelation caused a noticeable increase in the Rangers' pucker factor, but once they realized that the bunker complex was abandoned, they began to breathe a little easier. Salter reluctantly released the helicopters as he lay hidden in the dense cover.

Shortly after the team hit the ground, the sky closed over and it began to rain. The weather continued to deteriorate as the Rangers moved quickly into heavy cover just off the LZ to lay dog. After twenty long minutes of intense watching and listening, the patrol leader decided they had gotten in clean. He signaled for the team to break cover and move ahead to more thoroughly check out the bunkers that lay before them. Sergeants Salter and Jones were standing together next to the nearest bunker debating their next move when a tremendous explosion erupted at their feet, knocking both Rangers to the ground.

When the smoke and debris finally settled, the remaining Americans moved forward to help the team's two senior NCOs. They discovered that Sergeant Jones had died instantly after being hit in the chest by shrapnel from the unknown explosive device.

Salter, too, was dead. But the Rangers could find no wound

on him anywhere, until they prepared to move his body back to
the LZ and saw that the entire back of his head was missing.

As the surviving Rangers began to drag their slain comrades
behind cover, a heavy volume of automatic weapons fire
rained on them from several directions. The fire was so intense
that it forced them to leave the bodies of Salter and Jones
where they lay.

Within minutes there was heavy enemy movement on both
their flanks, in front of their position and behind them. They
were not merely heavily outnumbered, but completely surrounded. And to make matters worse, without the leadership of
Salter and Jones, the inexperienced soldiers were each fighting
a desperate personal battle to control the panic tearing at them.

When the NVA began firing RPGs (large caliber rifle
grenades) into their perimeter, the four surviving Rangers figured the battle was about all over for them; they would not be
able to survive without outside help. Spec 4 Herman Brown, a
black soldier from the deep South, stepped forward to take
over the reins of leadership on the team.

Brown immediately directed the remaining three Rangers
still with him to keep the enemy off his back while he established commo with the radio relay team several klicks away,
asking them to call back the two Cobra gunships that were
escorting the insertion slick.

Minutes later the two Cobras were making devastating gun
runs against the enemy positions. Brown took advantage of the
situation to hurriedly request a medevac to extract the bodies
of the two Ranger NCOs who had been killed in the initial
ambush. With an aircraft from Eagle Dustoff on the way to the
Rangers' location, Brown left his position and exposed himself
to enemy fire to crawl out and drag the bodies of his two dead
comrades back into the perimeter.

After recovering his dead, Brown continued to direct the
gunships against the enemy forces surrounding the team, preventing the NVA soldiers from maneuvering to put more
pressure on the trapped patrol.

When the dustoff aircraft finally arrived on the scene, it
hovered over the LZ and lowered a jungle penetrator for
the bodies. The recovery seemed to take forever, and as the

medevac banked away from the LZ, the rain slackened and a dense fog bank rolled in over the team.

The remaining four Rangers battled the enemy and waited desperately for their own extraction ship to arrive. But with the weather socked in around them, none of them expected to be rescued. As their ammo began to run low, the Rangers realized that unless help arrived in the very near future, they weren't going to make it out of this one.

Suddenly, Brown heard traffic on the PRC-25. He grabbed at the handset. The CO was high overhead in the C&C aircraft. Brown was to hang on because L Company volunteer reinforcements were on their way to Quang Tri to stage out for a rescue operation. With the patrol's prospects of survival suddenly taking a turn for the better, the four neophyte Rangers resolutely fought on.

Several minutes later the Rangers heard an approaching helicopter. Believing it was their relief force on the way in, the Rangers began to lay down a heavy base of fire. But the aircraft they had heard approaching was an LOH scout helicopter from the 2/17th Cav that had worked its way through the fog in a desperate attempt to reach the stranded team. The reaction force from Camp Eagle had not yet reached Quang Tri.

When the pilot finally spotted Brown's orange panel stretched out in front of the team, he maneuvered in to pick up as many of the trapped Rangers as he could carry. With a crew of three already aboard the aircraft, the pilot could only extract one of the Rangers at a time—and this he did rather quickly. With three more Rangers still on the ground and his helicopter taking heavy enemy ground fire, the scout pilot banked his aircraft away from the LZ. Struggling for altitude in the swirling fog, the courageous pilot headed straight for the Ranger radio relay team located on a mountaintop not far away. He would drop off his passenger there, then return to the LZ to pick up another Ranger.

When the pilot returned to the team for the second time, the enemy ground fire had intensified. But the undaunted scout pilot darted in over the Rangers' position and hung the tiny aircraft fully exposed over the LZ while Brown assisted his two comrades into the now overloaded helicopter. When the two

men were finally aboard, Brown attempted to hang from the
skids, hoping at least to get out of the circle of death he
was trapped in. But the pilot soon discovered that he was
overloaded—someone would have to get off. Brown realized
the predicament he'd put the helicopter in and let go of the
skid. Grabbing up his weapon, he waved the chopper away and
turned to face the enemy. He knew for certain at that moment
that he would not be getting out.

Miraculously, the NVA failed to take advantage of the single
American Ranger still inside the perimeter. They could easily
have overrun his position, but for some reason they held back.
Whatever their motive, Brown was still alive when the scout
helicopter returned a third time for him. Running in under
cover of the fog, the small scout aircraft hovered over the
battlefield just long enough to take the valiant Ranger on
board.

Spec 4 Herman Brown was awarded the Distinguished Service Cross for his valor and leadership that day. He stepped forward to take over the leaderless team, willingly assuming the
responsibility for the lives of those Rangers who still survived.
A short time later, with rescue imminent, the young Ranger
voluntarily remained behind so his comrades could get out
first. Alone on the ground, he accepted the hand that fate had
dealt him. He took up a firing position and waited for the
enemy's final assault. Not once did he imagine that he would
survive that day.

```
                    AIRBORNE
                     RANGER
        L                        75TH
        CO                        INF
```

Teams Anteater and Aardvark

On February 26, 1970, Lima Company infilled four reconnaissance patrols into the vicinity of the abandoned Marine forward combat base at Khe Sanh. Shortly after the four teams inserted into their AOs, things began to unravel in a hurry. One patrol immediately radioed for an emergency medevac for a Ranger who had been injured on the insertion and was unable to patrol. A medevac flight out of Eagle Dustoff soon picked up the injured man.

On the second day of the operation the weather began to deteriorate, and all four patrols found themselves hampered by low cloud cover over their recon zones. Then the same team leader who had lost the member of his team on the first day was forced to request a second medevac for a team member who had become violently ill. This left them with only four Rangers remaining on the team. In addition, the team leader was concerned that the helicopter activity in and around his AO had likely alerted the enemy to the presence of an American patrol in the neighborhood.

Not far away, Sergeant Jim Rodarte had to radio for a medevac; one of his teammates had just come down with a similar malady. Fortunately for the now shorthanded Ranger patrols, despite all the helicopter activity, the NVA had chosen to remain out of sight.

Team Anteater, led by Ranger Staff Sergeant Don McElroy, was having its own problems. The patrol, consisting of McElroy; Sergeant Andy Ransom, the assistant team leader; Sergeant John Fowler; Spec 4s Frank Johnson, Burgess Wetta, and Larry Dalton, was hopelessly lost. Not long after the team had inserted, McElroy was having a difficult time matching the local terrain features with the contour lines on his map. Rather than admit he wasn't sure where he was, McElroy led the team on, not realizing the danger he was putting them in. The patrol could see Highway QL9 to their south, right where it was supposed to be, but McElroy had no idea what section of the road they were viewing.

On the fourth day of the five-day patrols, the team leader of the understrength team once again had to radio the forward TOC at Quang Tri, this time to request a medevac for a man on his team who had just developed a severe case of stomach cramps and nausea. Now, with only three men remaining of the original six-man patrol, the team would be in big trouble if they made contact.

McElroy's patrol was still sitting back in the grass above QL9, the main road that ran from Quang Tri west into Laos. Sergeant McElroy, a newly acquired product of the Noncommissioned Officer's Course at Fort Benning, Georgia, was still lost. Either someone had come in and restructured their AO or McElroy's Team 2-4 was off their map completely. Unable to call in a marker round because of the proximity of the other three recon teams, McElroy decided to move his team down along the edge of the road in an attempt to get a fix on their position.

Team Aardvark, under the able leadership of Staff Sergeant Jim Bates, was set up in the elephant grass on the north side of QL9 just across the road from the old abandoned village of Khe Sanh. Sergeant Dave Weeks, another veteran Ranger, was the team's assistant team leader. Sergeant Mark Martin, Spec 4s Morgucz and McCreary, and PFC Buehrig made up the rest of the team.

Morgucz and McCreary were new in the Ranger company, and the two soldiers sought out each other's company. Now, with the patrol winding down, they sat next to each other in the grass on the east end of the patrol, keeping their eyes on the road and enjoying the scenery. The weather was pleasant and that part of South Vietnam was one of the most attractive parts of the country.

Suddenly, McCreary thought he saw something out in the grass to his left. Without alerting Morgucz, he forced himself to sit up a little higher to get a better view, and spotted the upper body and head of a soldier above the grass. Eyes wide with fear, the young Ranger elbowed Morgucz and nodded out toward the grass. When Morgucz realized that the black Ranger at his side had seen something, he, too, straightened up and raised his head to look over the cover they were hidden in. He saw two soldiers out in the grass to his left. It appeared they were trying to get a compass bearing on some hills to the north. Morgucz and McCreary were in a "situation." Bates, a legend in the company and an intimidating NCO on his good days, had told the two cherries not to open fire on the enemy unless they were fired upon first. At the time, the advice sounded good. But now, with two or more potentially hostile people less than twenty-five meters away, it didn't seem like such a good idea. Morgucz looked back to where Bates and Weeks were sitting along the rim of an old bomb crater and realized he wouldn't be able to attract their attention without alerting the two soldiers out in the grass.

Morgucz waited a few minutes, then raised up to get a second look, having already made up his mind that he would open fire if the enemy spotted him. That's when he recognized the two men as Johnson and Wetta from Team Anteater. Morgucz immediately thought, What in the hell are they doing in Aardvark's recon zone?

Now he had a "real" dilemma on his hands. He had to alert the rest of his team to let them know there were "people" in the grass to their left, and that these "people" were "friendlies." He also had to get the attention of the "friendlies" and let them know that they had people west of them—people who were on "their" side. This was one time that the element of surprise could get a whole lot of the wrong people killed in a hurry.

Morgucz finally got Bates's attention and moved over to tell him what was going on. He could see that Bates was immediately aware of the danger.

Bates reacted by calling out in a whisper, *"Johnson ... Wetta ... Don't Shoot! It's Anteater."* Fortunately for everyone concerned, it worked.

After the two teams had linked up and established a larger perimeter, setting up security along the road, Bates got together with McElroy and Ransom in the bomb crater to show them where they were on the map. While the patrol leaders had their strategy meeting, Team Aardvark's Fowler looked over at Morgucz and whispered, "You know who really runs this team?"

When Morgucz shook his head, Fowler replied, "Ransom!" It was obvious to Morgucz and McCreary that the members of Team Aardvark were not too happy with their shake 'n' bake team leader, McElroy.

The two team leaders decided that with the extraction set for the next morning, it was too late in the patrol to split up now. Aardvark and Anteater would stay together and set up an ambush along the highway. Just before the two teams had linked up, Anteater had discovered a huge ball of rice and an unlit marijuana cigarette lying innocently in the middle of the highway. Realizing that the enemy soldiers who owned these items had to be nearby somewhere, the two team leaders decided to ambush the road just west of the old village of Khe Sanh. Thirty minutes later the teams were set up in a line ambush in the grass along QL9.

Specialist Fowler and Corporal Johnson were outposted on the extreme east flank of the ambush. Sometime during the night, the last night of the patrol, the two Rangers were sitting side by side when they caught a brief whiff of the rotten-fish smell given off by NVA soldiers because of the fermented fish sauce they used as a condiment. Several minutes later they spotted what looked like a number of flashlights flickering on a nearby hill just east of the team's position. The low intensity lights remained on in the same vicinity for a short period of time, then began to go out. The two Rangers guessed that the lights probably belonged to an enemy unit preparing to bed down for the night. With a little luck the Ranger patrol would have some uninvited visitors in its kill zone sometime early the next day.

In the morning the Rangers remained fully alert and ready in their ambush positions until 0800 hours. They were scheduled to be extracted at 1000 hours, and it now seemed likely that the enemy wasn't going to show up, at least not along an open stretch of road in broad daylight. Bates gave the order to pick up their claymores and their equipment and move across the road into the dense brush on the opposite side of the highway to await arrival of the extraction slicks.

At 0945, Specialist Burgess Wetta and Corporal Frank Johnson were sitting together in thick cover on the east side of the Rangers' perimeter when Wetta thought he heard a noise out on the road. He alerted Johnson, but when he tried to pass the word to the rest of the patrol, he was unable to get anyone's attention; the remaining members of the twelve-man patrol were spread out in the brush along the road, most engaged in low volume small talk, whispering among themselves and far too relaxed for their own good in that part of South Vietnam. The knowledge that their impending return to the security of Camp Eagle was less than twenty minutes away might have lulled them into a false sense of security. Johnson, too, repeatedly tried to get their attention to quiet them down, but no one seemed to be paying any heed to the two Rangers out on flank security. While Johnson focused on alerting the rest of the patrol, Wetta carefully peered through the brush to his front to see if he could detect anything out on the road.

Suddenly, Johnson spotted a lone NVA soldier squatting out in the center of the road just east of their position. He slowly raised his weapon to open up on the enemy soldier when he noticed that Staff Sergeant McElroy and PFC Buehrig were sitting right in his line of fire. The two Rangers were both unaware of what was going down.

Johnson wasn't sure if it was some movement or a sound, but the NVA soldier spotted McElroy and Buehrig and immediately ducked down out of sight. Staying low to the ground, the enemy soldier ran back up the road toward a larger group of NVA that had apparently been moving up behind him.

On the other side of Johnson and Wetta, Paul Morgucz had

also seen the NVA soldier. He was shocked at the size of the man. Morgucz estimated that he was six feet tall or better. When he saw the enemy soldier spot McElroy and Buehrig, he knew the time had come for him to disregard Bates's instructions. Jumping to his feet, he opened fire at the fleeing soldier.

Rangers Wetta and Johnson had also realized the danger, and the two men jumped up, opened up on the fleeing NVA, then shifted their fire onto the cluster of enemy soldiers standing back up the road. Before the surprised NVA could react, Johnson heaved a frag into their midst, wounding two of them.

Johnson and Wetta had managed to put multiple rounds into the oversized NVA point man. Badly wounded, he ran across the road and fell into the bomb crater that had served as the Rangers' command center the night before.

While the rest of the NVA headed for the nearest cover, one of them hesitated long enough to stop and return fire, but managed to miss everyone inside the Rangers' perimeter. Other than Wetta, Johnson, and Morgucz, none of the other Rangers had yet spotted any of the NVA. They were now looking about, frantically trying to figure out what in the hell their comrades were shooting at.

Johnson and Wetta quickly shouted to inform the rest of the team where the danger was. When he heard what had just happened, Bates yelled, *"Oh boy, contact!"* The Ranger NCO had a reputation to live up to and combat was a big part of his agenda. From that moment the patrol was on full alert, waiting for the NVA to make the next move.

Twenty minutes later an LOH scout helicopter from the 2/17th Cavalry arrived on the scene. Bates got him on the radio and asked him to "box" their position. Without a second's hesitation, the pilot turned and buzzed down the road, firing a sustained burst from his machine gun into the brush along the far edge of the trace, then turned again and made a second run across the back side of the patrol's perimeter. Two more passes and the scout pilot had completed his mission.

Morgucz was stunned. He had never seen minigun fire

impact that close before. He swore under his breath that the rounds had passed within five meters of his feet.

As the aircraft shot past the team's location, the hotshot chopper pilot radioed that he had a body in the bomb crater across the road and east of the team's position. He also reported that there appeared to be three or four NVA rucksacks sitting abandoned in the middle of the dirt track.

After some animated discussion on the subject, Wetta, Ransom, Johnson, and Morgucz crept out into the open highway to retrieve the rucks. Wetta and Morgucz went after the two closest rucks, while Ransom and Johnson went after the two rucks farther up the road. Johnson reached the nearer of the two first, and knelt there next to it, covering Ransom as he leapfrogged forward to secure the last one.

Ransom reached the pack only to discover an NVA pith helmet lying in the road just beyond it. The Ranger assistant team leader smiled as he bent to retrieve it, and as he was bringing it up to put it on his head, the "dead" NVA soldier lying in the crater on the far side of the road suddenly returned to life, firing a single, unaimed round at Johnson that missed. However, the bullet did manage to hit Ransom, striking him between the thumb and forefinger of his right hand before exiting out the top of his wrist. The force of the round knocked the surprised Ranger off his feet and onto his back in the middle of the road.

Before anyone could fire at the enemy soldier, he dropped back down into the protection of the crater. Five seconds later the LOH was over the crater killing the "dead" NVA for the second time.

While the helicopter was dealing with the NVA in the crater, Johnson ran over to his injured teammate to cover him and see how badly he was hit. Satisfied that Ransom was all right, Johnson sent the wounded assistant team leader crawling back across the open road toward the Ranger perimeter, while he remained behind to provide cover fire. Before Ransom could reach the brush at the edge of the road, another NVA soldier opened up on him from a position farther up the highway.

Seeing that Ransom had escaped being hit a second time, Johnson spun around and returned fire, forcing the enemy soldier to flee for cover. With Ransom now safely inside the Rangers' perimeter, Johnson stooped to recover Ransom's rucksack and the two abandoned NVA rucks, then turned around and walked back to the patrol.

A short time later, the Cav scout helicopter returned to the Rangers' last location to extract the wounded assistant team leader. It circled the area a couple of times to check for any sign of enemy soldiers lying in ambush before setting down in the road opposite the Rangers' location. While Bates dressed Ransom's wound and got him ready to board the aircraft, Morgucz and Johnson moved to the east side of the landing site. They took up defensive positions at the edge of the brush to provide flank security in case some of the enemy soldiers decided to move back out to open fire on the helicopter.

With Ransom now safely on his way to an evac hospital at Quang Tri, a platoon-size reaction force from the Cav's Blues was flown in to search the AO for the remaining NVA soldiers. As they were getting into some semblance of a line to begin their sweep, the Rangers discovered that they were positioned out in front of the Blues' skirmish line. The pistol-wielding platoon leader commanding the reaction force started shouting orders in an abusive manner that obviously included the Rangers, and to make matters worse, the orders he had given were destined to get people killed. This didn't sit too well with Staff Sergeant James "Lobo" Bates, who had already decided that this "leg" officer wasn't going to tell his Rangers what to do. If he wanted to get his own men killed, that was his business, but no grunt second lieutenant was going to call the shots for Jim Bates's people.

As Bates and his Rangers stood up to confront this situation head on, a ChiCom grenade sailed over the top of the elephant grass and landed in the middle of the dirt road twenty-five meters away. The Rangers, who were closer to the grenade than the Blues, stood and watched it cook off. When it finally exploded, too far away to hit any of the Rangers, the lieutenant screamed, *"Who threw that grenade?"* When Bates slowly looked back over his shoulder and said, "NVA—" the loud-mouthed officer dove for the ground before Bates could finish his sentence.

When the lieutenant finally got his act together and got his people back on line, they swept perpendicular to the road up to the crater where the "dead" NVA was supposed to be lying. There was no one in the crater. During all of the excitement, the ballsy NVA had escaped into the brush along QL9.

The Rangers were incredulous. Wetta and Johnson had put rounds into him at a distance of only thirty meters. And when that didn't finish him off, the Cav scout pilot had filled his little crater with a three-second burst of minigun fire—enough to send anyone to visit his Buddha.

Johnson wanted to go into the brush after him—there were rules that had to be followed when you were a hunter. But Staff Sergeant Bates stopped him, ordering him to let the Blues handle it. But by the time the aero-rifle platoon managed to get itself reorganized and had swept through the brush around the crater, they were unable to find any sign of him.

Searching the captured enemy rucksacks, the Rangers discovered clothing, personal items, military hardware, and a large number of documents and maps. Some of the documents identified the NVA unit the Rangers had bumped into as a Communist Chinese engineer team that was sent to the area to survey QL9 for possible future military use. Among these documents were military orders, personal diaries, and an extensive map of the Khe Sanh area that appeared to be even more complete than the maps issued to the Rangers. This enemy map showed numerous, well-marked locations of NVA camp sites, transportation routes through the area, supply and ammo caches, and even the location of a reconnaissance mission that an L Company Ranger team had run in the vicinity on January 21. A number of the Rangers present had been on that particular mission, and found it demoralizing to think that the enemy had been able to piece together so much information about their patrol.

The team was extracted shortly afterward. Sergeant Ransom was later evacuated to Camp Zama, Japan, where neurological surgery was performed to save the nerves in his right hand. After the surgery, he was shipped back to an Army hospital in the States. The prognosis for full use of his hand was not good. Ransom's war in Southeast Asia was over.

The Rangers heard through the grapevine that the intelligence garnered from the documents and maps in the rucksacks they had captured was instrumental in the decision to invade Laos during Operation Lam Son 719. But grapevines are never truly reliable sources of communication, and they never learned if the rumor bore any semblance of truth.

The long range recon patrols into the northwest quadrant of I Corps in the vicinity of the abandoned Khe Sanh Marine base ushered in a new era of deadly missions for L Company—often beyond their own artillery fan. Lima Company, like its predecessors—1st Brigade LRRPs and F Company, 58th Infantry LRPs—had been reasonably lucky up to that point in the war. All three units had taken casualties, but the casualties had always been on the light side of moderate. But with the advent of intensive patrolling, in all types of weather, without adequate support, in some of the most remote areas of South Vietnam, that was about to change.

20

Team Grasshopper

In the Spring of 1970, L Company found itself running more and more heavy teams. This was not due as much to the nature of the missions being assigned as it was to the areas where they were conducted. An unusually large number of hot LZs and heavy contacts within the first few hours of insertion had created the need to strengthen the ability of the teams in the field to defend themselves. The heavy recon team was the answer.

Simultaneously, there was also a strong effort to develop new strategies to deceive the enemy into believing that he was dealing with something other than the conventional long range reconnaissance teams they were used to.

On April 8, 1970, Team Grasshopper, an eleven-man heavy team led by Sergeant Bernie Zentner, was assigned a reconnaissance patrol into a particularly bad AO. Other patrols had gone into the same area over the previous two months and had been shot out within hours of inserting. This time the Rangers inserted in four slicks, the last two being empty, to give anyone watching from a distance the idea that more than just a recon patrol had been inserted. The LZ was located on the finger of a major ridgeline, with a freewaylike trail running the length of the finger and a number of secondary trails spidering off the main trail. Unlike most enemy trail networks, this one had been relatively easy to spot during the overflight the day before.

Sergeant Steijen had been assigned to walk point for the patrol with a Kit Carson scout named Ut pulling his slack. Steijen, Ut, Spec 4 Paul "Blinky" Morgucz, and Sergeant Frank Johnson, were on the first slick into the LZ. They hit the ground running and immediately spotted a large number of NVA to their east sprinting downhill, away from the LZ.

An LOH scout helicopter covering the insertion spotted two more NVA on the trail above the LZ. The Rangers waited on the LZ for a few minutes to determine the enemy's intentions. When nothing happened, Sergeant Zentner decided to send a scouting party down the trail to the east in the same direction the larger group of NVA had disappeared into.

Rangers Steijen, Johnson, and the Kit Carson scout patrolled about a hundred meters away from the rest of the team before Ut observed several NVA on the move just ahead of them. Ut backed up slowly and reported to the two Rangers that he suspected a very large enemy base camp was located nearby.

The three men scampered back uphill to rejoin the recon team and to report the enemy sighting. It was obvious that the patrol had been spotted coming into the LZ and was compromised. They had lost the element of surprise, but could still salvage something out of the mission. Zentner decided that they would just have to outfox the enemy. The AO was hot, and the enemy would soon be out in force looking for them, so, after kicking around their options, the Rangers opted to beat them to the punch. They would move back down the hill to hunt the NVA and go after a body count. It would be the last thing the enemy would suspect.

Sergeant Zentner moved the team about five hundred meters from the LZ, then pulled his men into dense cover nearby and waited. It was nearly 1630, and they had already been on the ground for three hours. Zentner radioed quietly for the slicks to return to the LZ and fake an extraction, hoping the NVA would believe the Americans had departed.

As the first slick was climbing for altitude and the second slick was just pulling away from the LZ, an NVA .51 caliber heavy machine gun opened up on the extraction aircraft from a position less than seventy-five meters below the team. As the large caliber weapon pounded the helicopters, the Rangers heard the enemy soldiers laughing as they moved up the hill toward the hidden Rangers. Specialist Mike "Gringo" Blinston spotted them first, opening up and killing one before the NVA soldier could react. The remaining NVA immediately rushed the Rangers' perimeter.

Rangers Rob McSorley, Bernie Zentner, and Mike Blinston were in the direct line of the initial enemy assault. McSorley, reacting instantly, grabbed the M-60 from Zentner and opened up on the massed enemy soldiers, killing two outright, wounding several others, and throwing the enemy into confusion. In the heat of the moment, McSorley turned and yelled over his shoulder to his buddy, Frank Johnson, "Wow, I feel like John Wayne!"

Their frontal assault stopped, the NVA regrouped, then attempted to flank the Rangers. But McSorley was dealing out death with the M-60, while Johnson began lobbing multiple M-79 rounds that were air-bursting in the trees above the enemy. The NVA were forced to withdraw, giving up on the idea of flanking the team.

During the first twenty minutes of the enemy's initial assault, the patrol had difficulty establishing commo with the C&C aircraft circling off at a distance. When they finally established radio contact, they immediately requested gunship support.

A few minutes later the embattled Rangers had a Cobra circling overhead on station. McSorley, always ready with a bit of humor, commented on what a fuzzy feeling a friendly Cobra provided. Attempting to relay commo for the Ranger patrol, the Cobra pilot radioed in the team's contact, then dove down to place some suppressive fire on the enemy.

Suddenly, an RPG round exploded ten meters in front of the Rangers' small perimeter, showering the patrol with shrapnel. Fortunately, only Steijen was hit, catching a piece of metal in his left forearm.

Minutes later Mike Blinston took an AK-47 round through his left bicep. McSorley immediately spotted the NVA who had shot Blinston and killed him before he could duck back out of sight.

The firefight lasted for the better part of an hour, with small-arms fire and grenades being the primary unit of exchange. Finally, with darkness less than two hours away, Zentner decided to break contact and get back to the LZ. It was time for the patrol to grab its winnings and get out of town.

While the Rangers rounded up their gear and pulled back toward the LZ, Johnson remained behind to set up a claymore/willie pete package for their pursuers. Hidden in heavy cover, the young Ranger waited off to the side until nearly a dozen NVA were within his immediate kill zone. Then he squeezed the claymore's detonator and took down the entire group with a deadly blast of steel pellets and liquid fire.

Behind Johnson, the rest of the patrol had already moved nearly a hundred meters closer to the LZ, when McSorley, on point, ran headlong into a second enemy force maneuvering down on the Rangers from the high ground. The Ranger point man opened up, killing three NVA before his CAR-15 jammed. Before he could clear the malfunction, the remaining NVA in the party opened up, spraying him across the chest.

McSorley had been nearly ten meters ahead of his slackman and the rest of the patrol when he encountered the NVA column. Now the tough Ranger lay severely wounded ten meters out in the open with the NVA still firing up the team. Sergeant Bill McCabe was hit by an NVA bullet, which shattered his elbow and knocked him out of the fight. Zentner, coming up quickly in reaction to the enemy small-arms fire to their front, opened up with his M-60, dropping two more NVA.

By this time Johnson had caught up to Ut and Sergeant Gary Sands, who were waiting for him just up the trail from his successful one-man ambush. The four Rangers soon reached the rest of the patrol, just minutes after McSorley and McCabe had been hit. Getting word of their injuries, Johnson and Morgucz immediately headed to the front of the patrol.

Rob McSorley had been a good friend to Johnson and a mentor and hoochmate to Morgucz. Neither Ranger was about to leave him out in the open with NVA bullets flying overhead. But Sergeant Sands ordered them to stop and told both Rangers to remain in the rear to guard their back trail. Shouting that he would retrieve McSorley, Sands headed for the front of the patrol.

Minutes later Sands low-crawled ten meters across the fire-swept open area to reach McSorley, who, miraculously, was still alive. With enemy bullets buzzing past, Sands crawled back to the perimeter dragging the wounded and screaming McSorley behind him. Despite Sands's heroic effort, Ranger Rob McSorley died fifteen minutes later.

Above the Rangers' perimeter, the Cobra gunships began working their rockets and miniguns in closer then back out again, eventually silencing the enemy fire coming from below the Rangers' position. A short while later the heavy enemy fire coming from above them also grew quiet. Zentner took heart and yelled encouragement to the rest of his team. Arrangements were being made to extract them, and everyone had to hold on.

Finally it grew dark, and the danger of being overrun by the enemy was very real. Luckily for the Rangers, a C-130 Spooky flareship arrived on the scene and dropped parachute flares over the trapped Rangers for the better part of an hour.

When the Spooky finished illuminating the area, Johnson crawled out about twenty feet downhill from their perimeter, set up another claymore, then returned to his position. It was a good move because twenty minutes later Johnson, Morgucz, Ut, and Sands, who had just rejoined them, heard the NVA moving up from below. Johnson waited until the enemy soldiers were directly in front of the claymore before squeezing the clacker. The explosion devastated the enemy assault. With several more of the attacking force now slain, the NVA withdrew once again.

During the remainder of the night, staying just out of sight in the dense underbrush nearby, the NVA continued to maneuver around the trapped patrol. They were looking for a weak spot in the Ranger perimeter. The Americans kept them at bay with timely and accurate grenade tosses. Sands and Morgucz, both firm believers in the killing power of hand grenades, between them tossed out more than forty fragmentation grenades, killing and wounding a number of NVA who had moved within ten meters of the Ranger perimeter. Johnson, Bowland, and the Kit Carson scout killed several more with very accurate small-arms fire.

During the fight that night the enemy brought up more .51 caliber machine guns and opened fire on the circling slicks and gunships from two other nearby ridgelines. Surviving the next few hours was going to take a combination of skill, luck, and maybe a little Divine intervention.

Later that night a medevac helicopter attempted to hoist out the team's dead and wounded, but the enemy fire was too intense for the aircraft to remain on station. Before the aircraft departed, the peter pilot (copilot) was killed and the aircraft commander and the crew chief were wounded.

Just after midnight a Stinger gunship arrived over the patrol. The pilot requested that the Rangers mark their positions with a strobe light. One of the Rangers, Dave Hazelton, nicknamed "Canadian," moved into the center of the perimeter and took up a position lying on the ground on his left side. Extending his right arm, he held the flashing strobe skyward. He continued to do so through the remainder of the battle, lowering his arm only when there were no support aircraft on station.

The Stinger went into a short orbit over the trapped patrol, firing its miniguns in a tight arc around the Rangers' perimeter. During one of the Stinger's final gun runs, an errant burst of fire tore through the middle of the patrol without hitting anyone. That was a miracle!

At about 0020 hours, after the Stinger gunship had successfully suppressed much of the enemy small-arms and anti-aircraft fire, a pair of Huey slicks attempted to take out the casualties. The first slick moved in over the LZ and hovered directly above the team. The crew chief lowered a jungle penetrator, lifting out McSorley's body and the wounded McCabe. When the first aircraft had left the area, the second Huey edged in. The crew chief kicked out a pair of Maguire rigs, pulling out Steijen and Blinston, the last two wounded team members. That left six Rangers and their Kit Carson scout on the ground battling for their lives.

At 0205 hours, while a pair of Cobras worked over the surrounding area, another slick arrived on the scene and kicked out a ladder directly over the patrol's smoke-filled perimeter. With red, white, and green tracers still crisscrossing through the night, the remaining seven men booby-trapped their rucks and those of the dead and wounded who had already been extracted, then turned and climbed the swaying ladder into the waiting Huey.

The survivors arrived back at the Lima Company compound at 0315. They had been in heavy contact for over ten consecutive hours. Physically they were spent, and emotionally they were just beginning to feel the comedown that always followed a battle. The entire company had turned out to welcome them back. They were escorted to the mess hall by their jubilant comrades, where they were fed all the steak and eggs they could hold—a long-standing tradition for Lima Company Rangers returning from harm's way.

The team had lost one Ranger KIA, and three wounded. Four Cobra gunships and two Huey slicks had taken hits and sustained serious damage. The Stinger gunship had also been fired upon while supporting the trapped team. A medevac pilot was killed, while three other pilots and two crewmen were wounded. It was a tragic day for the U.S. Army, but the NVA had paid a much, much heavier price in manpower for the casualties and the damage caused.

A flight of U.S. Air Force fighter/bombers was ordered in that night to work over the battleground, and an infantry unit from the 101st Airborne Division was inserted the next day to search the area. The Rangers remembered to send word back that they had booby-trapped their gear, so none of the grunts would find himself on the short-arm end of a hot fragmentation grenade.

McSorley's loss was a serious blow to the company. The affable Ranger NCO was a brother, a teammate, and good friend to all. His death was doubly tough on his fellow Rangers because Sergeant Rob McSorley was a Canadian citizen who, unlike the rest of Lima Company, did not have to serve in Vietnam.

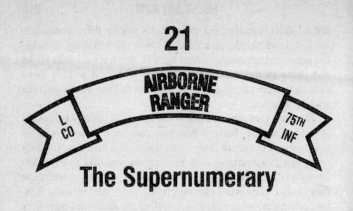

21

The Supernumerary

Not every day in L Company was all business. Sometimes a little humor managed to find its way into the Ranger compound. And it was always a good thing to see the veteran, hard-bitten Rangers cutting up and laughing, since laughter was the best remedy for the stress, tension, and anxiety they brought back with them from the field. Without a daily dose of levity, most of them would long before have surrendered to the pressures of their profession.

One such day occurred in early May 1970. The Ranger company had its own compound on the north perimeter of Camp Eagle. But the privilege of having one's compound on the outer perimeter carried with it the obligation of providing able-bodied soldiers to man the guard bunker on that portion of the perimeter during the hours of darkness. Every unit in the division that occupied a spot on the outer perimeter was responsible for that portion of the wire.

Since L Company had been attached to the 2/17th Cav, its four-man nightly guard post fell under the command and control of its parent unit's nightly officer of the guard. This boring and odious duty was offensive to the Rangers who drew it, and they treated it with the same respect they accorded KP duty and shit-burning details. Army SOP required those assigned to sentry or guard duty to report for inspection and to receive special orders prior to being posted.

Rangers in L Company, like most Rangers serving in Vietnam, had a real problem with U.S. Army standards and regulations. This was simply the product of the unconventional soldier's natural abhorrence of anything conventional. Most Rangers did not really mind manning the perimeter bunker one night every four to six weeks, although none of them believed that an NVA force short of a full regiment would be crazy enough to mount an attack on the Camp Eagle perimeter, especially through the Ranger compound. That would be sheer suicide! But to acknowledge the fact that Rangers were still part of the U.S. Army, they grudgingly agreed to comply. They just didn't look forward to the nightly routine of the officer of the guard's inspection and the formal posting of the guard.

Each evening, the Ranger company was required to send an armed four-man guard detail and an NCOIC to the Cav compound in full uniform, including the dreaded steel pot—a piece of equipment that was as out of place in a Ranger unit as an M-60 tank. Each Ranger in the guard mount was subjected to a personal inspection of himself, his flak jacket, and his weapon, usually conducted by an aviation warrant officer serving as the officer of the guard, who was even less inspired than the Rangers. After the inspection, the guard mount was given any special instructions and officially informed of the password and countersign. It wasn't an altogether unpleasant experience, just an ignoble one.

One evening, Spec 4 Herman Brown, a black Ranger, showed up for guard mount sporting a fresh haircut, spit-shined jungle boots, starched and pressed jungle fatigues, and with a weapon smelling strongly of cleaning solvent and gun oil. He was definitely standing tall and looking strac.

It was a well-known fact that no Lima Company Ranger had ever before shown up for a guard mount in full compliance with military regulations. In every case there was always some minor detail intentionally overlooked, which forced the OD to have to scrutinize each Ranger closely just to find it. It was just their way of saying, "Okay, dude, I'll do this despicable thing, but I'll be damned if I'm going to do it your way."

Spec 4 Brown, standing tall and strac, was definitely breaking new ground here. He was exceptional both in his appearance and in his demeanor, and everyone else in the guard mount paled in comparison. None of his fellow Rangers had the remotest idea what had come over him. He had failed to discuss this sudden total surrender to conformity with any of them, and was obviously too young and lacked enough time in service to be bucking for Sergeant Major of the Army!

When the officer of the guard, passing down the front rank of the guard mount, reached Brown, he stepped back in shocked surprise, studied Brown for a moment, and then broke into a huge smile. He had never before run across a soldier of Brown's caliber, and he was duly impressed. He snapped to and ordered the strac young Ranger to recite his general orders and his chain of command—the normal stumbling block for soldiers posted to guard mounts in a combat zone. But not for Specialist Fourth Class Herman Brown, who quickly reeled off his general orders, almost as if he'd been their original draftsman. Brown's clear and eloquent recitation of his chain of command was flawless, all the way up to the President of the United States—and beyond.

Undaunted by this miracle of modern warfare, the surprised warrant officer took Brown's weapon, checked the bore—which was immaculate—then eyeballed the chamber and magazine well, only to find that they, too, were spotless. When he finished, he released the bolt and held the weapon at port arms. Somewhat flustered by his inability to find a single flaw in Specialist Brown or his equipment, the young warrant officer decided he needed to say something derogatory. Noticing Brown's standard Ranger uniform, he made a comment concerning the Ranger's rather garish choice of camouflage fatigues over standard olive drab. It was a cheap shot, but it was better than nothing.

Smug, feeling that he'd just spoiled the young Ranger's effort to attain military perfection, the warrant officer couldn't help but grin. Then, with more flourish than thrust, he attempted to return Brown's weapon to him. Brown remained at attention and refused to take it!

Again the warrant officer tried to return the Ranger's

weapon to him. Again Brown refused to take it. This went on for several minutes, with Brown making no effort to accept the return of his weapon.

Finally, the flustered officer of the guard said, "Here, take your weapon." Brown's face showed no emotion as he answered slowly and deliberately, "I can't, sir."

A look of utter disbelief, then controlled rage, clouded the warrant officer's face as he responded angrily, "What do you mean you can't take this weapon? It's yours, isn't it?"

Brown kept his hands at his sides and answered again, "Sir, I have to take it back in the same condition I presented it to you."

This answer seemed only to confuse the officer of the guard even more. Once again he tried to hand the weapon back to the Ranger, standing rigidly at attention. Again Brown refused to accept it. Suddenly, the warrant officer looked back over his shoulder and whispered to a number of Cav troopers waiting their turn, "Well, what do I do?"

One of them answered, just loud enough for everyone in the formation to hear, "Sir, the bolt has to be locked to the rear, sir."

Now fully embarrassed, the officer of the guard turned back to face Brown, clumsily sliding the bolt to the rear and locking it. With an outward thrust he handed the weapon back to the Ranger, whose face still betrayed no expression. This time Brown accepted it.

While the warrant officer stood there in total defeat, head drooped and shoulders sagging, the young Ranger calmly rechecked the chamber, let the bolt go forward and pulled the trigger, then smartly executed an "order arms." He had made his point!

It was reputed that this was the only time that a Ranger ever served as a supernumerary of a guard detail in the history of the 101st Airborne Division.

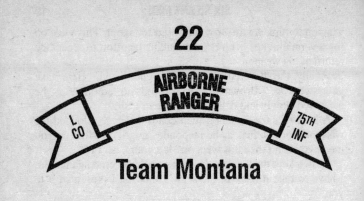

22

Team Montana

Lima Company had been running four to six recon teams at a time in the bush for nearly a month, which wouldn't have been so bad if the "bush" hadn't been in the vicinity of Khe Sanh, in the northwest corner of South Vietnam. On May 9, 1970, staging out of Quang Tri, five recon teams were inserted south of Highway QL9. One five-man patrol, led by Staff Sergeant Gary Sands, went in early that morning. With the team was Sergeant First Class Troy Rocha, who was on his first Lurp mission; Sergeant Larry Dalton, a new Ranger; Sergeant Frank Johnson; and Huan, a recently assigned Kit Carson scout. Huan had been a lieutenant in the North Vietnamese Army for thirteen years before surrendering to the Allies and becoming a scout.

With Johnson on point, the team moved quickly away from its LZ and immediately discovered a well-used trail with fresh sign indicating that a couple of LZ watchers had likely spotted the patrol inserting and made a mad dash for places unknown. Johnson followed the trail for approximately fifty meters before pulling the team into some dense cover to lay dog and listen for a while. Within minutes of going to ground, the team began to hear movement on the trail. After thirty minutes things finally quieted down. Waiting another ten to fifteen minutes to be safe, Johnson led the patrol back out onto the trail and moved them another fifty meters from the LZ before pulling off again, this time to set up an ambush.

That afternoon, Staff Sergeant Bates's team, about six klicks away from Sands's patrol, reported that they had just had a number of NVA walk right past them, but had to let them go by because they weren't yet set up for an ambush. Things were beginning to heat up quickly for the Lima Company patrols in the field; all of their RZs had plenty of fresh sign. Back at the staging area in Quang Tri, everyone had their fingers crossed that the shit wouldn't hit the fan everywhere at once.

At approximately 1630 hours Sergeant Jim Rodarte's team reported heavy enemy movement. A Cav Pink Team (Cobra and LOH observation helicopter) was sent in and fired up the area as the Rangers were pulled out and reinserted into another AO.

The following day Sands's patrol moved out of its ambush position early in the morning and followed the trail until it came to a wide, deep ravine. Johnson raised his hand to stop the patrol alongside the ravine. He motioned for the rest of the patrol to set up a defensive perimeter while he and Sands prepared to conduct a recon down into it.

The two Rangers soon discovered a high-speed trail that crossed a small creek running along the bottom of the ravine. In the mud were fresh tracks made by NVA sneakers. Johnson estimated the tracks were less than two hours old and had been put down by six enemy soldiers.

Johnson and Sands worked their way cautiously down the trail another fifteen meters, when they suddenly discovered an X made of leaves on the ground just ahead, an NVA trail sign indicating that a campsite or a rest area lay nearby. The two Rangers moved forward a few meters until Johnson spotted some kind of animal running down the hillside to their left and heading straight for them. The point man couldn't tell what it was because of the tall grass on the side of the hill, so he stepped back to see if he could get a better look at it. Suddenly, the two men heard a splash in the creek and the sounds of someone walking through the water. Whoever it was, he was between the two Rangers and the rest of their teammates.

Johnson turned and started to move toward the noise, then,

as he approached a bend in the trail six feet ahead, he suddenly came face-to-face with an NVA soldier. The man had his AK-47 at the ready, but Johnson was ready, and faster. He went for the enemy soldier's legs, hoping to wound him and take him alive. But the NVA had already started to turn and run, forcing Johnson to raise the aim of his weapon and put a round in the man's face. Mortally wounded, the enemy soldier staggered about ten meters before he collapsed and fell in the water. The two Rangers heard him thrashing around and fighting for breath.

Johnson and Sands moved ahead. The man had fallen face first into the creek and was sucking in water as he tried to breathe. He died as they walked up to him. Just as they reached the dead man, Sands whispered that he had spotted another NVA farther back in the stream when Johnson had fired up the first.

While Johnson pulled security, Sands searched through the dead man's ruck and found two sets of black pajamas, a girl's handkerchief, a bra, a ration of rice, a poncho, two poncho liners, and sandwich bags containing marijuana, heroin, and hashish.

Sands and Johnson finished checking the body, then moved cautiously back to where they'd left the rest of the team. After they linked up, Sands called in the contact, then instructed Johnson to lead them back to the LZ where they had come in.

At the LZ they were reinforced by Rodarte's patrol and a platoon of Blues. Johnson led them back to the site of the contact, then south to where they soon discovered an enemy base camp. It was the same camp Sands's team had found on their last patrol, except this time they'd come in from a different direction. They quickly searched the camp again and discovered that it had been used since the last time they were there.

At this point the Blues returned to the LZ to be lifted out, but Rodarte's team remained with Sands's patrol. The two team leaders felt that the AO was a little too hot for a five-man team, so they had called the TOC to request permission to merge the two patrols as a heavy team. Permission was granted; Sergeant First Class Troy Rocha didn't like the idea of the two recon teams joining forces, but he was not on the ground in the role of team leader, so he found himself overruled by Sands and Rodarte. The patrol, now eleven Rangers strong, moved silently into a dense stand of bamboo where they were still able to monitor the trail fifteen meters away and set up a defense perimeter.

During the early part of the night the patrol remained on fifty percent alert. Enemy soldiers passed by their location on several occasions, but did not appear to be looking for them. A little after midnight the movement out on the trail seemed to quiet down a little, so the patrol leader posted two men on guard at a time.

At 0430 hours on the morning of May 11, Sergeant Johnson was pulling guard shift when automatic weapons fire sounded from the direction of Staff Sergeant Ray Ellis's AO. A few minutes later he heard what sounded like six single pistol shots spaced about ten seconds apart. Concerned, Johnson tried to raise Ellis's RTO on the radio, but got no answer. Johnson then called the forward TOC at Quang Tri and asked the radio operator on duty to try to raise Ellis's team, but he, too, failed to get a response. Johnson woke the rest of the team.

Back at Camp Eagle, Sergeant First Class Jim Taylor, the first platoon's sergeant, had been awakened and informed of the situation up near Khe Sanh. He immediately asked for volunteers from among the Rangers still in the compound to mount a reaction force. Within the hour two slicks and a pair of gunships were on their way to Ellis's AO.

They reached the patrol area shortly after daylight and inserted on a small LZ close to Ellis's last reported position. At the site where the team had set up its night defense perimeter, the strong odor of gunpowder still hung in the calm morning air. Searching through the cover near the crest of the hill alongside a high-speed trail, they found the bodies of all six Rangers from Ellis's radio relay team. They had been killed to a man in their NDP while they slept.

Ellis had apparently set up his radio relay site on the crest of the highest hill in the area. It appeared that no one had taken the precaution to recon the immediate vicinity of the relay site, which would have led to the discovery that it was located right next to a major high-speed trail. Ellis's mission was to serve as

the radio relay for the other four Ranger patrols operating in the
bush around him. Apparently, Ellis had remained in the same
location for the two days his team was on the ground. From the
signs around their perimeter, it appeared that a small number of
NVA had walked right up to the Rangers as they lay sleeping
and killed them all. Three piles of empty brass around the
bodies indicated that only three enemy soldiers had fired.
Besides the bullets in their bodies, each Ranger had been shot
once in the head. Their weapons and one of the radios were
missing, but the rucks, web gear, and the second radio were
still in place. Ellis's body lay outside the perimeter, as if he'd
awakened during the shooting and attempted to get away. No
U.S. brass was found, indicating that the Rangers had not
returned fire. Sergeant Taylor later stated that he believed that
whoever was on guard had fallen asleep.

Killed in the ambush were Staff Sergeants Raymond
Ellis and Robert O'Conner, Sergeants Gary Baker and David
Munoz, Corporal George Fogleman, and Private First Class
Bryan Knight.

The Ranger reaction force secured the bodies and the gear of
their six slain comrades and brought them back to Camp Eagle.
It was a tragic day for Lima Company.

The remaining four patrols were left in the field to continue
their missions. However, they were advised to remain on high
ground in order to maintain commo with the forward TOC at
Quang Tri. Without a relay team operating from high ground
nearby, the patrols could easily find themselves without
commo, especially if they managed to get a mountain between
them and the TOC.

Around 1000 hours, shortly after Sergeant Taylor had completed recovery of the bodies, Staff Sergeant Sands decided to
take Ut, Vestal, and Johnson on a point recon to check out the
nearby river, where his team had made contact on their last mission. Sands left the remainder of the two teams under Rodarte's
command and told him they would return shortly.

Not far from their NDP Sands's patrol ran into a group of
NVA setting up an ambush. Ut was at point and he spotted the
NVA at the same time they saw him. Failing to notice the
Americans behind the Kit Carson scout, the enemy soldiers

hesitated to open fire, which gave the tiny scout the opportunity to open up first. He took advantage of it. But the NVA recovered quickly, returned fire, and wounded Ut in the calf. Another bullet tore through Sands's right pants leg without hitting him. The rest of the recon team then opened fire on the NVA, forcing them to break contact and retreat south. The three Rangers and their Kit Carson scout took advantage of the enemy's hasty withdrawal and dashed back up the trail to rejoin their comrades.

Another Cav Pink Team soon arrived to support the contact and to cover the medevac helicopter that came in to extract Ut. The Blues landed a short time later and swept the AO, finding only a cave in the side of a hill a short distance to the west. When the Blues failed to turn up any live enemy soldiers, their commander decided to extract them and the combined Ranger teams.

Bates's and Lewis's recon teams were also reporting heavy movement around them at the same time, so the TOC decided to pull them as well.

When the patrols returned to base, they discovered that they had just missed the seventy-five mph winds of a typhoon that ravaged Camp Eagle in their absence. A large number of hooches and other buildings were destroyed. In light of the major catastrophes that had befallen the Rangers both in the field and back at Camp Eagle, the Ranger company commander ordered the returning team members to spend the following day at Eagle Beach on the South China Sea, swimming, drinking, soaking up the sun, and trying to forget the tragedy that had befallen to them and their comrades the day before.

23

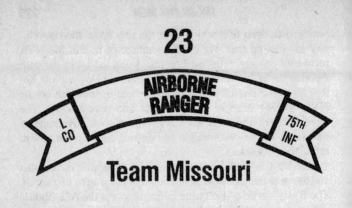

AIRBORNE RANGER

L
CO

75TH
INF

Team Missouri

With eight Rangers killed and more than a dozen wounded, May 1970 proved to be a tragic month for Lima Company. Enemy contact on missions had become the norm. There were no more cakewalk patrols. But the increased frequency of meeting the enemy in the field had little effect on most Rangers. Missions were still assigned with the same regularity, AOs were still selected based on the likelihood of finding the enemy in them. And in spite of the increased casualties, the company still managed to maintain at least four teams in the field at all times. Yet by the early summer of 1970 a number of subtle differences began to manifest themselves and to affect the Ranger operations.

New, inexperienced Rangers were assigned to operational teams much quicker than before. Teams with one or more cherry Rangers were being sent into high risk areas without the benefit of the "break-in" missions that were designed to eliminate costly mistakes and weed out those who were not up to the demands of long range patrolling. More and more creative techniques had to be utilized by the Rangers to deceive the enemy into believing they were dealing with anything other than a long range reconnaissance patrol. And there was a marked increase in heavy teams. In a number of instances reconnaissance teams were even inserted "with" an escort of

Blues—anything to increase the odds of staying alive long enough to carry out the patrol plan and complete the mission.

On May 27, Staff Sergeant Rowles and Sergeant Johnson went in heavy on an operation due south of Khe Sanh. The area was so hot that the combined Ranger teams went in to their LZ accompanied by a full platoon of Blues. The joint force patrolled about four hundred meters from the LZ before the Blues suddenly turned around and backtracked to the LZ and were extracted. The heavy Ranger team remained behind in ambush positions along a major trail they had discovered right off the LZ.

That afternoon it grew overcast and rained for a period of time as the Rangers remained in their ambush position over the trail. That night they spotted a number of NVA moving about with flashlights on the hill above them. The Rangers sensed that the enemy knew for certain they were present, but were unsure of the Rangers' location. The NVA unit remained in the area for quite a while, moving around and talking aloud just above the well-hidden Rangers. Unfortunately, without a Kit Carson scout they were unable to tell what the enemy soldiers were saying.

The next day the team leader decided to remain in place a little longer, hoping the enemy would come down off the hill and walk into their ambush; but when the Rangers' radio relay team was pulled out of the bush, they discovered they would have to relocate to higher ground or be without commo.

The Rangers packed up and moved out cautiously, working their way to the top of the hill where the NVA soldiers had spent so much time searching the night before. Just as they reached the top they received orders by radio to find the closest LZ and move to it so that Rowles could be lifted out. The company commander had just gotten word that his mother was dying back home, and he was to depart immediately on emergency leave.

Not wanting to waste time, the Rangers took a chance and quickly went back to their original LZ, where they waited with Rowles until a slick arrived to pick up the now thoroughly depressed Ranger.

With Rowles on his way back to Camp Eagle, the patrol

returned as quickly as possible to the top of the hill, only to discover that they couldn't reach anyone on the radio. After setting up a perimeter and spending the next two hours trying to pick up someone, they finally made contact on their URC-10 emergency radio with a U.S. aircraft returning from a bombing mission over North Vietnam. The pilot was happy to relay a message from the Ranger patrol to its base at Camp Eagle.

To create a sense of urgency in the company rear and to encourage the team's extraction and reinsertion into a new AO, one with better commo, the Ranger team leader falsely reported movement all around the team. Instead of an extraction, a Cav Pink Team was sent out to fire up the area. The team leader's false report of enemy movement in the vicinity of his position had backfired; instead of a fresh start in a new AO, the patrol would have to stay where it was even after calling so much excess attention to its location.

The NVA had clearly suspected the presence of an American recon team after the initial insertion. Then the patrol had returned to its original LZ to have Rowles extracted, making even more noise. Then the pilot of a fighter aircraft passing overhead relayed their message and gave their coordinates in the clear. And finally, a Cav Pink Team had just destroyed half the countryside in response to "movement." And if that wasn't enough to give the entire patrol terminal ulcers, the Rangers were sitting on the highest point in the area and couldn't get commo. Not a man in the patrol expected to survive the night.

Well, the entire patrol was still alive the next day, but they were still without commo. Was it possible that all of the NVA in I Corps had pulled back across the DMZ? There had to be some logical reason why the Ranger patrol was being ignored in spite of what must have appeared to be herculean efforts to draw attention to itself.

With their luck running so high, no one could understand why they were still having commo problems. Just when they began to feel they might survive the operation, four errant artillery rounds were walked into within two hundred meters of the patrol's position.

Johnson managed to raise another passing aircraft on the URC-10, and its pilot finally acquired commo for the team.

Johnson had the pilot relay a message asking if friendlies were firing artillery into their AO. The pilot radioed back that no one on their side had dropped any rounds in that area, and informed them that he had just received a message that they were to stay put.

A short time later the patrol listened on the radio as two more Lima Company recon teams were inserted into an area near the Ashau Valley. Led by Sergeants Delaney and Vestal, the teams immediately discovered that they, too, had no commo with the rear. Things appeared to be rapidly building toward a major catastrophe.

Soon, Johnson's patrol received a message that the team was probably going to be pulled in the next hour, then thirty minutes later another message informed them that a fixed-wing aircraft would remain on station overnight to act as an aerial relay station for each of the Lima Company recon teams in the field. Each patrol was assigned a coded check-in schedule to use during the night, when the aircraft was directly over their positions.

During the night of May 29, Delaney's patrol spotted three NVA. When they reported the sighting to Captain Stowers, the Lima Company CO, they got a surprise. A Cav Pink Team soon arrived on the scene and fired up the area where the enemy soldiers had been observed, but managed to chew up a lot of jungle without killing anyone. To make matters worse, instead of pulling Delaney's now thoroughly compromised patrol, Captain Stowers ordered them to continue the mission.

Sergeant Johnson's heavy team was finally extracted at 0800 hours the next morning and flown south to Firebase Birmingham. There they received additional orders to fly out to Firebase Whip, which was unoccupied at the time. They were instructed to establish a radio relay site on top of the abandoned firebase and handle communications for Delaney's and Vestal's recon teams still operating out near the Ashau Valley.

Firebase Whip was not much to look at. Shaped like a low-quarter shoe, the firebase had two distinct levels. The upper level was nearly flat across the top, then sloped down for forty or fifty meters to the west until it flattened out again before plunging down into the jungle below. There was very little concealment on the mountaintop, only a thin veneer of three-to-four-foot-high shrubs covering the slope between the two levels. The east side of the firebase was a sheer drop all the way to the bottom of the mountain. If the enemy was to attack, the assault would have to come up the west face.

Thirty minutes after the patrol landed on Whip, Johnson received a mysterious radio message from the Ranger CO warning them to set up in the tightest 360-degree perimeter they could form. No further explanation was given. Johnson was experienced enough to realize that someone had just discovered that his team was sitting in the middle of someone else's target. He also understood there were definite limits to just exactly how "tight" a 360-degree perimeter eleven men can form without being back-to-back.

The way things had been going for Lima Company lately, no one had to tell any of the Rangers on Whip that they were in a bad fix. Soon most of the Rangers began cracking jokes, clowning around, and laughing. It might seem unprofessional, perhaps even a little insane, to a casual observer, but to soldiers trying to accept the idea that their final fate has already been signed, sealed, and delivered . . . well, next to prayer, humor is probably their best deal.

Sergeants Johnson and Bowland were sharing one of the old, dilapidated bunkers that appeared to ring the top of the mountain. The bunkers' overhead cover had long ago been destroyed by the previous occupants of the firebase, probably to deprive nosy enemy soldiers of a place to hide if they got caught out in the open by American aircraft. The old bunkers would offer the Rangers some protection from small-arms fire, but they were little more than oversized catcher's mitts for mortars or grenades tossed in their direction.

Johnson, bored with relay duty, decided to have a little fun at Bowland's expense and pointed out to him that the NVA had to know there were only eleven men on top of Firebase Whip, that the Rangers had been seen coming in, and that the enemy would come after dark. He sardonically described how the final attack would begin. First there would be a surprise mortar barrage that would likely cause heavy casualties among the defenders. Then, under cover of machine gun fire designed to keep the survivors pinned down, the NVA assault forces would maneuver into grenade and satchel-charge range. It would all be over in a matter of minutes, and with only eleven men, there was absolutely no way for the Rangers to defend against it.

Bowland didn't at all appreciate Johnson's sense of humor. The hilltop grew quiet as the eleven Rangers traded their youthful horseplay for quiet contemplation—and maybe even a prayer or two.

A couple of hours had passed when Vestal's team called in to give its present coordinates. Johnson copied the information on his one-time pad, then relayed it on to the Ranger TOC back at Camp Eagle. When he was finished with the transmission, he located Vestal's coordinates on the map, then stood up in the bunker to shoot an azimuth to see where the patrol was located in relation to Firebase Whip. Suddenly, the team leader heard Vietnamese laughing and talking down below. Johnson dropped to his knees in the bunker, then slowly raised his head above the edge of the sandbags to scan the area. Walking across the lower level of the firebase, two NVA soldiers were moving directly toward the bunker occupied by the two Ranger NCOs.

At first Johnson thought they might be the point element for a larger NVA force trying to play a trick of some kind to get closer. Then he realized that whatever their plan, there was no reason to let them get any closer than they already had.

Johnson thumbed the selector switch on his CAR-15 from "safe" to "semi-auto" and whispered to Bowland, "Here we go!" Johnson keyed the radio handset and quickly called in a message, "We have two gunkies coming toward us. It might be a point for a larger unit. I'm going to initiate contact . . . right . . . NOW!"

Johnson rose to his feet and discovered the two NVA were now less than forty meters away and walking parallel to him. Without hesitating, he opened up and killed the nearest one outright, then wounded his comrade. The wounded NVA quickly ducked out of sight behind a nearby stack of logs. Some of the other Rangers, just becoming aware of the threat to their safety, stood and tossed several grenades in the vicinity of the stacked logs. After the explosions, Johnson yelled for the wounded enemy soldier to surrender. Instead, the NVA leaped to his feet and ran back the way he'd come. At sixty meters Johnson put three shots in the middle of his back, knocking him forward onto his face.

The patrol waited nearly fifteen minutes to see what else was coming. When nothing happened, Johnson sent Specialist Krause and another Ranger down to check the bodies. The two men returned shortly with the two NVA soldiers' weapons and rucks.

A few minutes later the patrol received the first good news of the day. A pair of slicks and a flight of Cobra gunships were on the way out to pull them off the mountain. For some reason, they were no longer needed to perform as a radio relay team for Delaney and Vestal. Johnson's Rangers would survive the day after all.

Back at the Ranger compound, Johnson's team learned that just after they had inserted onto the abandoned firebase, word reached the Ranger TOC from Division that an NVA battalion or regimental base camp was located at the foot of the mountain the patrol had occupied. The eleven Rangers had gotten out just in time; killing the two unsuspecting NVA soldiers had likely signed their death warrants.

Shortly after Johnson's patrol initiated contact, Delaney called in to report he had movement all around his position. Just before dark, his patrol and Vestal's were pulled.

The next day Division G-2 sent word to the Ranger company that the pair of NVA soldiers killed by Johnson had been among the force that wiped out Ellis's team on the eleventh. A diary had been found in the personal effects of one of the men that described the incident. There was even a crude sketch showing how the Rangers had been set up next to the high-speed trail.

24

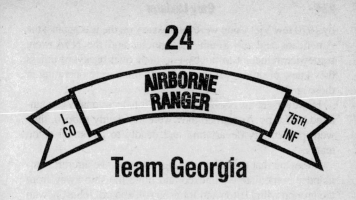

AIRBORNE RANGER

L CO

75TH INF

Team Georgia

On May 19, 1970, a heavy team led by Staff Sergeant Vestal was assigned a mission south of the Salad Bowl to locate and observe enemy elements reputedly moving into the rocket belt. The heavy team was to insert into a single-ship LZ on the side of a small fingerlike ridge in the mountains west of Camp Eagle. Vestal and four Rangers were on the first ship to infil. The remaining five Rangers rode in on the second slick.

As the first Huey flared to a hover just above the small hillside clearing, Vestal screamed for everyone to exit the helicopter from the left side. Staff Sergeant Roger "Ski" Lagodzinski was the first Ranger off the aircraft. Vestal, Huan—the team's Kit Carson scout—and Sergeants Dalton and Johnson were coming off right behind Lagodzinski.

Ten meters from the helicopter and running full out, Lagodzinski tripped a booby-trapped artillery round and was blown several feet into the air, landing in a heap eight feet away. Sticks, leaves, and debris peppered the aircraft as smoke curled up from the LZ and was sucked skyward in the Huey's rotor wash.

Late in the Vietnam War, especially in I Corps, booby-traps were seldom encountered by long range reconnaissance patrols. There were a couple of reasons for this: booby-traps are primarily a weapon used by guerrillas like the Viet Cong, and by 1970 few Viet Cong were left to carry on the war against the Americans and the South Vietnamese; and the NVA were somewhat reluctant to booby-trap their own backyard unless they knew of or suspected that enemy units were operating in those areas.

However, enemy booby-traps were still occasionally encountered by Lurps. And when they were accidently tripped, they were particularly devastating and deadly to the small recon teams.

Believing that the LZ was being mortared, the aircraft commander immediately panicked and lifted the ship away from the ground with Dalton and Johnson still aboard. Johnson, who had been out on the skid when the aircraft lifted out of the LZ, nearly tumbled out of the open bay as the ship banked sharply away from the clearing. Against the vehement protests of both Dalton and Johnson, the now thoroughly shaken pilot flew straight back to Camp Eagle, offering the excuse that the explosion had damaged his aircraft. The two Ranger NCOs were furious, but powerless to stop the young warrant officer; they had been forced to violate the Lurp creed: "Lurps don't leave Lurps behind. One goes in, we all go in."

The second helicopter, witnessing the explosion and the quick liftoff by the first slick, immediately aborted the mission. Its pilot would not risk his aircraft to insert the second half of the team. To make matters worse, the risk of booby-traps or mortars on the LZ prevented the chase ship and the C&C ship from landing to extract the remainder of the team. The three Rangers still on the ground would have to be lifted out by jungle penetrator or Maguire rig, and none of the aircraft at the scene were equipped with either.

Back at the LZ, Vestal and Huan had dragged the badly wounded Lagodzinski into some nearby cover and attempted to treat his wounds. Cobra gunships prowled low overhead, providing security for the three men left behind on the LZ. They would continue the air cover until the Rangers could be extracted or reinforced.

The explosion had shredded the inside of Lagodzinski's legs all the way to his crotch, perforating the femoral artery.

Lagodzinski was rapidly bleeding to death, and there was little that Vestal could do to prevent it.

Back at Camp Eagle, the helicopter had landed at the Ranger acid pad, and Johnson and Dalton were already busy installing Maguire rigs on the cabin floor. A close inspection by the pilots and crew chief immediately after touchdown revealed that the aircraft had suffered no physical damage from the explosion, so the aircraft commander had agreed to return to the LZ to extract the remainder of the team. But before the two Rangers could finish rigging the aircraft, a brief radio message came in from the C&C ship still at the scene reporting that a medevac helicopter had just arrived at the LZ and was extracting Lagodzinski, Vestal, and Huan.

Twenty minutes later, as the dustoff slick was on final approach to the helo pad at the 85th Evac Hospital at Phu Bai, the mortally wounded Ranger ran out of time. Ski bled to death in Vestal's arms.

Later, back at the Lima Company compound, a tearful Sergeant Vestal was taking Ski's death pretty hard. They had become good friends over the previous three months, and Vestal felt responsible for his death. A number of Rangers from Lagodzinski's tracker unit approached Vestal and revealed to him that Lagodzinski had felt that he was going to die. He'd already written a final letter to his parents and given away all of his personal possessions to his teammates. Then, nearing the end of his third tour in the Republic of Vietnam, he'd willingly gone out on his final patrol, bound by a profound sense of duty and loyalty to his team.

During the final three years of the war, the NVA exacted a very high price from the recon teams operated by U.S. Army Rangers, Special Forces, Marine reconnaissance battalions, and Marine force recon. Despite their losses, the recon units had to increase the number of patrols they fielded in order to screen the major U.S. infantry units standing down prior to their return to the States. President Nixon's Vietnamization program was beginning to see U.S. forces being replaced by South Vietnamese units, which in turn resulted in a natural reluctance on the part of unit commanders to risk their forces in operations against the enemy. It would be difficult to explain major casualties at a time when U.S. ground forces were being withdrawn from the war. So, small, mobile reconnaissance patrols were assigned to keep tabs on enemy troop movements without risking major, hard-to-explain casualties—a purely political move that constantly put the Rangers in harm's way.

Staff Sergeant Roger Lagodzinski was the seventh Lima Company Ranger to die in combat during May 1970.

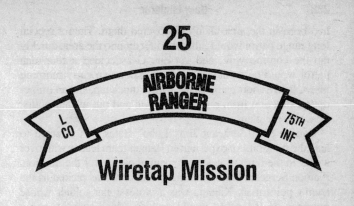

25

Wiretap Mission

On September 25, 1970, Division G-2 sent another warning order down to L Company. An aero-rifle troop from the 2/17th Cav had recently touched down out in the Ashau Valley to check out a reported NVA truck park. Instead they discovered a well-camouflaged string of light blue commo wire running through the brush parallel to an NVA high-speed trail. The Blues had not disturbed the wire. They had found no sign of the NVA truck park, so they got out of the general area as quickly as possible.

When G-2 learned of the Blues' discovery, they decided to have a long range patrol tap the enemy commo wire. Division couldn't very well send in an infantry company, or even a platoon, to perform such a task, because that would only draw the enemy's attention to the fact that Americans had been around their commo wire. It was bad enough that a platoon from the Blues had been stomping around the area. It was already a foregone conclusion that with thousands of enemy soldiers in and around the Ashau Valley, any U.S. ground element larger than a basketball team that ventured into it would be detected. So G-2 decided to give the area a couple of days to cool down, maybe even enough time to allow the "local" telephone company the opportunity to run a couple of wire checks on their lines, just to reassure themselves that the American patrol that had been in the area hadn't discovered them. Then a special long range patrol would infiltrate directly into the area, quickly tap the commo wire, and get out. G-2 decided a four-man patrol would be sufficient for the mission. An early morning insert, then a short patrol to the wire, a quick tap, and an immediate extraction from a nearby LZ—in and out in four hours. That was the plan.

Ranger Staff Sergeant Jim "Lobo" Bates was selected to lead the mission. An experienced Ranger team leader with over a year in the bush, Bates was a natural choice for the mission. Platoon Sergeant Harold "Ranger" Kaiama was picked as the team's point man. Kaiama was a professional soldier whose presence on the patrol would provide added stability and a backup if Bates went down. Second Lieutenant James Smith had also managed to secure a spot on the team. A West Pointer, and the son of an Army general, Smith was a fine officer, popular with the men and no slouch in the jungle. His selection was not challenged by anyone else on the team. The last man chosen, Spec 4 Ray Price, was an ex-Marine who had survived a thirteen month "hard" tour in 1967–68. Price had made it through the battle for Khe Sanh during Tet '68 without a scratch. A lot of his buddies weren't around to make the same boast. Price had reenlisted in the Army after discovering that civilian life didn't have a lot to offer. Back in uniform, the young Ranger struggled mightily to get back into the war. His father was career Air Force, stationed in South Vietnam, and a brother was in-country in an artillery unit. Price felt that he needed to be doing his part, too. He was the commo specialist on the team.

When the four Rangers loaded into their insertion aircraft and noticed all the extra space, it hit each of them for the first time that four men on a long range patrol instead of the normal six was a hell of a lot fewer than two; one man with a bad wound would cut the team's firepower by half and hobble it because at least one Ranger would have to carry the wounded man.

The insertion Huey and the chase ship raced up the valley barely sixty feet above the ground. With large numbers of NVA troops in the area, low and fast was the only way to fly. The two

aircraft played leapfrog and executed a number of false insertions. As the C&C aircraft circled high overhead, monitoring
the infiltration, a pair of Cobra gunships did their best to be
conspicuous out on the flanks. It worked.

The team hit the ground running in chest-high elephant
grass, moving on a direct line toward a distant stand of timber.
If they were in the right LZ, they were less than five hundred
meters from their target.

Soon they were out of the elephant grass and into an area of
dense underbrush. According to the Blues, the enemy commo
wire was along a trail just inside the trees, on the opposite side
of the underbrush. It was a likely spot for a trail, and an even
better location for a hasty ambush. The team was on full alert.

It took them less than an hour to reach the protection of the
trees. Right where it was supposed to be, Kaiama found the
trail. Just on the other side of the trail, he spotted the light blue
of NVA commo wire stretched among the dark green vegetation bordering the red-ball.

Kaiama took a good look around to make sure they were
alone, then stooped and followed the wire to where it ran
behind a large tree growing beside the trail. Setting up security,
Sergeant Bates began digging a shallow hole a few feet back
from the trail in which to bury the cigar-box-size transmitter.
At the same time, Lieutenant Smith began stripping the insula-
tion away from a short section of the wire to install the alligator
clips for the transmitter leads. With the transmitter in place, and
all indications of the excavation removed or covered, Kaiama
climbed up the back side of the tree to install the transmitter's
radio antenna, making certain that it was properly camouflaged
and invisible to anyone standing out on the high-speed trail.

With everything finished, the Rangers performed a final
check of the site, taking special care to sterilize the entire area
around the transmitter. After a test to make sure the transmitter
was turned on and functioning, the patrol was on the move to a
large clearing less than three hundred meters away. They had
been on the ground for less than three hours.

When they reached the designated PZ, they radioed for
extraction and discovered that the lift aircraft was only three

minutes away. Like a well-rehearsed play, the extraction ship identified the team's flash panel and swept in to pick them up.

That night an Air Force C-130 out of Thailand flew high over the Ashau Valley and recorded enemy land line transmissions picked up and transferred through the Rangers' wiretap. The signal would last for several days, until the enemy's detection equipment located the small signal drain on the wire. The NVA area commander would follow up by running a patrol along the length of the wire until they found the source of the trouble. There was little doubt that the enemy would not fail to find the tap, but in the brief period while the tap was good, important intelligence would be gathered that could possibly reveal enemy invasion plans, the location of enemy units, and the coordinates of their camps, staging areas, and supply depots. The bottom line was that wiretap missions could save American lives. Such missions were few and far between, depending on those occasions when the opportunity presented itself. But the ability to pull off wiretap missions, sensor implantations, Psyops missions, bomb damage assessments, and other off-the-wall assignments, was a constant demonstration of Ranger versatility.

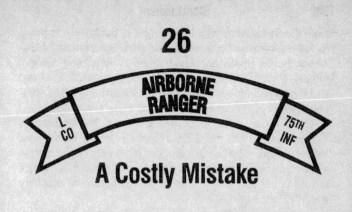

26

A Costly Mistake

Throughout the history of the 101st Airborne Division's LRP/Ranger companies, mistakes have proven costly. On nearly every patrol that had cost Ranger lives, the facts when reviewed showed that one or more of the team members had made a mistake. A mission in the Ashau Valley in November 1970 was no different.

It began like every other patrol, with a warning order coming down from Division G-2. This time the intel was more specific than usual. The five-man team, led by newly appointed team leader Staff Sergeant John Houser, was to locate the headquarters of the 803rd NVA Regiment.

It was a rough AO with a lot a steep ridges and correspondingly deep valleys. It lay on the west side of the Ashau, smack up against the Laotian border. It was a bad AO to break in a new team leader, especially with a couple of newly assigned NCOs filling in two of the remaining slots. Only Spec 4s Roger "Mitch" Costner and "Chief" Roubideaux had any experience to speak of.

Costner, Houser's ATL, was a big man, over six feet tall, but he was nothing compared to Sergeant Bob Drapp. At six-six, the recent transfer from a Screaming Eagle line company was awfully large for a recon man. The other new man, Staff Sergeant Norman Stoddard, Jr., a shake 'n' bake NCO fresh from the States, showed a lot of promise, but he was as green as his newly issued camouflage fatigues. Stoddard and Lieutenant James Smith happened to be cousins, and Smith's father—Stoddard's uncle—was a U.S. Army general. Stoddard and Drapp had hit it off pretty well since arriving at the company, becoming hoochmates and good friends.

The mission went in at first light on the morning of November 12, 1970. The LZ was a small clearing on the back side of a major ridgeline that dropped off steeply on the reverse slope all the way down toward the border with Laos. The patrol moved uphill and soon found fresh sign indicating that they weren't alone in the AO.

The team spent the next four days moving and watching. They covered a lot of ground, and everywhere they went it was the same—fresh sign but no enemy troops. Constant commo problems kept the team close to the high ground, preventing them from dropping down into the valley where they suspected the 803rd's regimental headquarters might be.

On the evening of the fourth day, Houser decided to move into an ambush position along one of the many trails the patrol had encountered. Since the team hadn't located the 803rd's headquarters, they would try to salvage something of the mission with an ambush the morning of the extraction. But no enemy soldiers passed through the patrol's kill zone that night or early the next morning.

At 0900 hours on the morning of November 16, the patrol's final day in the bush, Houser moved the team over the crest of the ridge and partway down the reverse slope. Below them was a steep cliff, with one small break in the cliff face where a steep slope provided possible access down into the valley below. Their take-out LZ was only a couple hundred meters above them on the crest of the ridge. Houser decided the spot was as good a place as any to lay dog until the extraction aircraft arrived at midday.

It was nearly 1030 hours. The five Rangers were set up in a tight defensive perimeter in heavy cover waiting for the word that the helicopters were on the way. As sometimes happens just before an extraction, security had gotten a little lax and a couple of the Rangers had given in to temptation to light up cigarettes—a no-no on any long range patrol.

Thirty minutes later Roubideaux elbowed Costner and began counting on his fingers ... one ... two ... three ... It took a couple of seconds for Costner to realize what his teammate was doing. Roubideaux was watching an NVA platoon coming up through the gap in the cliff directly below the Rangers' perimeter. The first of the enemy soldiers was already less than fifteen meters from the spot where Roubideaux and Costner sat hidden in the grass. The enemy patrol was much too close for either man to whisper a warning to the rest of the team. Costner turned and motioned for Stoddard to stay down. Roubideaux was the only one of the Rangers at the time who could actually see the enemy approaching.

As Costner began to respond to the threat, the NVA soldier closest to the Rangers' perimeter spotted Roubideaux and opened fire, missing the Native American but hitting Costner in the lower left leg. Stoddard, who had risen on his knees to see what was coming after Costner had signaled him to get down, then took a round through his chest.

Things happened quickly after that. Costner returned fire, killing the NVA who had shot him and Stoddard, and also dropping the man behind him. The remaining NVA, confused by what had just happened and seeing two of their own go down, turned and ran, firing back at the Rangers as they moved downhill. Costner and Roubideaux tossed a couple of frags after them, only to see the favor quickly repaid when a ChiCom grenade came flying in and landed at their feet. Thinking quickly, Costner grabbed it and pitched it downhill before it could go off.

Things got quiet for a while afterward. The Rangers could still occasionally hear movement in the gap down below them. It was obvious the enemy soldiers were maneuvering around them, but they did not appear to be attempting to force their way into the Rangers' perimeter.

After the enemy soldiers had withdrawn, Costner grabbed the seriously wounded Stoddard and dragged him back inside the Ranger perimeter, where the NCO's wound could be dressed. Stoddard was in very bad shape, showing all the symptoms of shock. This forced Houser to get on the radio and ask for an emergency medevac.

Lieutenant Jim Smith, Stoddard's cousin, soon arrived out over the team's location in a Huey equipped with a Maguire rig. It wasn't the best way to extract a man with a chest wound, but there had been no word about the medevac helicopter Houser requested, and Stoddard was going to die if he didn't get to a hospital within thirty minutes.

Hovering over the LZ, Lieutenant Smith kicked out a single sandbag-weighted Maguire rig. Costner and Roubideaux managed to get the badly wounded Ranger quickly snapped in. But as the helicopter began to lift Stoddard up through the trees, a heavy volume of enemy automatic weapons fire erupted from the valley directly below the Rangers' perimeter. Costner and Roubideaux both heard the chopper taking multiple hits and looked up in time to see Lieutenant Smith standing in the open door getting sprayed across the legs. Seconds later the door gunner on Smith's side of the helicopter got shot up so badly that he pitched headlong out of his "hellhole" and was left hanging from the helicopter only by his safety cord.

The aircraft began smoking as it fought to keep away from the LZ and the NVA ambush down in the valley. Stoddard, dangling eighty feet below the crippled Huey, suddenly had a round sever his lifeline, dropping him a hundred feet to the ground and killing him instantly. His body came to rest fifty meters downhill from the Rangers' perimeter.

Free of its burden, the wounded aircraft banked hard away from the hillside and disappeared out over the valley. It would be lucky if it made it to a friendly firebase.

Back on the side of the ridge, the remaining Rangers were expecting to be overrun at any minute. They were shocked instead when things began to quiet down. They could no longer hear the enemy moving around below them.

Houser radioed for a reaction force; the four of them would not be able to move downhill to recover Stoddard's body without drawing the enemy's fire. Their relay team radioed that the Blues were on their way in.

The aero-rifle platoon landed on the ridgetop above the team and quickly began to move down to the Rangers' perimeter.

Enemy small-arms fire opened up from below, wounding two of the Blues.

When the reaction force finally reached the Rangers' position, Houser pointed out the location of Stoddard's body. Several minutes later the combined elements moved downhill and recovered the dead Ranger.

As they moved back up toward the crest of the ridge, enemy fire broke out again from the valley below, wounding several more Cav troopers. Sergeant Drapp turned to see if he could tell where the enemy fire was coming from, only to catch an RPG round in his midsection, blowing him in two.

Costner saw and heard the explosion that hit Drapp. He knew instantly that Drapp was dead, but seconds later he heard his fellow Ranger crying for help. It took the oversized Ranger NCO nearly ten minutes to die.

Houser was on the radio again, this time calling in a fire mission on the NVA positions below. He would alternate between artillery, air strikes, and helicopter gunships for the rest of the afternoon in an attempt to break up the enemy troop concentrations and prevent their moving uphill into the American positions. Under the cover of a multiple plane air strike, some of the Blues and the rest of the Rangers moved back down to recover what was left of Drapp's body. A short time later a single Huey slick was able to get in to recover Stoddard's and Drapp's corpses and the more seriously wounded Blues. But Costner stayed in the bush with the rest of the team.

Later that afternoon, the weather began to change for the worse, and soon the valley was completely socked in. There would be no more aircraft for the rest of the day. Because of the poor visibility, Houser was restricted to calling in artillery for the remainder of the evening and throughout the night. But it was enough to keep the NVA from overrunning the nearly two dozen Screaming Eagles spread around the crest of the ridge.

Things were quiet the next morning. After the weather cleared somewhat, an LOH scout helicopter came in and set down on top of the ridge. Costner, now stiffening from his gunshot wound, climbed aboard and took a seat on a couple of stacked ammo boxes sitting against the aircraft's rear fire wall. During the extraction, the enemy forces hidden below the team once again opened up on the aircraft. The LOH pilot turned his miniguns downhill and kept them going until Costner was aboard and the aircraft was safely out of the area.

The tiny scout helicopter flew across the valley and set down on a secure LZ where two Delta model Hueys and a Cobra gunship were waiting. Costner climbed out of the LOH and into one of the Hueys, which immediately revved up its engine. A short time later the aircraft touched down at the landing pad outside the 85th Evac Hospital at Phu Bai. Costner was wheeled inside and triaged. It was decided to medevac him directly to the USS *Sanctuary* standing offshore from Danang. There, he ran into Lieutenant Smith, who was recovering from his leg wounds.

Roger Costner was awarded the Silver Star for his actions that day. He would return to the company five weeks later, only to be wounded again and medevacked back to the States. Lieutenant Jim Smith would also return to Lima Company. Unlike Costner, Smith would die in a tragic helicopter crash almost three months from the day that his cousin was killed.

27

Socked In!

From the end of 1970 and into early 1971, Lima Company Rangers ran a large number of long range reconnaissance patrols along the Laotian border from the northern Ashau Valley all the way to the mountains south and west of Khe Sanh in the northwest corner of South Vietnam. A Lima Company radio relay team became a permanent fixture at the newly occupied forward operations base at Lang Vei. The base, manned by Special Forces personnel and a large force of Nungs, would play a major role in the coming South Vietnamese incursion into Laos—Lam Son 719.

The Rangers continued to operate in the area until the invasion began. At that point Lima Company received orders to stand down at Camp Eagle and the Rangers were restricted to their compound. As Lam Son 719 drew to a close with the ARVN invasion force falling back into South Vietnam in a panic, Lang Vei was overrun for a second time, shortly after the Lima Company radio relay team was pulled back to Camp Eagle.

On February 15, 1971, a six-man long range patrol from Lima Company was inserted by ladder early in the afternoon on a five-day mission to monitor Route 547 near where it entered the Ashau Valley. The patrol—comprised of Ranger Staff Sergeant Asa Cook, team leader; Sergeant Adam Macias, assistant team leader; Sergeant Jim Barr; Lieutenant James Smith; and Spec 4s David Bush and Ken Wells—was being sent out to verify reports of enemy troop movements in and out of the Ashau Valley.

The insertion site was in an area of dense brush on the reverse slope of a minor ridgeline just two hundred meters north of the road. Once on the ground, the team lay dog just off the LZ for fifteen minutes, then moved slowly through the surrounding heavy cover until they reached a likely spot for an observation post overlooking the highway.

Like the LZ, the observation site was choked with very dense underbrush, forcing the team to burrow in on its hands and knees. While the patrol was setting out claymores and establishing security around their perimeter, they were informed by radio that a typhoon would be moving ashore that night near Phu Bai and would reach them out in the Ashau around 0300 the next morning.

Late that afternoon heavy, dark clouds moved into the valley and a slow, steady rain began to fall, socking in the Rangers and effectively grounding all U.S. aircraft over most of northern I Corps. Within an hour of the onset of the rain, the patrol began seeing parties of NVA, in groups of five to ten, moving in single file into the valley from the east. The enemy soldiers were well-equipped, wearing rubberized ponchos, shouldering heavy rucksacks, and carrying AK-47s. Before darkness finally shut down the Rangers' OP for the day, they had reported five such groups of NVA soldiers on the road below.

At 0200 hours, during Cook's hour and a half radio watch and just before the full force of the typhoon slammed into them, the young Ranger thought he heard music coming in over their radio. Turning his head to one side to shield the handset from the steadily strengthening wind, Cook clearly heard the lively strains of "Yankee Doodle Dandy" on the team's primary radio. Apparently, the NVA in the valley were jamming the Rangers' frequency.

The six Rangers spent a long, miserable night huddled close together in a futile effort to stay warm as torrential rains inundated their position. The typhoon's winds raged and gusted for several hours, often threatening to blow the team off the ridgeline. Their only protection from the high winds was on the forward slope down near the road. But the Ranger team leader opted to ride out the storm where they were.

The Rangers wondered how Division G-3 could possibly have overlooked a full-blown typhoon bearing down on I Corps the same day a mission was scheduled to go into the valley. But trying to second-guess anyone at Division staff was futile.

The second day was much like the first, the torrential rains continuing. However, the winds had abated somewhat, making observation of the road possible once again. Taking advantage of the cover afforded by the rain to scout the area around their observation post, the patrol discovered that they were sitting smack in the middle of a large network of well-used, high-speed trails.

On the third day of the mission, Cook, uncomfortable with the trail system they were sitting in, decided it was time to move to a new location. After covering some ground, he decided to split the team, keeping three Rangers back in the brush with him while sending two others out to scout to the east, parallel to the road. Barr and Wells made up the scouting party, with Wells taking the point position.

Working under the low cloud ceiling, the scouting party edged through dense fog and damp vegetation as they moved closer and closer to the road. About 150 meters from where they had left the rest of the team, the recon element located a large clearing that would serve as an ideal one-ship PZ when it was time for them to come out. They also discovered a much better OP site situated closer to the highway, with excellent cover and concealment. It also had the additional benefit of being within twenty-five meters of the new PZ. The Ranger scouting element marked the spot on their patrol map then turned around to rejoin their teammates back in the brush. Unknown to them, their four comrades had just observed a ten-man NVA patrol pushing quietly through the brush behind them.

Barr and Wells were just returning to the OP when they spotted their fellow Rangers kneeling in the brush, alert and ready to fire. Cautiously and on full alert, the two scouts slipped into the perimeter, expecting at any minute to be hit.

Cook quickly apprised the two returning Rangers of the enemy patrol they had seen. After Wells and Barr filled him in on the PZ they had located and the OP site they'd found, Cook ordered his teammates to prepare to move out immediately toward the PZ. Before they left, he called in an unscheduled sit rep, only to discover that their supporting aircraft were still grounded back at Camp Eagle due to inclement weather. This was bad news for the team, especially with enemy patrols scouting the same ridgeline the team was occupying. It was true that the Rangers had adequate artillery support from Firebase Veghel and Firebase Rifle, but if they were compromised by a large enemy force, there would be no gunship support, no medevac, no emergency extraction until the fog and low cloud cover finally broke. For all practical purposes the Rangers were on their own.

Cook put Macias on point and Wells at the rear, then ordered his team to move out. Wells tried to sterilize the patrol's back trail as the team pushed through the damp brush, but the ground was soaked; the Rangers were leaving tracks a blind man could follow.

Minutes later Wells heard movement on their back trail and passed word up through the patrol that they were being followed. Soon, all of the Rangers were hearing voices from behind them, then the muffled sounds of a large number of men moving slowly through the brush.

When the patrol finally broke out into the opening that marked the edge of the PZ, Cook ordered them to hurry across the clearing and set up in a semi-wagon-wheel defensive perimeter facing their back trail. Wells quickly discovered that he'd selected a bad position from which to fight, as an army of angry fire ants charged out of their nest and attacked the exposed flesh on his face and arms. Unable to move or brush them away, he bit down hard on his lower lip to avoid screaming in pain and waited for the first of the pursuing NVA to show up.

Suddenly, nearly a half-dozen NVA soldiers broke through the dense brush twenty meters from the team. Macias and Barr were the first Rangers to initiate contact, dropping two or three of the enemy soldiers with their opening bursts. Screaming

"Dinks ... dinks ... dinks!" the two Rangers dropped their empty magazines at their feet and jammed home new ones as a number of ChiCom grenades sailed out of the brush and landed among the patrol. One of the grenades exploded under Wells, flipping him on his back and wounding him in the penis. He knew instantly that this was a wound he would have to dress himself. Rolling over on his back, Wells tied a compression bandage–medium over the wound, then cursed himself for not packing a "compression bandage–small."

As the Rangers fought back desperately, word came over the radio that the weather back at Camp Eagle was beginning to break and the birds were cranking up. Now they only had to manage to stay alive for another twenty minutes until the cavalry arrived!

Immediately after throwing the grenades, some of the NVA began to maneuver to the left in an attempt to flank the recon team. The Rangers countered with a grenade shower of their own which momentarily put a stop to the enemy's flanking efforts.

Abruptly, the contact was over as quickly as it had begun. The NVA had pulled back and stopped the fight. The action had lasted less than two minutes, but it seemed like an hour to the harried Rangers.

A quarter of an hour later helicopters could be heard coming up Highway 547. The aircraft had taken off from Camp Eagle and flown nap of the earth down the highway all the way out to the valley. A 2/17th Cav heavy Pink Team arrived just ahead of the slicks and moved in close to put fire on the enemy's last known positions. Under the cover provided by the two Cobras, the extraction aircraft flared as it settled into the PZ and lifted the Ranger team out of danger.

Wells was the only friendly casualty of the encounter. It was the kind of wound that did more damage to the reputation than it did to the body. He would survive the wound and so would his "gun," but his ego would never be the same. The episode earned him a new nickname from another Ranger, Spec 4 David Walley, who would thereafter refer to the ex-Marine as "Sprinkler Man."

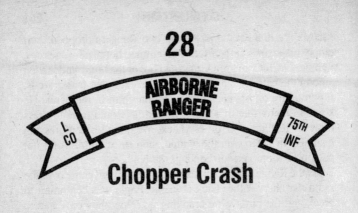

28

AIRBORNE RANGER
L CO
75TH INF

Chopper Crash

The monsoon rains were still falling in I Corps during mid-February 1971. Lima Company was running numerous patrols in the mountains surrounding Camp Eagle. The 101st Airborne Division was putting all of its aviation assets on the line to support Lam Son 719, and the division's Rangers were to watch the back door to Eagle while the division supported the Laotian invasion.

On February 18 a recon patrol from second platoon was in big trouble in the vicinity of Leech Island on the Perfume River southeast of Camp Eagle. The team went in early that morning to check out an access point frequently used by the NVA to funnel troops into the rolling piedmont below the division base camp and the southern approaches to Phu Bai. The team had gone in through a break in the weather, which had closed in on them again an hour later. With the return of bad weather came the enemy, and soon the team was reporting movement all around them. For the entire day the team remained hidden as enemy soldiers passed back and forth through the area. Then it happened—a quick, brief firefight, and the enemy withdrew, leaving Ranger Sergeant Gabriel Trujillo shot through the side. The wound was painful but not life-threatening.

The long range recon patrol remained in hiding the rest of the day, hoping that darkness would enable them to escape and evade before the enemy returned. Trujillo was able to move with the team, but the impact of running with a wounded man left everyone more worried than usual.

The low overcast ushered in the night an hour earlier than normal, and enemy movement in the vicinity of the team picked up again. The Rangers knew that the NVA were trying to get them to give away their position or to flush them from hiding. Concerned that the enemy would stumble across them in the darkness, the Ranger team leader radioed the TOC, reported that the patrol was in imminent danger of being discovered, and called for a medevac to make a night hoist extraction. But there would be no medevac until the weather broke. Flying at night in the mist and low cloud cover was suicidal. Captain Ohle, the Ranger CO, told the team to hang on and he would at least try to find a way to get Trujillo out. It wasn't long before he radioed the team and told them that Lieutenant Smith would be out in a Bravo Troop slick equipped with a Maguire rig to get the wounded Ranger.

Night extractions were always hairy, and this one would be compounded by low-hanging clouds and misting rain, and that there were no LZs in the immediate area of the team. This necessitated a "string," or STABO extraction. The wounded Ranger would have to be plucked from the jungle at the end of 120 feet of rope suspended from the helicopter.

First Lieutenant James Smith, second platoon's leader, was short. But the fact that he was due to rotate didn't keep him from volunteering to fly bellyman on the extraction ship. With the weather getting even worse over the team's location, Smith and a Ranger medic, Sergeant Steven G. England, boarded the Huey from Bravo Troop, 2/17th Cav, and flew out toward the Rangers' AO.

Using abandoned U.S. Army Fire Support Base Brick as a reference point, the aircraft flew slowly out to the team's location. When they finally spotted the Rangers' strobe light flashing in the vegetation below, the helicopter moved in quickly and Lieutenant Smith kicked out the rope. Before the NVA could respond, the chopper had the wounded Ranger on the line and was already climbing to lift him from the jungle. Soon, the Huey was feeling its way through the overcast past

Fire Support Base Tomahawk toward the U.S. Army medical facility at Phu Bai.

Due to the night and the poor visibility, the helicopter was forced to fly very slowly back toward Phu Bai, with Trujillo still dangling 120 feet below. As the Huey passed north of FSB Tomahawk, the ceiling was still too low to attempt a touchdown to bring the wounded Ranger inside the aircraft. The pilot decided to continue on to Phu Bai, but weather conditions along the coast were no better. As the aircraft approached the Phu Bai air base from the southwest, the aircraft commander from B Troop, 2/17th Cav, radioed that he was losing it and couldn't see the ground. He was experiencing vertigo, a total loss of one's sense of direction, even to the point of not being able to tell up from down. Unable to recover his senses or to correct the situation, the pilot flew the aircraft straight into the ground, killing everyone on board and the wounded Ranger dangling from the rope below.

As soon as the weather broke, a platoon of Blues from B Troop was flown out to secure the crash site and recover the bodies. The scene they found on arrival affected every trooper. The helicopter had not burned on impact, but had literally been torn apart, along with the passengers and crew. The necessary task of recovering the bodies was extremely gruesome. Sergeant England's body was located at the crash site along with the bodies of Trujillo and the aircraft crew. Lieutenant Smith's body was not found among the wreckage at the site, and a search of the immediate vicinity failed to turn it up. The Cav troopers went on line and began sweeping back along the flight path of the downed helicopter. With the help of a Cav LOH scout aircraft, Lieutenant Smith's body was finally located nearly a half mile from the crash site. From evidence discovered at the scene, it appeared that the Ranger officer had jumped or fallen from the helicopter shortly after the aircraft commander suffered vertigo.

It was a very sad day for L Company and for the Cav. The B Troop soldiers were shaken when they arrived back at Camp Eagle. The pilots and crew of the aircraft had been theirs, and many of them had known one or more of the dead Rangers. The traumatic experience of the recovery operation caused some of the Blues to harbor hard feelings toward the Rangers. They saw the episode as the sacrifice of four of their comrades who were risking their lives to pull a wounded Ranger out of the jungle, and the Rangers hadn't even had the decency to assist in the recovery of the dead, even though three of them were Rangers. But these were not the facts. Every Ranger in L Company had wanted to take part in the recovery operation, but Division stepped in to prevent it. Unfortunately, the word never managed to get back to the Blues. It would take several weeks to repair the rift that had been created.

The year 1970 had been costly in Ranger lives. With the war winding down and U.S. participation drawing to a close, no one expected 1971 to be a repeat of the previous year.

29

AIRBORNE RANGER

L CO

75TH INF

Friendly Fire

A week after the helicopter crash that killed Lieutenant James Smith, another Lima Company patrol was inserted into the rugged mountains southwest of Camp Eagle. On this particular patrol there was a newly arrived Ranger, Richard Lee Martin, who had previously served a tour stateside with O Company (Arctic Rangers), 75th Infantry, in Alaska. A good-looking, intelligent kid with a lot of drive and ambition, everyone in Lima Company took an immediate liking to Spec 4 Martin. He had all the makings of a superb Ranger.

Martin was assigned to a team not long after his arrival. With his past experience with Oscar Company, he picked up patrol techniques with relative ease. On February 19 his team received a warning order for a mission the following day. They were to go in on a normal reconnaissance mission back in the mountains southwest of Eagle. Because of the usual amount of enemy activity in the area, it would be a good break-in mission for the new Ranger.

On February 20, 1971, Martin's team infiltrated into a small clearing just off the side of a secondary ridgeline in a heavily forested and mountainous recon zone. The weather was damp and overcast, but still flyable. The patrol lay dog for thirty minutes after the insertion then radioed in that it had gotten in cold and was releasing the gunships and slicks to return to Camp Eagle.

Nothing happened during the first day of the patrol, but that night the team reported some movement around their NDP—nothing major, but definitely enough to let them know that someone was out there.

The next morning the weather closed in and a fine mist soon had the jungle wet and dripping. Again the team suspected they had movement around them. Because of the weather, it was difficult to ascertain what noises were natural and what noises were man-made, but the team leader decided that they had to move. Remaining too long in one spot was never good patrolling policy.

The patrol was moving along the side of the ridge parallel to the crest when it began to take enemy fire from above its location. The team went to cover immediately and returned fire as their team leader got on the radio and called for gunship support to help them break contact. But the weather continued to deteriorate, the already low ceiling dropping even closer to the ground, and the fine mist they had been experiencing turning into a slow, steady drizzle.

Still in contact with enemy forces, the Ranger patrol moved to an LZ and radioed for extraction, asking once again for gunship support. Back at Camp Eagle a number of Cav pilots monitoring the team's transmissions decided to risk the inclement weather to try to get the team out.

When the first Cobra gunships arrived on station, they were forced to drop down and fly into the AO under the three to four hundred foot ceiling, much lower than the altitude they were used to working in. But the action down on the ground was beginning to heat up, and the Rangers needed help immediately.

Flying just beneath the clouds, the two Cobras circled the area to get their bearings, then rolled in on the suspected enemy positions just as a dense fog bank settled into the area. The first 2/17th Cav pilot made a single rocket pass over the small clearing that the Rangers had selected for their extraction. Suddenly, over the pilot's radio, he heard the Ranger team leader cry, *"Break off, break off! You're hitting us."*

Immediately the Cav gunships broke contact and circled into a wide orbit while they tried to sort out what had just happened. The only logical explanation was that the descending fog bank had distorted the target so badly that the pilot failed to properly identify the Ranger team's location. But it was too late to correct the situation, the damage had already been done. One of the 2.75 inch rockets had impacted less than ten meters from the Ranger team's defensive perimeter, instantly killing Spec 4 Richard Martin.

By the time the Cobras arrived on the scene, the enemy unit had pulled back, enabling a Huey slick to work its way down through the fog bank to extract the patrol and bring out Martin's body.

Martin was the sixth Lima Company Ranger to die during that bloody week. The tragedy was even more unacceptable because none of the six Rangers had been killed by hostile fire. It was the harsh Vietnamese monsoon weather that had become the great slayer of American long range patrollers. These Rangers were not the first to die because of the weather, nor would they be the last.

30

AIRBORNE RANGER
L CO
75TH INF

Return to Ripcord

Fire Support Base Ripcord, located on a mountaintop east of the Ashau Valley, had been abandoned by units of the 3rd Brigade, 101st Airborne Division, under "extreme" pressure from overpowering NVA forces in midsummer 1970. During the following months, a number of long range reconnaissance patrols run by members of L Company in the immediate vicinity of the abandoned firebase proved that the NVA had not left the area after the battle ended; the mountains and valleys around the destroyed U.S. firebase were teeming with NVA soldiers. Contacts during recon patrols were both frequent and heavy.

Ranger Team 2-5 had worked the area several times prior to Lam Son 719 in March 1971. This major Allied offensive was designed to destroy NVA sanctuaries in Laos and disrupt the enemy's plans to invade South Vietnam. Great pains had been taken to keep the invasion a secret in order to surprise the NVA, but the enemy was waiting with a few surprises of his own.

With the bulk of the ARVN ground forces and U.S. aviation assets tied up across the border in Laos, the NVA units in and around the I Corps area took advantage of the situation to go on the offensive. One of these areas of intense enemy activity was at the northern end of the Ashau Valley in western Thua

Thien Province, specifically the area around Fire Support Base Ripcord.

Unoccupied since it was overrun and abandoned nearly a year earlier, the Ripcord area had become a hot spot for enemy sightings. Aerial scouts and division long range patrols seldom ended an operation without sighting or coming in contact with enemy forces.

The hills and valleys surrounding the destroyed U.S. fire-base had been off-limits to Screaming Eagle infantry units since the day the last American soldier departed the area under fire. Division LRPs had been allowed to go back in, but only at the risk of extreme peril. It was definitely not a place for the shy and uninitiated!

Team 2-5 had managed to remain intact as a team since November 1970, an oddity in a company that saw frequent team member displacement due to R&R, TDY, DEROS, wounds, injuries, and death. By sheer luck, all the members of Team 2-5 had arrived in-country at about the same time. They had lived together, trained together, and fought together. They also had the good fortune of getting along well together. There were no rivalries or personality clashes among the teammates, and without exception they liked each other.

Staff Sergeant William "Fido" Vodden was the team leader. A Canadian citizen, Vodden was a Ranger School graduate with tons of field experience. By anyone's standards he was one of the most well-respected team leaders in the entire company. He always carried his own radio on patrol.

Sergeant Charles "Chuck" Reilly was Vodden's assistant team leader. Another graduate of Fort Benning's Ranger School, Reilly soon found out that the training in the mountains of northern Georgia and the swamps of the Florida Panhandle did not hold a candle to the experience one received participating on a few long range recon patrols in the "Nam." Time in the bush was the only thing that really mattered. That's where one obtained the necessary experience to stay alive and healthy for a year in Vietnam. Reilly carried the patrol's other PRC-25.

Spec 4 Dave "Muldoon" Rothwell from Oregon was the team's grenadier, carrying the XM-203 grenade launcher mounted under the barrel of his M-16. Muldoon was a giant among his fellow Rangers, a massive six-four and 250 pounds—unloaded and unarmed.

Spec 4 Don Sellner walked point for the team when it was out on patrol. A veteran deer hunter from the Minnesota North Woods, Sellner was in his element in the forests of Vietnam. On missions he was so totally focused on his job that he often missed signals given by his team leader. Sellner was one of the best point men in the company.

Spec 4 Scott Whitmore from Alabama was the team's tail-gunner. Whitmore had an uncanny ability to sense when the team was being followed, and had refined his skill at sterilizing a back trail so well that his team usually found it nearly impossible to retrace their steps.

Spec 4 Philip Vogelsang was the team clown. A native of California, back in the rear he kept everyone in stitches. But in the field he was all business, as deadly as any of his counterparts.

Team 2-5 had seen more than its share of firefights. It had already pulled a number of missions in the Ripcord area, but had yet to run into any trouble there. Whether it was a testimonial to the team's skill or just plain old-fashioned luck, they never knew for certain. But if it was luck that kept them out of trouble, then their luck was about to change for the worse.

On March 1, 1971, Team 2-5 received a warning order for a mission scheduled to go in the next day in the vicinity of Ripcord. The RZ had taken a number of artillery barrages and air strikes, so it was no surprise when the overflight located a large number of potential LZs in the area. Vodden selected a rather small opening in the vegetation for the team's insertion LZ, figuring that the NVA would be less likely to sit on such an unlikely spot. He was right.

The patrol went in cold on the second. There appeared to be no sign of any NVA forces in the area, and no alarm bells were going off as the team lay dog off the LZ before moving out on patrol. During the first day of the mission, the team began to believe they were out on another cakewalk. There was no sign of the enemy, either hot or cold, in their RZ.

By the end of the fourth day the members of the patrol had

to force themselves to concentrate on what they were doing to maintain their normal degree of vigilance; nothing exciting had happened to keep their attention focused on the job. Trying to keep your mind on what you're doing is one of the worst problems on a cold mission. No one could understand why, operating so close to Ripcord, there was no indication that the enemy had ever been in the area.

On the final day of the mission, the team was informed that because of operations being conducted across the border in Laos, only a single UH-1H was available in the entire division; if the team missed the helicopter at the LZ or if anything went awry, they would have to remain in the field an extra day. Since the patrol had found no sign of the enemy, they radioed back that one helicopter would be enough. Who needs gunships when you're coming out of a cold AO?

The extraction was set for 1200 hours, less than four hours away. The patrol didn't have that much ground to cover to reach their exfil point, but they decided to move out early just to make sure they reached the LZ in time.

They had been on the march for an hour, and it was around 0900 when they found themselves moving along the base of a ridge they would have to climb to reach their designated pickup point. Suddenly, walking along a dried-up riverbed, they encountered what appeared to be giant stone steps cut into the hillside. Someone had decided to create an easy way to reach the top of the ridge, and since that was the direction Team 2-5 was heading, they decided to parallel the stairs as they ascended the hill.

They were moving cautiously uphill, alert, keeping an eye on the steps twenty meters to their left. That's when the Rangers noticed that all of the trees around them had insulated commo wire strung through their uppermost branches. Strands of wire ran everywhere. The area looked like a Bell Telephone training center. The Rangers immediately realized that there was likely a much better route to their extraction point than the one they'd chosen. However, before they could act on their realization, they discovered that the wire was not their only problem. They were face-to-face with a half-dozen, well-camouflaged bunkers less than forty feet away. Fortunately, the bunkers were unoccupied.

After the initial shock of finding themselves in the middle of some kind of enemy installation, Vodden decided to press their luck and check out what was back behind the bunkers. Cautiously, the patrol moved forward until it ran smack dab into what appeared to be a recently deserted NVA battalion-size base camp. Scores of bunkers were everywhere. Commo wire was stretched through the trees over the entire area. NVA uniforms and other items of clothing were hanging from clotheslines strung between the trees. Smoke was rising from a number of cooking fires. However, not a single enemy soldier was in sight. It was almost as if Goldilocks had suddenly entered the home of the three bears—except there were six Goldilocks and over three "hundred" bears. Well, at least the patrol had discovered where the stone steps led!

But where were the inhabitants of the enemy base camp? Surely they hadn't been chased away by the arrival of six U.S. Army Rangers? The patrol went into a quick huddle to discuss its next move, deciding among themselves to find a roundabout way to reach their extraction LZ, even if it meant heading in the opposite direction. The only thing that seemed to matter to any of them at the moment was to get out of sight and sound of the NVA base camp before its occupants returned. There was a general consensus among them to wait until "after" they were extracted to plaster the base camp with artillery.

Reilly called in a sit rep to give the dimensions of the enemy camp and its coordinates. When he finished transmitting the message, he told the relay team to stand by for further instructions.

There was still plenty of time to reach the extraction point before their Huey, but it didn't keep them from double-timing out of the area. The Rangers were concerned only in putting as much distance as possible between themselves and the enemy encampment.

The roundabout route to the LZ had consumed much more time than the Rangers had realized, and it was nearly 1200 hours when they reached their destination. The final push had left them exhausted and gasping. But at least there had been no sign of the enemy along the way, and for that they breathed a collective sigh of relief.

The extraction LZ was located on the side of a hill nearly devoid of overhead cover. The only vegetation offering effective concealment was the tall elephant grass choking the clearing. The open expanse was rather large for that part of the jungle, and there was plenty of room for a helicopter to land unobstructed.

The team set up security then collapsed in the grass to await arrival of the aircraft. While his teammates were resting, Vodden decided to take Sellner and Rothwell and go out on a short point recon to see what was at the top of the hill. There was still an NVA battalion wandering around out there somewhere, and he wanted to make sure they didn't wander into his team. If Vodden located them, he could return to the LZ to call in their coordinates and toss a few rounds of 155mm on their position. It would keep them ducking and weaving until the team got pulled out of the area.

Leaving his radio at the LZ with Reilly, Whitmore, and Vogelsang, Vodden moved up the hill, with Rothwell and Sellner close behind. The hill turned out to be much steeper than Vodden had first thought, and the three Rangers had some difficulty in reaching the top. At the apex was a small clearing which Sellner and Vodden reached without incident. But before Rothwell crested the hill to join them, all three men began to hear strange noises coming from the reverse slope. Rothwell stopped his forward progress just short of the crest, while Sellner and Vodden froze in position above him.

Coming up the back side of the hill was the missing battalion of NVA regulars. They had gone down into the valley that morning on a water run, and were only just returning. The front section of the strung-out column consisted of NVA soldiers walking in pairs, carrying huge canvas water bags suspended between them on long poles and carrying their weapons at sling arms. An armed guard on each side of the formation provided security. The two NVA were carrying AK-47s at port arms; however, it appeared none of the enemy soldiers had an inkling that there was an American long range patrol in the area. There was no point element preceding the water bearers. The NVA were slowly climbing the hills de carrying on casual conversation between each other as if there wasn't anything to worry about in a hundred miles.

The enemy column was headed straight for Rothwell who was only thirty meters away, hidden in some dense cover just off the crest of the hill. When Sellner and Vodder observed what was happening, they immediately moved behind some thick bushes near the crest and held their ground. The two Rangers were hoping that the NVA battalion would walk right past without spotting them. If it worked, Rothwell could wait until he was in the clear, then hustle back to the remaining Rangers waiting at the LZ and alert them to what was happening above them. Unfortunately for Sellner and Vodden, Rothwell had other plans.

The giant Ranger decided this was an opportunity too good to pass up. From his position in the brush he sighted down the barrel of his M-16 at the first two water bearers and sprayed them and their security guards with a long burst from his M-16. The two water bearers died instantly, their canvas water bags spraying water everywhere.

The one-man ambush so startled the enemy column that Sellner and Vodden had time to race back to Rothwell's position, grab him, and attempt to dash back down the ridge toward their LZ. But before the three Rangers could get fully out of range, the stunned NVA soldiers had recovered from their initial shock and began to hurl ChiCom grenades after the fleeing Rangers. It was likely they were more than just a little upset. After all, it had been a long trip down to the stream. It was even longer getting back to the top with a day's ration of water. Now to lose a couple of buddies and watch precious water soaking into the hillside—well, they were out looking for some revenge. However, they held back their pursuit, not knowing for certain the strength of the opposition they were facing.

Most of the enemy grenades had fallen far short of the fleeing Rangers, but one NVA with an arm like Roger Maris managed to lob his grenade right in the middle of the trio of Americans. They dove in different directions just as the grenade exploded. All three were hit, but Rothwell managed to catch the worst of it, taking shrapnel in the leg and shoulder.

But his last-second evasive action had at least succeeded in knocking Vodden out of the way of the blast, preventing injury to the patrol's team leader.

Naturally, the firefight on the hill above them had alerted the three Rangers still back at the LZ. During the initial contact, Reilly had radioed the relay team and requested an immediate extraction. Ranger Sergeant Nick Gibbone, pulling radio relay with his own team on a nearby U.S. firebase, radioed back that the "one and only" chopper left at the 2/17th Cav was on its way out to pick up the team, and he added, "You'd better be on it!"

Within minutes of the initial contact, the three Rangers bolted into the makeshift perimeter around the LZ. They were exhausted, scared, and wounded, but happy to be alive.

By now the NVA soldiers had crested the hilltop and were advancing, firing their weapons as they came on. Luckily for the Rangers, the enemy fire was passing harmlessly over their heads. However, it didn't change the fact that the NVA were moving closer and would soon be able to adjust their fire by sight.

The only advantage of a small unit in this type of situation is control. Because of their large numbers, the NVA had difficulty getting on line and remaining on line to carry out their assault. This wasted precious time, time the Rangers needed to escape. The Americans heard the NVA leaders shouting orders and yelling instructions as they struggled to move their soldiers into a combat formation. But the ordinary soldiers were still reeling in confusion and disorganization from Rothwell's surprise attack.

Ten minutes had passed since the first rounds were fired, and at least fifteen minutes more would pass before the Huey arrived to extract them. Time was critical, and the team began thinking of escape and evasion. But Vodden ended the talk of running by ordering his teammates to hold their position and wait for the chopper; if they made a dash for it, the NVA would run them to ground. The nearest LZ was several thousand meters away, and the enemy had the advantage of knowing the country far better than the Rangers.

The fight quickly turned into a battle of grenades. The

Rangers each tossed six to eight minifrags up the hill at the enemy soldiers moving toward them, and Rothwell was blasting rounds from the XM-203 grenade launcher one after another. The Rangers managed to make enough noise and throw out enough firepower to convince the NVA that they had run into the front end of an American battalion on the prowl.

The NVA slowed their assault fifty meters from the Rangers' perimeter because they were having difficulty locating the patrol's exact position, and the Rangers' grenades were keeping their heads down and preventing them from making a concentrated rush. To avoid giving their positions away, with the exception of Rothwell's grenade launcher, none of the Rangers had yet fired his weapon. The distinct sound of M-16s hammering away would tell the enemy exactly where they were, and if the NVA tried to assault their perimeter the Rangers would need every round they had. But the enemy was freely firing everything downhill at the suspected American positions, and throwing showers of ChiCom grenades. Some of the stick-handled fragmentation grenades began landing close to the team's perimeter, exploding less than five meters away.

Suddenly, the Rangers could make out the beautiful sound of a Huey slick droning less than a couple of miles out. Then they saw it coming straight in, even with the crest of the hill.

Reilly got on the radio, warned the pilot that he had a hot LZ and cautioned him not to come in with his guns blazing. There was too good a chance that the Huey would hit the friendlies with their sweeping M-60s.

The pilot radioed back that he could hear gunfire and said he would land but "only for five seconds, and you'd better all have your asses in the bird, because I'm taking off after that." To Reilly, it seemed a sensible request.

The pilot wasn't lying. A single smoke grenade, and the Huey was swooping in to extract the patrol. The aircraft hovered a few feet off the ground for all of five seconds. Then the door gunners opened up with everything they had. There was only one problem as the five seconds expired and the helicopter pulled away from the hillside in dramatic fashion—not everyone was on board.

Whitmore was outside the helicopter hanging from the skid,

holding on for dear life. Seeing his predicament, the Rangers formed a human chain, Vodden, Rothwell, and Reilly reaching down to secure Whitmore. There were a few anxious moments as the three men struggled to get their comrade aboard, but only with the additional help of the helicopter's crew chief were they able to pull the Ranger into the aircraft.

Muldoon, bleeding badly from his leg wounds, broke out in raucous laughter on the way back to Camp Eagle. Earlier he'd slapped a couple of bandages over his wounds, and the pain was not so bad that it overshadowed the sudden sense of relief that flooded through him at that moment. Soon the others were laughing, too. They had cheated death once again, and the payoff was the realization that they would soon be chugging cold beers back at the Ranger Lounge.

Several hours later, an LOH scout helicopter dropped down over the tree line at the top of the hill Ranger Team 2-5 had escaped from. The aircraft received some small-arms fire, but not before the pilot was able to spot the bodies of at least four dead NVA. The sighting was unusual because the NVA were known for their uncanny ability to pick up their dead during and immediately after a battle. It was quite possible that the enemy had temporarily left their dead where they'd fallen while they made another trip down to the valley to fetch water. Or perhaps they had fled the area in anticipation of the air strike that had destroyed their base camp later that same afternoon. Either way, Team 2-5 had turned a cold mission into a memorable success.

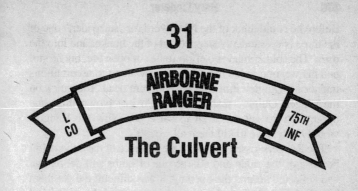

31

AIRBORNE RANGER

L CO · 75TH INF

The Culvert

Rangers were known for their versatility and their ability to adapt to any situation. But on March 16, 1971, Rangers from Lima Company were forced to handle a job that none of them could possibly have trained for.

A five-man patrol led by Ranger Staff Sergeant Jim Smith went in on a reconnaissance mission just north of Fire Support Base Bastogne, a large U.S. firebase overlooking Route 547—an improved gravel highway that ran from Camp Eagle to the eastern edge of the Ashau Valley. The eastern edge of the patrol's recon zone butted right up to the highway, so the Rangers decided to set up an OP just back from the road to determine if the enemy was using it during the night.

The second morning of the mission, the patrol spotted three NVA walking down the middle of the road. Sergeant Dave Quigley, Smith's ATL, prematurely opened up on the enemy soldiers, who escaped his fire by taking shelter in a large culvert that ran under the highway.

The Rangers could observe both ends of the culvert and knew that they had the three NVA trapped inside. It was an excellent opportunity for the team to pick up a body count, and even a possibility to capture some prisoners. With this in mind, Staff Sergeant Smith moved down closer to the road and began to shout *"Lai dai! Lai dai,"* ordering the NVA to "Come here."

269

Before he could think of the NVA word for "surrender," one of the three NVA suddenly stepped out of the bunker and into the open. The soldier made no effort to flee or open fire, but he still had his weapon in his hands. Without waiting to ascertain his intentions, Quigley immediately shot him dead. Too quick on the trigger, Quigley realized that he'd just blown their one opportunity to get the NVA to surrender. Now the Rangers would likely have to kill them all.

The Rangers tossed frags into the entrance of the culvert, but because of the angle and a large pile of limbs and debris that had collected around the opening, it was difficult the get them back far enough where they would do any good. An occasional burst of gunfire from deep within the culvert signaled that the NVA were still alive.

While the rest of the patrol kept up the grenade attack, Staff Sergeant Smith circled around away from the entrance to the culvert until he was able to get up on the highway above it. He moved quickly down the roadbed until he was directly over the culvert, then dropped to his hands and knees and crawled over to the edge.

It was dark inside, too dark to see anything of the two NVA. But from his position above them, Smith could toss a frag far back into the culvert. Taking out one of his last two grenades, the Ranger patrol leader leaned over and prepared to underhand the grenade into the culvert. As he did so, the weight of his rucksack shifted, flipping up over his head and pulling him over the edge. With a loud thump, he landed on his back in the dry creek bed. The ten-foot fall didn't cause any injuries, but it did knock the wind out of him. Plus, he was now lying at the mouth of the culvert, fully exposed to the two surviving NVA soldiers still inside.

As Smith fought to regain his breath and move away from the enemy soldiers' line of fire, the new man on the team leaped down into the streambed and began firing long bursts into the culvert with his M-16. If his intention was to keep the NVA from shooting Smith, it worked rather well. But it didn't prevent the NVA from returning fire at him. A short burst from inside the culvert hit the Ranger in the leg, knocking him to the ground. On his back, struggling to get a fresh magazine into his weapon, the young Ranger shouted to his teammates, "I'm hit, but it don't mean nothin'!" John Wayne was still alive in L Company.

Before the enemy soldiers could capitalize on the situation, both Rangers managed to scramble away from the entrance to the culvert.

A short time later, Ranger Lieutenants Paul Sawtelle and Jim Montano were returning to Camp Eagle after inserting a couple of patrols into the Ruong Ruong Valley not far to the south. When they heard that Smith's team was calling for a medevac, and that they had two NVA bottled up in a culvert, the two officers decided to lend a hand.

The officers reached the site before the dustoff arrived. Since the wounded Ranger had still not been medevacked, they hustled him aboard their own aircraft and gave the pilot instructions to get him to the 85th Evac at Phu Bai. Not wanting to miss out on all the fun, Sawtelle and Montano took the wounded man's place on the ground, where they joined the remaining four Rangers securing both ends of the culvert. Soon they, too, were putting fire into the entrances to keep the NVA pinned inside.

A short time later more helicopters arrived bringing in an aero-rifle platoon from Delta Troop, 2/17th Cavalry. The Cav troopers moved down the road and took up positions around the culvert, reinforcing the Rangers.

Once the combined American forces secured their positions, they ceased fire while Lieutenant Montano called Division G-2 for a Vietnamese interpreter. Nearly an hour passed before the Huey slick arrived with the interpreter.

After linking up with the Rangers and Blues, the interpreter crawled up and took a position just outside and little above the east entrance to the culvert. From that vantage point he shouted down for the two NVA soldiers to give up and come out, telling them they were hopelessly outnumbered. He also informed them that their companion had died in what was mistakenly thought to be an attempt on his part to escape the Americans. When this got no response, he further cajoled them, saying that if they lay down their arms and came out, they would be treated well and looked after. His story was not convincing enough to induce the enemy soldiers to comply; they responded by opening fire.

During the next fifteen minutes, the Rangers and Blues tossed nearly sixty fragmentation grenades and a good number of willie petes into both entrances of the culvert, without the slightest indication from the two NVA that they were willing to surrender. But when the two Ranger officers requested a Delta Troop machine gun crew take up position and put about five hundred rounds through the culvert, the two NVA sheepishly scrambled out of the culvert and surrendered. The six Rangers jumped down into the ditch where the enemy soldiers stood waiting and quickly secured them. When they were finished, three of the Rangers pulled the two prisoners out of the ditch and dragged them away from the culvert, forcing them down on the side of the road.

The two NVA were suffering from extreme dehydration. The streambed running under the road was bone dry and the NVA had no canteens with them. They'd had no water for ten hours, and between them they had taken over a hundred perforations from grenade fragments.

The Rangers immediately started IVs in both men and gave them water from their own canteens to drink. While Lieutenant Montano called for a medevac, the remainder of the Rangers stood guard to protect the two captives from a number of the Delta Troop soldiers who looked as if they didn't really want to see the POWs brought in. The Rangers knew that Delta Troop had taken some tough casualties a few weeks earlier, and they couldn't blame them for wanting to get a little payback.

Instead of a medevac, Colonel Gorman's personal helicopter soon set down on the road. As commander of the 2/17th Cav, Gorman felt he had direct control over the Rangers and their operations, and since L Company was attached to his command, he was probably correct in this assumption. On more than one occasion L Company patrols had been forced to step back in the shadows when certain Cav commanders took credit for Ranger successes. In some cases Cav leaders "forgot" that a six-man Ranger patrol had been alone on the ground, stirring up the bees, and they weren't doing it so the Cav could come in and steal all the honey.

The problem wasn't nearly as bad as it had been back in '68 when the Rangers' predecessors, the Lurps of F Company 58th Inf (LRP), were first attached to the 2/17th Cav. The Cav's support of the Lurps had been nonexistent to poor. Now, good leadership on the part of the Cav and a better understanding of how to use and support L Company's long range patrols had brought about a much better working relationship between the two units. Though far from being symbiotic, it still managed to get the job done.

After Colonel Gorman landed, he quickly secured the maps and postcards that the Rangers had confiscated from the captured NVA soldiers. When he realized that the two men needed immediate medical treatment, Colonel Gorman quickly returned to his aircraft with the two POWs. He bellowed that he would fly them directly to the 85th Evacuation Hospital at Phu Bai. No offer to accompany the colonel and "his" prisoners was extended to either of the Ranger officers.

However, the situation quickly changed when one of the NVA refused to relinquish his hold on Ranger Lieutenant Montano. Reluctantly, Colonel Gorman ordered Lieutenant Montano to climb aboard. At the evac hospital, the enemy POW still wouldn't release his death grip on Montano's hand, not even when they rolled him into the operating room and prepared him for emergency surgery.

Later, after the two NVA prisoners had been treated and properly interrogated, it was discovered that they were part of a recon element for an NVA regiment preparing to overrun Fire Support Base Bastogne. The Rangers had surprised them as they were moving up to ascertain the best access routes into the firebase. The two POWs finally divulged the nearby locations of their regiment, and immediately Division requested an arc light to destroy them. After two full days of intense B-52 strikes on the suspected enemy positions, a battalion from the 501st Infantry was inserted on a bomb damage assessment operation to police up the area and count all the bodies. Instead they walked into a hornet's nest and got the living hell shot out of them.

As expected, the 2/17th Cav received all the credit for stopping the NVA regimental-size assault on Fire Support Base Bastogne. It was recognition they "richly" deserved. Well, after all, Colonel Gorman did bring the prisoners in.

32

Team Indianapolis

In I Corps, especially in the Ashau Valley, long range reconnaissance patrols seldom outnumbered the enemy. That was a given, one the Rangers accepted. By stealth and surprise they were usually able to compensate for lack in number. But sometimes, individuals in positions of high command forgot the mission of LRRPs and ordered the special operations soldiers to perform duties they were not qualified nor trained to accomplish.

In 1971, with the war winding down and a general reluctance on the part of commanders to risk larger units in offensive operations against growing enemy strength, the remaining U.S. Army Ranger companies were often assigned patrol missions well beyond the scope of their capabilities.

On March 24, 1971, Ranger Team Indianapolis was inserted into the heart of the Ashau Valley. Their mission was to observe enemy vehicular traffic along Route 547, then establish an ambush on an NVA motorized supply convoy. Armed only with extra claymores and a half-dozen M-72 LAWs, the six Rangers were tasked to perform a mission that would have been risky even for a heavily armed, fully manned infantry platoon. But with American involvement in the war in Vietnam winding to a close, the U.S. high command felt that the loss of a half-dozen American soldiers would be much easier on the palate of an

275

already outraged American public than forty. They labeled their brilliant scheme "Economy of Force." To the soldiers in the field this simply meant, "Do more with less!" A wonderful idea if you weren't part of the "economy" end of the force.

Team Indianapolis inserted on a secondary ridgeline nearly a thousand meters north of Route 547. The patrol went in fast under the cover of a half-dozen slicks flying false insertions up and down the valley while four 2/17th Cavalry Pink Teams circled above a Psyops helicopter that was busily dropping propaganda leaflets.

The operation had been well planned and was designed to deceive the enemy as to what was actually going on in the valley. In the confusion of this aerial circus, three full six-man Ranger teams were to slip in unnoticed. The teams were to infiltrate unseen up to the road during their first day on the ground, then set up observation posts several hundred meters apart to monitor enemy traffic on the highway. The three patrols would be close enough to warn each other of enemy activity on the road, but not close enough to offer immediate support if one of them found itself outgunned.

At night they were to move up to the highway and establish linear ambushes along the road in an attempt to catch an NVA motorized convoy. Intelligence had reported the presence of a number of convoys and warned that they could possibly contain armored vehicles, which would make the ambushes even risker for the small Ranger patrols.

The Team Indianapolis OP/ambush location was to be just northeast of the abandoned Special Forces camp at Aloui, the site of major fighting early in the war. The remaining two Ranger teams were set up out in the valley on the intersecting north-south road.

Immediately after their insertion, Team Indianapolis dropped off the ridge, moving down into the valley and traversing a large number of unused farm fields. By then only bamboo- and cane-choked terraces, they were especially difficult to move through without making a lot of noise and leaving a visible trail. Signs of recent enemy activity were everywhere, but the patrol was under strict orders to maintain full radio silence until set up in the OP site. They had not even been permitted to call for a commo check after their insertion. The Rangers worried that they wouldn't have commo with the relay team when they finally reached the road.

Because of the unexpected overabundance of dense, nearly impenetrable cover and the patrol's requirement to move silently, they didn't reach the OP site during the first night. However, they did get close enough to the highway to be able to hear motor vehicles passing by in the dark.

The next morning the team moved out of their night defense position, with the goal of moving to their OP site next to the river and within twenty-five meters of the road. On the way to the site the patrol cut across a well-used high-speed trail and followed it into a recently abandoned enemy base camp. Setting up security, the Rangers nervously searched the bunkers and several aboveground structures. Among the litter in the camp was a number of American-made blue sweatshirts, miscellaneous articles of clothing, fresh human waste, and fresh blood on the handrails along one of the trails leading into the compound. After a cursory once-over, the patrol moved quickly through the camp and continued up to the highway. The focus of their mission was the road, not an empty NVA base camp standing in their way.

By noon the six Rangers had established an observation post in a cluster of trees on a slight rise fifty meters back from the road and about the same distance from the abandoned NVA base camp. On the Rangers' left flank ran a wide, shallow river.

During their second night in the field, two motorized convoys carrying a large number of NVA troops rolled down the road from across the valley. They came from the east and were heading west toward Laos. It was a definite indication that the NVA were pulling some of their forces out of South Vietnam to reinforce their efforts against the South Vietnamese government's Lam Son 719 offensive across the border in Laos.

The morning of the third day found Team Indianapolis reapplying camouflage face paint and still waiting for something to happen. After two nights in the bush they were just beginning to relax a little in the safety of their OP site, knowing that the most dangerous part of their mission would likely come with the hours of darkness. This false sense of security during daylight hours was difficult to combat and dangerous to ignore.

At exactly 0800 hours everything changed. An enemy patrol was spotted moving up the valley on the opposite side of the river. The NVA soldiers seemed to be heading in the general direction of the abandoned base camp behind Team Indianapolis. But as they passed the Rangers' position, the last man in the patrol unexpectedly left the others and moved directly down to the river. Without a moment's hesitation, he plunged in and crossed over at one of the deeper points in the stream, directly in front of the hidden U.S. long range patrol. The Rangers remained under cover, hoping the NVA soldier would stop before he reached them, or at least change directions. He didn't appear to be suspicious or even curious, only determined to reach the shore—at the exact spot where the Rangers lay concealed in the dense cover along the river.

The NVA soldier was carrying an AK-47 and wore a full bandoleer of ammunition across his chest. He was exceptionally large for a Vietnamese, weighing an estimated 160 to 170 pounds. The Rangers immediately suspected that he was Chinese.

The enemy soldier was just pulling himself up on the near shore and was less than six feet away when Spec 4 Ken Wells killed him with a single round from his M-16, knocking him back into the river.

Seconds after Wells shot the first NVA, another enemy soldier ran down to the riverbank opposite the Rangers. He stood there pointing animatedly across at the Rangers' position while shouting over his shoulder at his comrades. Wells, who had served an earlier tour with the Marine Corps and was an excellent marksman, fired another shot over the river and killed the second NVA, dropping him in his tracks.

Suddenly, a heavy volume of enemy small-arms fire erupted from the brush across the river and downstream from the Rangers' position. Unknown to the recon team, the enemy patrol had actually been the point element for an NVA company. At the sound of the first shot, the larger element had immediately deployed into the thick cover across the river and was maneuvering to flank the Rangers. The first burst knocked

Wells's weapon from his grip, destroying it in the process and wounding him in the right hand.

At the same time, the new man on the team, Corporal Joel Hankins, was struck in the back and mortally wounded by another burst of enemy gunfire. As more enemy rounds poured in on the Rangers, Hankins began screaming and writhing on the ground. Within minutes he was dead.

Soon each of the surviving Rangers had numerous bullet holes through their clothing and had equipment shot from their web gear. To make matters worse, there was no immediate indication that the enemy fire was going to let up.

Wells picked up Hankins's weapon and killed three or four more NVA soldiers attempting to cross the river. But many others had already moved up and were now throwing grenades at the embattled Rangers. A sudden explosion near Wells wounded him a second time, knocking him unconscious and out of the fight.

The situation along the river was growing desperate when a pair of Cobra gunships from the 2/17th Cav suddenly arrived on the scene and began making minigun runs on the exposed NVA. Caught in the open, the NVA had no choice but to break contact and flee back across the river to the cover of the trees, with the gunships following close behind.

A medevac helicopter came in minutes later and hovered over the river in an attempt to pull out Hankins's body. Two of the remaining team members grabbed the body and carried it out into the river, where they hoisted it up to the crew chief leaning out over the skids. On the first recovery effort the crew chief accidentally dropped the dead Ranger back into the river while trying to lift him into the open cabin, but on the second try Hankins's body was pulled into the dustoff helicopter and evacuated.

Wells, having recovered consciousness just in time to see Corporal Hankins's body fall from the medevac helicopter, opted to stay on the ground and go out with the remainder of his team.

Soon a Huey slick replaced the medevac out over the river, hovering low over the water to pick up the remainder of the patrol. As the Rangers moved out into the river from the shore, one of them stopped to search the body of the first NVA soldier that Wells had killed climbing out of the water. He quickly discovered a number of blasting caps in the dead man's shirt pocket. When he finished searching the body, the Ranger grabbed the oversized NVA's web gear and dragged him out to the waiting Huey. Reaching the slick with the body in tow, he threw it on board, then climbed in after it. The Ranger thought that the boys at G-2 might like to get a better look at this guy.

With the rest of the Ranger patrol finally on board, the extraction ship slowly lifted out of the valley and began the long flight back to Camp Eagle. Wells would recover from his wounds in time to depart on R&R, but would return to see more action before DEROSing back to the States.

Hankins, the new man on the patrol, was the sixth Lima Company Ranger to be killed in action in 1971. Eleven others would make the ultimate sacrifice before the unit's final year in Vietnam came to an end.

33

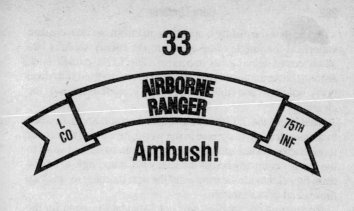

AIRBORNE RANGER

L CO

75TH INF

Ambush!

The success of any long range patrol operation is based on the patrol's ability to get on the ground without being compromised by the enemy; insertion is the most vulnerable time on any Lurp mission. When things went well during the insertion, the odds for a successful operation increased dramatically. But if things went badly during the insertion, a patrol's longevity can zero out in a heartbeat.

On April 5, 1971, a 2/17th Cav Pink Team, an LOH scout helicopter and a Cobra gunship, was flying a "hunter/killer" patrol over the heavily jungled mountains on the eastern side of the Ashau Valley. It had been a relatively slow morning for the Ashau—but things were about to heat up.

Popping up over a primary ridgeline, the scout helicopter caught a small number of NVA soldiers in the open. There was a mad scramble as the enemy troops tried to find cover. But the LOH pilot, realizing this was work for his big brother high overhead, immediately had his "shotgun" toss out a white phosphorous grenade to mark the target. While waiting for the Cobra gunship to dive to the attack, the LOH pilot spun around and opened up with his own minigun in an effort to keep the NVA from reaching cover. He succeeded in forcing the NVA troops to go to ground in a brushy clearing before they could reach the surrounding jungle.

In seconds the deadly Cobra dropped from the heavens and vaporized the jungle clearing where the enemy soldiers had taken cover, leaving no one alive. The LOH circled back around, hovering low over the carnage, and spotted four dead NVA soldiers and their equipment scattered around the clearing.

That night the 2/17th Cav's squadron commander decided that more than anything else in the world, he wanted to recover those enemy bodies and all their equipment, so he sent word to the Ranger company across the valley at Camp Eagle to have a team rappel into the clearing early the next morning to "pick up those dead gooks" for him.

Recovering enemy dead was not a standard mission for the Rangers, or anyone else, for that matter. And attempting such a recovery a full day after the action was both ill-advised and highly dangerous. Captain Ohle, Ranger company commander, called the squadron commander and, using exactly such words, told him so. But the colonel wanted his "battle trophies" and would not be put off by a mere captain. He did promise the Ranger CO that the team would have all the support it needed and that his personal scout helicopter would be on-site to do a close recon of the clearing and surrounding areas before the Rangers rappelled in. If an ambush was waiting, the helicopter would soon expose it.

Lieutenant Jim Montano, first platoon leader, learning of the mission, volunteered to go in with three of his men. This was immediately nixed by Captain Ohle. Due to the recent death of Lieutenant Smith and the unavailability of replacement officers, he could not risk losing another of his platoon leaders. So it was quickly agreed that Sergeant Billy Nix and three other Rangers would do the job.

Still worried about his men, Lieutenant Montano busied himself rigging the lift helicopter for the recovery mission while the four Rangers going in on the mission donned STABO rigs under their LBE. Everyone was nervous; the enemy had had an entire night to either remove the bodies or to prepare a welcome, and they were known to do both.

An early morning recon of the area confirmed the presence of the dead enemy soldiers and their equipment. And closer inspection indicated that there was no sign of an ambush in the nearby trees. Nevertheless, the Cav commander ordered a pair of Cobra gunships to lay on intense, suppressing fire in the surrounding jungle. After several minutes of this, with no counterfire or any other indication that enemy troops were dug in around the clearing, the mission was a "go."

The Huey slick containing the four volunteers and Ranger Staff Sergeant Leonard Trumblay flying bellyman maneuvered in over the clearing. The dead NVA were still visible down below. The chopper went into a hover sixty feet above the ground while Trumblay kicked out the four weighted sandbags carrying the coiled rappelling ropes. The four Rangers quickly hooked up to the dangling ropes, then moved out on the skids to begin their descent. Sergeant Billy Nix was the first Ranger to push off into space. But before he'd descended a dozen feet down the rope, the vegetation in the clearing beneath him was thrown back to reveal a long, U-shaped trench directly below the helicopter. The trench held a full dozen NVA soldiers armed with weapons pointing straight up at the helicopter. It was an ambush, and the hovering Huey with its passengers and crew were right in the middle of the enemy's "killing zone."

The first burst of automatic weapons fire came straight up through the floor of the helicopter, hitting both pilots, the crew chief, and Rangers Trumblay and Nix. The aircraft commander, hit in both legs, fought to maintain control of the ship. The copilot and crew chief were also hit in the legs and arms, rendering them ineffective. Trumblay, the Ranger bellyman, died instantly from several enemy rounds that blew up through his chest.

When the NVA soldiers sprang the ambush, Sergeant Billy Nix was in mid-rappel fifteen feet below the helicopter. Reacting quickly, he braked to a halt, which left him dangling in open space forty feet above the enemy. He must have presented a tempting target to some of the NVA gunners who now directed their fire at him. But the soles of a man's feet dangling directly overhead at a range of just over ten meters is not as large a bull's-eye as it may appear. Finally, a single bullet ripped through Nix's foot and exited his leg below the knee, causing a painful and serious wound. Undaunted, Nix again reacted quickly and, hand over hand, began to scale the rappelling rope back toward the questionable safety of the helicopter. With a final burst of nearly superhuman strength, fed by a massive dose of Ranger adrenaline, the Georgia-born NCO succeeded in reaching the edge of the helicopter's cabin floor, where he was quickly pulled inside.

The *ping . . . ping . . . ping* of enemy rounds striking the helicopter's aluminum airframe promised more casualties and the ultimate destruction of the aircraft, but the wounded pilot fought valiantly to control the ship until Nix was able to struggle back inside.

When Nix was finally aboard, the remaining door gunner and the surviving Rangers opened fire on the dug-in NVA beneath them, killing and wounding several. But having sustained dozens of hits through its undercarriage, airframe, tail assembly, cockpit, and main rotor blades, the helicopter was mortally damaged. The only thing that kept it aloft was the skill of its wounded pilot and the fact that the aircraft was new, having arrived in Vietnam only two months before.

Slowly, the aircraft managed to slip to one side as the pilot tried to pull away from the NVA kill zone. Finally, when he was away from the ambush site and the surrounding trees, he nosed the ship down to pick up enough airspeed to enable him to clear the area. For the next twenty minutes he nursed the crippled Huey back to Phu Bai while the uninjured Rangers in the cabin behind him did what they could for the wounded.

When the Huey finally settled down outside the evac hospital at Phu Bai, and the wounded and dead were tended to, the survivors found that the aircraft had taken over sixty hits. As for the remaining Rangers, well, they had just survived a well-planned, well-executed enemy ambush designed to destroy them and their aircraft. It was a miracle.

The new Huey was a total write-off, never to fly again. Three-quarters of the Cav air crew were permanently out of the war. Leonard Trumblay was dead, and Billy Nix was on his way back to the States and an early medical retirement. And for what? So that some rear-echelon O-6 could feed his vanity and his lust for war by getting to observe a few dead enemy soldiers up close!

This type of misuse of the Rangers was becoming common in the final years of the Vietnam conflict, and good men were dying foolishly to satisfy the foibles and fantasies of frustrated officers trying to milk the most from a failed war.

34

Blown Opportunity

In early April 1971 the focus of the Vietnam War was centered around the U.S.-supported South Vietnamese invasion of Laos—Lam Son 719. Nearly all of the aviation assets of the 101st Airborne Division had been committed to the effort, along with aviation units from all over South Vietnam that had been pulled together and placed under the operational control of the division. At that time, the consensus at Division Headquarters was that enemy activity in traditional hot spots like the Ashau and Ruong Ruong Valleys had dried up altogether because the NVA was rerouting its forces and supplies to the triborder region of Laos and the two Vietnams to counter the ARVN incursion into Laos. But the commander of the division's 2nd Brigade, whose AO included the Ruong Ruong Valley, decided this was not so. He suspected that the NVA was using this temporary lull in joint U.S./South Vietnamese operations in central I Corps to rebuild its strength in those areas. He even suggested that the NVA was employing motorized convoys to bring in massive amounts of war materials to build up the military stockpiles already in the valley. To prove his theory, the good colonel decided he needed a truck, an NVA truck, captured from the Ashau Valley. And the Rangers of L Company were to capture it.

Captain David Ohle, the Ranger company commander,

immediately put together an operations order designed to accomplish the task. A "can do" type of officer, Ohle accepted any assignment, no matter how difficult or impossible it appeared in theory.

The Ashau Valley had traditionally served as a safe haven for NVA forces operating on both sides of the border in central and southern I Corps. Over the years many stories had made the rounds among U.S. soldiers and Marines about the NVA's use of trucks, tanks, heavy artillery, and even Soviet-made helicopters in the Ashau Valley. Some were true, and some were likely the product of overactive imaginations, but U.S. military incursions and aerial patrols into the valley *had* found trucks and vehicle parts on more than one occasion. The valley definitely belonged to the NVA. Outsiders could visit—if they brought in enough military strength—but they couldn't remain. That was the Law of the Valley. It was Charlie's Law, and he enforced it with determination and enthusiasm.

The final operations order called for five six-man Ranger teams to insert west of the old highway, Route 547A, that ran north and south the length of the valley. The Rangers would go in with a company from the 1st Battalion, 502nd Infantry, to conduct sweep operations on the floor of the valley. Later in the day the grunts would be extracted while the Rangers moved into cover. Just before nightfall they would come out of hiding and infiltrate to the east until they reached the highway. Once there, they were to drop off a single team to the north and send another south to establish early warning and flank security positions, and then with the main party they would set up a three-team ambush on the road overlooking a culvert and a vehicle park.

The ambush teams would carry extra claymore mines, two M-60 machine guns, and a number of shaped charges that they would bury in the roadbed. When an NVA convoy entered the kill zone, the exploding charges would be the signal to spring the ambush. The eighteen Rangers were to shoot up any surviving vehicles and enemy personnel, then secure the kill zone long enough for a Chinook helicopter to sling-load out one of the enemy vehicles. The plan probably had a certain amount of tactical merit—that is, for any place other than the middle of the Ashau Valley.

First Lieutenant Paul Sawtelle drew overall command of the mission. A West Pointer from New York, Sawtelle was the kind of officer that men liked to be around. Unfortunately, as a combat leader he lacked experience for this type of mission. Lieutenant Sawtelle was new to the company, and leading a platoon-size commando operation on such a special assignment was not a typical mission for an officer in any of the LRP/Ranger units then serving in-country. But with the U.S. involvement in Vietnam winding down, MACV deemed it "politically correct" to avoid major unit confrontations with the enemy. Heavy casualties at this stage of the U.S. withdrawal were totally unacceptable to the U.S. military and to the American public. But risking a recon patrol or two, or even an entire Ranger platoon, would be far simpler to cover up if it ran afoul of the enemy than having a line company or battalion take heavy casualties. The term "expendable" crossed more than one mind among the Rangers who were still left in South Vietnam.

Back at the company, Lieutenant Sawtelle realized that the success of this mission could "make" his military career, and the word was that this fact was also not lost on several of the ranking officers up at Division. The destruction of an enemy motorized convoy within the borders of South Vietnam, and the recovery of a captured vehicle, would likely produce more stars than a Hollywood blockbuster film.

On the morning of April 15, 1971, five Huey lift ships from Bravo Troop, 2/17th Cav, settled in over a clearing five hundred meters west of the primary dirt highway that ran the length of the Ashau Valley. The thirty Rangers on board soon joined an infantry company from the 1/502nd already on the ground. For nearly two hours the Rangers conducted sweep operations with the infantry along the valley floor, but when the infantry moved down to a large clearing near the roadbed to be extracted later that afternoon, the Rangers were not with them. They had already gone to ground in deep cover two hundred meters back from the earthen highway.

After the grunts were gone and the surrounding countryside

had a chance to return to some degree of normalcy, the Rangers moved out cautiously to infiltrate to the highway to establish their ambush. But their advance was held up almost immediately by heavy underbrush and their need to make as little noise as possible while moving into position.

It was late when they finally reached the road. As soon as the Rangers broke cover, Lieutenant Sawtelle dropped off a single six-man team as his north flank security team, then turned south along the road to move to his ambush site. When he reached it, he quickly established a defensive perimeter, then sent the remaining six-man team two to three hundred meters to the south to set up the other flank security position.

The main party then moved down to the roadbed to set up its ambush, but it was already too late in the day to get the job properly done. They had only a single hour of twilight before full darkness set in. After that, the likelihood of encountering enemy patrols and troop movements on the road increased in direct proportion with the arriving darkness.

Fortunately, no enemy convoys passed that first night. However, hundreds of NVA infantry marched in columns down the middle of the road while the Rangers lay frozen to the ground a scant fifteen meters away. Using a Starlight scope to watch them from a distance, the Rangers could easily see them in the moonlight as they walked past almost close enough to touch.

Lieutenant Sawtelle began to have serious misgivings about hitting a convoy. With so many NVA infantry moving through the area, the Rangers could find themselves overwhelmed within minutes of blowing the ambush.

Just after daylight the next morning, a dozen members of the Ranger ambush party moved down to the road to set up their surprise party while the remaining six provided security. Working in the morning sun, the Rangers felt terribly exposed, even though it seemed that the NVA were only using the road at night. U.S. aerial surveillance flights still flew over the valley on a daily basis, making it too risky for the NVA to venture out in the open during daylight hours.

Still, enemy eyes were everywhere, and the Rangers had to set up the ambush quickly. While Lieutenant Suchke, the Rangers' explosives expert, set up the shaped charge under a rusty piece of corrugated PSP that the enemy had used to cover a shallow culvert, several other Rangers daisy-chained six claymores to a single electrical cord. They camouflaged the claymores and the wire, then fed it back toward their ambush site fifteen meters from the road. When everything was complete, the Rangers pulled back into the sparse underbrush overlooking the highway to take up their assigned positions over the kill zone. That's when they discovered, to their dismay, that the positions they occupied the night before were much too exposed under daylight conditions. So Lieutenant Sawtelle moved the patrol even farther back from the highway during daylight hours. He decided to hide his men in the brush fifty to sixty meters back from the road and move them back up into their ambush positions at dusk. There was nothing else he could do.

On signal, the Rangers left behind their six claymore mines facing the highway and pulled back into the heavier undergrowth that grew behind a low earthen berm fifty meters from the road. As they withdrew, they fed out the claymore wire behind them so they could still blow the ambush from their temporary position. Unfortunately, the wire ran out ten meters from the cover, forcing them to leave the claymore firing device unattended out in front of them.

Lieutenant Sawtelle dispersed his seventeen men in separate positions through the waist-high cover. He placed his two M-60 machine guns twenty meters out on his flanks atop two brush-covered mounds that might once have been large bunkers.

Five Rangers were at each machine-gun position. Lieutenant Sawtelle, along with Lieutenant Robert Suchke, Sergeant James McLaughlin, Corporal David Quigley, Spec 5 Asa Cook, and Spec 4s Ken Wells and John Perez, were spread out in a line between the two machine guns facing the highway. Though not actually close enough to the road to employ their claymores, the eighteen Rangers could still place effective small-arms fire into a kill zone of a hundred meters or so.

An hour later a ten-man NVA patrol moved down the road from the north. Six NVA, carrying AK-47s, were out front flanking the sides of the road. They were alert and moving cautiously, almost as if looking for something. Behind them fifty meters back were four more NVA. Two of them were armed with AKs, and two others were carrying RPD light machine guns.

As the NVA patrol slowly approached the kill zone, the Ranger M-60 gunner on the patrol's right flank was tracking them over his sights. At a distance of seventy meters, he knew that he could kill most of them before they could get off the exposed roadway and into the nearby cover, but he was hampered by Lieutenant Sawtelle's instructions during the premission briefing that only he or the detonation of one of the charges out on the road would signal the ambush to commence. No one else was to initiate it, under any circumstances. So, with his finger still on the trigger of his M-60, the gunner waited.

The two machine-gun positions and most of the Rangers hidden in the low grass could see the entire NVA patrol, but Lieutenant Sawtelle and his ATL, Sergeant McLaughlin, were only able to observe the road to their immediate front. They watched in silence as the first six enemy soldiers passed their position. The NVA appeared to be a road clearing patrol, sent out to sweep both sides of the highway.

Lieutenant Sawtelle saw them hesitate momentarily when they reached the culvert, then move out again as if nothing had happened. Ten meters down the road one of them looked back quickly, then shouted something over his shoulder. Could they have spotted the shaped charge? For a brief moment Lieutenant Sawtelle couldn't decide what he should do. If he initiated the ambush prematurely, the mission was compromised. If he let the patrol go by and the enemy soldiers had spotted the explosive charge, then the mission was still compromised, and the Rangers would be up to their asses in hostiles.

Sawtelle waited another minute while he continued to watch the six enemy soldiers. He could not be absolutely certain the NVA had spotted the charge. But the other Rangers in the ambush had also witnessed the actions of the NVA scouts as they passed the culvert, and they sensed that the enemy soldiers had suddenly become more alert—almost nervous.

They soon realized that the enemy patrol had indeed "made"

them. The Rangers waited for Lieutenant Sawtelle's signal to initiate the ambush.

As the six-man NVA element walked out of the kill zone, the remaining four enemy soldiers, now fully out of sight of Lieutenant Sawtelle and Sergeant McLaughlin, moved off the road. They were now walking parallel to it, searching the ground intensely. Soon they stumbled across the Rangers' claymore wire and turned to follow it back from the road toward the hidden American patrol.

Sawtelle and McLaughlin still did not see this second group of enemy soldiers. The two Rangers were still busy watching the first group of NVA as they moved farther down the road and out of the kill zone. But the remainder of the Ranger patrol were watching nervously as the four now fully alert NVA approached from their front. They waited anxiously for Sawtelle's signal to open fire, but instead, still unable to observe the second four-man NVA element, Lieutenant Sawtelle rose to his knees to watch the point element as it moved out of sight.

Suddenly, automatic weapons fire erupted from out in front of the Rangers' position. Lieutenant Sawtelle was immediately hit in the forehead by a single round, killing him instantly. McLaughlin, kneeling at his side, took three rounds in the chest and fell over backward. At the same time, the six NVA out on the road whirled around the began firing toward the Rangers hidden behind the berm.

Immediately, Sergeant Dave Quigley, carrying an AK-47, returned fire, possibly hitting one of the enemy RPD gunners to his front. A ChiCom grenade landed between Wells and Perez. Neither man saw it come in. Its detonation sent shrapnel into Wells's shoulder but missed Perez completely.

By this time the two Ranger M-60s had joined the firefight, wounding two more of the second NVA element and effectively silencing the RPDs. But the damage to the Ranger patrol had already been done. Lieutenant Sawtelle was dead and Sergeant McLaughlin was only minutes from joining him.

The remaining Rangers charged out of their hidden positions to fire up the surviving NVA, only to watch as the last of the enemy point element disappeared down the road and out of effective range. Miraculously, the badly shot-up RPD section had also managed to escape into the heavy cover on the opposite side of the highway. Wells, Perez, and Quigley moved quickly down to the road to search for bodies and found three blood trails going off into the elephant grass on the opposite side of the highway. The NVA machine-gun crews had not escaped untouched.

With three casualties and the element of surprise now lost, the original mission was compromised. Lieutenant Suchke, the company operations officer, took command of the main ambush party. He got on the radio and ordered the two flank security teams to pull back away from the highway and wait to be extracted. At the same time, he instructed his own people to blow their claymores and prepare the bodies of their dead for transport. The shaped charge would have to be left behind. The important thing now was to get the five Ranger teams out of the valley before the enemy had time to regroup and move up reinforcements.

Thirty minutes later six Huey helicopters and a pair of Cobra gunships arrived over the area. Within minutes the two flank security teams were recovered, then three slicks moved in to extract the ambush team and the dead and wounded Rangers.

The mission to destroy an enemy convoy and capture a vehicle was a failure. But it would not keep the brigade commander from trying again. Within two weeks, two more attempts would be made to accomplish the mission, each with Ranger casualties. This was another example of Rangers being misused in an operation not designed for their capabilities. Rangers in World War II and Korea, trained in company- and battalion-size commando operations, could have handled such an assignment, but in Vietnam Rangers worked best in the capacity of their Long Range Patrol predecessors. Trained to operate in six- to twelve-man teams, they were poorly tasked to perform offensive operations. Their successes in small ambushes and in defending themselves even when heavily outnumbered by enemy forces often misled brigade and division commanders into believing they were capable of conducting larger, more complex offensive combat operations. Unfortunately, their successes were more often than not attributable to the element of surprise and the Rangers' finely honed ability to direct artillery, gunships, and air strikes on enemy forces intent on destroying them. The title Ranger, conferred on February 1, 1969, by the Department of the Army, in no way prepared the Lurp companies for the task of tackling enemy convoys and large infantry units. The ignorance of LRP/Ranger capabilities by higher command resulted in a large number of unnecessary casualties among the U.S. Army Ranger companies during the latter part of the Vietnam War.

35

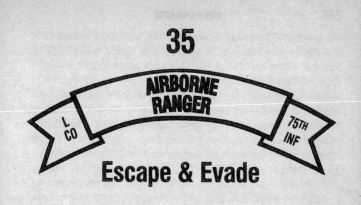

AIRBORNE RANGER
L CO   75TH INF

Escape & Evade

Three days after Lieutenant Paul Sawtelle and Sergeant James McLaughlin were killed in a futile attempt to ambush an NVA convoy in the Ashau Valley, Lieutenant Jim Montano's first platoon was sent into the same area to try one more time to complete the mission. Within hours he, too, was in contact and had to fight his way out, suffering one Ranger severely wounded. But incredibly, despite the heavy casualties, someone up at Division still believed the mission could be successfully completed. So for the third time Lima Company found itself tasked with knocking out an NVA motorized convoy in the middle of perhaps the deadliest enemy sanctuary anywhere within the borders of South Vietnam. Only this time the plan would involve the entire Ranger company.

At 1100 hours on the morning of April 23, 1971, ten Bravo Troop lift ships carrying ten six-man Ranger teams took off from Camp Eagle. Led by Captain Ohle, the sixty Rangers inserted into a large, grassy landing zone on the west side of the Ashau Valley. Once on the ground, the Rangers moved out in patrol formation toward a large culvert that had been constructed years before to prevent monsoon runoff from cutting the main road that ran through the valley. The Rangers had been instructed to secure the site, set demolition charges, and blow the culvert. Then shortly after the culvert was destroyed, the ten aircraft were to return and pick up only Captain Ohle and the second platoon. Hopefully, this would fool the NVA into believing that the Americans had come in to conduct a short raid on the road, had gotten it done, and pulled out.

But Lieutenant Montano's Ranger platoon would still be hidden somewhere away from the LZ in the thick elephant grass that seemed to grow everywhere. If the ruse worked, first platoon would move out a short time later and set up an ambush along the roadbed during the first hours of darkness. Their mission, like Sawtelle's, was to destroy an enemy convoy, then get out with a captured truck before the enemy had time to react. It would take timing, guts, and a lot of luck to pull off the mission. Lieutenant Sawtelle's team had failed to ambush an enemy convoy, but it did report exceptionally heavy enemy foot traffic on the highway during the night. This boded ill for the thirty Lima Company Rangers, who were expected to knock out enemy vehicles—maybe even armor— with no more than a few shaped charges, claymores, LAWs and an overabundance of raw guts. Even if they succeeded, there was a great likelihood that the NVA would be on them before they could be safely extracted.

Things began to go wrong at the very beginning of the mission. First, the lead aircraft led the entire formation into the wrong LZ: the Ranger company found itself on the ground three kilometers from its intended insertion point. That error in pilot judgment nearly resulted in the operation being scrubbed.

When Captain Ohle determined how far they would have to move overland to reach their designated target area, he decided that the chance of detection was too great to accept the risk. It was extremely dangerous to move in the open valley, but to do it in broad daylight with only sixty men was courting disaster. Too much time spent moving into an operational area would only invite detection and provide the enemy with the opportunity it needed to respond to the threat.

But Lieutenant Montano recalled spotting a second culvert on the highway, one much closer to the Rangers' position than the original target, on an overflight of the valley several weeks before. It was less than three hundred meters from their present location. Captain Ohle decided to amend the mission plan to accommodate the new target. In effect, nothing would have to be changed but the location of the ambush.

From that point on everything seemed to work to perfection. The Rangers moved up and secured the area of the road around the culvert, while a demo team under the command of Lima Company operations officer, Lieutenant Robert Suchke, set up their charges and successfully destroyed the target. Within the hour ten Huey helicopters arrived to extract Captain Ohle and second platoon.

As the helicopters lifted out with only three passengers aboard each ship, Lieutenant Montano and his twenty-nine Rangers lay hidden a hundred meters back in the shoulder-high elephant grass, where they would remain until just before dark, then move up to the road to establish the ambush.

Less than an hour after second platoon departed the valley, the single Huey slick bearing Ranger Sergeants Marvin Duren, James Champion, Fred Karnes, and Steve McAlpine, and Spec 4s Isaako Malo and Johnnie Sly, prepared to touch down on a shallow saddle on a ridgeline high above the Ashau Valley. They were to serve as radio relay team for Lieutenant Montano's ambush patrol operating out on the floor of the valley.

South of the saddle where Sergeant Duren's team had landed rose a steep promontory. To the north lay a narrow valley that ascended to a higher ridgeline on the far side. Unknown to the six Rangers, an NVA battalion, forewarned by the two days of heavy helicopter traffic that preceded the operation, knew something was about to happen and had set up housekeeping in a series of reinforced bunkers and fighting trenches on the promontory and along the opposite ridgeline. They were there waiting when the Cav helicopter carrying Duren's team touched down in the saddle. As the Rangers exited the helicopter they were met by a wall of small-arms fire that riddled Sergeant Duren, the team leader. The surviving Rangers dropped their rucks and sprinted in opposite directions for the safety of what little cover existed in the saddle.

As the action heated up around the now trapped Ranger team, down in the valley Lieutenant James Montano tried in vain to raise the team by radio. Little did he know that they were unable to answer his calls, or anyone else's, because their rucksacks along with both radios were out in the LZ where they had dropped them when the enemy had opened fire. Montano could only believe that they'd been wiped out in an ambush.

An hour into the battle, Spec 4 Johnnie Sly, a member of the relay team up on the mountain, crawled out into the saddle and made it back with one of the team's radios. During the next two hours, Lieutenant Montano directed the Ranger relay team by radio as it fought for survival.

When the 2/17th Cav commander, Colonel Gorman, arrived on the scene, he informed Montano that he was taking over the operation, and told the Ranger platoon leader to stay off the net. Montano tried to convince the Cav commander to come in and pick up his platoon since he was the closest U.S. ground element near enough to effect a reinforcement or rescue operation. But the Cav commander had other plans. He ordered Montano to avoid contact at all costs and further advised him to take his platoon someplace where he could stay out of the enemy's way until the relay team was rescued.

Montano was incensed by the colonel's apparent callousness. He knew that this early in the battle, he and his Rangers stood an excellent chance of fighting their way through to the team, but once the enemy forces consolidated around the besieged team and closed all the openings, nothing short of a miracle would suffice to get them out. But the colonel had already made up his mind and dismissed the idea, so Montano was forced to sit back in frustration and rage and listen to the battle unfold.

Soon, a Cav slick approached the LZ and, under heavy fire, touched down long enough to drop off Ranger Sergeant William Vodden. Vodden had volunteered to go out and take over the leadership of the team after he heard that Duren had been hit.

The Ranger NCO leaped from the aircraft and was met by the same reception party that had greeted his predecessor—and with the same results. Badly wounded, Vodden dropped behind a log and tried to return fire. As the Cav helicopter started to lift out of the LZ, enemy fire riddled it, causing the engine to seize. Out of control, the aircraft dove over the edge of the ridge and slammed into the side of the mountain, coming to rest upside down nearly three hundred meters from the crest.

Everything was going sour up on the ridge, and Lieutenant Montano and his Rangers could do nothing but listen over the radio.

The rescue effort raged for the rest of the day, but by nightfall the trapped Rangers and the surviving crew members of the Cav slick and an Eagle dustoff medevac chopper, which had been shot down in the LZ an hour after the first aircraft went down, were still up on the ridgeline fighting for their survival. Montano knew there was a very good chance that none of them would survive the night. But at the moment he had his own problems to worry about.

With the Cav's aviation assets tied up over the ridge, the Ranger platoon in the valley was on its own. Montano quickly realized they would have to stay out of trouble themselves or risk forcing the Cav commander to split his forces in an attempt to pull off a double rescue.

The stocky Ranger lieutenant waited until dark to take his platoon out into the sea of elephant grass to find a suitable place to hide. They finally located a bomb crater left behind by an earlier B-52 arc light. It was a huge crater, large enough to accommodate the entire platoon. When they found it, Montano had his point element move on past the crater, then circle back into it from the opposite side. If they were being followed by NVA trackers, they would be lying in ambush when the enemy soldiers followed the Rangers' trail past the crater.

Things quieted down up on the ridge that night. Support aircraft tried to keep the saddle illuminated to prevent the enemy from moving in close. Gunships patrolled the area, firing up enemy positions or any signs of movement.

Down in the valley, Montano and his Rangers lay quietly around the inside of the crater. Earlier they had moved out far enough to string a few defensive claymores around their position, but for the most part they were hoping to avoid contact.

Later that night, a C-130 "sniffer" flight out of Thailand flew high over the valley. Giving the call sign, "Bat Cat," the pilot informed Montano that he was on station and asked the Ranger patrol leader to mark his position. Montano did so with an infrared locator device. When the sniffer aircraft engaged its sensors to locate the signal, the pilot radioed Montano to report that he had a fix on him. But a few seconds later he called back to tell him not to move or make any unnecessary noise—there were enemy soldiers all around his position.

For three days the U.S. efforts to extract the team across the valley continued. Before it ended, the enemy would stop an infantry company from 1/502nd dead in its tracks, and then virtually destroy a Blues aero-rifle platoon from the 2/17th Cav. Reeling from the mounting heavy losses, the division commander decided that the Ranger team and the downed air crews were expendable. He ordered everyone out of the area. He was going to bring in an arc light to destroy the NVA who had chewed up so many American soldiers. Only the last minute rescue effort by Captain Ohle and five other Rangers saved the survivors from total annihilation.

The dead and wounded were lifted out on the fourth day. But the rescue effort was too late for some. Ranger Johnnie Sly lay dead near the LZ, and Malo and Champion had disappeared from the ridge. Ranger team leaders William Vodden and Marvin Duren, seriously wounded in the battle, were both fighting for their lives. A number of pilots and crewmen were also killed and wounded in the battle. Hardest hit was the thirty-two-man aero-rifle platoon, which lost twenty-two of its number killed in action. It was a costly defeat for the U.S. military operating in I Corps.

Montano's Rangers waited patiently for their own turn to be extracted. They'd been in the crater for three days, drinking stagnant rainwater they heavily flavored with halizone tabs to quench their thirsts. Nightly sniffer reports confirmed that they were far from being alone in the valley. The platoon was in the middle of a large number of sizable enemy formations, and to reveal their position now was nothing more than a quick invitation to serve as the main course at an NVA barbecue.

Midway through the fourth day of the battle it was first platoon's turn to be rescued. A flight of five Hueys, along with their escort Cobras, dashed in and plucked the Rangers from a hastily formed clearing near the crater. Even though they had never been fired upon, Montano's men had survived four very tough days in the middle of "Indian Country."

However, the final chapter of the operation had not yet come to an end, for as the Hueys and their accompanying Cobras were flying back to Camp Eagle, they were suddenly ordered to turn around and go back into the Ashau to secure a gunship that had gone down during the rescue operation two days earlier. The two pilots had been recovered immediately, but the Cobra was still out there. As far as it could be determined from the air, the enemy had not yet discovered the downed aircraft. Division wanted to attempt a recovery while it still had some assets in the valley.

As the flight of helicopters beat its way back to the valley, Lieutenant Montano couldn't help but wonder why it had taken so long to decide to recover the aircraft. Charlie owned the Ashau Valley, and he had enough people stationed throughout the area to know the exact location of the downed helicopter within minutes. Montano realized that he and his platoon could easily be flying into a well-prepared ambush.

Ten minutes later the five Cav slicks flared over the point of a low ridgeline and dropped the thirty Rangers into a bombed-out area near the Cobra. The platoon moved quickly through the waist-high brush and reached the ship in less than fifteen minutes. Surprisingly, it didn't appear that anyone had gotten there ahead of them. Montano set up security around the crash site while calling for a Chinook to fly in to sling-load the damaged Cobra back to Camp Eagle.

Suddenly, an NVA 37mm antiaircraft gun high up on a distant ridgeline opened up on the Rangers. The rounds passed high overhead, but it was still unnerving for the anxious Rangers. The enemy gunner continued shooting intermittently, yet never seemed able to come any closer. Montano finally determined that the NVA gun crew were likely unable to depress the barrel of their weapon enough to bring the Rangers under accurate fire.

The Chinook soon arrived on the scene, and presently the wrecked Cobra was dangling at the end of a cable on its way back to Camp Eagle. Minutes after the Chinook cleared the area, the Hueys returned to extract Montano's patrol.

However, the mission was still not over for the first platoon Rangers. As the formation neared Firebase Veghel, another urgent call came in ordering the Rangers to secure another downed helicopter, this time an LOH scout helicopter that had just gone down in the mountains west of Firebase Bastogne.

Once again the formation of five Huey slicks spiraled down to insert the Rangers. Landing one ship at a time in a jungle clearing a hundred meters from the downed aircraft, the weary Rangers moved forward to secure the LOH. As they neared the crash site they began to take sporadic small-arms fire from another ridgeline. Just as before, the gunfire was coming at the patrol from a long distance and was not accurate.

When the Rangers reached the abandoned aircraft, they hurriedly set up security and once again waited nervously around the wreckage until another Chinook arrived to pluck the little scout ship from the jungle. With this mission finally accomplished, the Rangers plodded back to the LZ and were lifted out.

Safely back at Camp Eagle, the first platoon Rangers dropped their gear at their bunks, heading first for the showers and then for the mess hall. It had been a grueling, stress-filled four days. There would need to be some time set aside to heal some of the physical and emotional stress that these young warriors had just gone through.

As Lieutenant Montano passed the TOC he was met by Ranger First Sergeant Neal Gentry, who motioned for him to wait up. When he reached the young officer, he said, "Lieutenant, we still have two MIAs out there." Montano hadn't realized until that moment that Sergeant James Champion and Spec 4 Isaako Malo had been left behind out on the ridge. Without a second's pause he answered, "What are we going to do about it?"

First Sergeant Gentry replied, "Are you prepared to lead the company back in to get them out?" Montano nodded and turned to round up his Rangers. But before the search and rescue mission was fully ready to go, Division ordered the Rangers to stand down. There would be no search and rescue mission. There had been enough casualties to account for during the operation, and Division high command didn't want to have to justify any others. B-52 strikes had saturated the area of the battle shortly after the last of the U.S. forces was extracted, leaving virtually no chance of finding anyone alive. If Montano did go in with an adequate force, finding the two men would be like looking for the proverbial needle in a haystack, and this particular haystack was infested with killer rats. No further rescue or recovery efforts were ever mounted to determine if the two Rangers had been either killed or captured during the operation.

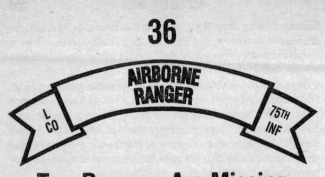

36

Two Rangers Are Missing

For a six-man Ranger patrol deep in enemy territory, everything has to go just right. When it doesn't, men die. On April 23, 1971, a Lima Company radio relay team led by Sergeant Marvin Duren was inserted by helicopter onto a ridge top on the eastern rim of the Ashau Valley in western I Corps. The team's mission was to set up a radio relay station for Lieutenant Montano's platoon on the floor of the valley, as described in the previous chapter, to ensure good communication with the Ranger TOC back at Camp Eagle. The team was to relay radio transmissions between the two elements, and to provide its own security while on the assignment.

The relay team's insertion into its primary LZ was aborted at the very last minute due to enemy ground fire directed at the insertion aircraft on its final approach. After the abort, Sergeant Duren decided to go in on the team's secondary LZ, a broad saddle in the middle of a major ridgeline flanked on the south side by an even higher mountaintop. Duren was glad that his team was going to remain on the high ground; radio relay elements had to get as high as possible to ensure reliable long distance radio communications.

Duren knew that if Chuck had his act together—and in the Ashau Valley, Chuck always had his act together. Lieutenant Jim Montano's Ranger platoon would be fighting for its life instead of trying to ferry out a Soviet truck for some paper tiger at Brigade.

But manning a six-man radio relay site in the heart of enemy country wasn't just another walk in the sun, either. Just eleven months earlier, Lima Company had lost an entire six-man radio relay team up north, near the abandoned Marine combat base at Khe Sanh. Transmitting too long from the same location too close to a major NVA trail had gotten that team triangulated, located, and terminated by a sophisticated enemy who was using Soviet radio directional locators to pinpoint radio transmissions. A brief flurry of small-arms fire a couple of hours before daylight had wiped out the relay team to a man. The Rangers hadn't even had the opportunity to return fire.

To add to the fun, just before his team departed Camp Eagle, Sergeant Duren discovered that there had been an unusual amount of air traffic over his relay site by Cav aircraft less than two days before the mission. Duren hoped that the traffic had not forewarned the NVA of the pending operation. If it had, there would likely be a welcoming party on the LZ.

As the helicopter settled into a clearing in the middle of the saddle, the six Rangers dropped to the ground, three on each side, and began to move quickly away from both sides of the aircraft. Immediately, NVA soldiers hidden in bunkers on the high ground across the saddle, and on another high point facing them across a small valley to their north, opened fire. In the hail of small-arms fire, the Rangers dropped their rucksacks and headed for cover. The volume of fire prevented the two separate elements from linking up on the ground, and the Rangers quickly found themselves split up on opposite sides of the LZ.

Duren was not with his five teammates when they reached cover. He'd been cut down out on the edge of the LZ in the opening burst of fire from an enemy AK-47. Hit twice in the right hip, once in the chest, and once in the stomach, the veteran Ranger team leader was out of the fight before it started.

As more NVA automatic weapons joined in, Duren was hit again in the spleen, appendix, left lung, left arm, and back. Firing from well-camouflaged bunkers, the NVA had waited until the helicopter dropped off the radio relay team and departed, then opened fire and pinned them down in the saddle.

At first, the remainder of the team were unable to reach their badly wounded team leader, but within minutes of the opening contact, Sergeant James Champion managed to put down enough suppressive fire with his M-203 grenade launcher to enable Sergeants Fred Karnes, the team's Senior RTO, and Steve McAlpine, an ex–Special Forces medic, to crawl out to where Duren lay and begin emergency medical treatment to save his life. McAlpine, under continuous heavy enemy fire himself, quickly started a saline IV in the team leader's neck to prevent his going into shock.

While Duren was being helped, Spec 4 Johnnie Sly left his cover to dash across the saddle and grab the rucksack containing the team's primary radio. Thanks to his courageous act, the team would at least have commo.

While preparations were being made back at the company area to rescue the trapped relay team, a Huey slick piloted by Captain Louis Spiedel from Bravo Troop, 2/17th Cav, was inbound with Ranger Staff Sergeant William Vodden, who had volunteered to take the place of the critically wounded team leader.

Spiedel approached the saddle keeping his aircraft low, below the rim of the ridgeline, popping up over the edge at the very last minute. As the Huey passed over the LZ, Vodden jumped out and ran across the saddle to join up with the rest of the trapped team. In spite of its nearly undetected approach to the ridgeline, heavy enemy ground fire hammered the Huey as it attempted to flare away from the LZ, forcing it to crash into the steep side of the ridge. The stricken aircraft rolled over and over again before finally coming to rest upside down in the thick undergrowth covering the side of the mountain.

Making certain the assistant team leader had everything under control, Sergeant Vodden looked up to see the door gunner from the downed Cav slick staggering across the LZ toward where the Rangers were maintaining a defensive perimeter. He looked badly shaken but under control. Then the helicopter crewman collapsed behind a log, got back to his feet, and fell again. Vodden knew he was in trouble. Abandoning his somewhat protected position, Vodden jumped up and ran out to retrieve the wounded door gunner, but on his way back to the Rangers' tiny defensive perimeter, Vodden was hit in the leg by an enemy round that shattered his femur.

As the Ranger NCO lay where he'd fallen, applying a pressure dressing to his leg, he spotted a medevac helicopter from Eagle Dustoff rapidly approaching the saddle. Piloted by Warrant Officer Fred Behrens and Captain Roger Madison, the Huey attempted to set down amidst a heavy volume of enemy small-arms fire to rescue the badly wounded Duren. McAlpine, the assistant team leader, and Spec 4 Johnnie Sly rose from cover and began to drag Duren toward the waiting medevac.

The dustoff crew chief leaped from the ship and ran to help, enabling the two Rangers to get the by-then unconscious Duren aboard. Amid a hail of enemy small-arms fire, the helicopter pulled away from the LZ, heading east toward the surgical hospital at Phu Bai.

While Duren was being extracted, the crew chief from Spiedel's downed Huey ran across the LZ and dropped to the ground at Vodden's feet. Excitedly, he reported that the two pilots from his chopper were both still alive, trapped upside down, their legs pinned in the wreckage.

When the crew chief stopped his story long enough to realize that the new Ranger team leader had himself already been seriously wounded and couldn't help, he mumbled his apology, then ran across the LZ to where the remaining Rangers had taken cover. But before he covered twenty feet, intense enemy small-arms fire turned him back. When he reached Vodden's position again, he hesitated momentarily to catch his breath then told the wounded Ranger that he was going back down to the wrecked bird to see what he could do for the pilots. Vodden nodded in understanding. If it had been his pilots trapped out there, he would have done the same thing. The crew chief then turned and disappeared over the edge of the saddle.

Meanwhile, the dustoff chopper piloted by CW2 Behrens had once again returned to the battle. Without circling, he brought his aircraft straight in, intent on medevacking the wounded Vodden and anyone else who'd been hit while he was getting Duren to the surgical hospital at Phu Bai. Flaring in fast over the LZ, Behrens slammed the Huey once again into the saddle amid the swirling smoke and debris of battle. Specialist Fourth Class Isaako Malo, the Ranger team's junior scout, along with Karnes, McAlpine, Sly, Champion, and the Cav door gunner, climbed quickly aboard the dustoff aircraft. Without realizing that Vodden and the Cav crew chief were still on the ground, Behrens struggled to get his heavily laden Huey into the air. As the helicopter slowly rose from the LZ, it became the target for every NVA gunner in the area. Behrens knew he was in trouble when he heard several loud metallic bangs. He was taking accurate ground fire from the enemy emplacements around the ridgeline. Suddenly, two rounds struck the young medevac pilot, one in his left foot, the other in his upper body. Then a third round struck his crew chief in the head, killing him instantly.

Fighting desperately to control the badly damaged Huey helicopter, Behrens seemed to be winning the battle until his engine failed. Though severely wounded and in tremendous pain, the aircraft commander still succeeded in autorotating his crippled helicopter back into the LZ.

The surviving crew members and passengers spilled out opposite sides of the downed Huey, some heading for Vodden's position, the rest ending up in a bomb crater fifty feet away from the crash site. Behrens, unable to keep up, limped away from the aircraft and collapsed behind the closest cover he could find.

A short time later the survivors of the crash who had made it to Vodden's location were joined once again by the crew chief from the downed Cav helicopter. He reported that the two pilots were still alive but were growing weaker by the minute.

During the entire operation, Cobra gunships from the 2/17th Cav had been making pass after pass over the dug-in NVA. The deadly gun runs were now the only thing that prevented the NVA from swarming out of their bunkers and overrunning the Americans trapped on the LZ. But the gun pilots could not keep the cover fire up much longer. And as darkness began to fall across the valley, the surviving Rangers and airmen on the ridge realized that there would be no rescue that day. Not one of them expected to make it through the night.

Soon the gunships, low on fuel and nearly out of ordnance, were forced to leave the battlefield and return to Camp Eagle.

With a heavy fog rolling in from the west, they would not be back that night. As the helicopters withdrew to the east, the enemy fire slowly dropped off and a strange silence settled over the smoking battleground.

As darkness moved in, the Cav crew chief announced once again that he was going to attempt to reach his ship's crash site for another attempt at freeing the two trapped pilots. His tremendous resolve strengthened by desperation, the young crew chief turned and disappeared over the edge of the ridge. Without a word the dustoff medic from Behrens's ship jumped to his feet and followed close behind.

The situation on the ridge remained unexpectedly quiet that first evening. The Americans talked quietly among themselves, discussing their chances for survival. They realized that the NVA would come with the darkness to finish the job. They accepted the fact that there was no way out, no escape . . . no hope of rescue.

The Cav crew chief and the dustoff medic returned a short time later, saying that it would take special tools to free the two pilots trapped in the wreckage of the Cav Huey. They both expressed great concern that the injured pilots would likely fall victim to the NVA after dark. There was little any of them could do to prevent it.

To everyone's surprise, the enemy remained in their bunkers throughout the night, seemingly satisfied to maintain the status quo. The Rangers understood that the NVA were likely using them as bait to draw more aircraft into effective range. The enemy knew that as long as there was anyone still alive on the ridge, the Americans would continue sending helicopters to get them out.

Karnes, Sly, and the other medevac pilot, Captain Madison, spent a sleepless night huddled in a bomb crater across the LZ from the others. None of the three knew for certain if anyone else still survived.

In the morning the three men decided to take matters into their own hands. They crawled around the top of the ridge trying to locate another radio. During this attempt, Sergeant Johnnie Sly was shot and killed by an NVA sniper.

When Karnes showed up a short time later with a radio,

Madison learned that an NVA battalion had been spotted by an aerial scout. The enemy unit was apparently moving up to reinforce the NVA unit surrounding the LZ.

Things began to look hopeless for the Americans scattered around the saddle. Captain Madison spent the rest of the day directing air strikes and gunship runs on the enemy positions, often bringing them right up to their own perimeter.

Later that day the two men received word that a reaction force of two aero-rifle troops from the 2/17th Cav had inserted just north of them and was attempting to reach their position. In addition, a pair of rifle companies from the 1/502nd Infantry had combat-assaulted into the valley below them and were moving uphill to link up with them. Just as the two men began to think they might yet survive this nightmare, the voice on the radio reported that all four elements of their rescue force had been stopped cold by heavy enemy resistance.

Toward the end of the second day Karnes and Madison made the difficult decision to attempt to E&E. As the two men moved to the west side of the ridge, they ran headlong into McAlpine, who had just left a badly wounded Isaako Malo hidden in a hole back off the military crest of the ridge. Unable to carry the hip-shot Ranger with them, the three men decided to leave him where he was hidden while they tried to make it to the Cav troops fighting for their survival a short distance away.

The trio moved slowly down the mountainside, turning north onto a secondary ridgeline then swinging back east again until they reached the rear of the Cav's perimeter. They were shocked by the carnage they found. Dozens of dead and wounded troopers lay about the rapidly shrinking perimeter. The NVA had mauled them badly on their insertion, killing ten of the Blues during their first ten minutes on the ground. The surviving Cav troopers were in no shape to rescue anyone else, and looked upon the arrival of the two Rangers and the pilot as a reinforcement of their own perimeter.

A short time later Captain Madison was medevacked off the mountain with a batch of the Cav's more seriously wounded. McAlpine and Karnes spent their second night on the ground with the remnants of the Cav reaction force.

CW2 Fred Behrens remained in hiding during the entire

second day of the battle. Fortified NVA bunkers and one- and two-man fighting positions were all around him. Wounded a third time by an NVA sniper, the tough pilot hugged the ground and cradled a Thompson submachine gun (.45 caliber) in his arms. He had managed to salvage his personal weapon when he abandoned his helicopter. But he would have traded it for a drink of cold water. Holding the Thompson close to his body, he felt better knowing that the enemy couldn't take him without a fight.

The NVA sniper had focused his full attention on finishing off the wounded American pilot, and seeing that he was only an aviator must have given him confidence. Forsaking the rules that all good snipers observe, the overzealous marksman decided to enter into a duel with the badly wounded pilot. He had to use up half his ammo, but Warrant Officer Fred Behrens came out of the duel the victor. With the enemy sniper no longer a threat, Behrens decided to save the rest of his ammo for when the enemy tired of waiting and decided to overrun his position.

During the day, friendly aircraft remained on station repeatedly strafing and rocketing the area around where Behrens lay hidden. Occasionally he would scream at the top of his lungs in a futile effort to alert anyone else in the area that he was still alive. Several times his yelling attracted the attention of the enemy and drew more small-arms fire down on his position. Behrens knew he wasn't alone. He was certain that somebody had to be out there directing the gunship runs. He finally breathed a sigh of relief when the Cobras suddenly adjusted their strafing runs away from him.

In the late evening the medevac pilot watched frozen in fear when, during a lull in the action, a number of khaki-clad NVA soldiers came out of their bunkers to drag off their dead and wounded.

Vodden, Champion, and the Cav crew chief tried to remain out of sight and under cover, as each movement now seemed to draw enemy fire. The medic had not returned from a trip out to the wrecked medevac helicopter in an attempt to salvage a canteen of water. The Cav crew chief continued making periodic checks on the two injured pilots still trapped in the wreckage of the downed Huey slick, giving them moisture from a few pulpy roots he managed to find. He reported that they were in very bad shape and getting worse by the hour. By some inexplicable miracle, the enemy had not yet discovered them.

The three Americans, believing they were the only ones left alive on the ridge, decided among themselves that Champion and the crew chief would attempt to escape and evade. The crew chief was armed with only a revolver. Champion wasn't much better off. He had lost his web gear and rucksack, and the stock of his M-16 had been shattered by an NVA bullet. Vodden divided up his remaining frags and magazines with Champion and gave the young Ranger his map and compass.

At dusk on the second day the two men set out. But a short time later the crew chief returned to Vodden's position, explaining that he'd decided to stay and look after the injured pilots. An hour passed, then the two men heard brief but heavy firing in the valley below their position. Vodden sighed and bowed his head, telling the crew chief that they had just heard Sergeant James Champion's "last stand."

During the second night, Behrens lay terrified, holding his breath and waiting to die as a number of enemy soldiers came out and began searching the saddle for dead and wounded Americans. Amazingly, the NVA walked within a few feet of the wounded pilot without finding him.

A short distance away from Behrens's hiding spot, Vodden lay in a crater, with the crew chief, nursing his own wounds. On two different occasions the Ranger team leader had fired at the silhouette of a man standing above them on the edge of the crater. Both men had disappeared when he fired, but Vodden was not certain that he'd hit either one. But each time he fired, just for good measure, he tossed a grenade into the brush above the lip of the crater.

On the third day a scout helicopter suddenly appeared overhead followed by several Cobras making their deadly rocket runs. When the gunships had finally expended their ammo, low flying fighter/bombers arrived on the scene and dropped their ordnance with pinpoint accuracy on the enemy forces dug in around the LZ.

The Cav crew chief once again took advantage of the distraction provided by the Cobra gunships and slipped off the ridge to check once more on his pilots. When he returned an hour later, it was to sadly announce that his aircraft's copilot had died sometime during the night.

Off in the distance the two men spotted a long string of Huey helicopters approaching. They knew that more help was finally on the way. For the first time in three days they began to hope . . . to believe they might somehow survive this terrible nightmare.

Early in the afternoon, Vodden and the crew chief heard small-arms fire up the ridge from the saddle, and someone yelling something unintelligibly in English. Then, miraculously, two Lima Company Rangers suddenly appeared almost specterlike out of the brush and moved toward them. Ranger Sergeants Dave Rothwell and Don Sellner, part of a small Ranger rescue force, had finally reached the two survivors. With their help, the Cav crew chief and Sergeant Vodden were quickly medevacked off the ridge.

Karnes and McAlpine remained inside the tiny Cav perimeter until the morning of the third day. When a small contingent of Rangers landed and quickly linked up with them, the two men volunteered to join up with a five-man reaction force under the command of the Ranger commanding officer, Captain David Ohle. The team consisted of Sergeant Dave Quigley, Sergeant Herb Owens, and two other Rangers. Karnes and McAlpine offered to lead them back up to the ridgeline.

It was a decision borne of desperation. General Tarpley, the division commander, had just ordered an arc light to be put in on the ridgeline, scheduled for sometime late that afternoon. When they heard the news, Captain Ohle and most of the Rangers still in the company immediately volunteered to go in ahead of the B-52s to try to rescue and evacuate anyone who might have survived the three days of intense fighting on the ridgeline.

The rescue force moved up the side of the ridge, inching cautiously toward the saddle. Nearing the LZ, the seven Rangers suddenly came under intense enemy small-arms fire from a large number of NVA hidden in reinforced bunkers. Everyone but Quigley was immediately pinned down, unable to move any closer to their objective. Taking full advantage of this sudden and unexpected window of opportunity, Quigley rushed through the area alone until he reached the LZ. He immediately stumbled upon Sly's body near the downed medevac.

Then Quigley discovered Warrant Officer Fred Behrens, by then more dead than alive, looking a lot like a piece of Swiss cheese, from all the holes that were in him. It appeared to Quigley that the NVA gunners had used him as a target to zero in their weapons. Miraculously, Behrens was still conscious, and when he saw Quigley, he asked him for something to eat. Quigley rummaged through his rucksack and dropped off a can of apricots and a canteen of water then moved on to look for others.

Captain David Ohle was also succeeding in fighting his way past the NVA bunkers and soon caught up with Quigley. The two Rangers flanking the edge of the saddle looked down and spotted the Cav chopper overturned in the trees three hundred meters down the hillside, smashed like a pancake. Unknown to the two Rangers, the aircraft commander, Spiedel, was still alive, and was ultimately rescued, but he would later lose both legs at the hips as the price for his survival.

When the remainder of the Rangers finally broke through the circle of NVA emplacements, Owens and Quigley linked up and searched the rest of the ridgeline for Champion and Malo. They found a damaged weapon but no sign of either man. With the day drawing to a close, they were forced to give up and move back to the saddle to help extract the dead and wounded. There was not enough time to run a more extensive sweep of the entire ridgeline, and the sheer number of enemy soldiers still in the immediate vicinity of the ridge made the possibility of bringing in a larger reaction force even more treacherous.

By nightfall, with the exception of Champion and Malo, all of the casualties and the survivors had been located and extracted from the scene of the battle. There was no more time to look for the two missing Rangers. The B-52 arc light mission had been laid on for 2200 hours.

Two years later, in the spring of 1973, Spec 4 Isaako Malo

was released from captivity by the North Vietnamese government, along with a little more than three hundred other American POWs. To this day he will not discuss the events of the ill-fated operation nor the circumstances of his capture. But the emotional and physical scars of his torture at the hands of the NVA are plain for anyone to see.

Staff Sergeant James Champion is still carried on the Ranger rolls as "Missing in Action." But most of those who survived the battle believe that he never reached the valley floor.

37

LZ Watchers

L Company's effectiveness against the NVA in the western border areas of I Corps had been somewhat ignored by the hierarchy at Division HQ, but duly noted by the enemy commanders who sought desperately to develop new strategies to cope with the American long range patrols that invaded their sanctuaries.

One of their measures was to post LZ watchers on every clearing, sandbar, bomb crater, abandoned crop field, and open area that could be utilized as a helicopter landing zone. This was a tremendous manpower drain for the enemy, but the simplicity of the plan was exactly what made it so effective. Between 1969 and 1971, with increasingly larger numbers of U.S. forces standing down and preparing to return to the States, the enemy was able to assign more and more of its soldiers to duty as LZ and trail watchers.

By 1969 the NVA knew a lot about how long range patrols operated. They knew that most patrols were inserted by helicopter, usually touching down in some type of opening or clearing surrounded by thick cover, although on some occasions the Americans would also infiltrate teams by means of rope ladder or by rappelling. The NVA also knew that because of the danger of resupplying a patrol in the field, the patrols seldom spent more than five days on the ground. The enemy understood that because of this restriction on the number of days in the field, most patrols were inserted close to the areas they were to patrol. To the enemy this meant that they could counter the effectiveness of U.S. LRPs if they could simply put every possible helicopter landing site within a three-day march of their base camps under constant surveillance.

Since the concept of "Economy of Force" was rapidly becoming the standard practice of all U.S. commands during the final years of the war, small reconnaissance patrols were growing more common and were the popular choice as the primary military force to be sent against enemy units operating in the field. And as more long range patrols infiltrated into the enemy's sanctuaries, contacts on the landing zones and along the enemy's high-speed trails became more and more frequent. Such encounters were usually brief but often deadly.

On May 7, 1971, Staff Sergeant Riley Miller received a warning order to get his team ready for a six-day reconnaissance mission into a heavily mountainous area just north of the Ruong Ruong Valley. The overflight showed the RZ to consist of heavy jungle and rugged terrain. Miller selected a primary LZ in a small clearing near the end of a finger running down from the main ridgeline that bisected the AO.

The team went in at 1500 hours. It was a hot, sunny day, and every member of the five-man patrol was soaked with sweat long before the sounds of the departing Huey had faded in the distance. Staff Sergeant Miller, team leader; Sergeant David Bush, assistant team leader/point man; Sergeant Dave "Pig Pen" Quigley, Senior RTO; Spec 4 Paul Morgucz at drag; and a new cherry, still without a name or a reason to be remembered, moved off the LZ and lay dog in the thick underbrush bordering the clearing.

An enemy high-speed trail ran from the east side of the clearing back across the face of the ridgeline. Below them the Rangers could just make out a break in the undergrowth on the downhill side of the clearing. It appeared to be another trail running from the end of the finger down to the "blue line" in the valley below.

Bush whispered to Miller that he'd been to that very spot before. He remembered the clearing out on the finger, and combat-assaulting into it with Charlie Company, 2nd Battalion, 502nd Infantry—his old unit—just eight months before. He whispered to Miller that he was the one who'd personally hacked out the trail that ran from the end of the finger down to the blue line. Bush said he had done it when he was walking point at the head of a water detail, and admitted that the exertion had caused him to suffer a serious bout of malaria that got him medevacked out of the boonies that very same day.

Convinced that Bush was telling the truth, Miller told him to move out following the trail that ran across the finger. Miller said he wanted to put some distance between the patrol and the LZ by nightfall, and it was already going on 1600 hours.

Bush moved out on point and immediately sensed that something wasn't right. He couldn't tell what was causing the hair to stand up on the back of his neck, but he was sure there were gooks in the area. More cautious now than before, Bush worked his way slowly and carefully along the trail. He could feel that the patrol was going to make contact any minute.

When the team had covered three hundred meters, Miller told Bush they'd come far enough. It was getting late in the day, and Miller wanted him to locate a good place to hole up for the night. Just ahead Bush spotted another clearing, smaller than the one they'd inserted into. He turned and told Miller they should check it out. Miller agreed, and looked over his shoulder to order Quigley to stay back in the brush with Morgucz and the new guy while he and Bush moved up to scout the clearing.

With Bush in the lead, the two Rangers moved cautiously out into the clearing in a crouch, weapons moving back and forth. Alarm bells began going off in Bush's head, but only he seemed to hear them.

Suddenly, automatic weapons fire opened up on the two Rangers from the opposite side of the clearing. The unmistakable deep, throaty *takka takka takka* identified the weapons as AK-47s. Bush and Miller realized immediately that there were only a couple of assault rifles firing at them. They figured it was nothing more than a pair of trail watchers.

Abruptly, Bush was jolted and knocked backward, almost as if someone had punched him hard in the chest. He realized instantly that he'd been hit, and hit hard, but the pain was not too bad—at least not bad enough to prevent him from returning fire.

Miller moved up alongside him and opened fire, then Quigley and Morgucz and the rookie joined in from behind them. Suddenly, Bush felt light-headed and wobbly. He knew for sure that he'd stopped a bad one. He turned around and told Miller he'd been hit, and the two Rangers quickly rejoined the rest of the patrol. The cherry, who was a medic, moved up and began to dress Bush's wound.

While attending to Bush, the Ranger medic informed him that the round went in just above his heart and exited through his left shoulder. The wound was a "through and through" hitting no bones or vital organs before it passed out of his body. The medic told Bush that he'd just gotten the proverbial million dollar wound. Grimacing in pain, Bush replied, "I'd take a helluva lot less for it right now."

A short time later an Eagle dustoff aircraft arrived over the team's location. It set down briefly in the clearing and extracted the wounded Ranger. An hour later a second slick came in to pick up the remainder of the team.

At the 22nd Surgical Hospital in Phu Bai, Bush was stabilized and emergency exploratory surgery was performed to determine how badly he'd been wounded. As a result, it was decided to medevac Bush to a hospital in the States. He departed Phu Bai and was flown directly to a hospital in Danang, where he underwent more treatment. Finally, he ended up in Guam by way of the Philippines. It was the last stop on his way home. Sergeant David Bush would spend some time there before being sent to a hospital in the States, where he would eventually make a full recovery. He never returned to Vietnam.

38

AIRBORNE
RANGER

L
CO

75TH
INF

Saved by a Nose

Sometimes long range patrols escaped ambush and annihilation by the thinnest of threads. In most cases the survivors attributed their good fortune to luck, intuition, or Divine intervention. Today, most Vietnam-era Rangers will tell you that you make your own luck. Of those who attribute their survival directly to their almost supernatural powers of intuition, you'll find that most of them left any vestiges of a sixth sense in the trash barrel at the DEROS point with the rest of their war contraband. And if pressed for an answer, a good number of them will admit that they're not altogether sure that over in Vietnam, God wasn't Buddhist. But once in a while you still run across a story that tells of a miraculous escape from disaster and stands on its own in the realm of truth.

In early June 1971, Lima Company got a warning order for a recon mission north of the Triple Forks area. Since most of the company's teams were already out in the field or just coming in, Lieutenant Montano volunteered to go out as the sixth man on an otherwise incomplete team. This was not unusual, since officers had often accompanied teams in this manner. But Montano had led numerous patrols on his own, and the fact that he deferred to the existing team leader in this case showed the value he placed on team integrity.

The mission was scheduled to go in at first light on the

morning of June 10, 1971. The insertion went well, the team making it quickly into heavy cover not far off the LZ. As soon as they dropped down in a circle to lay dog, they smelled the overpoweringly strong odor of nearby Vietnamese soldiers. Not to say that Vietnamese soldiers smelled badly—only differently. Their nearly exclusive diet of rice flavored with exotic spices and *nuoc mam* sauce imbued them with a certain, distinct aroma—somewhere between rotten fish and fresh bird droppings—that distinguished them from the meat-and-potato-consuming Americans. Likewise, the Vietnamese found Americans a little on the "smelly" side, too—registering somewhere on the odor spectrum between dog shit and rancid meat.

Anyway, the recon team knew that there were NVA forces in the neighborhood as soon as they got a whiff of what was blowing downwind. The Ranger leader kept his team in the middle of the dense cover for nearly an hour, and when nothing had happened, he moved them out into the surrounding trees. It didn't take long to find fresh enemy sign. The team's point man soon discovered fresh tracks moving away from the patrol's LZ. Someone had watched the Ranger patrol come in, and they were probably down by the river at that very moment snitching to their pals.

Undaunted by the fact that the NVA likely knew of their presence, the Ranger team leader sent his point man ahead, following the fresh tracks right down to the river. When they reached the shore they discovered that the stream wasn't very wide, no more than twelve to fifteen meters, nor did it appear to be overly deep. They radioed the situation in to their TOC and sat back to await instructions.

It didn't take long. The Cavalry squadron commander had decided he wanted to know what was happening on the other side of the river. Without considering the safety of the small recon team he was expecting to take all the chances, he ordered them to cross the river and check out the opposite shore.

Montano, recognizing the young team leader's predicament, was nearly tempted to step in and take over control. After all, no one could expect a young buck sergeant to stand up to a full colonel and refuse to comply with his order, but that's exactly what he did. The Ranger team leader calmly told the Cav commander that he suspected a trap and he wasn't going to take his team across the river. When the colonel heard the Ranger TL's refusal, he got on the radio and began to threaten him. But about that time members of the team spotted several enemy soldiers maneuvering around on the opposite shore and called for gunships.

When the Cobras arrived and began to make their gun runs down the opposite shoreline, they were greeted with a large volume of 12.7mm and 37mm antiaircraft fire coming from hardened positions on the far side of the river. The enemy had set up a well-planned, superbly camouflaged helicopter trap, but sprung it prematurely. They had planned to lure the American long range reconnaissance patrol across the river before they pinned it down with small-arms fire. When the recon team called for gunships and an emergency extraction, the enemy soldiers would have been waiting for the helicopters with their big stuff. It would have been a massacre.

When the NVA prematurely blew their ambush, the Rangers asked for reinforcements. Division broke in and said no. Instead, the fast-movers were sent in to take out the AAA. Without waiting for the Rangers to eyeball the results, Division HQ ordered them to return to their LZ and wait for extraction. With the war winding down, no one was really looking for a pitched firefight anymore.

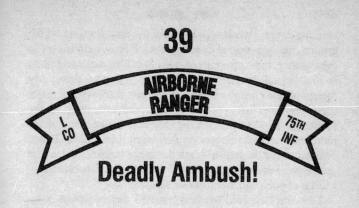

39

AIRBORNE RANGER

L CO · 75TH INF

Deadly Ambush!

By the early summer of 1971, Lima Company's role as the "eyes and ears" of the 101st Airborne Division was beginning to wind down. Few reconnaissance missions were coming from G-2, and the missions that did manage to filter down to the company were a variety of off-the-wall assignments usually involving heavy teams. One of these was a last minute request to check out the report of caves being used by the enemy along a stream in the Tri-River area northeast of the Ashau. The caves were located in a deep gorge and had been spotted by a scout helicopter flying aerial recon in the area. The pilot had also reported seeing the smoke from cooking fires coming from the same location.

Newly arrived Lieutenant David Grange III, son of Major General David Grange, Jr., and the late Lieutenant Paul Sawtelle's replacement, immediately volunteered to lead a nine-man Ranger patrol into the area to check out the target. Among the Rangers volunteering to accompany him were Sergeants Adam Macias and Ken Wells, Spec 4s Albert Bartz and Danny Dominguez, Corporal Charles Sanchez, and Private First Class Steven Ellis.

The actual insertion was scheduled for late in the afternoon of June 12. The designated LZ was an abandoned U.S. firebase located atop nearby Hill 714 not far from the deep gorge that held the caves. Two Huey slicks put the nine Rangers on the ground during a routine insertion. As the Hueys circled off in the distance, the patrol moved quickly off the exposed hilltop in the general direction of the caves. Not more than thirty meters off the crest the patrol's point man discovered a major high-speed trail that appeared to run in the same direction the Rangers wanted to go. Much to the concern of some of the more experienced Rangers on the patrol, Lieutenant Grange decided to use the trail to reach the gorge quicker. At least he put his two most experienced men in the key patrol positions—Macias at point and Wells at rear security.

The patrol covered the first hundred meters moving cautiously as they searched for fresh signs of recent enemy activity. So far everything was going as planned. They were making good progress toward their goal, and they had not yet discovered anything—excepting the trail—that indicated the presence of enemy forces in the area.

Two hundred meters from the top, with night approaching, Grange signaled Macias to find a suitable spot to set up a night defense perimeter. Soon the veteran NCO located a good site and moved the patrol fifteen meters off the trail into a dense thicket. It was a good choice. The location offered both excellent cover and concealment. While Grange called in to report the patrol's position and coordinate a number of artillery pre-plots with the fire control officer at Firebase Veghel, the remaining Rangers silently put out their claymores then settled back for what they hoped would be an uneventful night.

The next morning found the team up early, anxious to get on with the patrol. Lieutenant Grange ordered them to down a quick breakfast then pull in their claymores and prepare to move back out onto the trail. He was eager to continue the mission down to the stream at the base of the mountain.

Everything was abnormally quiet for the first hundred meters or so. Then suddenly, at the front of the patrol, the team's point man, Sergeant Macias, stepped around a sharp bend in the trail and came face-to-face with a pair of NVA soldiers. The men were sitting behind a tripod-mounted .30 caliber machine gun set up directly in the middle of the trail.

Macias knew immediately that this was no chance encounter. The enemy soldiers had been waiting for him.

He immediately screamed *"Ambush!"* and opened fire at the two NVA gunners. Without waiting to see if he'd hit anyone, Macias began the well-rehearsed immediate action drill for "contact, front." He quickly folded back on his slack man, dropping the now empty magazine from his weapon and jamming home a fresh one. Before his backup could bring up his own weapon to fire, all hell had broken loose to the Rangers' immediate front and along their left flank. The patrol was in the kill zone of a well-planned, L-shaped ambush. The enemy had done its homework well and now had the Rangers at their mercy.

Before Macias had taken three steps, Ellis and Sanchez were killed outright and four of the remaining seven Rangers had been wounded.

Each of the remaining three Rangers dropped to one knee and tried to establish fire superiority over the enemy ambushers, while at the same time attempting to move the wounded off the trail. But the NVA soldiers along the ridge above soon spotted them and began dropping ChiCom hand grenades down on the trail. Many of the grenades failed to detonate, but enough still managed to explode among the patrol that some of the wounded were repeatedly struck by shrapnel.

The battle raged for a full twenty minutes, with the Rangers desperately trying to establish fire superiority, but the enemy was too numerous, too strong, and too well-entrenched to be beaten back by only small-arms fire.

Lieutenant Grange, hit in the right calf during the opening burst of enemy gunfire, had snatched up the radio and crawled off to the side of the trail. While heavy enemy small-arms fire raked the kill zone, the young officer called the radio relay team and calmly reported the ambush, requesting Cobra gunships immediately. He was told to hang on, that it would take twenty minutes for the Cobras to reach the team.

Grange knew instinctively that he and his Rangers didn't have that much time—twenty minutes was an eternity in the kill zone of a well-organized, L-shaped ambush. He would have to figure another way to keep himself and the remainder of his team alive until the gunships could reach them.

Artillery was the only viable answer. Within minutes of the ambush being initiated, Lieutenant Grange called in his nearest preplot from the evening before and soon had volleys of 105mm rounds crashing along the ridgeline above them. Adjusting by sound alone, he walked the rounds back into the enemy positions located above the team. He kept them dropping until the Cobras finally came up on the net and reported that they were only two minutes out and closing fast.

When the gunships radioed again to report that they were on station, Grange reluctantly called off the artillery and directed the gunships in on the enemy positions. After the toll taken by the deadly artillery barrage, the fast-moving gunships proved too much for the NVA. In the open without prepared, hardened fighting positions, they were soon forced to break contact and withdraw from the battlefield.

Under the cover of the supporting Cobras, Wells crawled forward and began emergency medical treatment on the wounded Rangers. Only he and Bartz at the end of the patrol had escaped injury. Wells hurriedly finished with the dressings then moved in to coordinate the medevac extraction. With dustoff helicopters on the way into the patrol's position to pull out the dead and wounded, Wells and Bartz positioned themselves where they thought they could most effectively provide security in case the NVA returned.

The medevacs finally arrived and wasted no time maneuvering in over the patrol's position. Each aircraft took its turn hovering over the trail and slowly lowered its jungle penetrator down into the gorge to haul out the Ranger casualties. Wells and Bartz coordinated the evacuation and were the last two Rangers extracted.

The aircraft commander of the overloaded medevac helicopter carrying Wells and Bartz, four wounded Rangers, and all of their gear, was not used to ferrying so large a load. Nor was he used to carrying soldiers who were not wounded, so on the way back to the surgical hospital at Phu Bai the pilot told his crew chief over the intercom that he was going to have to drop off Wells and Bartz at the first friendly position they came to. Unfortunately, he forgot to inform the two Rangers.

Soon, the Huey was circling down toward a raw cut bisecting the surrounding hills. The Rangers aboard the aircraft knew that it had to be a section of Highway 547. The aircraft flared to a quick touchdown as it dropped off the two Rangers, along with the patrol's equipment and weapons, right in the middle of Highway 547. The spot was outside Firebase Birmingham, located just inside the mountains west of Camp Eagle.

At first Wells and Bartz didn't think too much about being dropped off out in the middle of nowhere. As the two Rangers stood hunched over in the swirling dust storm caused by the departing Huey's rotor wash, they watched through squinted eyes as the aircraft lifted away from the road and rapidly flew off to the east. But it was only after the two soldiers realized that Firebase Birmingham had been abandoned that they understood what kind of sling their young asses were now in.

It had been around noon when the medevac pilot touched down in the middle of the highway. He'd offered no real explanation, just a simple "get off here, another chopper will pick you up later." So the two Rangers sat expectantly in the middle of the red clay road amid a large pile of rucksacks, CAR-15s, M-16s, and a couple of M-79s. They waited for nearly two hours, totally unsure of what they should do next. They had all of their teammates' gear, with the exception of the one piece of equipment they really needed—the radio.

By mid-afternoon the two Rangers were beginning to suspect that "someone" had forgotten about them. Still not knowing what they should do, but realizing they had to do something, they moved all the weapons and gear off the road and hid them in some dense cover alongside the highway. It didn't really accomplish much, but it made Wells and Bartz feel better about their predicament. Not long afterward the two Rangers decided that they, too, should probably find some cover for themselves, just in case the ever-present NVA came along and discovered that Firebase Birmingham was no longer abandoned.

By late afternoon the now thoroughly dejected Rangers

moved back up to the edge of the road. It had just occurred to them that if the NVA couldn't find them, then neither could they be spotted by a passing helicopter.

Back at the company area, Lieutenant Jim Montano, Lieutenant Grange's counterpart from first platoon, suddenly realized that Grange's entire team had not been accounted for. Hurriedly checking with the evac hospital at Phu Bai and then with Graves Registration, he discovered there were still two Rangers missing somewhere between the Tri-Rivers area and Phu Bai. When he finally located the aircraft commander who had flown the last medevac that brought out the wounded, he discovered that the pilot had dropped off Wells and Bartz in the middle of the boonies outside an abandoned U.S. Army firebase and inadvertently forgotten to tell anyone else.

Lieutenant Montano immediately went into a rage. He couldn't believe the stupidity that had just put two of his Rangers in this type of jeopardy. To make matters even worse, it took the tough, young officer nearly two more hours on the land line to get a helicopter from the 2/17th Cav in the air and on the way out to Firebase Birmingham to pick up the two forgotten recon men.

Lieutenant David Grange would later receive the Silver Star medal for his part in directing accurate artillery fire on the enemy positions within minutes of the deadly ambush. His quick actions were credited with saving the team from total annihilation. Sergeant Ken Wells deserved the same award but received only the Army Commendation medal with V device for his unselfish efforts in treating the wounded and for seeing to their successful evacuation from the battlefield. Spec 4 Albert Bartz received no decoration at all.

40

Full Company Operation

In mid-July 1971, Lima Company went through a major command shake-up. Popular company commander, Captain David Ohle, along with First Lieutenant Robert Suchke, the operations officer, were leaving the unit for new assignments. While waiting for the arrival of Captain William Robinson, a West Pointer and the new company CO, Ranger First Sergeant Neal Gentry got word from Division that a captured NVA soldier had just coughed up information on the location of a suspected NVA hospital in the 3rd Brigade Area of Operations. Division soon sent word down to Lima Company's Tactical Operations Center requesting that the Rangers put together an operation to go in and find the complex. This was not to be a reconnaissance mission, but a full-fledged raid.

Gentry immediately went to find First Lieutenant James Montano, the first platoon leader and currently the ranking officer in the company. When he finally discovered Montano conducting team training down by the helicopter pad, he quickly drew him aside and explained the nature of the mission from Division. When he was done with the details, he asked the young officer if he thought he was man enough to take the entire company out on the operation. Jokingly, Gentry mentioned that Platoon Sergeant Harold Kaiama had sworn that he

was going to get a Medal of Honor before his tour was over
and the old soldier was running out of time.

Montano, also nearing the end of his tour, jumped at the
chance to lead the entire company into action. He had already
led more than his own share of tough recon and hairy combat
patrols. One more wasn't going to make any difference.

When the second platoon leader, First Lieutenant David
Grange, heard the news of the coming operation, he immediately volunteered to accompany Montano as his executive
officer even though Grange was still on profile with staples in
his leg. His wounds were not severe enough to send him home
but serious enough to keep him on limited duty. Now, with a
full month of riding time left on his medical profile, he decided
that he couldn't miss an opportunity to go out on an operation
with the entire company. He was typical of the gung ho officers
serving in Lima Company during its final year of the war.

The operation went down on July 17 with the company
going in on a single ship LZ against the side of a mountain just
below its narrow pinnacle. Montano's slick went in first and
immediately took heavy small-arms fire from above the LZ
near the pinnacle.

Two Cav Pink Teams responded immediately, going in and
"lighting up" the pinnacle to take some pressure off the
approaching slicks. As they pulled out of their gun runs they
reported "dinks running everywhere." Soon every gunship in
the squadron was out there over the battleground, getting its
teeth into the action. With the assistance and support of the
heavily armed Cobras, all ten Huey slicks made it into and out
of the LZ.

With sixty Rangers on the ground around the LZ, Montano
ordered Grange to take one team and move up to secure the
pinnacle while he took the remaining nine teams and moved
down into the valley to destroy the NVA hospital.

The pinnacle was only 150 meters above the LZ and had
been pounded pretty heavily by the gunships. The Cobra flight
leader had reported that his aircraft had killed eight to ten NVA
and driven the remaining defenders down the back side of the
mountain. Grange's team reached it without firing a shot.

Montano's Rangers were a full klick and a half from the suspected location of the hospital. He was anxious to cover the ground before the NVA had a chance to prepare a reception party. The enemy would defend the hospital with everything they had at their disposal, fighting to buy time while the medical staff and rear echelon personnel evacuated. He also knew that the longer it took the Rangers to reach it, the tougher the fight would be to take it.

As Montano's Rangers dropped down the ridge, they began to encounter fresh enemy sign everywhere. Numerous signs and signals were carved on trees along the trails, some that looked amazingly similar to contour lines on a topo map. Not knowing for sure if the signs warned of booby-traps or ambushes up ahead, Montano was forced to slow his force to a crawl while he sent point patrols to check out the trails more carefully. Patton techniques could lead to Custer outcomes.

It soon became obvious that at their present rate of movement the small Ranger force would not be able to reach its objective until just before dark. And the last thing Montano wanted was to get caught in the middle of an NVA hospital complex at night. The local morgue would be full of dead Rangers by morning. Instead Montano decided to halt the company where it was and move it off the trail into some thick cover. They were still five hundred meters above the NVA field hospital, and if things went well during the night, they would go in and hit it at first light the next morning.

An hour later a single Huey slick arrived to bring in a much needed resupply of water, trip flares, and extra ammo for Montano's Ranger force. First Sergeant Gentry was on board with the supplies and decided to spend the night in the bush with his Rangers. If the NVA was to come after them during the night, an experienced Ranger of Gentry's caliber inside the perimeter could save a lot of lives. Besides, Montano had known Gentry too long, and knew better than to fight the old warhorse. Secretly he was glad that Gentry was there.

Just before dark Montano sent out a patrol to sweep the area around the company's perimeter. They soon found a cemetery with six to eight bodies buried in it. The Rangers said the place was really spooky, and they felt as if they were being watched. With the evening shadows lengthening, the patrol moved back, looking over its shoulder the entire way, and rejoined the rest of the company.

During the night, Montano's Rangers could see numerous campfires and lanterns blazing brightly down in the valley. From up high on the pinnacle Grange's team reported the same thing. It was obvious that the enemy was making no effort to conceal his presence in the valley, nor was he trying to minimize his numbers. No, there were a lot of people down there, and they weren't running.

Just before midnight the enemy launched about a dozen of its monster 240mm rockets at the Ranger perimeter. Even more inaccurate than their smaller 122mm cousins, the large rockets hit everywhere but inside the Rangers' perimeter. However, the glowing flashes of the rockets as they left their launch stakes were spotted by the observant Rangers, and soon Montano had deadly air strikes plastering the enemy's launch points.

The next morning word came down early from Division ordering the Rangers to return immediately to the LZ for extraction. With the element of surprise lost, the sighting of numerous campfires and lanterns in the vicinity of the hospital during the night, and the presence of the 240mm rockets, Division rightfully decided that there was a larger enemy force waiting for them down in the valley than fifty-five Rangers could handle.

The Rangers hurriedly picked up their claymores and trip flares, broke camp, and headed back to the LZ. Grange's team was already there waiting for them, and within thirty minutes all the Rangers were extracted.

It was fortunate that the operation was aborted at the last minute. It was another example of higher command attempting to use a recon element for a mission it was not trained to handle. Vietnam-era Lurp/Ranger companies were tasked primarily to gather intelligence, conduct ambushes, prisoner snatches, and small-unit raids. To attempt to use them in company strength as a commando or raider unit was both irresponsible and foolhardy. It was not a mission they were trained for.

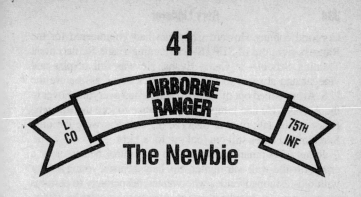

41

AIRBORNE RANGER
L CO
75TH INF

The Newbie

In line companies during the Vietnam War the story was always being told about how the new guys usually got zapped. This was based on the premise that new men made more mistakes and usually got killed the fastest. But on six-man long range patrols the reverse was typically true. The most experienced Rangers, who were often the team leaders, were the most likely to die when a mission went sour. They were the ones who exposed themselves in order to determine the enemy's strength and position. They were the ones who controlled the battle and directed the actions of their teammates. It was usually the team leaders who called in supporting air and artillery fire on the enemy. And they were always the first in and the last out when inserting and extracting.

But sometimes in spite of the best efforts of more experienced Rangers to keep them safe, at least long enough to have a shot at surviving the game, new Rangers still managed to get themselves killed before they had a chance to learn all the ropes. It was always painful losing a buddy. And it was a real tragedy to lose a comrade who was short or near the end of his tour. However, losing a new man, before anyone really got to know him—well, the pain healed a lot faster.

In late July a replacement arrived at Lima Company. He was a good-looking kid, the son of a retired Army first sergeant.

Corporal Johnny Howard Chapman had volunteered for the
Rangers right out of SERTS—Screaming Eagle Replacement
Training School—at Camp Evans. He was full of piss and
vinegar and anxious to get out and kick some ass before the
U.S. Army pulled out of Vietnam and turned everything over to
the ARVNs. He had jumped at the chance to join the Rangers.
From all the talk over at SERTS, the Rangers were the only
Screaming Eagles still out looking for a fight.

Johnny Chapman wasn't an out of control berserker or a
crazy, off-the-wall war fighter. No, he was just a young soldier
with old-fashioned values who wanted desperately to earn his
spurs in combat. Maybe it was an attempt to impress his father,
or maybe he had a girl back home. But as soon as he cleared the
mandatory two weeks of company P-training and was assigned
to a team, he sent home a Polaroid photo of himself dressed in
cammies wearing the Ranger scroll and black beret. The only
problem was that he had not yet won the right to wear the
Ranger colors. He still had to be accredited.

Shortly afterward Corporal Chapman went out on his first
mission, a three-day reconnaissance patrol along the Ba Long
River up north near Quang Tri. His team had gone in early on
the morning of August 20, 1971, and had struck pay dirt, discovering a well-used high-speed trail within thirty minutes of
inserting.

They started to follow the trail, hoping that it would lead to
an enemy base camp, when Chapman triggered a booby-
trapped NVA grenade. It went off low and to his side, spraying
him with hundreds of pieces of shrapnel. There was nothing
anyone could do to save him. Within minutes the young soldier
was dead.

With the Ranger team now fully compromised, the helicopters were called back to extract the patrol. They came out of
the bush thirty minutes later, bringing with them the body of
their dead teammate.

When the team arrived back at the Ranger compound,
Chapman's platoon leader, First Lieutenant James Montano,
interviewed the survivors to find out as much as he could about
exactly how Chapman's death had occurred. Satisfied that he
had the facts straight, he began the unpopular task of writing a

letter to Chapman's parents explaining how their son had died
and telling them what a wonderful soldier he'd been. Unfortunately, with only a month in the unit, Montano had had very
little time to get to know the young trooper. And since
Chapman had not yet been awarded the L Company scroll and
beret flash, Montano avoided mentioning anything about the
young man being a Ranger in his letter.

Shortly after sending his letter of condolence to Corporal
Chapman's parents, Lieutenant Montano received a return
letter from the family requesting that the uniform and beret that
their son had been wearing for the photograph be located and
shipped home immediately. It had not arrived in the box with
the rest of the dead soldier's personal items.

This new revelation presented a major problem in that Corporal Chapman had not lasted long enough to meet the requirements for acceptance into the Rangers. By all acceptable
standards he had been killed during the probationary period
required before a new replacement became a full-fledged
Ranger.

This resulted in a serious predicament for the Ranger lieutenant. When he discovered that young Corporal Chapman had
prematurely mailed home a snapshot of himself in full Ranger
regalia, he knew that the family would accept nothing less than
their dead son's uniform—the one he wore in the photo. Montano couldn't get the dead soldier accredited, so he did the only
thing he could do to handle the situation. He ordered some of
Chapman's teammates to dummy up another beret and Ranger
uniform with the proper insignia, and then sent them to
Chapman's parents with another letter of apology for not
including them the first time.

Rangers always took care of their own. Although Chapman
hadn't fully paid his dues for membership in this exclusive fra-
ternity of men, his family would not be left with a tainted
memory of a fallen loved one.

Corporal Johnny Chapman would be the last L Company
Ranger to die in Vietnam. With the 101st Airborne Division
preparing to stand down in preparation for its return to the
United States, the role of its Ranger company was also
changing. A smaller number of replacements were coming into

the unit. As DEROSs, ETSs, and WIAs continued to take their toll of company personnel, fewer operational teams were available for missions. The end of the Screaming Eagle's illustrious Lurp/Ranger tradition was in sight.

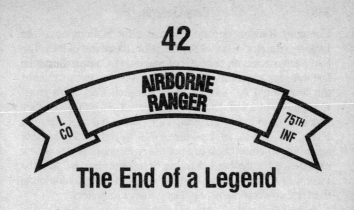

42

The End of a Legend

In early November 1971 word came down through the channels that the 101st Airborne Division was going home. This scuttlebutt caused much consternation among the Rangers assigned to L Company. There had been rumors for months but nothing to confirm it. Many of those who served on the recon teams didn't fully understand the ramifications of the division standing down prior to its return to CONUS. What would happen to those Rangers still in the early phase of their tours? Would they go home, or would they be reassigned to another unit still serving in the Republic of Vietnam? It was a good question which, at the time, didn't have many answers.

Soon the official word was given that all Rangers serving in L Company, 75th Infantry, with more than six months remaining in-country effective November 15, 1971, would be reassigned to another unit to complete their tours. They were offered a number of selections to choose from. Those with less than six months would be granted an early out from overseas duty in the Republic of Vietnam and returned to CONUS for reassignment or separation from the service.

Within two weeks members of the company began to depart for new duty stations. Not surprisingly, most of the Rangers selected assignments to the few U.S. units still conducting combat operations in South Vietnam. More than forty L

Company Rangers departed en masse for H Company, 75th Infantry (Ranger), 1st Cavalry Division, based just outside Ton San Nhut airbase on the edge of Saigon. H Company was the last Ranger company to leave Vietnam. For the next six months the war would be good to these Rangers. Duty with Hotel Company was a walk in the sun compared to the missions they had been previously assigned in I Corps. No mountains to hump, VC instead of hard-core NVA to fight, and stateside amenities to come back to after every mission. It was a new experience for the hard-charging Screaming Eagles. And the forty well-trained I Corps Rangers were a welcome addition to the 1st Cav's complement of Long Range Patrollers.

A half-dozen L Company Rangers volunteered for the brigade reaction force of the 5th Division (Mechanized) operating just below the DMZ. Within two months they would all be dead, victims of a tragic helicopter crash.

A number would report to various line companies around the country. But with the war winding down everywhere in South Vietnam, few military units were looking for replacements.

By November 15, 1971, all personnel to be reassigned had moved on to their new duty stations. A skeleton crew under the command of Captain William Robinson and First Sergeant Neal Gentry remained behind to stand down the company. There was equipment and weapons to be disposed of, records to be updated and sent back to the States, reports to be written, all the necessary activities and functions required to remove a unit from the active military roles of the United States Army.

In late November the company area at Camp Eagle was closed down. Ray Price, the acting motor pool sergeant, Danny Dominguez, Lou Distretti, and several other Rangers convoyed the company vehicles, loaded with the last of the equipment and weapons to be turned in, down to Danang. It was a sad day for L Company. Without a home and the tools of battle, their function as a military unit had come to an end. A few of the short-timers ended up going back north to Camp Evans, where they waited out their last days pulling perimeter guard and trying to get a full body tan before catching their "freedom bird" back to the States.

There was no parade, no final formation, no company party.

The proud history of the 101st long range patrollers came to an ignoble end, simply fading away. Within months of the division's return to CONUS, the Ranger company would only be a memory in the minds of those who wore the scroll and the black beret. Company L, 75th Infantry (Ranger), had completed its rendezvous with destiny.

Epilogue

AIRBORNE RANGER
L CO
75TH INF

I attended a 101st Airborne Division Association reunion at Fort Campbell, Kentucky, in the summer of 1974. The division was back from Vietnam, and U.S. military participation in the war was over. I was four years out of the Army, had completed a B.S. degree in business management and marketing, and was in my second year of law school at St. Louis University. South Vietnam was about ready to fall to the communists and life was good.

Another 101st Vietnam vet, Nick Borusiewich, a buddy from my high school days, joined me for the five-hour trip down to Hopkinsville. When we arrived, we were guided into a large auditorium to register with our unit representative. Nick soon found the sign marked *1/501st* and headed off in that direction. I spent the next twenty minutes trying to find F/58th (LRP) or L/75th (Ranger), but to no avail. Finally, frustrated at my inability to find my buddies, I took the REMF way and asked for directions. I was shocked when no one there had ever heard of either of the units I'd served in. Two short years after the division's departure from Vietnam, no one remembered the name of the Screaming Eagle Long Range Reconnaissance Company. I felt betrayed and outlawed by the parent unit I had been so proud to serve in. How could the 101st Airborne Division have forgotten about us in two short years?

In 1985, one of my buddies from Nam called to tell me that the guys were planning a big reunion and we were forming our own association. It caught me off guard. I had put Vietnam behind me and was getting on with my life. But I had to go see the guys one more time. So late in June 1986, I found myself walking into the lounge at the Holiday Inn on the north side of Fort Campbell. I had almost turned back a dozen times. But now it was too late. I was there and I couldn't get out of the confrontation.

Ti Ti Tercero and Dave Biedron recognized me first. They were with a group of ten or fifteen guys huddled around a table at the back of the lounge. I had my back to them, waiting for the bartender to mix me a scotch and water. When the two voices from my distant past spoke up—voices that I remembered as if I'd just heard them yesterday—I looked up in the mirror, afraid to turn around and face them. My eyes widened in surprise as the faces came flooding back. They were all there, maybe a little heavier, their features a little softer, but it was the same bunch of guys I had fought beside, partied with, joked, and cried with seventeen long years before. I finished the drink and turned to face them. I was ready now, but would they accept me again? Stupid question! I was one of them, part of them, and they were part of me. For the first time in nearly twenty years I felt whole again. I moved across the lounge to join them.

Two days later the division passed in review on the parade field for our benefit. Seeing all those young studs honoring us popped our chests out like bantam roosters. And when they took us over to the drop zone for a special demonstration—again for our benefit—things got even better. We soon learned that a Long Range Surveillance detachment had recently been activated at Fort Campbell to give the division a Long Range Reconnaissance capability. Captain Barry Lowe was its first commander. A body builder, Lowe, like his men, was a stud, and he treated us with the respect and courtesy that no officer showed us in Nam. Many of his young Lurps mixed with us, begging for the war stories, wheedling us for some of the old trade secrets we'd long since forgotten. Spec 4s Kurt Donaldson, Ken Newsome, and John Campbell were all ears. Tough young soldiers from a new generation who impressed us with their dedication, esprit, professionalism, and drive, as much as we seemed to impress them with our experience and our camaraderie. The nation is in good hands with young men like these.

And then Lieutenant Colonel David Ohle, commanding officer of the 2/17th Cav, stepped up to speak. He was of our generation . . . and this new generation, too. He had served in Lima Company as a platoon leader and then come back to spend six more months as the Ranger CO. Now, here he was at Fort Campbell, commanding the 2/17th Cav, our parent unit in Nam and now the parent unit of the LRS detachment. History has a funny way of coming full circle.

Colonel Ohle's welcoming speech to our 150 Vietnam-era Lurp/Rangers was our first official welcome home. We returned the favor by presenting him with the L Company 75th Ranger guidon that one of our number had plucked from a trash barrel at the Phu Bai airbase when the division was standing down. Thanks to one man's foresight, the guidon was back home now, where it belonged.

As I sat in the bleachers with my long lost comrades, watching the guidon fluttering so proudly in the breeze, my heart nearly burst with pride for the first time in years. All the love, all the bonding, all the camaraderie was still there . . . still strong . . . and I knew then that it would never be lost again.

It's been over ten years since that reunion. We've had others, none quite so memorable, but each one rich and unique in its own way. The families are involved now, and that's the way it should be. It keeps us honest, on our best behavior. It's a neat feeling bringing our military family and our civilian families together. There's a freshness about it that makes everything dirty seem clean, makes all the bad memories seem trivial. Somehow it seems to lessen the impact of war's personal trauma.

We're a proud bunch, all of us. Each generation served with pride, integrity, and valor, and we served well. They tried to take that away from us when we came home, and without the support of each other we let them do it to us again and again. But not anymore. We're whole again. A little grayer, a little heavier, perhaps a little tired. The pride's back, the integrity is back, and the valor . . . well, the valor was never gone.

Appendix 1

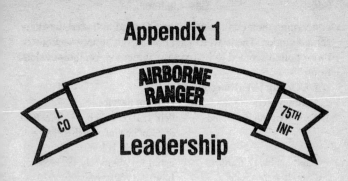

AIRBORNE RANGER

L CO

75TH INF

Leadership

The performance of every military unit mirrors the leadership of its commander and his subordinates. The degree of esprit, dedication, loyalty, skill, respect for superiors, and obedience to lawful orders of those men who serve is in direct proportion to those same attributes in those who lead them.

L Company, 75th Infantry (Ranger), was no different from any other military unit. Those men whose names appear on the rolls were a mix of race, creed, education, and social position. Their ability to work together was a testimony not only to their dedication to each other, but to the perceived loyalty of those who led them.

Most of the officers who led this company in battle were more than qualified, and their performance, like that of their men, was top of the line. But there were notable exceptions. The same can be said of the first sergeants, usually professional NCOs whose job it was to make sure that the company's administrative and logistical needs were met. As with L Company's commanders, most of its first sergeants performed above and beyond the call of duty, but again there were exceptions.

I polled a large number of those veterans who served in L Company during its two-and-a-half-year Vietnam odyssey. I discovered that there was a general consensus among them concerning their evaluation of the COs and first sergeants they served under. There were exceptions, but ninety percent of those polled seemed to be in close agreement on their evaluations.

L CO/75th INF (Ranger)

Commanders	Dates of Service
Capt. Kenneth R. Eklund	Feb. 1, 1969 to Feb. 13, 1969 (CO of F Co/58th Infantry [LRP] Aug. 1, 1968 to Feb. 1, 1969)
Capt. Lannie D. Cardona	Feb. 13, 1969 to July 19, 1969
Capt. Robert A. Guy	July 19, 1969 to May 20, 1970
Capt. James D. Stowers	May 20, 1970 to Aug. 15, 1970
Capt. David Ohle	Aug. 20, 1970 to Aug. 29, 1971
Capt. William Robinson	Aug. 20, 1971 to Dec. 7, 1971

L CO/75th INF (Ranger)

1st Sergeants	Dates of Service
1st Sgt. James G. Farrington	Feb. 1, 1969 to Mar. 12, 1969 (1st sergeant of F Co/58th Infantry [LRP] Dec. 10, 1968 to Feb. 1, 1969 —suffered heart attack and was relieved of duty for medical reasons)
1st Sgt. Clarence J. Cardin	Mar. 12, 1969 to May 18, 1969
1st Sgt. Robert F. Gilbert	May 18, 1969 to May 16, 1970
1st Sgt. William J. Unzicker	May 16, 1970 to Jan. 14, 1971
1st Sgt. Neal Gentry	Jan. 14, 1971 to Dec. 15, 1971

My poll revealed that the commanding officers who garnered the most respect and the highest praise from the men who served under them were Captains Eklund, Guy, and Ohle. All were rated as exceptional officers who put their troops first and themselves second. The Rangers interviewed readily admitted that if a life threatening "situation" developed endangering a patrol in the field, any of these three officers would have left no stone unturned to get them out—including jeopardizing his own career.

Captain Cardona was seen as distant, aloof, unable to accept the fact that those "special" soldiers who served under him were different and had to be trusted and given more latitude in calling their own shots. While probably an excellent line officer, Captain Cardona was a poor choice to command a company of Long Range Patrollers.

Captain James Stowers was totally out of place as commander of L Company. Never comfortable in this role, Stowers combined his absence of ability with a lackluster command presence, coming away with an overall rating as the worst commander ever to lead L Company. Along with a first sergeant who had difficulty in attaining even this degree of respect from those who served under him, these two "leaders" were instrumental in nearly destroying the company as a viable combat force. Unhappy, dissatisfied soldiers make for a weak command. The men of L Company, 75th Infantry (Ranger), under Captain James Stowers and First Sergeant William Unzicker were definitely unhappy and highly dissatisfied soldiers. Stowers was relieved from duty not quite three months into his command when he lost the SOI code book, maps, artillery frequencies, and other valuable operational information while preparing to insert eight Ranger patrols in what was supposed to be a critical reconnaissance operation. The items were left unsecured in the Command & Control aircraft during the insertion and fell out, unnoticed, high over enemy territory. Captain Stowers was relieved of command the next day.

Captain William Robinson served as company commander for less than four months, and had the unpopular duty of standing the unit down for deactivation. Because, during his command, the unit saw decreasing levels of combat and a deterioration of commitment from supporting units, we won't rate Captain William Robinson one way or another.

My poll revealed roughly the same popularity spread among the first sergeants. Farrington, Gilbert, and Gentry were lauded as exceptionally qualified by most of those who served under them. Unfortunately, First Sergeant Farrington was stricken by a heart attack early in his assignment. But during the brief time he was the company "First Shirt," the Rangers of L Company loved him like a father. Perhaps his only fault was that he was too easygoing and too understanding.

First Sergeant Clarence Cardin was a man who probably possessed all the administrative skills necessary to handle the job, but lacked the personality and the presence to fill the slot.

During his assignment as the top enlisted man in L Company, 75th Infantry (Ranger), several halfhearted attempts were made to "take him out." Instead of questioning the reason behind the attempted fraggings, Cardin only became more and more distrustful, contemptuous, and finally even paranoid of everyone in the company, forcing him eventually to withdraw from those who served under him. The true culprits were never uncovered.

First Sergeant Robert Gilbert was the consummate professional, totally dedicated to his job, willing to put his life—but not necessarily his reputation—on the line for his Rangers. Overloaded with ability and command presence, Gilbert was a controversial figure among L Company's top NCOs. Those who served during his "reign" either loved him or hated him. Halfhearted attempts were also made on First Sergeant Gilbert's life, but these were likely the efforts of one or two disgruntled and troubled Rangers. The company thrived under Gilbert's leadership.

First Sergeant William Unzicker's popularity fell somewhere between Lyndon Johnson's and Ho Chi Minh's. He combined with Captain Stowers to drive from the company anyone who did not see eye-to-eye with their philosophies. During their "reign," many of the unit's finest team leaders and veteran patrollers voluntarily or involuntarily left the company, forced out by unprincipled and unreasonable demands made upon them. Reassignment was Stowers's and Unzicker's way of dealing with what they saw as obstinacy and rebellion. Numerous examples abound of a particular first sergeant's "requests" of Rangers heading on R&R that they accept $500 MPC from him—supposedly with no strings attached. The only stipulation was that they send $400 of the total amount to an address back in the States. The extra $100 was a gift from him for their R&R. Many of the Rangers went along with this scheme, never questioning the source of the funds but always bothered by its implications. No one was sad to see Unzicker go, nor has he been invited to any of the company's reunions.

First Sergeant Neal Gentry was perhaps the all-around best of the "First Shirts" who ran the show at L Company. As professional as First Sergeant Robert Gilbert and as popular with many of the Rangers as First Sergeant James Farrington, Gentry was bigger than life. Few Rangers interviewed had anything negative to say about Neal Gentry. He was a strict disciplinarian, but he was a professional soldier.

Besides this array of company commanders and first sergeants, the Rangers saw a number of outstanding junior officers and senior NCOs who earned their scrolls and the respect of those they led serving as executive officers, platoon leaders, and platoon sergeants in L Company. First Lieutenants Jim Jackson and Bob Suchke were both highly competent executive officers who performed outstandingly, coordinating patrols, inserting teams, and sometimes running missions. Lieutenants Owen Williams, John Gay, David Grange, Jim Montano, Jim Smith, and Paul Sawtelle were a group of real "studs" who willingly put in their time in the bush, usually as the "sixth" man without rank or position. But when called upon to command "heavy" teams or Ranger platoon-size operations, they led as well as they followed.

Platoon sergeants like the legendary Richard "Bernie" Burnell, Ron Bowman, Jim "Contact" Johnson, Harold "Ranger" Kaiama, Troy Rocha, and others provided professional seasoning to a batch of inexperienced soldiers. These senior NCOs led by example, molding their young wards quickly into a special breed of soldier. From their ranks came the solid foundation upon which the L Company developed and thrived.

Appendix 2

Long Range Patrollers

In researching the seven-year history of the Lurp and Ranger companies of the 101st Airborne Division in Vietnam, one soon discovers no common trait that defines seven generations of Long Range Patrollers save their service. In researching this book and reading the works of my compatriots, Rey Martinez and Kenn Miller, I kept trying to stereotype the sort of individual it took to operate behind enemy lines on small reconnaissance teams. I reasoned some common characteristic inherent in the men must have possessed them to volunteer for that kind of duty. I knew that it wasn't unique to the Vietnam War, for we have always had men willing to serve in special operations units.

The more I searched, the more futile were my results. When I asked an individual I was interviewing what made him volunteer to be a Lurp or a Ranger, the answers I received were as varied as the personalities of those who gave them. Over a period of time, all of my preconceived notions began to fall by the wayside. There was simply no common characteristic shared by those men who had worn the LRRP, LRP, or Ranger scrolls over their Screaming Eagle patch.

They were a proud bunch, of that I could be sure. But their pride was where all similarities ended. In reading Rey Martinez's work on the First Brigade LRRPs, I was amazed to discover the stringent steps taken to secure only the most qualified individuals for the first long range reconnaissance patrols formed in 1965–66. Professional, career soldiers filled the ranks of the early teams. Led by E-6s and E-7s, these patrols embodied the spirit of the Alamo Scouts of World War II. Draftees and first enlistment soldiers were an oddity in the provisional LRRP detachment. As a result, many of the early Lurps were well-known, if not already legendary, among their peers. They were men who had already proven themselves "before" they had to prove that they were qualified to be an LRRP. Most of them were products of blue collar America— blacks, whites, and browns—they were men who had joined the service in search of a career. And keep in mind, they were the cream of the crop from probably the finest U.S. combat brigade ever to go into battle.

Their replacements a year later came from the same stock as their predecessors. The only difference was that most of the replacements were Spec 4s and E-5s with a few months of combat time in Vietnam. Nearly all had enlisted in the Army and gone through tough training and garrison duty stateside or in Europe before arriving in Nam—not necessarily career soldiers, but still professionals. The newcomers fit in well with the "old-timers" who were beginning to rotate back to the States. Most of the original LRRPs would be back, many to die in combat serving with Special Forces or line units. Many of these newcomers, however, would not return to the States at the end of their tours. Most of them extended their tours one or more times, not for the cushy jobs available to most soldiers who signed on for another six months in-country, but for another tour in the LRRPs. Was it the camaraderie that they couldn't leave behind, or were they perhaps a little insane? Maybe it was a little of both! But for whatever the reason, they were an outstanding batch of young and fearless warriors.

The next generation of LRRPs earned the name the "Old Foul Dudes" for their total disregard for convention and their willingness to challenge any foe and accept any dare. What an assemblage of mismatched personalities they turned out to be! A mixture of convicts, social and educational dropouts, spoiled rich kids, orphans, streetwise city kids, and backwoods yokels, this group of LRRPs was the opposite of what an elite military unit should be. In the rear they were prone to drunkenness, brawling—often among themselves—whoring, and avoiding anything that remotely resembled labor. They would eat anything that would hold still long enough to be seized with the teeth. One of them once bet that he could urinate over the hood of a three-ton truck. He won that bet and hosed down one of those who bet against him. They were a rough-and-tumble lot, but, God, were they good in the field!

The division Long Range Patrol company that came to Vietnam from Fort Campbell in 1967 was a group of Recondo-trained rookies who initially thought they knew all the answers. The company's senior NCOs had been instructors at the 101st Recondo School back in Kentucky, and they also believed they knew all the answers. But they were few in number and could only provide the initial leadership as patrol leaders, forcing the rookie NCOs to take over the division teams before they were ready.

In a tragedy of bad judgment and injured egos, little effort was made by either side to marry up the field-experienced brigade LRRPs with the highly trained division LRPs. Much of the lore that had been collected during more than two hard years of service by the brigade LRRPs was lost as its members were routinely discouraged from transferring to division LRPs. Those who did were regarded as pariahs and made to feel second class, their talents unwelcome. Many soon transferred out of the unit. Part of the blame was their fault; their cocky attitudes were a slap in the face to every division LRP they encountered. It was a marriage that was never consummated.

But the division LRPs drove on, learning everything about long range patrolling all over again from scratch. The first year was a tough one. Until the division finally found a home in I Corps and the teams could settle in to accomplish what they'd been trained to do, actual long range reconnaissance patrols were few and far between.

The next large batch of replacements joined the company in May/June 1968. Many were replacements fresh from airborne training in the States who were coming to the unit to replace LRPs who had come to Vietnam with the division with more than six months but less than a year to serve in the military. It was a mixed lot of draftees and enlistees, many with two or more years of college. Most were middle class and white. Many played high school athletics. Few planned to make a career of the military. Others were transfers from 501st Signal Battalion, Division Pathfinders, and line companies, men who were looking for a little action or desperate for a way to get out of the field. That was probably the last generation of Lurps who believed we could still win the war.

The next influx of Lurps was also the final group to join the unit as "Lurps." Arriving in late November and December of 1968, it was a group similar in makeup but younger than the generation that preceded it. They were coming into the division LRPs at a time when most of the original division LRPs were DEROSing. Their arrival was also on the tail end of a heavy team mission that resulted in four KIAs and eight WIAs, of which only three would return to the company. The combination of DEROSes and casualties had nearly depleted the company of experienced personnel. February 1969 was a rough time to transition into a Ranger company. It also resulted in the first influx of legs and shake 'n' bakes—graduates of stateside noncommissioned-officer schools.

For the next three years the company would receive replacements from a number of sources—the bulk coming in directly from Stateside Training Command. NCOs experienced in combat became rare as more and more junior noncommissioned officers opted to get out of the service rather than risk a second or third tour in Vietnam. There was little doubt by 1969 that we were looking for a graceful way to exit Vietnam. Fortunately, many Rangers completing a tour of duty were extending, some because they liked it, but many more because the U.S. government was offering "early outs" to soldiers in Vietnam with three and later six months remaining in the service. For many of those who had been drafted into the military, spending a few more months in Vietnam was far more preferable than six to eight months of garrison duty back in the States. So, homegrown NCOs began to vie with stateside shake 'n' bakes for team leader slots. The results were predictable. A number of outstanding team leaders came out of

L Company—Ray "Zo" Zoschak, Jim "Lobo" Bates, William "Fido" Vodden, Dave "Lazy Day" Hazelton, James "Jungle Jim" Rodarte, James "Bugs" Moran, and Jeff "Pengun" Paige were some of the best. A disproportionate number of team leaders were killed and wounded on operations, demonstrating that the Lurps were always in the thick of battle.

During the entire history of the unit, cultural and racial equality were out of balance among the Lurp/Ranger units of the 101st Airborne Division. In 1965–67, some of the unit's finest team leaders and NCOs were blacks. Sergeants Ron Weems, Larry Forrest, and Lester Hite are 1st Brigade legends. From 1968 to the end of the division's involvement in the war, blacks played a minor role on the teams. However, many of the unit's outstanding senior NCOs were blacks. Sergeants James Champion, Troy Rocha, Aubrey Batts, and Milton Lockett, to name a few, were true leaders. One of the company's three Distinguished Service Crosses was awarded to Sergeant Herman Brown, a black from North Carolina.

There were always a large number of Mexican-Americans and Latino-Americans, particularly Puerto Ricans and Cubans, in the company. They were able team leaders and outstanding soldiers. Sergeants Manuel Ortegon, Albert Contreros, Nick Caberra, Joe Gregory, and Rey Martinez were outstanding team leaders. Rudy Lopez, Carlos Quinones, John Perez, Ramon Lopez, and Tony Castro all served admirably. Contreros was awarded a Distinguished Service Cross posthumously.

Native Americans also gravitated to the Lurps and Rangers in numbers far beyond their cultural/racial position. Lurps Edwin Lee, Brian Lewis, Bill McCabe, Riley Cox, Billy Walkabout, and Ranger Tommy Roubideaux were valuable assets to any Long Range Patrol. Walkabout was the unit's third recipient of the Distinguished Service Cross, and had been considered for the Medal of Honor. Riley Cox was presented a Silver Star for his actions on November 20, 1968. Several witnesses, including this writer, believe that the award should have been higher.

Samoans, Guamanians, Filipinos, and native Hawaiians were also proudly represented by outstanding NCOs such as Sergeants Vincente Cruz, Marvel McCann, Jeff "Pineapple"

Ignacio, and Isaako Malo, the only Lurp/Ranger in the Vietnam War to survive capture at the hands of the enemy.

Several Canadians also served with L Company during the latter part of the war. Sergeant William Vodden was one of the finest team leaders to wear a Screaming Eagle patch. Sergeant Dave Hazelton saw more than his share of action. And Ranger Sergeant Rob McSorley, one of the most popular men in the company, died a hero's death, blunting an NVA attack on his team.

Two of L Company's officers are presently serving as generals in the U.S. Army. Brigadier General David Grange and Major General David Ohle are still on active duty. Robert Guy and James Montano retired from the military as colonels, James Jackson as a major. A large number of NCOs retired from the Army as sergeant majors and command sergeants major. The list is too numerous to name them all.

Only two men served in all three Long Range Patrol units of the 101st Airborne Division during the Vietnam War. Sergeants Kenn Miller and James Brandt each survived more than two and a half years of long range patrolling. Miller went out on more than eighty patrols. Brandt was a close second with over seventy.

There is no commonality among the men who served in the 101st Airborne Division's LRRPs, LRPs, and Rangers. They are a diverse bunch. Some are in prison, many are dead, and more and more are dying each year—young men, still in their forties and fifties. Many of them have severe physical, emotional, and mental problems that have prevented them from leading whole and productive lives. They are society's dregs, its rejects—used up and wasted in the prime of their lives. No one cares anymore—no one except their "brothers" who served with them. We still try to do what we can, but it's always tough. Distance, time, and lack of finances always make it a personal sacrifice—but we cope, we drive on, and we get the job done.

Most of us returned to society after the war, completed our educations, married, got jobs, raised kids—everything we were supposed to do. We might even be your next door neighbors. We're fine, upstanding citizens—people you would be proud to call your friends. But we're all a little different from the everyday citizen. We've been there, and seen the "elephant." It's left us a little different, somehow—marked men. It's not necessarily a bad thing, but it's something we're constantly aware of. For those of you who read this and don't understand—well, I guess you just had to be there.

Appendix 3

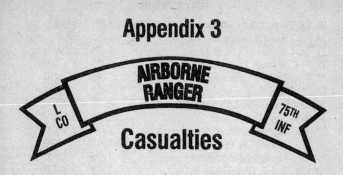

AIRBORNE RANGER
L CO · 75TH INF

Casualties

1st Brigade LRRPs, 101st Airborne Division
F Company, 58th Infantry (LRP), 101st Airborne Division
L Company, 75th Infantry (Ranger), 101st Airborne Division

Killed in Action

Rank/Name	Unit	Date
1. SFC Donald Stephen Newton	1/101	2/26/66
2. PFC Francis DeSales Wills	1/101	2/26/66
3. SSG Donovan Jess Pruett	1/101	4/3/66
4. SGT Percy W. McClatchy	1/101	8/13/66
5. SP4 David Allen Dixon	1/101	5/15/67
6. SP4 John Lester Hines	1/101	9/15/67
7. PFC George Buster Sullens, Jr.	1/101	11/1/67
8. SGT Patrick Lee Henshaw	1/101	12/19/67
9. SP4 John T. McChesney III	1/101	1/23/68
10. SGT Joseph E. Griffis	1/101	1/31/68
11. SP4 Thomas Wayne Sturgal	F/58	3/22/68
12. PVT Ashton Hayward Prindle	F/58	4/23/68
13. SGT Thomas Eugene Riley	F/58	6/2/68
14. SP4 Terry W. Clifton	F/58	11/20/68
15. SGT Albert D. Contreros, Jr.	F/58	11/20/68
16. SP4 Arthur J. Heringhausen, Jr.	F/58	11/20/68
17. SGT Michael Dean Reiff	F/58	11/20/68
18. SSG Dean Julian Dedman	L/75	4/23/69

19. SGT Keith Tait Hammond   L/75   5/5/69
20. SSG Ronald Burns Reynolds   L/75   5/8/69
21. SGT William Lincoln Marcy   L/75   5/20/69
22. PFC Michael Linn Lytle   L/75   10/26/69
23. SSG James William Salter   L/75   1/11/70
24. SGT Ronald Wayne Jones   L/75   1/11/70
25. SP4 Rob George McSorley   L/75   4/8/70
26. SGT Gary Paul Baker   L/75   5/11/70
27. SSG Raymond Dean Ellis   L/75   5/11/70
28. SSG Robert Lee O'Conner   L/75   5/11/70
29. CPL George Edward Fogleman   L/75   5/11/70
30. PFC Bryan Theotis Knight   L/75   5/11/70
31. SGT David Munoz   L/75   5/11/70
32. SSG Roger Thomas Lagodzinski   L/75   5/19/70
33. SSG John Thomas Donahue   L/75   5/22/70
34. SP4 Jack Moss, Jr.   L/75   8/25/70
35. SP4 Lawrence Elwood Scheib, Jr.   L/75   8/29/70
36. PFC Harry Thomas Henthorn   L/75   8/29/70
37. SGT Lloyd Harold Grimes II   L/75   9/25/70
38. SSG Norman R. Stoddard, Jr.   L/75   11/16/70
39. SGT Robert George Drapp   L/75   11/16/70
40. SGT Steven Glenn England   L/75   2/15/71
41. 1LT James Leroy Smith   L/75   2/15/71
42. SGT Gabriel Trujillo   L/75   2/15/71
43. SP4 Richard Lee Martin   L/75   2/21/71
44. SP4 David Roy Hayward   L/75   3/22/71
45. CPL Joel Richard Hankins   L/75   3/26/71
46. SSG Leonard James Trumblay   L/75   4/6/71
47. CPT Paul Coburn Sawtelle   L/75   4/16/71
48. SGT James Bruce McLaughlin   L/75   4/16/71
49. SP4 Johnnie Rae Sly   L/75   4/24/71
50. SSG James Albert Champion   L/75   4/24/71
51. SGT Gary Duane Cochran   L/75   5/8/71
52. PFC Steven John Ellis   L/75   6/13/71
53. CPL Charles Anthony Sanchez   L/75   6/13/71
54. CPL Johnny Howard Chapman   L/75   8/20/71
55. SP4 Hershel Duane Cude, Jr.   L/75   9/18/71
56. SP4 Harry Jerome Edwards   L/75   1/20/72

May they rest in peace!

Appendix 4

What They're Doing Today

Company L, 75th Infantry (Ranger)

Gary Linderer—Resides in Festus, Missouri, with his wife and two remaining sons. The author of *The Eyes of the Eagle*, *Eyes Behind the Lines*, and *Six Silent Men—Book III*, he also is the executive editor of *Behind the Lines*, a bimonthly journal on U.S. military special operations.

Kenn Miller—Lives in San Gabriel, California, with his wife and two children. The author of *Tiger the Lurp Dog* and *Six Silent Men—Book II*, he is a senior editor of *Behind the Lines*.

Larry Chambers—Resides in Ojai, California. He is divorced and is the author of *Recondo* and a number of books in the investment field.

Larry Closson—Lives in Springfield, Illinois, with his wife. He is the head agent for the Illinois Department of Conservation.

James Schwartz—Resides in Chicago, Illinois. He is divorced and works as a manager in telemarketing.

Ron Rucker—Lives in Bossier City, Louisiana. He is divorced, unemployed, and is a totally disabled veteran.

Riley Cox—Resides in Bailey, Colorado, with his wife. He is totally disabled from wounds received in Vietnam.

Joe Bielesch—Died at his home in Philadelphia of a massive heart attack in February 1995.

Dave Bennett—Lives in Huntington Beach, California, with his wife and children. He is an executive in the commercial heating and cooling industry.

Captain Kenneth Eklund—Resides in Concord, California, with his wife and youngest son. He is a totally disabled veteran.

John Sours—Lives in Golden City, Missouri, with his wife. He works in the field of special education and manages his own farm.

Ray Zoschak—Died in a traffic accident on the New Jersey Turnpike in 1972.

First Sergeant Clarence Cardin—Died of a heart attack in 1979.

First Sergeant Neal Gentry—Died of a heart attack in 1990.

Dave Weeks—Lives in Sterling Heights, Michigan, with his wife. He is an employee of the Chrysler Corporation and an NCO in the Michigan National Guard.

Frank Johnson—Resides in Reno, Nevada. He is married and serves as a police detective with the Reno Police Department.

Rich Fadeley—Lives in Columbia, South Carolina, with his wife. He is in construction.

First Sergeant Bob Gilbert—Resides in Columbus, Georgia, with his wife. He is retired from the U.S. Army and works for the government as an investigator.

Captain Robert Guy—Lives in Athens, Georgia, with his wife. He retired from the U.S. Army as a colonel.

Captain David Ohle—He is married and currently a major general on active duty in the U.S. Army.

First Lieutenant David Grange—He is married and currently a brigadier general on active duty in the U.S. Army. He once commanded the 75th Ranger Regiment.

First Lieutenant James Montano—Resides in Huntington Beach, California. He is divorced and recently retired from the U.S. Army as a colonel.

Frank Anderson—Resides in Rancho Mirage, California, with his wife. He is an E-7 in the U.S. Army Reserves.

Bruce Bowland—Lives in Dunnellon, Florida, with his wife. He is a totally disabled veteran.

Michael Penchansky—Resides in Island Park, New York. He is an elevator repairman.

Charles Reilly—Resides in Anaheim, California. He is a business marketing executive.

James Bates—Stationed at Fort Polk, Louisiana.

Ken Wells—Lives in West Hempstead, New York, with his wife. He is a totally disabled veteran.

Burnell Zentner—Resides in Esparto, California, with his wife. He is a rancher.

David Biedron—Resides in Chicago, Illinois, with his wife. He is an athletic director for the Chicago parks system.

Herman Brown—Lives in Savannah, Georgia.

Marvin Duren—Resides in Lebanon, Ohio. He is totally disabled as a result of his wounds.

Dave Hazelton—Resides in Ontario, Canada.

Mark Martin—Lives in Littleton, Colorado.

Paul Morgucz—Lives in Summit, Illinois, with his wife and children. He is medically retired from the railroad after undergoing a liver transplant.

Ken Munoz—Resides in Galveston, Indiana, with his wife and son. He works for General Motors.

Phil Myers—Resides in Belton, Texas. Retired as a CW3 from the U.S. Army, where he flew Apache gunships.

Billy Nix—Lives in Marietta, Georgia. He is partially disabled and works for the Veterans Administration.

Jeff Paige—Resides in Shelby Township, Michigan. He is a widower.

Larry Saenz—Resides in Sterling Heights, Michigan. He works in special education.

Isaako Malo—Lives in the state of Washington. He was released from captivity by the North Vietnamese government in 1973.

David Bush—Resides in Hamilton, Ohio, with his wife. He works for Ralston Cereals.

Albert Bartz—Took his own life in 1989.

Ray Price—Resides in Golden, Colorado, with his wife and son. Retired from the U.S. Army as a CW3 and received his doctorate degree in Management and Quality Improvement in 1997.

Ned Norton—Died of leukemia in 1992.

Gary Bandy—Lives in Leaburg, Oregon, with his wife and two young sons. He is a carpentry contractor.

Roger Costner—Lives in Wichita, Kansas, with his wife and two sons. He works for Cessna Aircraft as a flight mechanic.

Glossary

AAA   Antiaircraft artillery

AC   Aircraft copilot

acid pad   Helicopter landing pad

AFB   Air Force Base

air burst   Explosive device that detonates above ground

aerial recon   Reconning a specific area by helicopter prior to the insertion of a recon patrol

air strike   Surface attack by fixed-wing fighter/bomber aircraft

AIT   In the U.S. Army, Advanced Individual Training that follows Basic Combat Training

AK   A Soviet bloc assault rifle, 7.62 caliber, also known as the Kalashnikov AK-47

A Troop or **Alpha Troop**   Letter designation for one of the aero-rifle companies of an Air Cavalry squadron

AO   Area of Operations, specified location established for planned military operations

ao dai   Traditional Vietnamese female dress, split up the sides and worn over pants

ARA   Aerial Rocket Artillery

Arc light   A B-52 air strike

Artillery or **arty fan**   An area of operations that can be covered by existing artillery support

ARVN   Army of the Republic of (South) Vietnam

arty   Artillery

ATL   Assistant team leader

A Team   Special Forces operational detachment that normally consists of a single twelve-man team composed of eleven enlisted men and one officer

ARTO   Assistant radio/telephone operator

baseball   Baseball-shaped hand grenade with a five meter kill range

BCT In the U.S. Army, Basic Combat Training every trainee must complete upon entering service

BDA Bomb Damage Assessment

beat feet Running from danger

beehive Artillery round filled with hundreds of small metal darts designed to be used against massed infantry

berm Built-up earthen wall used for defensive purposes

Big Pond Pacific Ocean

Bird Dog A small fixed-wing observation plane

black box Sensor device that detects body heat or movement. They were buried along routes used by the enemy to record their activity in the area

black PJs A type of local garb of Vietnamese farmers also worn extensively by Viet Cong guerrillas

blasting cap A small device inserted into an explosive substance that can be triggered to cause the detonation of the main charge

blood trail Spoor sign left by the passage or removal of enemy wounded or dead

Blues Another name for the aero-rifle platoons or troops of an Air Cavalry squadron

body bag A thick black plastic bag used to transport American and Allied dead to Graves Registration points

beaucoup or **boo koo** French for "many"

B Troop or **Bravo Troop** Letter designation for one of the aero-rifle companies of an Air Cavalry squadron

"break contact" Disengaging from battle with an enemy unit

"bring smoke" Placing intensive fire upon the enemy. Killing the enemy with a vengeance

bush The jungle

"buy the farm" To die

C-4 A very stable, pliable plastique explosive

C's Combat field rations for American troops

C&C Command & Control

CA Combat assault

cammies Jungle-patterned clothing worn by U.S. troops in the field

cammo stick Two-color camouflage applicator

CAR-15 Carbine version of the M-16 rifle

Cav Cavalry

CCN Command & Control (North), MACV-SOG

Charlie, Charles, Chuck GI slang for VC/NVA

cherry New arrival in-country

ChiCom Chinese Communist

chieu hoi Government program that encouraged enemy soldiers to come over to the South Vietnam side

Chinook CH-47 helicopter used for transporting equipment and troops

chopper GI slang for helicopter

chopper pad Helicopter landing pad

CIDG Civilian Irregular Defense Group. South Vietnamese or Montagnard civilians trained and armed to defend themselves against enemy attack

clacker Firing device used to manually detonate a claymore mine

CO Commanding officer

Cobra AH-1G attack helicopter

cockadau GI slang for the Vietnamese word meaning "kill"

Col. Abbreviation for the rank of colonel

cold An area of operations or a recon zone is "cold" if it is unoccupied by the enemy

commo Communication by radio or field telephone

commo check A radio/telephone operator requesting confirmation of his transmission

compromised Discovered by the enemy

contact Engaged by the enemy

CP Command post

Cpt. Abbreviation for the rank of Captain

CS Riot gas

D Troop or **Delta Troop** Lettered designation for one of the aero-rifle companies of an Air Cavalry squadron

daisy chain Wiring a number of claymore mines together with det cord to achieve a simultaneous detonation

debrief The gleaning of information and intelligence after a military operation

DEROS The date of return from overseas service

det cord timed burn fuse used to detonate an explosive charge

didi Vietnamese for "to run" or move quickly

diddy boppin' Moving foolishly, without caution

DMZ Demilitarized Zone

Doc A medic or doctor

double canopy Jungle or forest with two layers of overhead vegetation

Doughnut Dollies Red Cross hostesses

drag The last man on a Long Range Reconnaissance Patrol

dung lai Vietnamese for "don't move"

dustoff Medical evacuation by helicopter

DZ Drop zone for airborne parachute operation

E&E Escape and evasion, on the run to evade pursuit and capture

E-1 or **E-2** Military pay grades of Private

E-3 Military pay grade of Private First Class

E-4 Military pay grade of Specialist Four or Corporal

E-5 Military pay grade of Specialist Five or Sergeant

E-6 Military pay grade of Specialist Six or Staff Sergeant

E-7 Military pay grade of Sergeant First Class or Platoon Sergeant

E-8 Military pay grade of Master Sergeant or First Sergeant

E-9 Military pay grade of Sergeant Major

ER Enlisted Reserve

ETS Estimated Termination of Service

exfil Extraction from a mission or operation

extension leave A thirty-day furlough given at the end of a full tour of duty, after which the recipient must return for an extended tour of duty

FAC Forward Air Controller. Air Force spotter plane that coordinated air strikes and artillery for ground units

fast mover Jet fighter/bomber

firebase or **fire support base** Forward artillery position usually located on a prominent terrain feature, used to support ground units during operations

finger A secondary ridge running out from a primary ridgeline, a hill, or mountain

firefight A battle with an enemy force

Fire Fly An LOH observation helicopter fitted with a high intensity searchlight

fire mission A request for artillery support

fix The specific coordinates pertaining to a unit's position or to a target

flare ship Aircraft used to drop illumination flares in support of ground troops in contact at night

flash panel A fluorescent orange or yellow cloth used to mark a unit's position for supporting or inbound aircraft

field Anywhere outside "friendly" control

FO Forward Observer. A specially trained soldier, usually an officer, attached to an infantry unit for the purpose of coordinating close artillery support

FNG "Fucking new guy." Slang term for a recent arrival in Vietnam

foo gas or **phou gas** A jellied gasoline explosive that is buried in a fifty-five-gallon drum along defensive perimeters and when command-detonated sends out a wall of highly flammable fuel similar to napalm

freak or **freq** Slang term meaning a radio frequency

ghost or **ghost time** Taking time off, free time, goofing off

grazing fire Keeping the trajectory of bullets between normal knee to waist height

grease Slang term meaning "to kill"

Green Beret A member of the U.S. Army Special Forces

ground pounder Infantryman

grunt Infantryman

G-2 Division or larger intelligence section

G-3 Division or larger operations section

gook Derogatory slang for VC/NVA

gunship An armed attack helicopter

HE High explosive

H&I Harrassment and Interdiction. Artillery fire upon certain areas of suspected enemy travel or rally points, designed to prevent uncontested use

heavy team In a Long Range Patrol unit, two five- or six-man teams operating together

helipad A hardened helicopter landing pad

Ho Chi Minh Trail An extensive road and trail network running from North Vietnam, down through Laos and Cambodia into South Vietnam, which enabled the North Vietnamese to supply equipment and personnel to their units in South Vietnam

hooch Slang for barracks or living quarters

horn Radio or telephone handset

hot A landing zone or drop zone under enemy fire

HQ Headquarters

Huey The Bell UH helicopter series

hug To close with the enemy in order to prevent his use of supporting fire

hump Patrolling or moving during a combat operation

I Corp The northernmost of the four separate military zones in South Vietnam. The other divisions were II, III, and IV Corps

infil Insertion of a recon team or military unit into a recon zone or area of operation

Indian Country Territory under enemy control

immersion foot A skin condition of the feet caused by prolonged exposure to moisture that results in cracking, bleeding, and sloughing of skin

incoming Receiving enemy indirect fire

indigenous Native peoples

intel Information on the enemy gathered by human, electronic, or other means

jungle penetrator A metal cylinder lowered by cable from a helicopter used to extract personnel from inaccessible terrain

KCS Kit Carson Scout. Repatriated enemy soldiers working with U.S. combat units

Khmer Cambodian

Khmer Rouge Cambodian communist

Khmer Serei Free Cambodian

KIA Killed in Action

Killer team A small Lurp/Ranger team with the mission of seeking out and destroying the enemy

LAW Light Anti-tank Weapon

lay dog Slang meaning "to go to cover and remain motionless while listening for the enemy." This is SOP for a recon team immediately after being inserted or infilled

LBJ Long Bien Jail. The in-country military stockade for U.S. Army personnel convicted of violations of the U.S. Code of Military Justice

lifer Slang for career soldier

LMG Light machine gun

LOH or **Loach** OH-6A light observation helicopter

LP Listening post. An outpost established beyond the perimeter wire, manned by one or more personnel with the mission of detecting approaching enemy forces before they can launch an assault

LRP Long Range Patrol

LRRP Long Range Reconnaissance Patrol

LSA Government-issue lubricating oil for individual weapons

Lt. Abbreviation for Lieutenant

LTC Lieutenant Colonel

LZ Landing zone. A cleared area large enough to accommodate the landing of one or more helicopters

MAAG Military Assistance Advisory Group. The senior U.S. military headquarters during the early American involvement in Vietnam

MACV Military Assistance Command Vietnam. The senior U.S. military headquarters after full American involvement in the war

MACV Recondo School A three-week school conducted at Nha Trang, South Vietnam, by cadre from the 5th Special Forces Group to train U.S. and Allied reconnaissance personnel in the art of conducting Long Range Patrols

MACV-SOG Studies and Observations Group under command of MACV, which ran Long Range Reconnaissance and other classified missions over the borders of South Vietnam into NVA sanctuaries in Laos and Cambodia

mag Short for magazine

Maguire rig A single rope with loops at the end that could be dropped from a helicopter to extract friendly personnel from inaccessible terrain

Main Force Full-time Viet Cong military units, as opposed to local, part-time guerrilla units

Maj. Abbreviation for Major

MARS Military/civilian radio/telephone system that enabled U.S. personnel in Vietnam to place calls to friends and family back in the United States

Marine Force Recon U.S. Marine Corps divisional Long Range Reconnaissance units similar in formation and function to U.S. Army LRP/Ranger companies

medevac or **dustoff** Medical evacuation by helicopter

MG Machine gun

MIA Missing in Action

Mike Force Special Forces mobile strike force used to reinforce or support other Special Forces units or camps under attack

Montagnard The tribal hill people of Vietnam

MOS Military Occupation Skill

MP Military Police

MPC Military Payment Certificates. Paper money issued U.S. military personnel serving overseas in lieu of local or U.S. currency

M-14 The standard issue 7.62 caliber semiautomatic/automatic rifle used by U.S. military personnel prior to the M-16

M-16 The standard issue 5.56 caliber semiautomatic rifle that became the mainstay of U.S. ground forces in 1967

M-60   A light 7.62 caliber machine gun that has been the primary infantry automatic weapon of U.S. forces since the Korean War

M-79   An individually operated, single-shot 40mm grenade launcher

NCO   Noncommissioned officer

NDP   Night defensive position

net   Radio network

NG   National Guard

no sweat   With little effort or with no trouble

Number One   The best or highest possible

Number Ten   The worst or lowest possible

nuoc mam   Strong, evil-smelling fish sauce used to add flavor to the standard Vietnamese food staple—rice

Nungs   Vietnamese troops of Chinese extraction hired by U.S. Special Forces to serve as personal bodyguards and to man special strike units and recon teams. Arguably the finest indigenous forces in Vietnam

NVA   North Vietnamese Army

ONH   Overnight halt

OP   Observation post. An outpost established on a prominent terrain feature for the purpose of visually observing enemy activity

op   Operation

op order   Operations order. A plan for a mission or operation to be conducted against enemy forces, covering all facets of such mission or operation

overflight   An aerial reconnaissance of an intended recon zone or area of operation prior to the mission or operation, for the purpose of locating access and egress points, routes of travel, likely enemy concentrations, water, and prominent terrain features

P-38   Standard manual can opener that comes with government-issued C-rations

P's or piasters   South Vietnamese monetary system. During the height of the Vietnam War, 100P was equal to about eighty-five cents

P-training   Preparatory training. A one-week course required for each new U.S. Army soldier arriving in South Vietnam, designed to acclimatize new arrivals to weather conditions and give them a basic introduction to the enemy and his tactics

pen flare   A small spring-loaded, cartridge-fed signal flare device that fired a variety of small, colored flares used to signal one's position

peter pilot   Military slang for the assistant or copilot on a helicopter

PFC   Private First Class

Pink Team   An aviation combat patrol package comprised of an LOH scout helicopter and a Charlie-model Huey gunship or an AH-1G Cobra. The LOH would fly low to draw enemy fire and mark its location for an immediate strike from the gunship circling high overhead

pith helmet   A light tropical helmet worn by some NVA units

POW   Prisoner of War

PRC-10 or **"Prick Ten"**   Standard issue platoon/company radio used early in the Vietnam War

PRC-25 or **"Prick Twenty-five"**   Standard issue platoon/company radio that replaced the PRC-10

PRC-74   Heavier, longer range radio capable of voice or code communication

Project DELTA   Special Forces special unit tasked to conduct Long Range Patrols in Southeast Asia

Project GAMMA   Special Forces special unit tasked to conduct Long Range Patrols in Southeast Asia

Project SIGMA   Special Forces special unit tasked to conduct Long Range Patrols in Southeast Asia

PRU   Provincial Reconnaissance Units. Mercenary soldiers who performed special military tasks throughout South Vietnam. Known for their effective participation in the Phoenix Program, where they used prisoner snatches and assassinations to destroy the VC infrastructure

PSP   Perforated Steel Panels used to build airstrips, landing pads, bridge surfaces, and a number of other functions

point   The point man or lead soldier in a patrol

Puff the Magic Dragon   AC-47 or AC-119 aircraft armed with computer-controlled miniguns that rendered massive support to fixed friendly camps and infantry units under enemy attack

pulled   Extracted or exfilled

punji stakes   Sharpened bamboo stakes, embedded in the ground at an angle, designed to penetrate into the foot or leg of anyone walking into one. Often poisoned with human excrement to cause infection

Purple Heart   A U.S. medal awarded for receiving a wound in combat

PX   Post Exchange

radio relay   A communications team located in a position to relay radio traffic between two points

R&R   Rest and Recreation. A short furlough given U.S. forces while serving in a combat zone

Rangers   Designation for U.S. Long Range Reconnaissance Patrollers after January 31, 1969

rappel   Descent from a stationary platform or a hovering helicopter by sliding down a harness-secured rope

reaction force   Special units designated to relieve a small unit in heavy contact

redleg   Military slang for "artillery"

REMF   Rear echelon motherfucker. Military slang for rear echelon personnel

rock 'n' roll   Slang for firing one's weapon on full automatic

Round-eye   Slang for a non-Asian female

RPD/RPK   Soviet bloc light machine gun

RPG   Soviet bloc front loaded antitank rocket launcher used effectively against U.S. bunkers, armor, and infantry during the Vietnam War

rear security The last man on a Long Range Reconnaissance Patrol

RT Recon team

RTO Radio/telephone operator

ruck Rucksack or backpack

Ruff-Puff or **RF** South Vietnamese regional and popular forces recruited to provide security in hamlets, villages, and within districts throughout South Vietnam. A militia-type force that were usually ineffective

saddle up Preparing to move out on patrol

"same-same" The same as

sapper VC/NVA soldiers trained to penetrate enemy defense perimeters and to destroy fighting positions, fuel and ammo dumps, and command and communication centers with demolition charges, usually prior to a ground assault by infantry

satchel charge Explosive charge usually carried in a canvas bag across the chest and activated by a pull cord. The weapon of the sapper

Screaming Chickens or **Puking Buzzards** Slang for members of the 101st Airborne Division

SEALs Small U.S. Navy special operations units trained in reconnaissance, ambush, prisoner snatch, and counterguerrilla techniques

search & destroy Offensive military operation designed to seek out and eradicate the enemy

SERTS Screaming Eagle Replacement Training School. Rear area indoctrination course that introduced newly arrived 101st Airborne Division replacements to the rigors of combat in Vietnam

SF U.S. Special Forces or Green Berets

SFC Sergeant First Class (E-7)

Sgt. Abbreviation for Sergeant

shake 'n' bake A graduate of a stateside noncommissioned or commissioned officer's course

short-timer Anyone with less than thirty days left in his combat tour

short rounds Artillery rounds that impact short of their target

single canopy Jungle or forest with a single layer of trees

sit rep Situation Report. A radio or telephone transmission, usually to a unit's tactical operations center, to provide information on that unit's current status

Six Designated call sign for a commander, such as "Alpha Six"

SKS Communist Bloc semiautomatic rifle

Sky Pilot Chaplain

sky To run or flee because of enemy contact

slack Slang for the second man in a patrol formation. The point man's backup

slick Slang for a lightly armed Huey helicopter primarily used to transport troops

smoke A canister-shaped grenade that dispenses smoke used to conceal a unit from the enemy or to mark a unit's location for aircraft. The smoke comes in a variety of colors

Snake Cobra helicopter gunship

snatch To capture a prisoner

Sneaky Pete A member of an elite military unit who operates behind enemy lines

snoop and poop A slang term meaning "to gather intelligence in enemy territory and get out again without being detected"

socked in Unable to be resupplied or extracted due to inclement weather

SOI Signal Operations Instructions. The classified code book that contains radio frequencies and call signs

Spec 4 Specialist Fourth Class (E-4)

Spectre An AC-130 aircraft gunship armed with miniguns, Vulcans, and sometimes a 105mm howitzer, with the mission of providing close ground support for friendly ground troops

spider hole A camouflaged one-man fighting position frequently used by the VC/NVA

Spooky AC-47 or AC-119 aircraft armed with Gatling guns and capable of flying support over friendly positions for extended periods. Besides serving as an aerial weapons platform, Spooky was capable of dropping illumination flares

spotter round An artillery smoke or white phosphorous round that was fired to mark a position

SSG Staff Sergeant (E-6)

staging area An area in the rear where final last minute preparations for an impending operation or mission are conducted

stand down A period of rest after completion of a mission or operation in the field

star cluster An aerial signal device that produces three individual flares. Comes in red, green, or white

starlight scope A night vision device that utilizes any outside light source for illumination

Stars and Stripes U.S. military newspaper

stay behind A technique involving a small unit dropping out or remaining behind when its larger parent unit moves out on an operation. A method of inserting a recon team

strobe light A small device employing a highly visible, bright flashing light used to identify one's position at night. Normally used only in emergency situations

TA Target Area. Another designation for AO or Area of Operations

TAOR Tactical Area of Responsibility. Another designation for a unit's Area of Operations

TAC Air Tactical air support

tailgunner Rear security or the last man in a patrol

TDY Temporary duty

tee tee or **ti ti** Very small

ten forty-nine or **1049** Military Form 1049 used to request a transfer to another unit

thumper or **thump gun** Slang terms for the M-79 grenade launcher

Tiger Force The battalion reconnaissance platoon of the 2/327th, 101st Airborne Division

tigers or **tiger fatigues** Camouflage pattern of black and green stripes usually worn by reconnaissance teams or elite units

time pencil A delayed fuse detonating device attached to an explosive charge or a claymore antipersonnel mine

TL Team leader

TM Team

TOC Tactical Operations Center, or command center of a military unit

toe popper Small pressure-detonated antipersonnel mine intended to maim, not kill

Top Slang term for a First Sergeant meaning "top" NCO

tracker Soldiers specializing in trailing or tracking the enemy

triple canopy Jungle or forest that has three distinct layers of trees

troop Slang term for a soldier, or a unit in a cavalry squadron equal to an infantry company in size

Tri-Border The area in Indochina where Laos, Cambodia, and South Vietnam come together

tunnel rat A small-statured U.S. soldier who is sent into underground enemy tunnel complexes armed only with a flashlight, knife, and a pistol

URC-10 A pocket-sized, short range emergency radio capable only of transmitting

VC Viet Cong. South Vietnamese communist guerrillas

Viet Minh Short for Viet Nam Doc Lap Dong Minh, or League for the Independence of Viet Nam. Organized by communist sympathizers who fought against the Japanese and later the French

VNSF South Vietnamese Special Forces

warning order The notification, prior to an op order, given to a recon team to begin preparation for a mission

waste To kill the enemy by any means available

White Mice Derogatory slang term for South Vietnamese Army MPs

WIA Wounded in Action

World Slang term for the United States of America or "home"

WP or **willie pete** White phosphorous grenade

XF Exfil. Extraction from the field, usually by helicopter

xin loi/sin loi Vietnamese for "sorry" or "too bad"

XO Executive officer

X-ray team A communication team established at a site between a remote recon patrol and its TOC. Its function is to assist in relaying messages between the two stations

Yards   Short for Montagnards

zap   To kill or wound
zipperhead   Derogatory name for an Oriental

The bloody history of the 101st LRP/Rangers
by one of its own.

SIX SILENT MEN
Book One
by Reynel Martinez

In 1965, the 1st Brigade of the 101st Airborne Division
was detached from the division and assigned to
Vietnam. Reynel Martinez provides a personal account
of the first faltering steps of the brigade's provisional
LRRP unit as the men learn how to battle the VC and
NVA while surviving the more pernicious orders of their
own, occasionally thoughtless, high-level commanders.
SIX SILENT MEN: Book One provides an often bloody
but always honorable chronicle of courage under fire.

SIX SILENT MEN
Book One
By Reynel Martinez

Published by Ivy Books.
Available in your local bookstore.

The compelling chronicles continue in

SIX SILENT MEN
Book Two
By Kenn Miller

After working on their own in Vietnam for more than two years, the 1st Brigade LRRPs were ordered to join forces with the division once again in the summer of 1967. It was a bitter pill to swallow for this formidable band of soldiers, but swallow it they did as they went on to become one of the most highly decorated companies in the history of the 101st.

SIX SILENT MEN
Book Two
By Kenn Miller

Published by Ivy Books.
Available in your local bookstore.

They did it—
and saw it—
all. . . .

THE EYES OF THE EAGLE
F Company LRPs in Vietnam, 1968
by Gary A. Linderer

Gary Linderer volunteered for the Army, then volunteered for Airborne training. When he reached Vietnam in 1968, he was assigned to the famous Screaming Eagles, the 101st Airborne Division. Once there, he volunteered for training and duty with F Company 58th Inf, the Long Range Patrol company that was "the Eyes of the Eagle."

F Company pulled reconnaissance missions and ambushes, and Linderer recounts night insertions into enemy territory, patrols against NVA antiaircraft emplacements and rocket-launching facilities, the fragging of an unpopular company commander, and one of the bravest demonstrations of courage under fire that has ever been described. *The Eyes of the Eagle* is a riveting look at the recon soldier's war. There are none better.

THE EYES OF THE EAGLE
F Company LRPs in Vietnam, 1968
by Gary A. Linderer

Published by Ivy Books.
Available in your local bookstore.

The suffering and the courage.

EYES BEHIND THE LINES
L Company Rangers in Vietnam, 1969
by Gary A. Linderer

In mid-December 1968, after recovering from wounds sustained in a mission that saw four members of a twelve-man "heavy" team killed and five more sent back to the States, Gary Linderer returned to Phu Bai to complete his tour of duty as a LRP.

The job of all-volunteer Rangers was to find the enemy, observe him, or kill him—all the while behind enemy lines, where discovery could mean a quick but violent death. Whether inserting into hot LZs, ambushing NVA soldiers, or rescuing downed air crews, the Rangers demanded—and got—extraordinary performance from their dedicated and highly professional troops.

EYES BEHIND THE LINES
L Company Rangers in Vietnam, 1969
by Gary A. Linderer

Published by Ivy Books.
Available in your local bookstore.